Visual Design in Dress

THIRD EDITION

Marian L. Davis

Florida State University

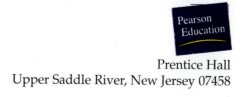

Prentice Hall
Upper Saddle River, New Jersey 07458

Library of Congress Cataloging-in-Publication Data
Davis, Marian L., [date]
   Visual design in dress / Marian L. Davis. — 3rd ed.
     p. cm.
   Includes bibliographical references and index.
   ISBN 0-13-112129-4
   1. Costume design.   I. Title.
TT507.D35   1996
746.9'2—dc20   95-46111
                                          CIP

Acquisitions Editor: Elizabeth Sugg
Director of Production and Manufacturing: Bruce Johnson
Managing Editor: Mary Carnis
Interior Design: Inkwell Publishing Services
Cover Design: Jayne Conte
Cover Design Director: Marianne Frasco
Manufacturing Buyer: Edward O'Dougherty
Page Layout: LPM Services
Color Insert Layout: Inkwell Publishing Services
Line Illustrations: Marian L. Davis

Published by Prentice-Hall, Inc.
A Simon & Schuster Company
Upper Saddle River, New Jersey 07458

© 1996, 1987, 1980 by Marian L. Davis

Printed in the United States of America

10 9 8 7 6 5 4 3 2

ISBN 0-13-112129-4

PRENTICE-HALL INTERNATIONAL (UK) LIMITED, *London*
PRENTICE-HALL OF AUSTRALIA PTY. LIMITED, *Sydney*
PRENTICE-HALL CANADA INC., *Toronto*
PRENTICE-HALL HISPANOAMERICANA, S.A., *Mexico*
PRENTICE-HALL OF INDIA PRIVATE LIMITED, *New Delhi*
PRENTICE-HALL OF JAPAN, INC., *Tokyo*
PRENTLCE-HALL OF SOUTHEAST ASIA PTE. LTD., *Singapore*
EDITORA PRENTICE-HALL DO BRASIL, LTDA., *Rio de Janeiro*

Contents

v

Preface

CONTENTS

Visual Design in Dress is a text, manual, and reference for the teacher or consultant who advises others on personal appearance, for the student of clothing design who needs a thorough grasp of visual design elements and principles, for the professional who occasionally needs a quick, graphic reference, and for the consumer who wants to know how to achieve a desired look. It is for both sexes and all races, ages, and figures.

The third edition updates approaches and illustrations, and reorganizes some areas for easier and more logical sequence. It condenses and simplifies explanations where possible and adds tables and charts to speed and ease reference and show relationships. Ethnic as well as historic example illustrations are included in each chapter, and the last chapter's international focus demonstrates the universal uses and timelessness of the elements and principles. Class activities are included at the end of each chapter to help teachers help students master application of book concepts.

Special features include the analysis of design as process and product; a concept of clothing as a visual tool to increase cultural acceptability; the study of illusions; comprehensive illustrations of garment styles; facial shape and effects of hairstyle for both sexes and all races; effects of various lighting on fabrics and colors; chart of skin and hair color for all races; chart of common colors and their names; chart of physical, psychophysical, and psychological color effects; color profile charts; textile properties as they work into garments; analysis of pattern by source, interpretation, and arrangement of motif; conceptual definitions and analysis of each element and principle and their uses in dress; concepts and techniques of "reinforcing" and "countering"; "advancing" and "receding"; "physical" and "psychological" effects; and a quick tour of visual design in international dress.

The text is amply illustrated with photographs, charts, and line drawings, which are intended as simple, informative diagrams, not fashion illustrations. Styles come and go—and come again in fashion. Most clothing examples are of recent and contemporary Western dress, but other cultures and historic periods are also included to demonstrate the fundamental nature and timelessness of the elements and principles.

Unit I examines the sensory and behavioral contexts within which clothing design works, explores the visual illusions on which many effects rely, and analyzes interactions of functional, structural, and decorative levels of clothing design. Unit II examines each element according to (1) conceptual definition, (2) its aspects and their variations, (3) potentials and limitations, (4) physical and psychological effects, and (5) ways of using it in dress.

Unit III groups principles as linear, highlighting, and synthesizing, in general order of increasing complexity. For clarity and quick reference, each principle has its own chapter, with a format of (1) conceptual definition, (2) physical and psychological effects, (3) elements to which it applies, (4) relationship to other principles, and (5) structural and decorative ways of introducing it in clothing. The book as a working tool allows the reader to find a topic quickly in the same order in each chapter. At first glance some treatments might seem repetitive, but each is in a different context from a different point of view. Showing how each principle relates to others clarifies that interaction, creating an appreciation and a sense of perspective of the versatility of elements and principles.

Unit IV integrates elements and principles in clothing in social and cultural contexts. It describes those settings and their fashion terminology and concepts. It suggests ways of applying elements and principles to create desired illusions and effects for specific figure areas or moods, and it demonstrates their versatility and universality around the world.

ACKNOWLEDGMENTS

To the extent that later editions of a work are based on the first, gratitude still goes to those who contributed to its development. For constructive responses to early drafts, the writer expresses gratitude to Dr. Emmy Hookham, Miss Margaret Robers, Dr. Wanda Montgomery, Miss Helen Strow, Dr. Mary Gephart Donnell, Dr. Joanne B. Eicher, and at University of Nigeria, Nsukka, Mrs. Mabel Ibeanu, Mrs. Patricia Ogbugu Tetenta, Sister Mary Okolo, Mr. Joseph Eze, Mr. Omeje, and my other students who helped me help them.

For later versions, gratitude goes to friends, relatives, and Florida State University colleagues who left me alone for the nights, weekends, holidays, and vacations needed for writing and creating illustrations; to Mrs. Eleanore Adam and Dr. Carol Avery of the College of Human Sciences; to Dr. John Fox of the Physics Department for his valued assistance in the chapter on light; to Dr. Mary Mooty; to Miss Rose Pearson and Mrs. Kay Stops for typing; to Mrs. Barbara Shikarpuri for her extensive typing and editorial assistance; to those students whose thoughtful questions and curiosity helped me clarify presentations in all editions, and for the third edition to Ms. Deborah Simpson and Ms. Pamela Wallheiser of the Multimedia Laboratories for their photographic help. Gratitude also goes to the commercial firms, trade associations, international airlines, travel offices, museums, friends, and colleagues who graciously made clothing photographs and charts available and whose names appear under each photograph or chart provided.

My expression of gratitude would be incomplete without recognizing those who encouraged my creative pleasure in art and clothing design, even while my interests were expanding into other areas. Foremost among these are my parents, Mr. and Mrs. C. H. Davis, for their lifelong help and encouragement; Miss Harriet Green for her years of help and encouragement as home economics extension agent and friend; the 4-H movement, in which I grew up and which provided many practical, developmental opportunities; and the Columbus Gallery School of Fine Arts, Angela's Modern School of Fashion Design, Coats and Clark, Inc., and the Ohio State University, all of whose scholarships helped develop background.

It is a sincere pleasure and privilege to express the foregoing, not just a formality. Any shortcomings are the writer's responsibility, and thanks go to those named, and more unnamed, whose assistance contributed to this volume.

M.L.D.

I Setting the Stage

Any subject can be better understood if studied in the context of its creation and use. Visual design in dress seen in context is one example of one type of design product created through the same fundamental design process used to create everything. As such it fits into a framework and finds its place among all designed and used products. Unit I analyzes the contexts into which clothing fits, shows its place and role in them, and discusses how we experience their effects visually.

Chapter 1 stretches one's concept of design as process and product. Clothing is only one example of many design products that we see, smell, feel, hear, or taste every day. Yet we also use clothing for physical, psychological, social, economic, and emotional reasons or purposes. Understanding these contexts helps us clarify the nature clothing should have. Knowing that it is created by the same process that produces every other product in the world provides a framework to understand its

creation and similarities to other products in daily life.

Chapter 2 narrows the broad view of design as process and product to focus on the three aspects of clothing necessary to succeed in the applied world. These are *functional*, which addresses the physiological and performance roles of dress; *structural*, which involves the configuration of a garment and the way it is assembled to meet its purposes; and *decorative*, the aesthetic aspects relating garment appearance and practicality.

Chapter 3 shows how visual impressions influence one's social acceptability and explores the role of optical illusions in creating appearances that increase acceptability. These illusions use the elements and principles of visual design discussed in later chapters to create culturally desired effects to increase both wearer acceptability and garment performance. Thus the stage is set. A framework and context are established within which visual design in dress can be studied in perspective.

1

1 Concepts of Design

What do you think of when you hear the word "design"? Many people think of a high fashion dress or flowered wallpaper. Both are true, but design only as decorative art is a *very* narrow concept. Stretching your concept of design will

1. strengthen understanding of what all of design really is and can be;
2. increase enjoyment and appreciation of each kind of design;
3. demonstrate how each kind of design fits with others, and how they interact and complement each other; and
4. help you master the use of design.

Design is two things: process and product. Verb and noun. As process it is planning, organizing to meet a goal, carrying out according to a particular purpose, creating. As product it is the end result, an intended arrangement that is the outcome of that process or plan. As process and product studied here, it includes everything intentionally created by man.

DESIGN AS PROCESS

Some art is pure—"art for art's sake"—but most creations in the daily world are for a practical purpose and use. Design as process is planning to meet a goal, and thus applies to everything intentionally created for a purpose. The steps and order of the process are essentially the same regardless of the end product. These steps are very similar to management as a planning process.

Many people do not regard themselves as creative, but when they understand the nature of the product and the steps of the process, they can create. Practice in translating an idea into reality for any one product increases your ability to realize other ideas, if you follow the process steps that apply. There are many variations of the process, from general to specific applications, but there are six basic steps.

1. Set the Goal. The first step is to decide what the last result or product should be. The goal may be very broad and general, such as a piece of writing, or a garment; or very specific such as a poem or a wedding dress. Setting the goal focuses efforts, suggests a range of possible media, and eliminates impossible and aimless paths. Often a clothing designer will get an idea for a garment from an event or another source; but once the inspiration is crystallized, it then becomes the goal. Thus, a generalized goal establishes a range of possibilities, eliminates irrelevancies, and suggests a direction of focus. Specifics of a goal may be established at the outset or may arise out of inspiration, creative experimentation, or recognized needs along the way.

2. Examine Outside Influences. Outside influences are the given conditions of use and the characteristics of the user that influence the development and properties of the goal product: purpose, occasions, locations, settings, resources, restrictions, users, and other factors. *They are all external to the product; none of them describes the product itself,* but all of them must be recognized and considered *before the design is begun.*

For example, the architect must know whether the purpose of a proposed building is for business, education, worship, food processing, or constructing airplanes before he or she can even think of blueprints. He or she must know the composition of the soil; the characteristics of users; zoning laws and building code requirements; climate; the availability of money, supplies, and labor; and many other factors that do not describe the product but which must be taken into account before realistic planning can progress.

The clothing designer must consider the likely user's age, sex, size, weight, figure, preferences, any special needs or problems, and budget. For conditions of use,

the designer must know the intended occasion, climate, season, and availability of resources. If the work is custom, the customer's personal preferences, coloration, and other individual factors are known. But the designer may work for a commercial firm that caters to a market of a particular size range (such as children's wear), a price level (such as budget), or special occasion (such as weddings), and those will become the outside influences. Considering these outside influences suggests the qualities the product must have to perform. If the bathing suit designer has not recognized and considered the influences of water, friction, movement, sand, sun, and chlorine on the needs of the bathing suit, the design will likely fail. Hence, the outside factors show the conditions the product must face, and so set the stage for the next step to describe product performance requirements.

3. Establish Criteria. Criteria tell what the product *must or must not do* to fulfill its purpose and meet the needs determined by the outside influences. For example, the architect's outside influences (such as the purpose of conducting business), suggest the criteria that people must be able to enter and exit, move about, and see. They must have work and meeting space and equipment, a comfortable temperature, fresh air, and the like. The raincoat designer's outside influences (wet, windy weather) suggest criteria that the product must keep the wearer dry yet allow air circulation; not be damaged by water; withstand friction, strain, and motion; be easy to put on and take off and care for; be roomy enough to put over other clothing without being bulky; be attractive, and the like. If anticipated weather is cold, the coat must also be warm. Note that these are verbs: actions the product must or must not do.

Often an industry or governmental agency sets minimum acceptable performance standards; in other cases functional criteria are voluntary. Clothing involves both. For example, certain children's wear is required by law to meet government flammability standards, whereas other standards, such as fit, are more arbitrary.

Once the goal is set, the outside influences are examined, and the criteria they suggest are established, much of the "designing" is already done. The range of feasible choices is narrowed, and the next step has its focus: decide what "ingredients" will make the product perform to meet its criteria and purpose.

4. Make the Plan. In this step the designer selects the supplies and ingredients and their specifications and plans their use for the product to meet the criteria, to perform. (This is the step that many people perceive as "designing," but it is unrealistic and frustrating to sit with a blank paper without a goal, considered influences, and criteria.) Now, when the first three steps are done, the designer is ready to ponder the concept and contents of the product itself. *The plan is the recipe, the blueprint, or formula to meet the criteria.* In the plan the designer selects and matches the substances and specifications of the product to the criteria they are intended to meet.

For clothing, the design plan answers the following questions: How will the garment function to meet its purpose? Where will the openings be? How will they work? How will the designer provide for moving, ease, stretching, and bending? What fit is intended, and how will it be achieved? How will the structure of the garment relate to the structure of the body? What specific fabrics will be used? What linings? Buttons? Zippers? Interfacings? What weight? What fiber content? Which of the elements and principles of visual and tactile design will be used and how? And why? What colors? How will the back relate to the front to make a unified whole? Where will structural lines be? Will it be washable? Sometimes a fabric provides inspiration for a garment, but the preceding questions still must be answered before the designer's sketch and pattern, the plan, can be created.

For example, a coat designer examining outside influences of winter season and cold climate sets a criterion of warmth. For this criterion the plan of specifications might include long sleeves, wool for its insulating properties, and a high collar.

The parts of a well-designed garment must seem to belong together, the right thing seeming to be "naturally" and effortlessly in the right place in the right way. The garment does not betray the designer's effort and detailed care in planning the proportions of the bodice in relation to those of the skirt, or the width of a pleat underlay, or the distance between buttons. It is in this step of the process that the designer calls upon the tools of visual and tactile design. Although following chapters concentrate on that step and those tools, they need to be viewed in the context of the total process. Wise use of fabric textures, colors, line, shape, and other elements of design according to principles of design will show how thoroughly the outside influences have been considered and will determine how well the criteria will be met for a successful product.

5. Carry Out the Plan. This step brings the design from plan to reality. If the item is well designed for its purpose, few, if any, changes are needed along the way. Details may need adjusting or new ideas may occur to improve work as it progresses. Some may be incorporated without risk to what is already done; others may suggest rethinking the whole project and backing up to previous steps. Fortunately, clothing manufacturers can make a sample to ensure that the pattern specifications produce a result reflecting the designer's intentions. If modifications are needed, they can be done before volume production of the final model is begun.

6. Evaluate the Product. This step uses the set criteria to judge the characteristics and performance of the product to meet the goal. Many companies use standardized tests and quality control laboratories to ensure that standards are met. But with garments, the final evaluation is in the wearing. Does it fit? Is it comfortable? Does it wear well? Is it easy to care for? Do fasteners open and close easily and stay closed when they should? Are they placed to avoid gaps? Is there adequate provision for body movement and ease? Are the lines and colors becoming to the wearer? Does the garment meet special criteria, if any? Is the texture appropriate to its use? Is the manufacturing and retail cost in line with its quality? These and many more questions may be asked and answered, both to evaluate a particular garment and to explore new ideas for future improvements.

Design as a process may be entered or left at any point along the way. The home sewer who knows how to drape and draft patterns and has her own dress form may go through the entire process from original idea to finished garment. Most commercial firms specialize in a particular age group, price range, and/or garment type, such as sportswear, lingerie, hosiery, or bridal. Hence for these firms, specialization has already established the goals, outside influencing factors, and criteria. The firm may plan the pattern and fabrics and also construct the garment in volume, or the volume construction may be contracted out to another firm once a sample is approved. Some firms specialize in only one step of the process. For example, making belts is the whole process for a firm that produces belts, but only part of one step for a firm that makes garments. Or within a garment firm, the sample-maker concentrates on that one task, which is part of the larger process of producing garments for market.

Even the individual consumer selecting a ready-made garment off a store rack (with care, not impulse) is involved in the design process. In selecting a product of a commercial firm, the consumer is in the process of designing the composition of a wardrobe, having considered the wardrobe goal, personal characteristics, the money available, and other factors.

The design process chart, Table 1-1, is by no means complete, even for examples in the categories described; but it does show the similarity of the steps and sequence in the design process regardless of the product.

DESIGN AS PRODUCT

Having seen the universality of the process, using the same steps in the same order to lead to any product, let us now explore the range of design products. Design as man-made product falls into two major categories: sensory and behavioral. Many products, however, include aspects of both.

Sensory Design

Sensory designs include those products experienced through the physical senses: sight, sound, taste, touch, smell. The main purpose of a sensory design product is the sensory experience itself.

Many products are experienced through several senses at once. Sculptures are both seen and touched. Prepared dishes can be appetizing in flavor, attractive visually, and satisfying in touch (e.g., crisp or soft). Pills have a smooth or grainy surface feel as well as a sweet or bitter taste. Clothing fabric is felt on the outside as well as on the inside against the skin and is also seen on the wearer. Occasionally it is also experienced as sound, as with the soft swoop of satin, the rustle of taffeta, the rubbing of corduroy, the crackling of leather, or the jangle of beads; or as smell, as in suede and leather goods or the fragrance of sandalwood beads. But clothing as a sensory design product is most often and most importantly experienced as visual and tactile design. Table 1-1 shows two examples of sensory design in process; Table 1-2a shows sensory design types, examples, plans, and titles of planners.

Behavioral Design

Behavioral design deals with patterns or ways of doing things, events, or actions in time (as opposed to tangible sensory products). It can be found in every area of human endeavor, but most often involves the "behavioral" sciences of economics, sociology, psychology, religion, government, education, anthropology, law—and such activities as transportation, advertising, communications, time use, and service industries. To be sure, unplanned human events occur, many of them accidentally, but every planned behavior is also a design product. The main purpose of a behavioral design product is the action or condition resulting from an action. For example, an election results from the planned behavior, the action of a campaign. (Even though one may *hear* slogans and *see* posters, they are means to a behavioral end product, not ends in themselves.)

DESIGN LEVELS: MACRO AND MICRO DESIGN

Behavioral design products, and sometimes sensory design products, occur at various levels. "Macrodesign" deals with over-all characteristics, large-scale or major features, dominant themes or generalities of a product. "Mid-range" design deals with concerns of moderate scope, between macro and micro. "Microdesign" deals with details, subcategories, small-scale or minor characteristics. For example, economic macrodesign describes the plan of a whole system, such as "closed," "open," centrally controlled or free enterprise. Marketing patterns, currency, and banking systems exemplify mid-range levels; one person's budget plan exemplifies microdesign. Clothing production, distribution, consumption, and use employ all three levels.

Whether a design is macro or micro is sometimes relative; one behavioral event may involve several of the levels. Or one event may involve several behavioral areas, such as a wedding ceremony containing religious, cultural, and social facets. But seeing the various types and levels of design helps you see clothing design in a wider design context and develop a perspective toward it. Political, social, religious, and cultural designs often involve specific clothing prescriptions and behaviors. Economic, educational, and communications designs may allow greater clothing behavior flexibility and a wider range of examples; yet certain of their events, such as educational graduation exercises with academic regalia, may still be very clothing specific. Table 1-2b shows examples of various types and levels of behavioral design, plans, and designers.

Combinations

Many products involve both sensory and behavioral design, because design may be perceived through the senses and then interpreted behaviorally. For example, a poem with a certain audible rhyme and meter is also designed to carry a certain meaning that may be psychologically or emotionally interpreted. A perfume perceived by smell is not only pleasant in sensory experience but often intended to suggest emotional reactions.

The same is true of clothing. While it is perceived visually and tactilely, it is often interpreted behaviorally. A woman may choose a dress shape she regards as attractive in order to be socially accepted by her peers. A visually perceived garment color may be behaviorally interpreted to identify the wearer as a bride, a ruler, someone in mourning, or of a certain rank. Airlines and other firms use the visual cues of uniforms (sensory) to provide occupational identification (behavioral). These behavioral interpretations of sensory designs are done according to the culture in which they are practiced, since one's cultural background determines how one perceives and interprets experience and visual cues.

Hence, clothing as visual and tactile sensory design fits into and interacts with many other kinds of sensory and behavioral designs. These positions and relationships provide a context and perspective for further study in later chapters which focus on the visual aspects of dress.

TABLE 1-1 Design Process Chart and Selected Examples

Step in Design Process	BEHAVIORAL DESIGN		SENSORY
	Type	Possible Example	Type
1. Set goal.	Party	Birthday dinner for adult	House (Visual and Tactile)
2. Examine outside influences.	Space available; money, time for preparation available; preferences of guest of honor; date, etc.	Table seats 10 or trays for 16; $50 available; time available to shop and prepare meal and cake; guest of honor likes little fuss, likes chocolate, etc.	Client's family size and composition, activities, income, likes and dislikes; climate, land type and amount; zoning ordinances, easement restrictions; money available, etc.
3. Establish criteria.	Must be within budget; must end early; might include birthday cake; decorations must be simple, etc.	Cost no more than $50; end at 10 P.M.; no more than three courses; dessert should be birthday cake; party should have happy atmosphere, etc.	Appropriate size, cost, location; must be family-oriented; materials must suit climate, needs, etc. Must meet zoning requirements, etc.
4. Make plan.	Make out menu; plan table for 10, seating arrangement; make shopping list; plan time; invitations, costs, decorations, etc.	Time: 7 P.M.; menu: baked ham, sweet potato, green peas, tossed salad, rolls, butter, chocolate birthday cake, coffee and tea; table setting with blue dishes and white cloth, arranged for 10; decide invitations, list, etc.	Make plan of exact room sizes, floor plan, window, floor, wall treatments; plan and select materials; decide on electrical, heating, and cooling, light, plumbing, ventilation systems; ensure all legal requirements are met, etc.
5. Carry out plan.	Put plan into action: prepare food, table, have party, etc.	Send invitations; shop, prepare food; set table; greet guests, serve food, act as host or hostess; ensure that all enjoy; clean up, etc.	Prepare site and foundation, construct house, etc.
6. Evaluate.	Does it meet criteria?	Was party a success? Was the food good? Was seating comfortable and table appropriate? Guest of honor pleased? Party within budget? End on time? Invitations sent on time? Clean-up efficient, etc.?	Does it meet criteria?

TABLE 1-1 Design Process Chart and Selected Examples *(continued)*

DESIGN	SENSORY DESIGN	
Possible Example	*Type*	*Possible Example*
City home Family: parents and 2 daughters, 11 and 10; all like active sports; combined income $43,000; like to read; mother teaches; children belong to clubs; family has 1 car, 1 dog; area zoned residential, etc.	Garment (Visual and Tactile) Child's size, height, weight, age, coloration, motor coordination, likes and dislikes; climate, season, occasion; money available, etc.	Child's Dress Age 3½, 38" high, weighs 34 lbs.; is learning to help dress self, very active, dislikes fussy clothes, likes yellow; semitropical climate, late spring, school, not wealthy, etc.
Must have quiet areas, away from activity areas, be moderate in size, efficient, and have smooth traffic flow. Must be economical to heat, cool, and light; have yard for children to play; have space for guests; be in budget, etc.	Must be appropriate garment size, versatile style. Must have safety features, self-help features that grow with the child. Must be attractive, washable, cool, comfortable, etc.	Must be size 4, provide easy access and self-help, coolness, comfort, convenience, softness, help to tell front from back; must cost under $10.
Small ranch-style floor plan, wood frame, brick exterior walls, gas heat, sash windows, bedrooms at one end of house, living, dining, and kitchen at other end, workshop in garage, fireplace in family room, walls insulated, etc.	Decide on specifics of functional, structural, and decorative garment design; decide what visual effect is to be, what visual elements and principles are to be used and how. Decide specific lines, colors, fabric textures, structural and decorative shapes, use of space and light, pattern, according to visual design principles and functional criteria.	Size 4, small flower print. Yellow cotton broadcloth, sleeveless and collarless for coolness and ease of dressing. A-line with wide hem and no waistline (to grow with child) opening down front with large buttons (for self-help), 2 square pockets on front at hip (functional and to help distinguish front from back in self-help). Plan cost, etc.
Build home according to plan, zoning requirements, easement specifications, safety codes, etc.	Construct garment.	Select or draft pattern, prepare fabric, lay and cut pattern, assemble and finish garment, press, etc.
Is it within budget, comfortable, safe, attractive, appropriate in size, arrangement, and materials? Does family like it, etc.?	Does it meet criteria?	Does it work? Is it comfortable, easy to get into and out of, easy to care for, safe, cool? Will it show soil easily? Will it grow with the child and help her practice dressing herself? Is it attractive and correct size? Does the child like it, etc.?

TABLE 1-2a Examples of Sensory Design Types

Sense	Design as Type	Design as Product	Design as Plan	Designer as Creator
Sight	visual	painting	sketch	artist
		dress	pattern	fashion designer
		building	blueprint	architect
		dance	arrangement	choreographer
Sound	auditory	music	score	composer
		spoken poem	poem	poet
		alarm system	plan	engineer
Taste	gustatory	sugar pill coatings	formula	chemist
Touch	tactile	statue	model	sculptor
		fabric	pattern	textile designer
Smell	olfactory	perfume	formula	chemist
		food dish	recipe	chef

PRODUCT AND PROCESS: CREATIVITY

The design process shows that realistic observation of outside influences and needs, and logical thinking and order, remove a great deal of the supposed "mystery" of design or "creativity." One who thoroughly understands design as product and process and has mastered the use of appropriate materials can be "creative." Marvelous inspirations get nowhere if the designer cannot bring them to reality.

Some people see the problem as how to get a new idea. The creative person is often regarded as "someone who is good at getting ideas." Getting ideas, however, is not so often a matter of inventing something totally new, as of using old things in new ways, or seeing the familiar in a new light. One can cultivate a sensitivity that explores the potential of the ordinary, that sees an exciting shape in a mundane button, that nourishes imagination by *practicing* it.

One way of seeking such inspiration might be called "cross-sensory interpretation." In it, designs intended for one sense organ are interpreted through another: a flavor (olfactory and gustatory) inspires a poem (auditory); a satin (tactile) inspires a scent (olfactory); a song (auditory) inspires a picture (visual).

This is a long-used technique that has provided ideas for many artists. Walt Disney's film "Fantasia" is a classic example of visualizing sound. In it famous musical works are interpreted in line, color, shape, light, and pattern in motion as music progresses. Many words are used in both music and art vocabularies, such as rhythm, balance, and harmony, or orchestral "color" and "texture." Musical compositions with titles like "Deep Purple" and "Rhapsody in Blue" suggest the close relationship between visual and auditory design. This process of visualizing sound is called *synesthesia*.[1]

If you were a composer, what would a sunset sound like? If you were an artist, how would Gershwin's "American in Paris" look? If you were a clothing designer, what would Chanel No. 5 perfume look like? What mood is conveyed? Links between olfactory and auditory design have described fragrances as musical compositions, and associate perfumes with tactile fabric moods.[2] Can such moods be translated into a visual design? Into garments? Let your imagination soar, and practice cultivating new ways of seeing familiar things to increase your pool of ideas.

[1]Faber Birren, *Color Psychology and Color Therapy* (Secaucus, N. J.: The Citadel Press, 1950), pp. 162–163, 192–193.

[2]Ann Marie Fiore, "Multisensory Integration of Visual, Tactile, and Olfactory Aesthetic Cues of Appearance," *Clothing and Textiles Research Journal*, Vol. 11, No. 2 (Winter 1993), pp. 45–52.

TABLE 1-2b Examples of Behavioral Design Types and Levels

Behavioral Area	Macrodesign	Mid-range Design	Microdesign	Microdesign As Action Plan	Designer As Creator
Political	democracy, monarchy	campaign, succession, tax systems	election slogan, local caucus	strategy	political strategist, speech writer, legislator
Economic	free enterprise, central control	banking and currency, production programs	personal accounts, daily quota	budget	fiscal planner, economist
Social	kinship systems, mores	social program, social clubs	meeting, party	agenda, program	organizer, planner
Education	primary, secondary, and higher system organization	school districts, college organization	lesson, class times	curriculum, schedule, lesson plan, syllabus	educational planner, teacher, administrator
Religious	monotheism, polytheism, denominations	mission programs, organizational structure, diocese	specific ceremony (wedding, baptism, funeral), ritual	ceremony, plan, ritual order	clergy, synod, conference
Communication	network organization, language	TV series, literature	speech, play, poem, books	pilot, draft, script	writer
Cultural	ethnic system, belief systems	folkways, norms, major traditions, symbolism	"rite of passage," "body language," food customs	traditions, ceremonies, customs, rituals	parents, elders, officials

Another technique for creating new ideas in clothing superimposes two transparencies on each other like a double exposure photograph and creates a new idea from the combination. Described as "homospatial process," it can also be applied using different senses.[3]

PRODUCT AND PROCESS: SOCIETY AND ENVIRONMENT

Because clothing is an example of applied design, even the most exciting, original idea must show awareness of its practical purpose and environment. We shall not examine the sociopsychological, behavioral

aspects of clothing in depth, but there are social and economic questions that affect responsible clothing design as both process and product. The designer of usable products does not create in isolation, but brings natural and human resources to both the social and physical environments where the product either does or does not work. What factors now and in the future will affect how clothing designs work? To what extent can the designer influence these factors?

Much of the Westernized world has become dependent on the convenience and easy care of synthetics. Many of these are petroleum-based, and oil supplies seem uncertain, increasingly expensive, and wanted primarily for fuel and other products. What will this mean to the clothing designer and consumer?

Some designers have turned, or returned, to natural fibers. Yet many fertilizers and insecticides used for their produc-

---

[3]Albert Rothenberg and Robert S. Sobel, "A Creative Process in the Art of Costume Design," *Clothing and Textiles Research Journal*, Vol. 9, No. 1 (Fall 1990), pp. 27–36.

tion contain petroleum products, and tractors and sprayers require fuel, thus intensifying the problem. Some compounds leave harmful residues after their beneficial role has ended. If the world's population continues to explode, land presently used for producing natural fibers will be needed for living space and food production.

Some designers put faith in improved technology, but it, too, needs judicious use. New concepts often show valid promise, but potential may be distorted. For example, the idea of disposable paper clothing showed promise if low cost made it feasible. A dress was introduced at 99¢, and mass production and consumption might have reduced its price to 40¢. Instead, the cost of disposable clothing ranged from $20.00 to $149.50, more than much nondisposable clothing. Thus, the basic validity of an idea was negated by the urge to capitalize on a novelty.[4]

The finite resources of our planet call into question the concepts of disposability and planned obsolescence. The historical assumption that "more is better" demands a fresh look at both the clothing industry and consumer. Designers, retailers, and consumers alike must question their own long-range impact on resources and environment if policies and practices foster a sponge-like mentality in which a person soaks up everything possible for instant gratification and then discards the residue with little concern for the consequences.

The clothing designer and consumer are involved in the idea of instant gratification, which pervades advertising. But the more each knows about design process and product, the greater the satisfaction in the product use and the less reliance on gimmicks that depend on consumer ignorance or insecurity. The consumer who knows the elements and principles of visual design and their effects in dress has no need for the $49.95 "home dial-amatic necktie selector," which tells which tie to wear with what suit.[5] The consumer who knows basic color theory and how it works has no need for "color advice" tied to clocks, seasons, astrological signs, keys, gems, or personality "types."[6] The consumer must be educated, thoughtful, wary, and decisive so that offers of "assistance" in decision making and the desire for instant gratification do not mean manipulation and behavior control as well as a depleted budget.

Then the question is who controls the market: designers and manufacturers by what they make available, or consumers by what they choose and reject? Generally, firms try to anticipate market demands, but at the same time they try to influence customers' wants in their direction. Influences are reciprocal, and an informed, careful consumer will seek responsible designers to create safe and healthy, as well as attractive, clothing.

Innumerable social questions influence design decisions in different cultures, time periods, socioeconomic levels, and occupations. For example, how do standards of decency and exposure among different religions, occasions, or cultures affect clothing design? As cultures evolve, ideas of beauty change. How do these changes affect clothing design when the physical demands of climate and activity remain similar? When does a clothing-assisted, healthy self-image change into self-obsession, narcissism, and hollow vanity? And, finally, how can the fashion industry play a socially and economically responsible role in any changes?

These are only a few of the clothing-related social questions that designers, manufacturers, and consumers must face. With no clear-cut answers to such questions now, the nearest approaches seem to try to achieve balances and work toward solutions.

---

[4]Victor Papanek, *Design for the Real World* (New York: Bantam Books, 1973), pp. 33, 100.

[5]*Ibid.*, p. 100.
[6]Judith Rasband, *Color Crazed* (Provo, Utah: n. pub., n.d.), pp. 1–16.

SUMMARY

Design is two things: process and product. Design as process deals with active steps in planning and creating anything new. No matter what the product, the process follows the same steps in the same order: (1) Set the goal, (2) examine outside influences, (3) establish criteria, (4) make a plan, (5) carry out the plan, (6) evaluate based on the criteria. The process allows for experimentation and may be entered or left at any point along the way; one person or company in clothing design may carry out the entire process or specialize only in certain parts of it.

As man-made product, design is described in two major categories: sensory and behavioral. Sensory design is perceived through the senses, and is classified as visual, auditory, olfactory, tactile, and gustatory. Many products involve several senses; clothing is most often experienced as visual and tactile. Behavioral design is planned action. It can be seen in religion, economics, and every other area of human endeavor on large-scale levels, as "macrodesign," at mid-range levels, or as detailed, small-scale "microdesign." Clothing is tangible, sensory design, but it may often be used for and interpreted as part of behavioral design or purposes.

To increase one's originality and creativity, one can seek new ways of using old, familiar media and practice "cross-sensory interpretation." Sensitizing oneself to a wide range of experiences and translating them into other forms of expression increases creativity.

When clothing is the end product, even the most exquisite creativity must be viewed from the perspective of the real world of physical and behavioral resources and environment. Clothing is applied design, practical as well as beautiful. Both designer and manufacturer must anticipate natural resource needs, availability, cost, technology, and probable customer needs and preferences. Ideas such as disposability, planned obsolescence, and instant gratification demand examination by both clothing producer and consumer. Social, cultural, economic, and other behavioral changes will affect the contents, but the basic characteristics of product and process remain, so that social responsibility and creativity can work together.

CLASS ACTIVITIES

1. Choose a clothing or related product, such as a bathing suit, raincoat, umbrella, or maternity dress as a design process goal, and discuss how it would be taken through design process. What outside influences must be taken into account? What special needs are operating for the use or occasion? What functional, structural, and decorative criteria will these influences suggest? What styles, materials, notions, trims, specifications, and construction techniques will best meet these criteria? How will it be evaluated?

2. Bring to class a garment you consider a *poor* example of a design product. Then (a) analyze how it probably arrived at that stage. Identify what may have gone wrong at what stage: Were outside influences adequately identified and considered? Were probable criteria realistic and practical? Were the fabrics, notions, and trims chosen consistent with the criteria, goal, and purposes of the garment? Do some process steps seem to have been omitted or addressed out of order? (b) If you were designing this garment, what would you change? Why?

3. To experiment with cross-sensory interpretation, play an instrumental music recording. With eyes closed, imagine what kinds of lines the music suggests: Curved? Wavy? Straight? Angular? What kind of spaces do you see? Open and empty? Or small, broken, and filled? What kind of geometric shapes do you see? Circles? Rectangles? Triangles? Ovals? Curvelinear or straight-edged shapes? What specific colors do you see? What kinds of textures do you see?

Rough? Smooth? Supple? Brittle? Can you translate that touch into a fabric? Is the music patterned or plain? Busy or simple? Sophisticated or sporty? Now translate your abstract visual responses to the music into a garment. The same stimulus music will likely inspire as many different garments as there are students in the room.

4. With the class divided into groups, give each group a component of a garment; fabric, a button, a zipper, a belt, interfacing, etc. Let each group analyze how that component is the product of a complete design process from that manufacturer, while at the same time it is only one part of the process of another product, a total garment.

5. Choose or bring a specialized garment to class, such as a wedding gown, fireman's jacket or nurse's uniform, and analyze it as a sensory design product. Then in discussion take it through the design process as a tool or part of a behavioral design. What are the needs of the event? Which criteria will make it succeed? How is the garment a part of the plan to meet event criteria?

6. Collect data to compare the environmental impact of two garments; one of polyester or other synthetic fiber, and one of cotton. Which takes more land and/or resources to produce? How do their costs compare? What are the advantages and/or disadvantages of each?

2 *Aspects of Clothing Design*

No matter how beautiful, a garment that pinches, stifles movement, has awkward fastenings, or does not work will hang unused in the back of the closet. To be successful, a garment must be well-designed in three respects: (1) function, (2) structure, and (3) decoration, *in that order of importance.* Successful garments blend these three aspects so well that they seem naturally to be unified, each aspect growing out of and complementing the others. Parts of a garment, or whole garments, may incorporate two or all three aspects. Well-designed garments look like what they are, and do it attractively. A party dress masquerading as a work dress succeeds as neither. A garment conveys a "message" most effectively by expressing it "honestly" and pleasantly, often as the "attractive understatement."

The *purpose* of a garment is distinct from its functional, structural, and decorative design. A garment may have a purpose, or reason for being, in any or all three design aspects. Its functional, physical purpose may be to allow the wearer to ski comfortably and safely, to sit comfortably, or to move and survive in space. Its structural purpose is to allow it to fit and to perform. Decorative, visual purposes might be to increase night visibility, or the attractiveness of the wearer, or to provide visual identification of a nurse or policeman, qualities that can only be seen. While the main *purpose* of a garment may be for appearance, it must still fit and perform; appearance cannot compensate for the absence of function and structure.

The steps in the design process—establishing the criteria, planning, carrying out, and evaluating—are all taken in terms of functional, structural, and decorative design. A designer sets functional criteria for what the garment must or must not do. Plans for the structure and construction of the garment provide for

15

meeting functional criteria, and plans for decorative aspects must meet both functional and aesthetic criteria. In actual use, the completed garment is evaluated in terms of its combined functional, structural, and decorative criteria.

For example, the gown in Figure 2-1 appears splendid decoratively. Functionally, however, the large ruff would restrict head movement and vision such as looking down for steps; the voluminous skirt and sleeves could hinder movement, be heavy, and risk getting caught in doors or car- riages; and the stiff, tight bodice might restrict internal organs as well as movement. Conversely, the garment in Figure 2-2 is structurally fitted without being tight, bulky, or heavy, functionally allowing freedom of movement and air circulation and protection. At the same time, the decorative pattern is blended into the functional and structural design.

The visual blending has been described as "apparel body construct (ABC)" or "the visual form presented by the interaction of apparel on the human body; ... a

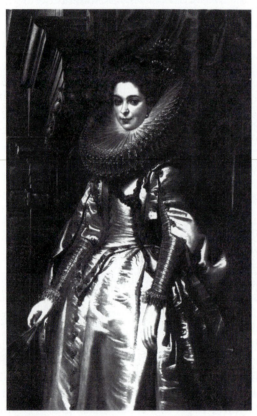

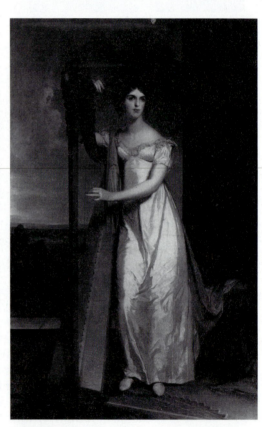

FIGURE 2-1 This sumptuous gown uses a variety of structural forms; the bodice and inner sleeves follow body contours, whereas the ruff, outer sleeves, and skirt deviate from body contours enough to affect functionality and mobility, making this primarily a decorative, ceremonial gown. (*Marchesa Brigida Spinola Doria,* by Peter Paul Rubens; c. 1606; National Gallery of Art, Washington; Samuel H. Kress Collection.)

FIGURE 2-2 The tubular sleeve and dress forms conform to figure forms with simple styling and soft textures to allow functional freedom of movement and comfort, as the decorative neck ruffle visually reinforces the structural neck edge. (*Lady with a Harp: Eliza Ridgely,* by Thomas Sully; 1818; National Gallery of Art, Washington; gift of Maude Monell Vetlesen.)

concept of a physical object based upon sensory data."[1]

When you have studied the following functional, structural, and decorative design aspects, return to these portraits and note additional design evaluation points in all three areas and how they do or do not blend. Practice that combined evaluation with examples and illustrations throughout the book and in the clothes you wear.

FUNCTIONAL DESIGN

Functional design deals with how something works physically, how it performs. In clothing, functional design refers either to parts of or to whole garments. A functioning pocket holds things; functioning zippers and buttons and buttonholes open and close; belts buckle and unbuckle, allowing the wearer to get in and out of a garment.[2] Fake parts are merely decorative and do not provide the function they appear to give. Some functions are common to nearly all complete garments; other functions are specialized for particular occupational, sport, or other needs.

General Needs

1. Movement. All garments must provide for movement and changes in body measurements that come from reaching, stretching, and bending. Back shoulder measure may increase 13 to 16 percent, and sitting may increase the hip 4 to 6 percent. Bending the elbow may increase the arm length by 35 to 40 percent and circumference at the elbow by 15 to 22 percent. A bent knee may increase leg length by 35 to 45 percent and knee circumference by 12 to 14 percent.[3] Some garment parts, such as wed-

ding gown trains or flaring ice skating skirts, are designed to emphasize body movement.[4] Designers must plan for these changes to maintain mobility.[5]

2. Protection. Functionally, clothing can protect against extreme temperatures, wind, moisture, radiation, insects and other creatures, thorns, fungi and bacteria, plant secretions, chemicals, excessive friction, and the like. Specialized clothing may also offer protection against electrical shock, gas, or extremes of air or water pressure.[6]

All garments should help prevent the wearer from becoming a human torch. According to the Southern Burn Institute there are some 12,000 deaths, 50,000 serious cripplings and maimings, and over 300,000 hospitalizations yearly from burns. Studies cited by the Institute indicate that ignited clothing increases the extent and seriousness of such injuries. Burn surgeons report finding definite burn injury patterns that relate directly to the type of fabric *and styling*. "Because clothing designers often specify fabrics and trim and create the styling, it is especially imperative that they understand flame-retardant criteria, so that they do not unwittingly create problems."[7] This problem is important for every consumer, but especially for infants, young children, the elderly, and the handicapped—those who are most vulnerable, immobile, and least able to care for themselves. Even with research on flame-retardant fabrics, designers assume a great responsibility in keeping garment styles as safe as possible.

3. Environmental Modifier. All garments are physiological modifiers between the body and its physical environment. Cloth-

---

[1]Marilyn Revell DeLong, *The Way We Look: A Framework for Visual Analysis of Dress* (Ames, Iowa: Iowa State University Press, 1987), p. 3.

[2]Susan M. Watkins, *Clothing: The Portable Environment* (Ames, Iowa: Iowa State University Press, 1984), pp. 185–86.

[3]*American Fabrics*, No. 95 (Fall 1972), p. 22.

[4]DeLong, *The Way We Look*, p. 47.

[5]Watkins, *Clothing: The Portable Environment*, pp. 144–45, 167–68, 179.

[6]Ibid., pp. 35–42, 58–61, 91–92.

[7]Southern Burn Institute and Rehabilitation Center, Invitation to 3rd National Flame-Free Design Conference, March 1974.

ing regulates energy flow to and from the body by its permeability, resistance to evaporation, insulation, absorbency, or effect on heat transfer by conduction, convection, radiation or evaporation.[8] Fourt and Hollies note that clothing "interacts with and modifies the heat-regulating function of the skin and has effects which are modified by body movement." They regard clothing "fabrics as mixture of air and fiber, in which the fiber dominates by weight and visibility, but the air dominates by volume."[9] This combination of air and fiber is the designer's tool for creating a functional environment to interact with the body's skin and motion.

4. Health and Safety. Clothing should allow the body to be functionally safe from hazards. Extreme extensions of long scarves, flowing sleeves, or flaring pant legs can be dangerous around wheels, revolving doors, or moving machinery. High platform shoes, extremely high heels, tight boot tops, or tight sandal straps can all affect balance, support, and mobility. They can distort distance judgment necessary for curbs, stairs, and driving.

Any garment or part that reduces control over one's immediate body environment is a hazard. Tight straps, belts, pants, or girdles affect circulation, posture, and comfort, and may damage internal organs. Functionally well-designed clothing eliminates as many safety hazards as possible and provides comfort, efficiency, and safety.

Special Needs

The usual image of the intended consumer is that of a physically normal teenager or adult using daytime or evening outerwear. These groups are a major segment of the clothing market, yet there are millions of people with special clothing needs. Some are created by temporary conditions—such as a broken arm, pregnancy, or a special occupation—and some needs, such as those resulting from certain disabilities, may be permanent.

People with special needs also require and deserve professional and consumer attentions. They, too, must be able to function as much as possible and feel attractive and gain social acceptance. The elements and principles of visual design can create illusions and physical and psychological effects for them as well as for any other person.

Among those requiring special consideration are those in certain occupations, children, pregnant women, the elderly, and the handicapped. For each of these groups, good functional design and step 2 of the design process—considering wearer characteristics and needs—become especially important.

1. Occupational/Sports. Special occupational clothing has received increased attention but more is needed. The survival of astronauts or deep-sea divers depends quite literally on their clothing. Astronauts' space-walking suits consist of eleven layers of materials that must protect them from "hard vacuum," extreme heat and cold, possible micrometeoroids, and electromagnetic radiation. These layers must allow movement, temperature and humidity control, pressure retention, and impact protection, all without any failure.[10] Clothing that assists workers' jobs, such as distributing the weight of portable television cameras, is also gaining attention.[11]

Protective occupational clothing concerns for industrial, military, and medical personnel also increase as needs change. Firefighters require protection from extreme heat and fire. As environmental awareness increases, farmers, truck drivers, and toxic

---

[8]Watkins, *Clothing: The Portable Environment*, pp. 3–5.

[9]Lyman Fourt and Norman Hollies, *Clothing: Comfort and Function* (New York: Marcel Dekker, Inc., 1970), p. 31.

[10]Sandra Kay Ehlers Park, "Shuttle Space Clothing," *Journal of Home Economics*, Vol. 80, No. 1 (Spring 1988), p. 12.

[11]Susan M. Watkins, "Designing Functional Clothing," *Journal of Home Economics*, Vol. 66, No. 7 (Nov. 1974), pp. 33–38; *Clothing: The Portable Environment*.

waste disposal and hazardous materials teams need protection from chemicals and pesticides. Military and law enforcement personnel need protection against ballistic, mechanical, bacterial, and gas risks. Medical personnel need protection from germs, bacterial and viral agents such as AIDS, and radiation. Anticontaminate garments protect sensitive environments such as processing food, pharmaceuticals, and microchips.[12]

Clothing for active sports must provide protection, comfort, absorbency, and freedom of movement, as well as visual identification. One boy was condemned to a lifetime coma from an injury received while wearing the supposed "best" football helmet available, one which was shown not even to have been tested for absorption of kinetic energy.[13]

2. Proper Use. Often uneducated consumer choice or use is as much a problem as improper design. One gasoline truck explosion resulted from a spark caused by static electricity in the driver's clothing. Similar problems with static electricity in nurses' uniforms worn near operating room oxygen tanks have resulted in strict hospital regulations. Newspapers almost daily contain items of injuries caused by improperly designed or used clothing. Both the designer and the consumer have a critical stake in safety.

3. Action Potential. Different purposes require different kinds and amounts of motion. For example, a bathing suit should functionally provide freedom of movement, snug fit with comfort and flexibility, quick drying, minimum weight or volume increase when wet, and resistance to damage by water, sun, salt, or chemicals. Even finer distinctions of functional criteria would operate between bathing suits intended for racing and those for sunbathing.

Some garments are functionally designed for much action, others for very little, and still others for versatility of varying activity. As Fourt and Hollies note, clothing such as traditional "Sunday best," which stressed appearance, allowed little action or else became most uncomfortable and restrictive. "The quiet comfort ideal is closely tied to ceremonial rather than functional clothing...."[14] Thus, the purpose and function of a garment determine how much action potential is to be designed into it.

4. Children. Children are curious, inexperienced, and vulnerable. In general they need protection against flammability, sharp edges, toxic dyes, sudden extreme temperature changes, loose buttons or trims, excessive fuzziness, drawstrings that could strangle, and long ties and belts. They need the learning assistance of self-help features and those that grow with them. They enjoy bright colors and trims with which they can identify if they are old enough. However, younger children are less concerned with appearances than with comfort and mobility. Safe, functional, and visually attractive children's wear is a continuing need.

5. Pregnancy. Maternity wear presents unique challenges in some cultures. The Indian *sari*, African skirt wrapper, and Philippine *malong* are marvelously versatile in that they need only be wrapped or draped to accommodate the expanding figure. In cultures in which pregnancy is a prized condition women emphasize its appearance, whereas in other cultures women seem to delight in camouflaging it as long as possible. In Westernized cultures where clothing is fitted to the body, a maternity garment must expand with the figure and accommodate increased perspiration. It should provide absorbency, loose fit, comfort, layers for temperature control; it must avoid any constriction (see Figures 2-3a, b).

[12]William C. Smith, "The Protective Clothing Market," *Industrial Fabrics Review,* Vol. 65, No. 5 (Sept. 1988), pp. 49–54.

[13]Victor Papanek, *Design for the Real World* (New York: Bantam Books, 1973), pp. 97–98.

[14]Fourt and Hollies, *Clothing: Comfort and Function,* pp. 4–5.

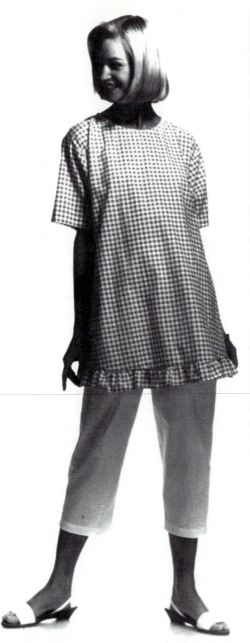

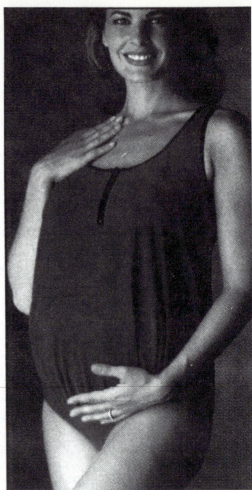

FIGURE 2-3b Maternity swimwear combines two special needs: the activity needs of swimming and the shape, comfort, and expansion needs of pregnancy. (Courtesy of Christina U.S.A. Inc.)

FIGURE 2-3a Maternity wear must expand with the figure, be absorbent, loose, and comfortable. (Courtesy of **McCall Pattern** Company.)

6. The Elderly. The percentages of elderly people in populations around the world are rising as life expectancies increase, and even though they form a relatively small market, it is a significant one. The fairly low, fixed incomes, fixed preferences, and increasing immobility of many of the elderly often mean minimal consumption. Yet mental and psychological capabilities and interests often continue while physical capabilities decline. Joint and finger stiffness, stooped shoulders, upper arm and neck flabbiness, thickened waists, all suggest incorporating clothing features to accommodate these physical changes comfortably and attractively.

Such features might include front rather than back openings, velcro rather than snap or button fastenings, and use of several lighter layers rather than one heavy layer of clothing. Age brings lessened body-temperature control and increased susceptibility to hypothermia (extreme body-heat loss). Research has shown that many elderly people perceive clothing as a useful tool to increase their control over body temperature.[15]

Some firms do make "matron," or "half-sizes," but more attention has often been given to aesthetic needs than to functional ones. Oriental and other cultures revere age whereas Western cultures generally prize youth and disdain age. Social attitudes are often reflected in the amount of attention given to clothing for the elderly.

7. The Handicapped. Handicaps defy generalities because each type presents its own unique needs. Temporary handicaps, such as a broken leg, have a different range of needs from permanent paralyses, amputations, blindness, mastectomies, incontinence, birth defects, or wheelchair confinement. Mental and emotional illnesses or severe retardation often have physical aspects that affect clothing needs. Whatever the situation, clothing should not further complicate a handicapped person's problems. It should generally be flame-resistant, washable, soft, absorbent, and have easily accessible and simple openings. It should also be attractive to lift morale as well as physical appearance. Research on meeting clothing needs of the disabled is growing but merits more attention.[16]

While most of our attention has been on outerwear, the special design needs such as shoes, hosiery, underwear, and accessories for all ages and occupations also require conscientious designer attention.

---

[15]Carol E. Avery, Ruth Pestle, and Pamela M. Radcliffe, "Hypothermia, Use of Textile Items, and the Elderly," *Clothing and Textiles Research Journal,* 4, No. 1 (Fall, 1985), pp. 53–59.

[16]Elizabeth Echardt May, Neva R. Waggoner, and Eleanor Boettke, *Independent Living for the Handicapped and the Elderly* (Boston: Houghton-Mifflin Company, 1974), Chaps. 7, 8, 9, App. D.

STRUCTURAL DESIGN

The structural design allows a garment to function. It determines what textures and notions it will contain, the construction lines and shapes of parts, how they are put together and will relate to each other and to the body, how the garment will fit, where and how it will open and close, and how it will allow for movement, protection, air circulation, and safety. Frank Lloyd Wright's architectural maxim that form follows function also applies to dress. The most successful designs are often those that meet their functional criteria and purpose with the simplest form, and because of their structural honesty and apparent simplicity, have the greatest visual beauty and timelessness.

Structural design must agree both with the garment's function and with the structure of the human figure. Perhaps the major challenge of clothing design is to translate a flat, two-dimensional fabric into a three-dimensional creation, a hollow structure capable of containing the volume of the human form and conforming to its contours at the same time that it allows for motion, dimensional change, and protection. Researchers have suggested classifications of garment interaction with the body as enclosed (wrapped, suspended, preshaped, or combination), attachments to the body or its enclosures, and hand-held objects.[17]

A garment must allow for movement and ease, yet hold its shape. How it does that will depend largely on manipulation of the visual design elements (line, space, shape, and texture), which are discussed in later chapters. Textural qualities of the fabric and grain use within parts and at seams are important. When problems arise in an otherwise well-designed garment, they may stem from asymmetrical body features, off-grain fabric (warp and filling yarns not at

---

[17]Joanne B. Eicher and Mary Ellen Roach–Higgins, "Definition and Classification of Dress," in Ruth Barnes and Joanne B. Eicher, eds., *Dress and Gender: Making and Meaning* (Providence, R.I.: Berg Publishers, Inc., 1992), p. 18.

right angles to each other), or construction problems such as faulty pattern layout or unbalanced or unevenly sewn seam lines.[18] Any of these conditions can hinder movement, comfort, or appearance.

The structure and flexibility of the fabric affect the fit, flexibility, and structure of the garment. Contemporary active lifestyles and demand for snug yet flexible garments stimulate development of active wear that fits, is light and washable, and holds its shape, yet moves with and contours the body. To address these needs, researchers have explored garment pattern design considering the relationship between body movement and differing fabric flexibility.[19] Care requirements and performance, shrinkage, or fading of interior notions and linings as well as face fabric affect structural success and must be considered as an integral part of the design (see Figures 2-4a, b, c). The numbers, kinds, locations, and directions of construction lines and

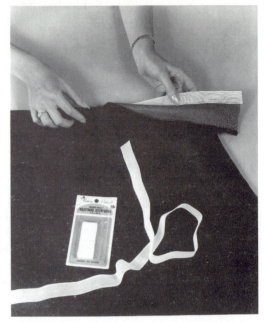

FIGURE 2-4b Interfacing and belting affect performance in functional and structural design. (Courtesy of Belding Lily Company, subsidiary Belding Heminway Company, Inc., Box B, Shelby, North Carolina.)

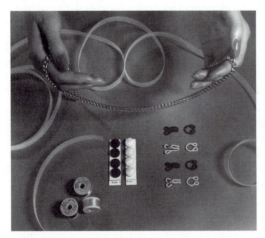

FIGURE 2-4a Notions needed for construction must be considered an integral part of design. (Courtesy of Belding Lily Company, subsidiary Belding Heminway Company, Inc., Box B, Shelby, North Carolina.)

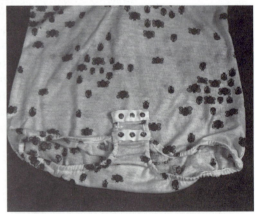

FIGURE 2-4c Notions like body suit snap tape allow versatile structural design. (Courtesy Belding Lily Company, subsidiary Belding Heminway Company, Inc., Box B, Shelby, North Carolina.)

---

[18]Carolyn L. Moore, "Factors That Affect Undesirable Garment Drape," *Journal of Home Economics,* Vol. 84, No. 3 (Fall 1992), pp. 31–34.

[19]Beate Ziegert, "A New System for Designing Active Wear," *Human Ecology Forum,* Vol. 16, No. 2 (Spring 1987), pp. 15–18.

shapes determine functional fit and visual composition. Thus, the structural design of a garment affects both its functionality and its appearance.

Sewing beginners sometimes choose styles with few seams or darts believing that they will be easy to construct, but often the student learns the hard way that any structural seam, dart, gather, or pleat also allows the opportunity to manipulate fit. Conversely, fewer seams or darts reduce opportunities to control fit; so placement and contour of each is more critical and requires greater skill and precision. Thus, those garments that appear the simplest often demand the greatest drafting and draping skill.

Any construction technique such as a seam or dart that is visible is decorative as well as structural. Each structural part should be "honest"—to its purpose, to the other parts of the garment, and to the body that supports it—to retain functional, structural, and decorative harmony.

DECORATIVE DESIGN

Decorative design is for appearance only. It affects neither fit nor performance. However, it can contribute to the overall purpose of the garment by identifying a team member, for example, or a fireman, or by visually flattering the wearer's good points and concealing figure problems. Decorative design is the least important of the three aspects of design. It is subordinate to and must agree with both functional and structural design. Functional openings, belts, pockets, and buttons, or structural seams, darts, and gathers may also be decorative because they provide visual stimuli as well as fit and performance. But design that deals exclusively with visual effect is decorative only.

There are three general ways to incorporate decorative design into a garment:

1. By the color or pattern in the fabric itself before it is cut (Figure 2-5). Color and

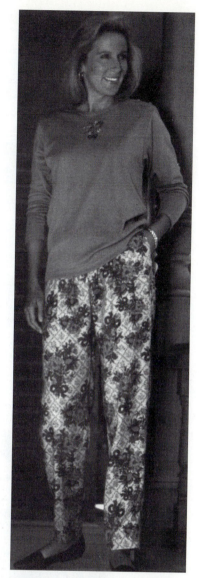

FIGURE 2-5 Decorative design introduced by fabric color and pattern before fabric is ever cut must be placed with care on the structural design. (Courtesy of Mark, Fore & Strike.)

fabric pattern, which are nearly always decorative, are discussed in greater detail in Chapters 8 and 10.

2. By construction details. Examples include top-stitching, piping, trapunto, and quilting (Figure 2-6), tucking (Figure 2-7), shirring (Figure 2-8), binding,

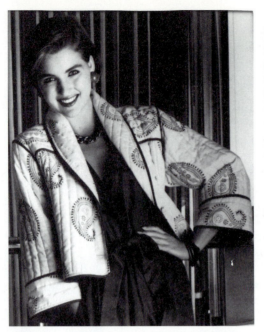

FIGURE 2-6 Topstitching, piping, quilting, and trapunto are construction details that contribute to decorative design. (Courtesy of Cotton Incorporated.)

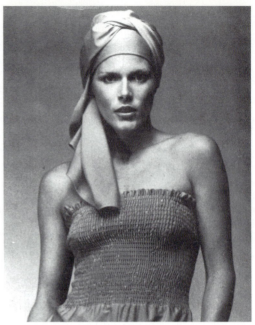

FIGURE 2-8 Elasticized shirring affects fit and appearance. (Photo courtesy of Du Pont, in Klopman "Qiana.")

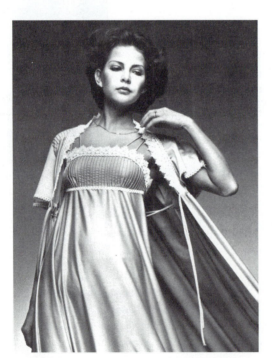

FIGURE 2-7 Tucks add decorative surface interest. (Photo courtesy of Du Pont, in Klopman "Qiana.")

ruffles, quilting, fagoting, hemstitching, drawn work, smocking, and piping (Figure 9a–h). Even though these details are sewn into the garment, their effect on fit or performance is usually minor and their primary purpose is decorative. Even some structural parts, such as collars and cuffs, may be more decorative than functional. Sewing techniques may be both structural and decorative if they affect fit (shirring, especially if elasticized, smocking, or tucks) or warmth (all-over quilting or trapunto).

3. By decorative trims or fabrics applied to the surface of the structurally completed garment. Examples include lace and eyelet edgings and insertions, soutache and other braids, bias binding, ribbon, rick rack, fringe, tassels, pompoms, decorative frogs, buttons, appliqué, embroidery, decorative bows, glass or other beading, sequins, gimp, and other applied trims (Figures 2-10a–k, 2-11a–r, 2-12, and 2-16 to 2-19). Some items, such as buttons, may also be functional (Figures

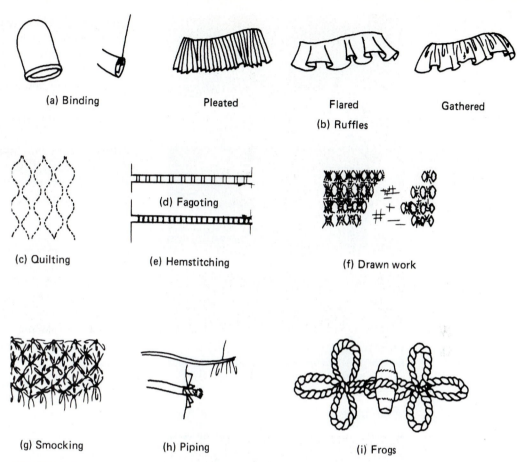

(a) Binding   Pleated   Flared   Gathered

(b) Ruffles

(c) Quilting   (d) Fagoting   (e) Hemstitching   (f) Drawn work

(g) Smocking   (h) Piping   (i) Frogs

FIGURE 2-9 Decorative structural details and trims.

2-13, 2-14, and 2-15). The designer, buyer, teacher, and consumer should recognize names and types of trims and know how to use them.

Many well-designed garments provide enough pleasing visual stimuli in structural lines and shapes, interesting fabric colors, and imaginatively used textures so that little more decorative design is needed. If it is used, several criteria should be considered.

Uses and Purposes

1. Decorative design should agree with functional and structural design. Even a bold, inspiring fabric pattern should seem to emerge from a structural design. Applied trims that have a clear, logical relationship to the structural design provide a visual and psychological satisfaction that they "belong." However, if a trim is attached at random—goes from nowhere to nowhere and has no apparent relationship to structural design—then it has no rationale for inclusion. Not only should an applied trim follow structural lines, but it should be appropriate in size, shape, and texture to the garment and parts of the body where it is used.

2. Decorative design should never be used to camouflage poor workmanship or structural design. Such use often betrays its purpose and may call attention to the reason it was considered necessary.

3. Decorative design should neither be, nor appear to be, tacked on as an after-

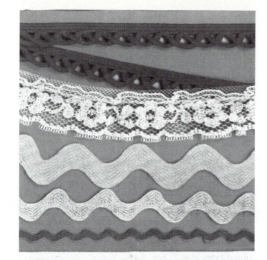

(a) loop braid

(b) lace ruffling

(c) jumbo rick rack

(d) regular rick rack

(e) mini rick rack

(f) twill tape

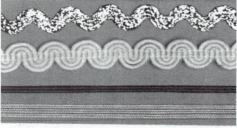

(g) metallic rick rack

(h) scroll braid

(i) soutache braid

(j) middy braid

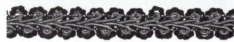

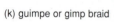

(k) guimpe or gimp braid

FIGURE 2-10 Braid and rick rack. (Courtesy WM. E. WRIGHT CO., Trims.)

thought. It is most successful if it seems to "grow out of" the structural design and complements it and the wearer.

4. "Honesty" of garment design suggests that parts that appear to function actually do, and so are both functional and decorative. These include pockets, buttons and buttonholes, belts, ties, frogs, and other methods of closure.

5. "Understatement" in the use of decorative design often shows a control and restraint that are visually inviting. Lavish use of decoration often looks cluttered and suggests indecision about where to put it or when to stop. Too much decorative design also detracts attention from a focal point, creating visual confusion or a spotty effect.

6. Often the less the decorative design and the more abstract it is, the more versatile the garment. Trims showing chickens, postage stamps, or pots and pans define specific moods and occasions, thus restricting use of a garment. The most versatile garments have simple but well-designed structure, adaptable textures, and small amounts of abstract decorative design. They may be dressed "up" or "down" with accessories for many occasions.

Placement

1. Because the purpose of decoration is to attract attention, it should be placed on the body where one wants attention drawn. Usually the face and neck are attractive and "safe" focal points. One would avoid placing a decorative accent on a part of the body whence attention is to be diverted.

2. Trim should be placed where it is unlikely to be subject to friction, strain, snagging, or pressure. For example, avoid putting three-dimensional trim—such as buttons, bows, or beading—on the seat, back, or the back of the legs, where they will be impractical and uncomfortable. Large bows or flowers at the hips or chin might interfere with movement.

3. Large or heavy trims, even if appropriate to the size of the body and garment part, should be well-anchored close to the body. Flowers, bows, and ties that dangle and flop away from the body are dangerous and look awkward, out of balance, and out of place.

BLENDING FUNCTIONAL, STRUCTURAL, AND DECORATIVE DESIGN

Having identified and analyzed functional, structural, and decorative characteristics and criteria brings us to combining them into a blended whole. Each aspect belongs naturally and attractively to the others.

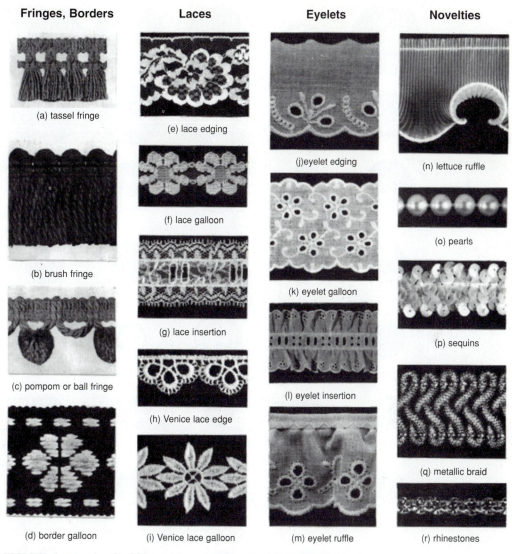

Fringes, Borders	Laces	Eyelets	Novelties

(a) tassel fringe

(e) lace edging

(j) eyelet edging

(n) lettuce ruffle

(b) brush fringe

(f) lace galloon

(o) pearls

(c) pompom or ball fringe

(g) lace insertion

(k) eyelet galloon

(p) sequins

(h) Venice lace edge

(l) eyelet insertion

(d) border galloon

(i) Venice lace galloon

(m) eyelet ruffle

(q) metallic braid

(r) rhinestones

FIGURE 2-11 Applied linear trims. (Courtesy WM. E. WRIGHT CO., Trims.)

Decorative design accents and supports structural design which allows the garment to fit and function. Figure 2-20 provides an excellent example of blending in a special need garment: an international airline flight attendant's uniform in which each aspect of design is well-applied and beautifully blended to meet needs likely encountered in airline service. Functionally, the two-piece uniform provides warmth and protection by the coverage of the style, yet provides freedom of movement by loose sleeves, gently fitted bodice, and front skirt pleats and opening for walking. The cotton texture is sturdy for serviceable wear, yet soft and absorbent for comfort and coolness, and easily cleanable from possible in-flight needs. It is safely fitted close to the

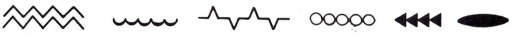

FIGURE 2-12 Decorative stitching.

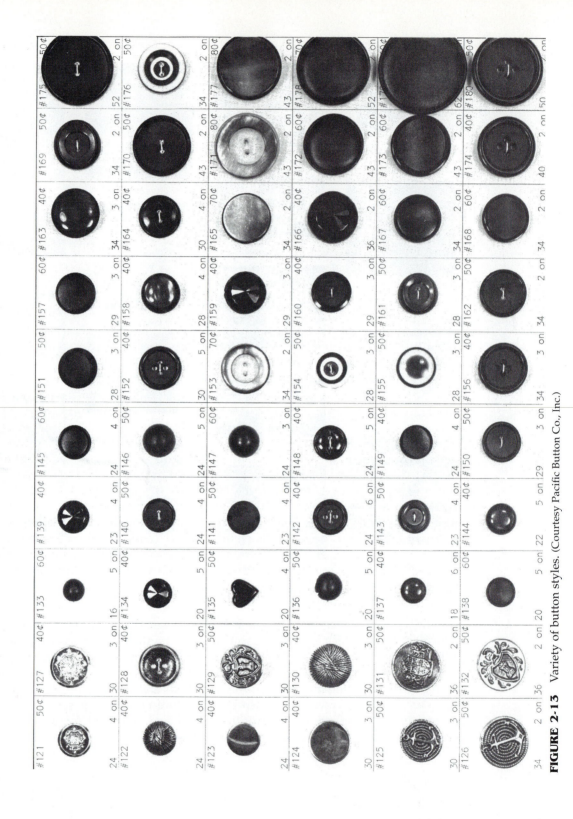

FIGURE 2-13 Variety of button styles. (Courtesy Pacific Button Co., Inc.)

28

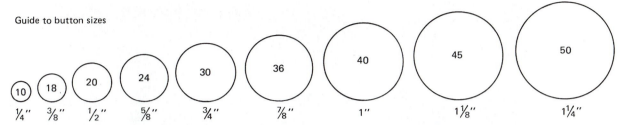

Guide to button sizes

| 10 | 18 | 20 | 24 | 30 | 36 | 40 | 45 | 50 |

¼″ ⅜″ ½″ ⅝″ ¾″ ⅞″ 1″ 1⅛″ 1¼″

FIGURE 2-14 Button sizes are described as "lines," as shown. (Courtesy Pacific Button Co., Inc.)

figure without bulk or appendages that would be hindrances or dangerous in tight airplane spaces. Structurally, the tubular forms agree well with the body that supports it and are smooth and compact. The front jacket and skirt openings allow easy access. The texture also provides body to hold the style and flexibility for movement.

Decoratively, the fabric pattern and colors present traditional Southeast Asian dress styles. Together they provide an ethnic identification that delightfully blends classic and current, and does so in traditional colors that are calming and soothing to passengers. The fabric pattern is pleasant, versatile, and practical. Its border well supports the structural design as it follows and accents the structural neckline and center front, and jacket, sleeve, and skirt hems. It draws attention to the face and neck with other locations echoing support. All decorative design is in the fabric and styling, avoiding any extra surfaces or appendages that could hinder performance. The criteria for each aspect of design appears well met and beautifully blended to present a practical, comfortable, unified, functioning airline uniform which at the same time uniquely and attractively identifies the airline, demonstrating a successful blend of functional, structural, and decorative design.

Faster-paced lifestyles also increase functional, structural, and decorative design demands on special needs clothing such as fast-food restaurant uniforms. One example has cited functional criteria including freedom of movement, temperature control, comfort, safety, easy care, sanitary, storage provision (pockets), and accommodation of pregnant workers. Structural criteria included ease of dressing, accessible and adjustable closures, durability, sizing for young and mature figures, and relatively close fitting. Decorative criteria included identification of the restaurant and wearer's role (hostess, manager, or counter-worker), color coordination with restaurant interior, back as well as front aesthetic interest, and classic appearance suitable for a range of ages and figure types.[20] Achieving such a blend of the three aspects of design is essential for garment success whether in special needs or everyday wear.

---

[20]Jane E. Workman, "Improving Uniform Design For Foodservice Workers: Criteria Prototypes," *Journal of Home Economics*, Vol. 83, No. 3 (Fall 1991), pp. 17–22.

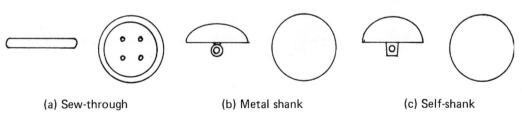

(a) Sew-through   (b) Metal shank   (c) Self-shank

FIGURE 2-15 Button types.

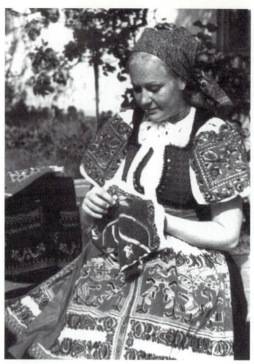

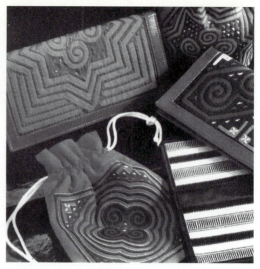

FIGURE 2-18 These intricate traditional Thai appliqués show a surface-applied decorative design. (Courtesy of Thai Airways International Limited.)

FIGURE 2-16 The rich embroidery on this traditional Czech costume follows and fills the structural shapes for a lush, over-all effect. (Courtesy of Czechoslovak Airlines.)

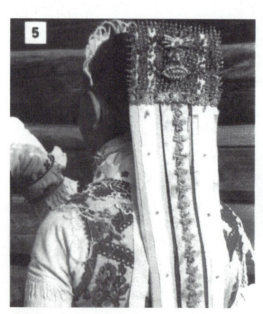

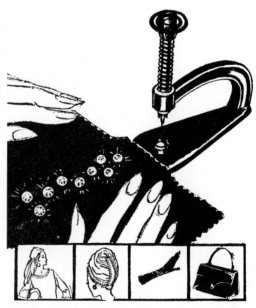

FIGURE 2-17 The applied lace, beading, lace, and ribbons add rich decorative design to this traditional Czech festival headdress. (Courtesy of Czechoslovak Airlines.)

FIGURE 2-19 Trim setters assist in applying rhinestones, studs, and other similar trims. (Courtesy A. H. Standard Co., Brisk-Set of 28 West 38th Street, New York, New York 10018; under Patent No. 3,483,603; other patents pending.)

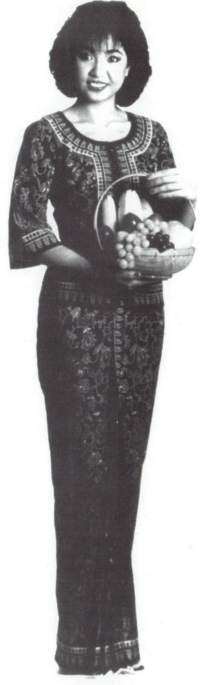

FIGURE 2-20 The traditional "sarong kebaya" is beautifully adapted to modern and specialized needs of an airline flight attendant, combining cultural and airline identity with function, grace, and practicality in a lovely blend of functional, structural, and decorative design. (Courtesy of Singapore Airlines Limited.)

SUMMARY

Clothing design involves three aspects: functional, structural, and decorative, *in that order of importance.* Each aspect must succeed and interact with the others for a garment to fulfill its purpose. Criteria, plans, execution, and evaluation for design process are all given in terms of functional, structural, and decorative criteria. A whole garment or part may exemplify one, two, or all three aspects of clothing design.

Functional design deals with how things work or perform. Some functions—such as motion, protection, health and safety, and warmth or coolness—are common to all clothing or parts. Other functions apply only to specialized needs, such as those for special occupations or sports, children, pregnant women, the elderly, and the handicapped.

Structural design determines garment contours, construction, and closings that affect fit and allow functional performance. It agrees with the structure of the human form supporting the garment and is subordinate to functional design.

Decorative design is for appearance only. It may serve various visual purposes, but affects neither physical fit nor performance and is subordinate to both function and structure. Decoration may be incorporated in fabric color or pattern, in nonfunctioning construction details, or by applied trims.

CLASS ACTIVITIES

1. Study examples of several types of garments to compare *different structural* means of meeting *similar functional* needs. What are different structural methods of providing functional needs?
   (a) Openings/closures? (zippers, plackets, buttons and buttonholes, snaps, velcro, etc.) Which is most appropriate for different body areas? Degrees of action? Garment types? Why?

(b) Freedom of movement? (loose fit, ease, fullness, stretchy fabric, etc.) Which is best for sports, business, casual, or dressy use? Why?

(c) Walking? (bifurcated styling, gathers, pleats, slits, short garments, etc.) Which is most appropriate for certain events, activities, age, climates, etc.? Why?

(d) Physiological modifiers? (loose fit, ease, layering, fiber content, fabric structure, etc.) Which is most effective for insulation? Ventilation? Reflection? Absorption? Certain climates? Why?

(e) Protection and safety? (compact styling; fiber content; fabric structure; coverage; avoidance of constrictions, extensions, or reduction of body control, etc.) Which is most appropriate for certain conditions? Climates? Activities? Why?

2. Bring to class and analyze a garment you consider either a very *good* or a very *poor* example of functional design in one or more of the following areas: movement, physical modifier, protection, health and safety; or special needs of occupational, sports, action potential, children, pregnancy, elderly, or handicapped. What makes it a good or poor example? If it is poor, what would you change to improve it for its purpose?

3. Choose one of the special needs listed in activity 2 as outside influence and use design process to create functional, structural, and decorative criteria for a garment.

4. Make three copies of one structural design picture. Show how you might incorporate decorative design on one with fabric pattern and color, on one with construction details, and on one with applied trims. Compare their effects. How do the different techniques influence placement of decoration? How do techniques influence effects? Care requirements?

5. Find a good and a poor example of *blending* functional, structural, and decorative design. Use general and any relevant special need criteria to analyze what distinguishes them.

6. List your personal criteria for a successful garment. Why are these important to you? How have they changed in the last five years? Why?

3 *Culture, Illusion, and Clothing*

Since a well-designed garment is a successful blend of the functional, structural, and decorative aspects, functional and structural design must always be kept in mind while working with decorative design. Why is the visual component so important? Why do we study it? Why is so much money spent on it? Why has a whole industry developed around it?

From many possible answers, two major reasons emerge. First, the eye can be fooled; the world is not always as it appears. Second, we want to be wanted, to be accepted by others important to us. Our appearance influences that acceptance (or rejection), and cultural values determine what constitutes acceptable appearance. Here optical illusions and cultural values come together. In many cultures, people recognize and use visual illusions to manipulate and bring their appearance closer to a visual ideal. In short, visual illusions in dress are used to control appearance and increase cultural acceptability.

CULTURE, PERSONAL APPEARANCE, AND ACCEPTABILITY

Acceptability or rejection results from daily cultural experiences that condition our responses. These include not only illusory visual cues, but also ideas of beauty, ugliness, and utility. Clothing is an excellent example of these ideas, to which we are culturally conditioned from birth.

People usually see clothing as an object of both beauty and utility, but members of one culture may rave over a dress as exquisite while people of another culture may find it ugly. What one culture treasures as indispensable, another discards as useless trash. As Anderson noted, "... design problems are not solved in a vacuum. The logical idea behind the expression 'form fits function' is intruded upon by the structure of ... society.... The designer must study both to solve design problems."[1]

Culturally conditioned ideals of beauty have varied drastically from one society to another and at different periods of history. For example, the voluptuous, well-rounded female figure idealized by one culture or historical period may be seen as just fat and flabby by another. Or the tall, sinuous model admired by one society may be ridiculed as skinny and starved by another. A figure asset in one culture may be a figure fault in another. As Roach and Eicher note, "... whatever the physical attribute, it only becomes a beauty problem in reference to some cultural ideal."[2]

Not only does each society have its own ideal of beauty, but within each culture ideals and fashions change with time. Further, the individual in any given society changes with age, physically and in tastes and preferences. Browsing through a department store from junior to misses to women's to matron departments reveals as much about *personality* changes through the life cycle as it does about size changes. Many of these personality changes are learned.

Kinds of Learning

There are two general *kinds* of learning—cognitive and affective—and two general *ways* of learning—consciously and through conditioning. Understanding these shows how our visual ideals develop.

Cognitive learning deals with the factual, intellectual, or mental. For example, the statement "This dress hem stops at the knees" describes an observable, provable fact. A statement is made, a condition is in-

dicated, a mental idea is established, but no judgments are made.

Affective learning deals with feelings, attitudes, values, beliefs, emotions, and subjective judgments. Examples would be, "A dress hem at the knees is too short and indecent," or "It is too long and dowdy." All these affective reactions inject value judgments of good and bad, of desirable or undesirable. These are learned along with, or sometimes before, cognitive information. Cognitive and affective are so often and unconsciously intertwined throughout life that it is difficult to recognize and untangle each in practice. To do so is critically important, however, because affectively learned values determine what we do with cognitively learned facts: whether we ridicule, cherish, ignore, distort, believe, reject, or even perceive them as facts.

The family and culture first and most deeply determine these feelings and values. These early developing values and attitudes set a lifelong stage that vitally affects the child's self-image, sense of worth or rejection, tolerance, prejudice, curiosity, suspiciousness, and the like. What is your reaction to a stranger dressed very differently from you? You may feel that your reaction is entirely dependent on the stranger's appearance, but your perception depends as much on the set of attitudes and feelings you bring to the viewing as it does on the way the person is dressed.

As children grow, they learn actions and attitudes about clothing that will gain acceptance by those important to them. These people are often called "significant others," because they have the power to satisfy—or withhold satisfaction from—a person's physical and emotional needs. Much of the significant others' behavior in conveying clothing ideals is based on their own already existing ideals; thus the cultural pattern is continued.

Ways of Learning

Conscious teaching, the most obvious way of learning, is the intentional effort to impart

---

[1]Donald Anderson, *Elements of Design* (New York: Holt, Rinehart and Winston, Inc., 1961), p. 12.

[2]Mary Ellen Roach and Joanne B. Eicher, *The Visible Self* (Englewood Cliffs, N.J.: Prentice Hall, Inc., 1973), p. 102.

knowledge and ideas. It involves study, lecturing, reading, guided experiments, demonstrations, and other conscious instructional or learning techniques. It is the approach on which all "educational" systems are based, and constitutes what most people think of as "learning"—something that comes from a book, the classroom, or from specific instruction, such as "this is the way to wear this."

Conditioning, the other major way of learning, is often not explicit, as is instruction. More often it is suggested, implied, insinuated, subjective, subtle, or even unconscious, resulting from unlabeled and repeated observations or imitations. It is a gradual realization of what is regarded by significant others as proper or improper. It is the kind of awareness that one "catches on to" when a pattern is sensed in repeated actions. It is the gradual and insidious "making one's own" or internalizing an ideal or value. Often we do not even realize we have it until some event calls it into play. Then our unconsciously conditioned response seems natural and automatic: "*Of course* that's how to wear it," one says, as though no other way were conceivable. Or one thinks "Nobody told me, I just knew," but not knowing *how* one knew. Conditioning is growing up in one's own culture and unconsciously absorbing its values as the result of many small, related, often seemingly minor experiences. Thus, one may look at something and think "pretty" or "ugly," believing the quality to be in the object rather than in one's own opinions, and not knowing how those opinions were reached.

A friend may say she chose a particular dress, "because I like it." But if you ask, "Why do you like it?" reasons may include "Because it makes me feel good" or "It suits me." Asking "why" to those reasons may lead to difficulty in thinking of a specific reason because there have been so many small, forgotten feelings that have evolved over years. They have become so much a part of our unconscious, culturally conditioned selves that none of us can thoroughly or objectively explain our behavior. Conditioning

is of critical importance and invites much more educational recognition because of its profound influence on formal learning of behaviors, including dress behavior.

Affective learning often happens through conditioning, and cognitive learning through intentional teaching. Early affective conditioning within the family and culture has the greatest impact; it more often and more deeply determines *initial* feelings, attitudes, and values about dress and its use. Often before they even start school, human beings have culturally conditioned

1. opinions about clothing,
2. concepts of beauty and ugliness,
3. ideas of what constitutes acceptable appearance,
4. degrees of susceptibility or resistance to visual illusions,
5. concepts of ways to gain acceptance.

Human beings can change; so early conditioned learning may be reinforced, modified, or reversed by later conditioning and teaching. However, later learning is influenced by initial learning, a fact which helps explain why dress habits may be difficult to change once they are firmly established. We often feel "funny" the first time we wear a garment very different from our accustomed dress.

Aesthetic and Cultural Purposes of Dress

The choice and use of clothing are often intended to promote acceptance of the wearer as well as meet functional needs. Most people want to be wanted, to be accepted by others, and first impressions of appearance are very influential. Until there is some other communication, visual appearance may be the only cue inviting a reaction. A favorable social response is more likely if the visual impression is pleasant; so most people dress to please those important to them, including those who claim to dress only to please themselves, since what pleases them is also culturally conditioned by their previous interaction with others.

Because interpretation of visual cues is largely culturally conditioned, similar cues may evoke very different reactions in different cultures. For example, the widening effect of horizontal stripes may be appealing in one culture and repulsive in another. Even similar use of the same element in the same culture may result in strikingly different effects. For example, using line in exactly the same way on seven different figures will give seven different effects, as anyone who has ever seen the back of a row of uniformed men or women of varying sizes and shapes can testify. Uniforms often emphasize figure differences more than likenesses because they provide a common basis for comparison (Figure 3-1).

Such differences can make clothing design recommendations slippery business; there are not always exact rules without exceptions. Some factors of "beauty" may have widely accepted "formulas," such as the symmetry of formal balance or the "golden mean" ratio of proportion. But because most uses of art elements and principles are highly subjective and culturally varied, just stating a guideline or principle does not guarantee success in its use. Even "success" is often individually and culturally defined.

Because concepts of "attractive" are also culturally conditioned, the wearer ultimately decides what effects to cultivate according to personal cultural values and aspirations. Written advice on the use of visual design elements and principles is aptly described by Roach and Eicher as "prescriptive literature."[3] Knowing what effects certain uses of line, shape, color, texture, or illusions are likely to have tells the designer or wearer how to manipulate them to attain the desired look. However, the wearer is still the one to make the final decision. Advice may tell how to look thin or fat, but one must decide which way one wants to look. Traditional uses of "should" or "shouldn't" often implied what the wearer should want as well as how to get it. This is an excellent example of affective conditioning, whereby an advisor assumes that a particular effect is wanted, and by prescribing means for its achievement, insidiously helps create that want. However, in this book a "should" or "shouldn't" is appropriate *only if* the wearer wants the effect; it does not tell the wearer to want a particular effect.

"Desirable" visual effects come and go, and prescriptions tied to them quickly become obsolete. However, if one knows which methods produce which effects, one can change effects as often or seldom as desired. Illusions play a major role in creating

---

[3]*Ibid.*, p. 20.

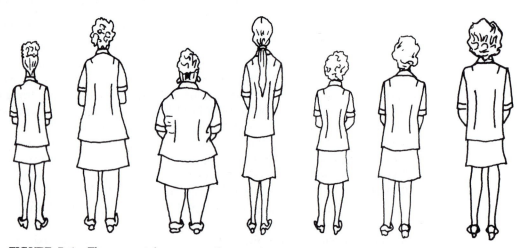

FIGURE 3-1 The same style on seven figures gives seven different effects.

these effects. Controlling these illusions is much easier if we understand what an illusion is and what causes it, especially since some causes are also culturally conditioned.

CAUSES OF ILLUSIONS

The reasons that humans (and some animals) perceive illusions have intrigued and eluded scientists for centuries. Indeed there are still many puzzles unsolved, but enough is known to generalize that there are two major causes of visual illusions: physiological and learned. Some illusions may contain aspects of both and it may be difficult to distinguish one from the other.

Physical Bases

Physically based illusions result from the physiology of the eye, nerves, and brain; that is, they are not learned and exist potentially in all normally sighted human beings.

Physical body changes, state of health, and aging can affect susceptibility for some illusions. But there is still much to learn about physiological bases of illusions. For example, researchers don't yet know why the eye and brain spontaneously reverse apparent fronts and backs of transparent objects or figures and ground. Understanding visual perception is still a fascinating challenge.

Learned Bases

Understanding how illusions are learned is an equal challenge, and researchers offer several explanations. Illusions may be caused by "imperfect solutions available to [the mind] faced with problems of establishing reality from ambiguity."[4] Or they may arise from mental processes that "under normal circumstances make the visible world easier to comprehend."[5]

These theories suggest tantalizing questions: Since perception includes both stimulation and interpretation, what does an image *mean*? The fact that meanings are learned invites the question raised by Gregory: whether most distortions originate in the brain, rather than in the eye.[6]

Part of the answer is that man must literally learn to see and to interpret visual images. For example, those receiving sight only late in life have very little susceptibility to illusions; they have not learned the "perceptual habits which [underlie] such illusions."[7] People in cultures lacking flat representations of three-dimensional objects (pictures, photographs, drawings, or diagrams) cannot "read" meaning from pictures. One study of two races showed that illiterates of both races were not subject to many visual illusions, but "educated" people in both races were.[8] Hence learning is critical to interpreting visual cues.

The deceptive part about this culturally conditioned learning is that it leads to the development of automatic and unconscious assumptions and expectations that the perceiver does not recall having learned. So he or she falsely assumes these expectations to be both "natural" and shared by all others. For example, a tribal chief arrayed in ceremonial dress and anticipating respect might wonder at being ignored or getting only amused or suspicious stares in midtown Manhattan or Hong Kong, where people have not learned the meaning of his visual cues, nor he theirs.

People who don't realize that assumptions are learned often subscribe to "phenomenal absolutism," which holds that the world actually is the way it appears—to them. This is an example of ethnocen-

---

[4]Richard L. Gregory, "Visual Illusions," *Scientific American,* Vol. 219, No. 5 (Nov. 1968), p. 75.

[5]*Ibid.*, p. 66.

---

[6]*Ibid.*, p. 66.

[7]Marshall H. Segall, Donald T. Campbell, and Melville Herskovits, *The Influence of Culture on Visual Perception* (Indianapolis, Ind.: Bobbs-Merrill, Inc., 1966), p. 81.

[8]J. O. Robinson, *The Psychology of Visual Illusion* (London: Hutchinson & Co. Publishers, Ltd., 1972), p. 111.

trism—the belief that one's own notions of one's own culture are "best," "true," "normal," "basic," or "natural"—which leads to the making of automatic value judgments on all other ways according to that bias.

On the other hand, "cultural relativism" holds that each culture has evolved its own concepts of "best," "true," and "normal" over centuries of defining and meeting its own needs, including those for functional and symbolic clothing. This philosophy recognizes that concepts are learned, not inborn, and tries to understand others' behavior from the others' points of view—if care and time be taken to learn them. People who have learned this approach will not ridicule those who dress or act differently from themselves. Hence, one's perceptual assumptions, expectations, and susceptibility to certain illusions are not only learned, but learned according to one's culture.

Some studies have shown that non-Westerners are more susceptible to the horizontal-vertical illusion. Westerners appear more susceptible to geometric illusions[9] because of cultural habits of interpreting straight lines and angles, unlike "circular" cultures in which most lines are curved.[10]

Similarly, members of cultures lacking pictures to represent three-dimensional objects are less susceptible to pictorial illusions than those accustomed to interpreting flat pictures as objects. In one such culture, students had difficulty understanding Western commercial clothing patterns and construction diagrams; how could those intersecting lines on flat paper have anything to do with a garment? When forest residents—whose visual experiences did not include distant vistas—were first shown pictures representing distant objects, they perceived them as small rather than as distant.[11] The practice needed to learn visual interpretations until they become automatic also develops a susceptibility to some illusions.

Thus, environment and cultural experiences shape how we learn to see;[12] we see what we have learned to look for.

Multiply-Based Illusions

Some illusions have both physiological and cultural causes. Some visual phenomena are labeled "laws" and presumed to be universal. However, some of these "laws" are being questioned. For example, the Gestalt psychological "law of closure" (Figure 4-1j), holds that a row of dots or broken lines is universally interpreted as a line or shape, but that perception may be more cultural than physical, and hence not a universal law at all.[13] The "law of visual perception," in which the stimulus is interpreted as the simplest structure that can give meaning, is also questioned. Some studies have shown the effect to be true at first glance; but with prolonged viewing, the eye (or brain) tends to introduce complexity, either by grouping small shapes or subdividing compound ones.[14] People are also said to interpret visual stimuli patterns as "wholes."[15] But to interpret an image as a "whole something," that thing must be familiar from experience, from cultural learning. All visual symbolism—letters, numbers, words, insignia, logos, traffic signals, or other—is based on culturally learned meanings of "wholes." If the cause of an illusion is mostly cultural, perception may differ vastly for viewers from different cultural backgrounds.

Other multiply-based illusions related to dress illustrate Piaget's observation that people tend to establish visual centers of gravity,[16] or focal points, in a composition, a phenomenon important in using emphasis in garment organization.

[9]Segall et al., Influence of Culture, p. 81.

[10]Richard L. Gregory, Eye and Brain: The Psychology of Seeing (New York: McGraw-Hill Book Company, Inc., 1972), pp. 160–61.

[11]Ibid., pp. 161–62.

[12]Segall et al., Influence of Culture, p. 212.

[13]Ibid., p. 60.

[14]Rudolf Arnheim, Art and Visual Perception (Berkeley: University of California Press, 1971), p. 44.

[15]Rudolf Arnheim, Toward a Psychology of Art (Berkeley: University of California Press, 1972), p. 62.

[16]Robinson, Psychology of Visual Illusion, p. 143.

Illusions and Culture

Why is it important in clothing design whether an illusion is physically or culturally based? If it is physically based, every person, regardless of experience, is subject to it and will have similar, predictable reactions on which the designer, buyer, and consumer can rely. However, if the illusion is culturally learned, then people with varying cultural experiences will have different susceptibilities and perceptions, making their reactions to various designs more unpredictable. This helps explain why some people think a particular garment is beautiful and flattering, and others see it as boring or ugly. It also helps the designer create for a particular market.

A few people seem to have all the "right" physical attributes admired by a certain culture at a certain time. However, many people want to change their appearance to increase their acceptability. Depending on the culture, some may diet, exercise, dye hair, sharpen teeth, or surgically change some "unsatisfactory" aspect of the figure. The optical illusions possible in clothing have become popular in conveying desired effects, camouflaging a "fault," or emphasizing a "good" point. Design elements use visual illusions to create a culturally approved appearance that will enhance personal acceptability. Thus, visual, decorative design and illusions are important in dress because they help increase personal acceptability for people of all shapes, colors, and sizes.

In some cultures, clothes are often designed as though there were only one mythical "ideal" or "average" figure: that of the dress form in the designer's workroom. Real people have figure, coloration, and preference differences that, however slight, make rigid analysis or universal application of guidelines unrealistic. The individual seamstress or custom designer can cater to these personal differences, but most commercial firms and pattern companies cannot. Thus, companies establish size ranges for differences in fit and style. They try to keep proportions similar as they grade sizes larger or smaller, but visual effects resulting from differences in proportion may be as great between the largest and smallest sizes of the same style as between two styles of the same size. This is where knowledge of using visual design and optical illusions to create culturally desired effects is valuable. The wearer should know what visual effect he or she wants to create and how to use visual design and illusions to do it.

Mastering these illusions allows us to manipulate them to control the appearance of dress and create our own ideas of beauty. To do this, we must know the types of illusions, what phenomena happen, and how to control them.

VISUAL ILLUSIONS

Just what is a visual, or optical, illusion? Illusions depend on visual perception, which has two aspects: One is a sensory awareness of a visual image or cue, and the other is a mental recognition of that visual image as representing an actual object. Hence, visual perception means choosing the best interpretation of available visual cues.[17]

Illusions result when we mistake visual cues for the objects they represent, or when misinterpretation of a visual cue "makes us commit a mistake in dealing with the physical world," such as walking into a mirror.[18] Hence, visual illusions are simply misinterpreted or misapplied visual cues,[19] but they have powerful effects in dress that are based on complex mechanisms easier to control if we know the various *kinds* of illusions relevant to dress. Some kinds happen spontaneously; others we can create and control. Some create culturally desirable effects, and so are intentionally employed. Others create distractions or visual confu-

---

[17]Gregory, "Visual Illusions," p. 75.
[18]Arnheim, *Toward a Psychology*, p 154.
[19]Segall *et al.*, *Influence of Culture*, p. 77.

sion, and so are generally avoided. Knowing which is which and how they work enables using desirable ones and avoiding accidentally creating unflattering ones.

Illusions do not happen with a single element in isolation; they occur as lines, shapes, spaces, and colors interact with each other. The types of illusions, phenomena, and clothing examples are shown here to set the stage for further study of illusions as applied to each element in its chapter.

There are two major types of illusions: "static," or not moving, and "autokinetic," or appearing to move. Several types of static visual illusions relate critically to dress both positively and negatively: geometric, depth and distance, after-image, simultaneous contrast, and irradiation. Autokinetic illusions are generally distracting and confusing; so the designer and consumer should be able to recognize and identify them so they may be avoided in clothing.

STATIC ILLUSIONS

Geometric Illusions

Geometric illusions—"carpentered," size and space, and direction—deal with two-dimensional flat lines, distances, angles, spaces, and shapes. Many examples could fit well into several categories. Some researchers refer to one type as "carpentered world" illusions, common to cultures with right-angled books, buildings, and objects seen in perspective.[20] Such illusions occur when the length, shape, or arrangement of lines, angles, and spaces are misinterpreted. In dress they affect apparent height, weight, shape, length, width, or size—all characteristics important to the consumer.

1. "Carpentered" Illusions. These include lines, spaces, angles, interruptions, and intersections that cause illusory lengths, widths, or distortions. Some are useful, and some cause distortions generally best avoided in clothing. Among the useful ones

FIGURE 3-2a Müller–Lyer.

is the *Müller–Lyer* illusion in which a line with angled extensions at each end appears longer than another line of equal length in which the angled lines at each end double back (Figure 3-2a). In dress, the one with extensions will lengthen the figure area (Figure 3-2b, c and Figure 6-35g, n) whereas the one doubling back will be less lengthening (Figure 3-2d).

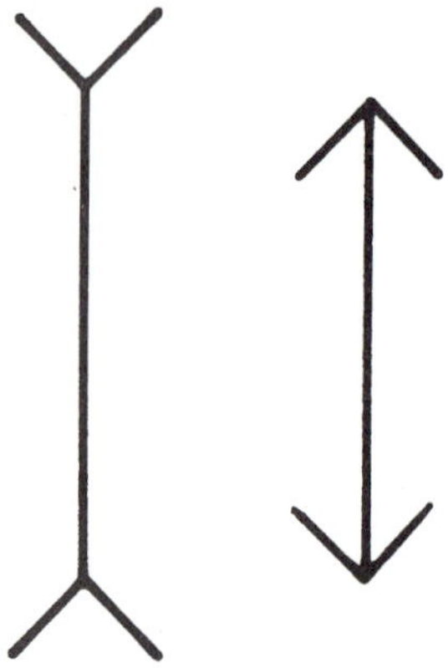

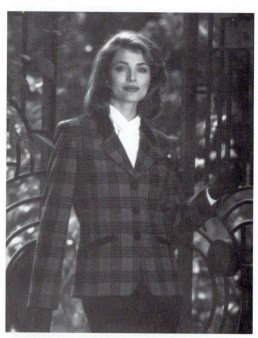

FIGURE 3-2b The jacket V-neck and lower edge V use the Müller–Lyer illusion, creating diagonal extensions that make the center vertical opening line seem even longer. (Courtesy of Pendleton Woolen Mills.)

---

[20]*Ibid.*, p. 84.

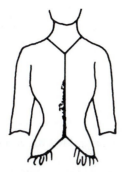

FIGURE 3-2c The diagonal extensions of the center front vertical seem to lengthen the entire bodice and the center line itself.

The *horizontal-vertical* illusion (Figure 3-3a) makes a vertical line seem longer than a horizontal one the same length (Figure 3-3b). The effect is even stronger when a shorter vertical line intersects a longer horizontal one (Figure 3-4a, b). This illusion makes it easier to create lengthening effects.

The *Sander parallelogram* (Figure 3-5a) demonstrates Western tendencies to interpret diagonals and nonright-angled figures as rectangles seen in perspective and misjudge distances as a result. Because the left section is larger, line A–B is seen as longer although line B–C actually is. In dress this tendency may make diagonals seem longer than neighboring horizontal or vertical lines, thus lengthening or widening a figure area (Figure 3-5b).

Apparent angle sizes are influenced by the spacing of surrounding lines (Figure 3-6). In

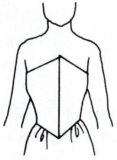

FIGURE 3-2d The diagonals doubling back toward the other end seem to shorten the center vertical and make the bodice area seem shorter than if the diagonals were not there.

FIGURE 3-3a Horizontal-vertical.

Figure 3-6a, the inner angle seems larger where the outer lines are closer, and in 3-6b, smaller where the lines are farther away, making wider angles. This illusion may be translated into dress in many ways; for example, a V neckline may appear wider when edged by a narrow collar than by a wide collar (Figure 3-6b, c).

Dress often makes use of *subtle curves,* which can also be illusory (Figure 3-7a). The more curve of a circle that is used, the rounder it seems. The less of a total curve

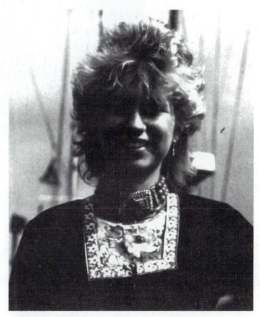

FIGURE 3-3b The vertical lines of the neckline appear longer even though the horizontal one actually is. (Courtesy of the Netherlands Board of Tourism.)

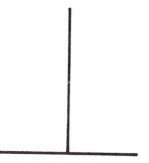

FIGURE 3-4a
Horizontal-vertical intersecting.

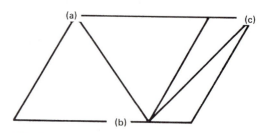

FIGURE 3-5a Sander parallelogram.

that is used, the flatter it seems (Figure 3-7b). Thus the sharpness of a curve or the amount of the circle included influence the feeling of roundness it conveys. The above illusions deal with lengths, widths, areas, or curves.

Another useful type of geometric illusion is "displacement" of which the *Poggendorf* is an example. In it lines are interrupted at an angle that distorts apparent continuation of the line. The center line is

the continuation although the lower one appears to be (Figure 3-8a). In dress structure, a midriff yoke or belt might interrupt an angled line begun by a bodice dart; so slightly moving a skirt dart or pleat could make it appear to be a continuation (Figure 3-8b). Figure 3-12 shows a fabric pattern use.

Less useful geometric illusions include a group in which intersecting lines distort shapes or other lines, and would likely be distracting in clothing. They most likely occur in unwanted distortions between stripes, plaids, chevrons, or other geometric fabric patterns and structural garment

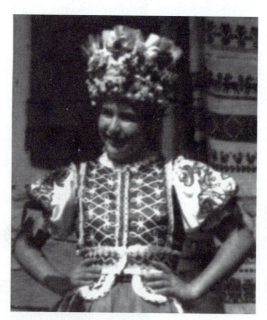

FIGURE 3-4b The shorter center vertical bodice line intersecting the longer horizontal upper belt edge makes the vertical line appear longer in this Czech festival costume. (Courtesy of Czechoslovak Airlines.)

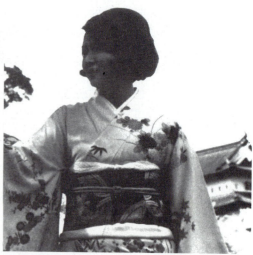

FIGURE 3-5b The diagonal of the overlapping kimono may help lengthen the upper bodice area as the horizontal upper edge line of the obi seems even shorter than it is, using one type of the Sander parallelogram effect. (Courtesy of Japan National Tourist Organization.)

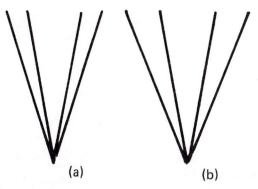

(a)   (b)

FIGURE 3-6   Comparative angles.

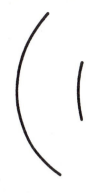

FIGURE 3-7a   Arcs

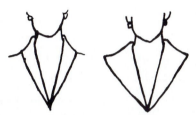

FIGURE 3-6c   Narrow lapels may make a V neck seem wider, and wider lapels will narrow the center section even though they may widen the shoulders.

lines, making the garment appear poorly constructed.

The *Zollner* illusion (Figure 3-9) shows intersecting lines making lines that are really parallel appear angled toward or away from each other. This illusion was first observed in a fabric pattern,[21] and it would make a distracting one.

In the *Wundt* illusion (Figure 3-10) the heavier horizontal parallel lines appear to cave in, whereas they seem to bulge out in the *Hering* illusion (Figure 3-11a) because of the differences in angles of the opposing intersecting lines. The "push" is greatest where the lines radiating from a point intersect the horizontal lines at right angles, making them seem to bend. In clothing, if the horizontal lines were a belt, it would appear unevenly cut, and in the Hering il-

---

[21]M. Luckiesh, *Visual Illusions* (New York: Dover Publishers, Inc., 1965), p. 76.

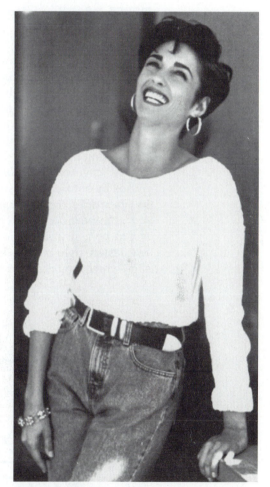

FIGURE 3-7b   The smaller the circle, the more curved a given length will seem. The sharper curve of the inner pocket edge conveys more roundness than the flatter curve of the neckline, even though the neckline is longer. (Courtesy of Levi Strauss & Co.)

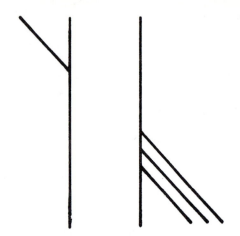

FIGURE 3-8a Poggendorf.

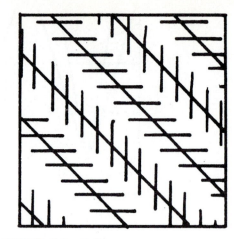

FIGURE 3-9 Zollner.

lusion would enlarge the waist or other area as well as bend the lines (Figure 3-11b). Figure 3-12 deftly avoids the Hering illusion because the diagonal shapes within the horizontal stripes go at different angles and stop at the edges of the stripes without intersecting them.

An *angular distortion* (Figure 3-13a) caused by obtuse angles superimposed on a square makes the lower left corner of the square appear pointed. A clothing example would be a striped fabric pattern (decorative design) used on a pocket (structural design) which would distort the structural de-

sign and suggest poor workmanship (Figure 3-13b).

2. Size and Space Illusions. These are very useful geometric illusions in which the eye incorrectly estimates distances or sizes where comparable images or areas are placed close together. Any slight actual differences appear exaggerated.

Illusions explored by *Aubert* show that *filled space* seems larger than identical empty space (Figure 3-14a, b). Line segments may seem shorter or longer depending on surrounding lengths (Figure 3-15). A variation of this illusion often appears in dress when the total figure seems wider if a center panel is wide compared to outside sections (Figure 3-16a, c), and seems thinner if the center panel is narrow compared to the outer panels (Figure 3-16b, d).

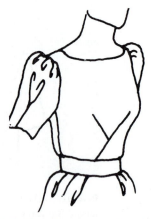

FIGURE 3-8b The pleat at the right, below the midriff, can appear to be the extension of the bodice dart above the midriff, even though it is offset.

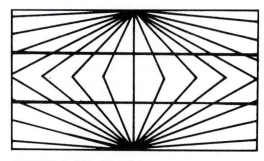

FIGURE 3-10 Wundt.

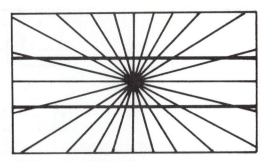

FIGURE 3-11a Hering.

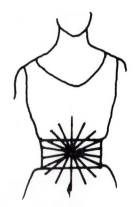

FIGURE 3-11b The radiating lines intersecting the belt edges at right angles push the lines apart, making them seem to curve outward, thus enlarging the abdominal area. In the same way, lines radiating from the neck would make a straight shoulder yoke line seem to sag.

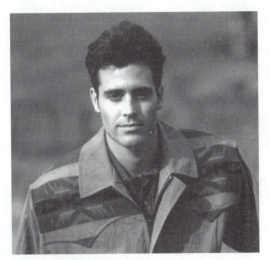

FIGURE 3-12 (left) The three decorative horizontal stripes on the yoke avoid the Hering illusion. Even though the lines in the outer stripes may seem to radiate from the center stripe motif, they go at varying angles and do not intersect any of the stripes. However, the Poggendorf illusion may make some of the lines within the upper and lower stripes appear to be continuations of each other even though they are not. (Courtesy of Pendleton Woolen Mills Menswear.)

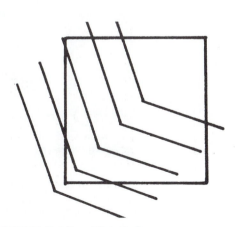

FIGURE 3-13a Distorted square.

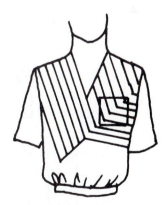

FIGURE 3-13b The fabric pattern angles large enough to invite comparison with garment structural lines lead the obtuse angles to point and distort the right-angled structural lines of the pocket, making it seem poorly constructed.

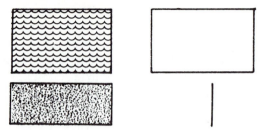

FIGURE 3-14a   Aubert filled space.

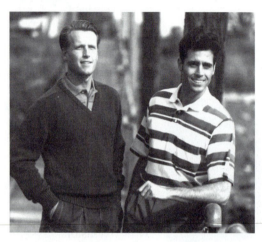

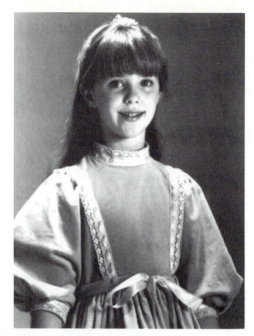

FIGURE 3-16c   Size differences are often exaggerated and then generalized to the entire figure, as in this bodice with a wide center section in relation to narrow side sections making the entire bodice seem wider. (Courtesy of Cotton Incorporated.)

FIGURE 3-14b   The space inside the silhouette of the shirt on the right seems larger because it is "filled" or subdivided by fabric pattern, whereas the "empty" space makes the sweater on the left seem smaller even though it has long sleeves. Prolonged viewing of the light/dark pattern contrasts of the stripes could create a shape as well as color after-image which is lessened by the break created by the collar. (Courtesy of Pendleton Woolen Mills Menswear.)

FIGURE 3-15   Line segments.

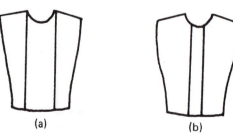

(a)   (b)

FIGURE 3-16   Varying width panels.

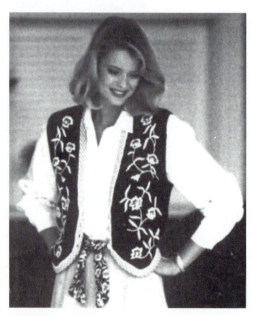

FIGURE 3-16d   When a center section is narrower compared to outer sections, the entire figure seems thinner. (Courtesy of Mark, Fore & Strike.)

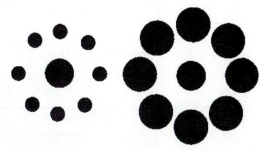

FIGURE 3-17 Titchener and Lipps circles.

Size differences are exaggerated in the *Titchener and Lipps* circles (Figure 3-17) when the larger circles make the center one seem smaller, and smaller circles make the center one seem larger. In clothing, a full, bulky style may make a neighboring fitted area seem small, as in Figure 6-34m in which the puffy sleeves and full skirt make the midriff waist appear even smaller, or Figure 6-34g in which the bouffant skirt makes the bodice seem smaller.

Arrows or points in circles control direction of attention and apparent size. The inward arrows shrink the left circle, and the outward arrows expand the right circle (Figure 3-18). In clothing illusions this is most likely in fabric patterns or trims that focus inwardly and reduce (Figure 2-11e) or thrust outward and expand (Figure 2-11i).

3. Directional Illusion. This illusion is generally one to avoid because it may make the figure appear to lean when a strong linear directional feeling *within* a figure is attributed to the *whole* figure (Figure 3-19). In clothing, strong interior diagonal lines going in one direction in fabric pattern may make the whole figure seem to be leaning in that direction (Figure 6-9). This is why diagonal lines in dress need opposing diagonals for balance (Figures 6-35f, g, l).

Depth and Distance Illusions

A second major category of static illusions includes depth and distance which occur mostly because we have learned to interpret flat images, such as paintings and photographs, as the three-dimensional objects they represent. Then when visual cues are ambiguous, they may be interpreted in several ways. These include: (1) foreshortening, convergence, perspective, and representing three-dimensional objects by flat, two-dimensional images; and (2) ambiguous figures in (a) figure/ground reversals and (b) spontaneous change of position. In dress these illusions are most likely to emerge accidentally in fabric patterns such as scenic vistas or "op art" which may cause two- and three-dimensional and size perceptions, and become distracting. Being able to identify them allows avoiding unwanted illusions.

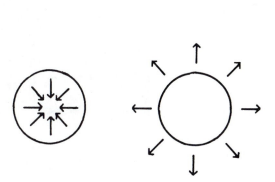

FIGURE 3-18 Arrow effects of size.

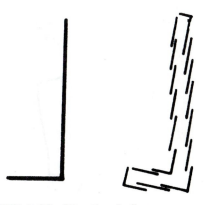

FIGURE 3-19 Directional effects.

1. Foreshortening of Receding Horizontals, Convergence, and Perspective. These illusions derive from change in perspective and size as we view objects from greater distances. Some cultures portray same-sized objects as larger if closer, and smaller if farther away; so we learn to link distance and size. If two objects are the same size, but one has surrounding cues that suggest distance, we interpret that object as being larger. Figure 3-20a is easy to see as a sidewalk of equally sized squares appearing smaller as they recede, while (b) lacks the depth. In the *Ponzo* or "railroad" illusion, the upper bar appears larger (Figure 3-21) and in *same-sized boxes* the upper box appears larger (Figure 3-22), both because their surrounding cues of greater distance suggest that they should look smaller if they were really the same size. But being the same size makes the "farther" ones appear larger. These illusions are most likely in scenic prints which are seldom recommended for clothing use because of likely distortion of structural design and distractions.

2. Ambiguous Figures. These have two subcategories: (a) figure/ground reversals, and (b) spontaneous change of position. Both are most likely to occur in fabric pattern when the visual cues are few or ambiguous, thus allowing more than one

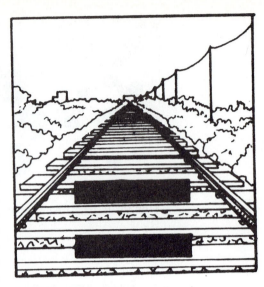

FIGURE 3-21   Ponzo or railroad.

interpretation which can be distracting and distorting.

Usually the smaller area in a composition is seen as figure and the larger area as background regardless of light and dark areas or apparent flatness (Figure 3-23). In clothing, the effect is heightened if the figures are distinct and seem clearly "in front of" the background (Figures 3-24a, b).

Figure/ground reversals happen when vague or few visual cues allow a shape, often curved, to be interpreted either as foreground shape or background space, and perception switches back and forth. The viewer may be able to switch interpretations at will, but he cannot perceive an area as

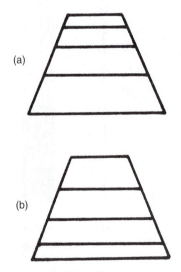

(a)

(b)

FIGURE 3-20   Sidewalk.

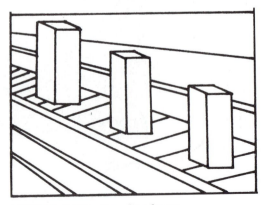

FIGURE 3-22   Receding boxes.

FIGURE 3-23 Shape and space perception.

both figure and ground at the same time. One of the best known figure/ground illusions is the *reversible goblet* (Figure 3-25) which can be seen either as the silhouette of a goblet or as two faces. The convex curve of one becomes the concave curve of the other.

Spontaneous change of position occurs in two types when visual cues allow several interpretations of a flat image. In the first type, the object stays the same, but the angle of viewing suddenly changes as in the *Necker cube* (Figure 3-26) which appears as a transparent cube, sometimes viewed

from below and other times viewed from the top. The *reversible cubes* illusion (Figure 3-27) sometimes appears as a receding stack of cubes viewed as lighted from above, sometimes as an arching ceiling of cubes lighted from below, rarely as a flat surface of diamonds.

In the second type, the vantage point stays the same, but the object itself seems to change. The *duck/rabbit* illusion (Figure 3-28) can be seen either as a rabbit facing left or a duck facing right.

Because ambiguous-figure illusions in dress are most likely to occur in fabric pattern, the designer and consumer must decide whether their effects are desirable or distracting.

After-Images

After-images are images we see *after* we have been looking at a stimulus long enough to tire the retina. Then when we look away,

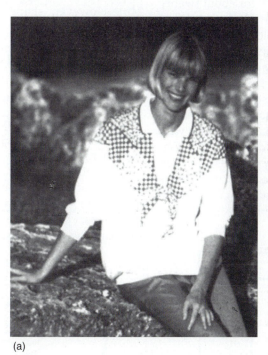 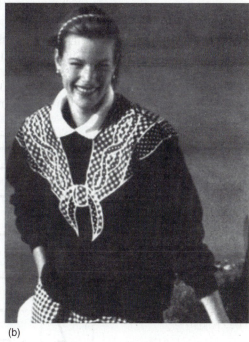

(a)   (b)

FIGURE 3-24 Though the colors of the appliquéd "scarf" outlines are similar in (a) and (b), they are both easily seen as smaller, distinct figures "in front of" the larger areas whether the backgrounds are light or dark. The light background of the shirt in (a) may create an after-image darkening the complexion, whereas the dark background of the shirt in (b) will make an after-image lightening the face. (Courtesy of Mark, Fore & Strike.)

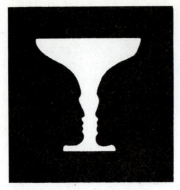

FIGURE 3-25 Reversible goblet.

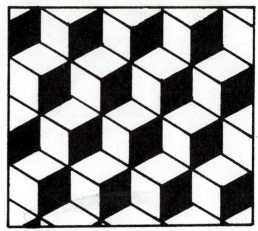

FIGURE 3-27 Reversible cubes.

the eye may continue to see the same thing, or a "positive" after-image, which gradually disappears or is replaced by the opposite quality or "negative" after-image which continues until the eye is "rested."

After-images happen most with shape and color. Shape after-images are positive, and color after-images are negative. Stare at the triangle in Figure 3-29 for about twenty seconds and then at the black dot. What shape appears? What color is it? The white (negative) triangle (positive) may be lighter than the paper. After-images of bright light are usually positive, such as seeing bright spots after looking at flash bulbs or the setting sun; then change to negative. Sometimes negative after-images appear with lines. Stare at the lower curved line in Figure 3-30 for about twenty seconds, and then look at the upper line. An after-image makes the straight line seem to curve slightly upward.

After-images are physically based, not learned; so all normally sighted people are susceptible. Color after-images are very useful in clothing, as viewing a light garment may make a face appear darker (Figure 3-24a), and looking at a dark garment may make a face appear lighter (Figure 3-24b). However, shape and line positive after-images need care to avoid light and dark fabric pattern shapes (Figure 3-14b) being echoed where not desired.

Irradiation

There are at least two types of irradiation, one of which is very useful in clothing, and the other is very distracting. Both are based on perception of a light area being diffused beyond, or "spilling over," actual shape edges into darker areas. Over-stimulated nerves react beyond the area of actual stimulus causing light areas to appear larger at

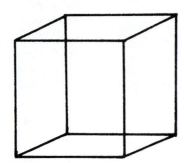

FIGURE 3-26 Necker cube.

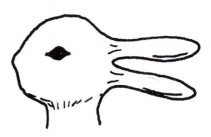

FIGURE 3-28 Duck and rabbit.

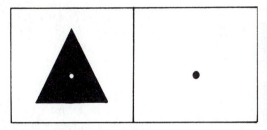

FIGURE 3-29 Shape and value after-image.

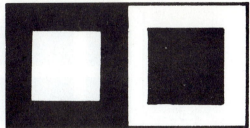

FIGURE 3-31 Irradiation: expansion.

the expense of neighboring darker ones[22] (Figure 3-31). This version is one reason light areas look larger and dark areas look smaller, a very important illusion in dress (Figures 3-24a, b). Figure 3-32 uses irradiation to make the light areas stand out, seeming to expand into the black as it shrinks into a background, thus accenting the key features of the picture. But a distracting version of this same illusion (Figure 3-33) creates an effect of shadows where the white bars cross,[23] and should be avoided in fabric pattern.

Simultaneous Contrast

Simultaneous contrast is the exaggeration of differences (contrast) while being viewed (simultaneous). It occurs with color when opposing hues, values, and intensities placed next to each other increase each other's apparent differences. Dull colors intensify brighter colors; complements brighten each other; dark colors make light colors look lighter and light colors darken dark ones further (Figure 3-34). Here, the grey on the white looks darker than the

FIGURE 3-30 Curved and straight line after-image.

grey on the black. Hold a string along the straight, center edge and the illusion is even stronger[24] (see also Chapter 8). After-image, irradiation, and simultaneous contrast are physically based, and all are powerful illusions often used in dress.

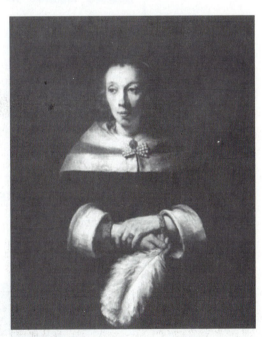

FIGURE 3-32 Irradiation advances and enlarges the white collar, cuffs, and feather against the black bodice, which appears to recede; simultaneous contrast heightens impact of dramatic light/dark contrasts. (*Portrait of a Lady with an Ostrich-Feather Fan*, by Rembrandt van Rijn; c. 1660; National Gallery of Art, Washington; Widener Collection.)

---

[22]Luckiesh, *Visual Illusions*, p. 121.
[23]*Ibid.*, p. 118.

[24]Gregory, *Eye and Brain*, p. 72.

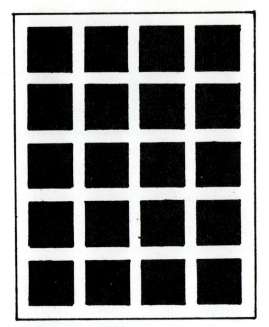

FIGURE 3-33 Irradiation: shadows.

The seventeenth century dress in Figure 3-32 uses both simultaneous contrast and irradiation dramatically. The dark garment and background make the white collar and cuffs seem even lighter, and they in turn deepen the black.

AUTOKINETIC ILLUSIONS

Autokinetic (self moving) illusions appear to flicker, undulate, waver, or otherwise move. In clothing they can be very distract-

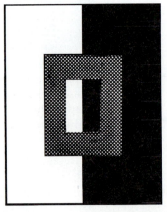

FIGURE 3-34 Simultaneous contrast.

ing, even uncomfortable, and so are described to allow recognition and avoidance. They involve two kinds of apparent movement: (1) a moving object stops but appears to continue moving, and (2) a still object appears to move. The latter is most likely to happen in fabric patterns of fine lines as shadowy shapes seem to undulate over the lines (Figure 3-35).

Color-induced movement happens in "chromatic aberration" when the eye lens constantly refocuses to accommodate bright long and short wavelength hues, and they appear to quiver or vibrate (see Figure 8-24 in color insert). This is described further in Chapter 8.

USING ILLUSIONS

We have seen different types of illusions related to clothing and their physical or learned bases. Matching these can help predict likely viewer susceptibility even though (1) there may be exceptions, (2) some appear to have multiple bases, and (3) much is yet unknown about illusions. Most normally sighted people generally experience physically based illusions, and most Westerners also experience learned illusions.

Dominantly Physically Based

Figure/ground reversals

Spontaneous change of position

After-images

Irradiation

Simultaneous contrast

Autokinetic

(a) Fine stripes   (b) McKay's rays.   (c) Herringbone

FIGURE 3-35 Autokinetic.

Dominantly Learned

Geometric carpentered world

Size and space

Directional

Foreshortening of horizontals

Some illusions can be controlled in clothing to introduce culturally desired effects. Others need to be known and recognized to avoid accidentally creating culturally undesirable, confusing, or distracting effects in dress. Many of the "avoidable" ones are most likely to emerge in fabric pattern or its interaction with structural design rather than in structural design alone.

Generally Useful

Müller–Lyer

Poggendorf

Horizontal-vertical

Sander parallelogram

Comparative angles and arcs

All size and space illusions

Shape/space perception

Color after-images

Size irradiation

Simultaneous contrast

Generally Avoided

Zollner

Hering

Wundt

Distorted square

Directional

Foreshortening/convergence

Figure/ground reversal

Spontaneous change of position

Shape/line after-images

Shadow irradiation

Autokinetic

With understanding of the phenomena as a foundation, the useful illusions will be explored further in chapters on the elements they use: geometric and size and space illusions in chapters on space, line, shape, and pattern; and after-images, irradiation, and simultaneous contrast in the chapter on color. When elements, principles, and other interactions have been examined, their collective use in creating and controlling illusions is brought together in "Applied Illusions" (Chapter 28) showing a range of ways to achieve specific effects.

Art Elements and Principles in Structural and Decorative Design and Illusions

The art elements and principles are the designer's tools used to create desired visual effects and illusions. The elements are the ingredients, and the principles are the guidelines to manipulate the elements. Together they provide a large and powerful resource of media to apply to both structural and decorative design. Their visual effects and illusions may be new ones, or may strengthen or camouflage existing ones.

One might compare element and principle use in clothing design to preparing a dish: The elements such as line and color as visual ingredients compare with eggs and sugar as food ingredients. Principles compare to the recipe telling how to use the ingredients.

Thus, an element of visual design is a basic ingredient, substance, component, or medium from which a visual design is made. They are: line, space, shape or form, light, color, texture, and pattern. Each element has its own characteristics, which no other single element can duplicate.

A principle of visual design is two things: (1) it is the verb/process: the guideline, the technique, the method of manipulating an element of visual design for a specific effect; and (2) it is the noun/product: the term that describes the visual effect resulting from successful application of that method. For example, when the methods and techniques of balancing are successfully applied, the resulting visual effect is one of equal distribution of weight, or balance. Thus, a principle is both a process and a product.

We have seen that physiologically-based illusions are timeless and universal: they happen to all normally sighted people worldwide and throughout history. Element and principle visual effects are the same: their existence and effects span centuries and continents. A vertical line, for example, was as lengthening and narrowing in 320 B.C. Greece or Egypt as it was in A.D. 1510 in China or India, or 1997 in Europe, or will be in 3056 in Brazil.

While *effects* stay the same, it is their *combinations, relationships,* and *desirabilities* that change with cultures and historical periods. *It is these changes that create "fashion" in which desirability of certain combinations and relationships comes and goes in a given culture.* These three factors will change many times during the professional and personal life of the designer and consumer. The designer will be much better prepared to create or cope with such changes if the designer commands knowledge to use the timeless and universal elements and principles to create desired changes. That means knowing how to recognize and use them, not just in current Western fashions, but any time, any place. To encourage this broader view, *illustrations show historical and ethnic as well as current Western examples,* even though it is assumed that the reader is "Westernized" to some degree since this edition is in English and deals primarily with Western dress. Cultural value judgments are generally avoided, and a global, timeless view is stressed.

Elements are discussed in Unit II, and principles in Unit III. Since some of them are mentioned before each is discussed in its own chapter, they are all briefly defined here.

Visual design element. Basic component, medium, ingredient, or material of art used to create a visual design.

Line. An elongated mark; a connection between two points; the effect made by the edge of an object.

Space. Area or extent. A particular distance; the total area to be organized; the area within, around, or between shapes or forms. May be two-dimensional (flat) or three-dimensional (with volume).

Shape. The outline of an object; the area or space enclosed by a real or imaginary line. Two-dimensional objects are often referred to as shapes, three-dimensional ones as form.

Light. Electromagnetic radiation that makes things visible; radiant energy permitting visibility.

Color. Light waves perceived according to the visible hue spectrum; experienced as colored light rays emanating directly from a light source, or as light reflected from pigmented surface.

Texture. Visible and tactile quality of any surface or substance, such as fabric surface and body.

Pattern. Arrangement of lines, spaces, or shapes on or in a fabric.

Visual design principle. Guideline, technique, or method of employing a visual design element; the visual effect of its successful application.

Repetition. Use of the same thing more than once; the same thing arranged in different locations.

Parallelism. Use of lines or rows of shapes lying on the same plane, equal distances apart at all points and never meeting.

Sequence. Following of one thing after another in a particular order; a regular succession.

Alternation. A repeated sequence of two and only two things changing back and forth in the same order.

Gradation. A sequence of adjacent units usually alike in all respects except one, which changes in distinct and consistent steps from one unit to the next.

Transition. A smooth, flowing passage from one condition and position to another, without an observable point of change.

Radiation. Feeling of movement steadily bursting outward in all directions from a visible or suggested central point.

Rhythm. Feeling of organized movement; regulated intervals of staccato or flowing, continuous movement; usually involves repetition.

Concentricity. Use of progressively larger layers of the same shape, all having the same center and usually parallel edges.

Contrast. Feeling of difference; opposition of things for the purpose of showing unlikeness. May involve different elements or different qualities of the same element.

Emphasis. Feeling of dominance; creation of a focal point or most important center of interest.

Proportion. Result of comparative relationships of distances, areas, amounts, degrees, or parts. May be linear or two- or three-dimensional. Occurs on four levels: (1) within one part, (2) among parts, (3) between part and whole, (4) in clothing, between garment and wearer.

Scale. Comparative relationship of size regardless of shape; a consistent relationship of sizes to each other and to the whole.

Balance. Feeling of evenly distributed weight resulting in equilibrium, steadiness, repose, stability, rest.

Harmony. Feeling of agreement; consistency in mood; a pleasing combination of differing things used in similar ways around a common theme; a pleasing effect mid-way on a continuum between boredom and conflict.

Unity. Feeling of completeness; sense of cohesion or oneness; an integrated totality. Something complete and harmonious within itself; a relationship resulting in finished wholeness.

SUMMARY

Visual aspects of clothing design have become important in the clothing industry for two fundamental reasons: First, the eye and brain are subject to optical illusions; second, people want to be wanted. Every society has culturally conditioned ideals of beauty which may be achieved by manipulating optical illusions to create desired visual effects.

Cultural conditioning shapes our concepts of beauty, ugliness, and utility. Although these concepts change with time, we respond according to values we have learned. Learning is of two kinds, cognitive and affective, and is arrived at by conscious teaching or by conditioning through suggestion and implication. Facts about dress may be cognitively and consciously learned, but desire for certain clothing appearances is more often affectively conditioned. Decorative or visual design in dress has become important because it provides a means of making oneself more acceptable to others by creating culturally desirable visual illusions and effects.

Visual illusions are misinterpreted visual cues. Static illusions occur when the image is still; autokinetic illusions, when it appears to move. Major types of static illusions include geometric illusions that result from misjudging angles, spaces, and shapes, and involve "carpentered," size and space, and directional illusions. Illusions of depth and distance generally result from the cultural practice of interpreting a two-dimensional image as a three-dimensional object. They include foreshortening of receding horizontals, perspective, convergence, and ambiguous figures, such as figure-ground reversals and spontaneous change of position. After-image, simultaneous contrast, and size irradiation happen spontaneously. Some illusions have physical causes, some are culturally learned, and some may have several causes.

Some illusions are considered more useful than others in creating culturally desirable effects in clothing or between clothing and the body. These include many geometric and size and space illusions, color after-images, size irradiation, and simultaneous contrast. Those to recognize and avoid accidentally introducing include certain geometric, directional, depth and distance, shape after-image, shadow irradiation, and autokinetic illusions.

The designer uses art elements and principles to create desired illusions and effects. Basic element and principle effects are worldwide and permanent. "Fashion" comes as their combinations, relationships, and desirability change in different cultures and periods. Designers require thorough knowledge of elements and principles to control their use and effects any time and any place.

CLASS ACTIVITIES

1. With fashion magazines and department store or mail order catalogs for the class as a whole, or a set for each of several groups, compare fashion ad copy with factual catalog descriptions. Identify whether writing is cognitive or affective. Discuss whether the messages are being conveyed with conscious statement or conditioning implication. What is the effect of each? How would you compare the techniques and effects of communication?

2. Using a sample garment and the class in three groups, have one group describe the garment in cognitive terms and the second describe it in appealing affective terms. Without the third group having seen the garment, they may read both descriptions and choose "which garment" they would prefer and why. Then the class as a whole compares both writings and the garment and discusses how choices are influenced.

3. With the class in groups, each group is assigned a figure characteristic that might be culturally considered a "problem." Then discuss (a) what kind of visual effect will counter or hide that problem, (b) which kind of illusion can create that desired effect, (c) how could it be incorporated in clothing, and then (d) design a garment or outfit applying that illusion to the problem and evaluate its effect.

4. With the class in groups, each group is assigned a different illusion to find in Chapter 6 style line drawings or photographs throughout the book, fashion magazines, catalogs, pattern books, historic or ethnic sources, or actual garments. Explain how that style is an example of that illusion and what effect it is having on the figure.

5. Compare the effects of the phenomenon of a "pure" illusion in the text and its applied adaptation in a garment or picture.

6. On a paper or poster showing three identical silhouettes, students subdivide the interior space of each using a different carpentered world or size and space illusion. Compare their effects and whether they would be best introduced structurally or decoratively. Or, use different placements and applications of the same illusion in each silhouette and compare effects.

II Elements

This unit introduction shows characteristics common to all elements, it sets the stage to study each in its own chapter, and it provides a basis for later understanding of their interactions.

The elements of visual design have been defined as the basic ingredients or components from which a visual design is made. They are: space, line, shape or form, light, color, texture, and pattern. Professionals and consumers who use the elements need command of their aspects, variations, concepts, and vocabulary. They must know both the potentials and the limitations of each element.

Certain uses of an element give a certain effect under many conditions; other uses produce a certain effect only under specific conditions. Although the elements are unique and fundamental, they are not always mutually exclusive. For example, shape cannot exist without line and space. Color depends on light. All these elements show their influence on pattern, which technically is not a single element but an arrangement of other elements on or in a surface. Understanding each element heightens awareness, not only of their individual potentials, but of their interactions and the magnificent array of their possible combinations.

Certain conditions that apply to all elements are introduced here to show points they have in common even though examples differ with each element. They all (1) have several aspects or facets, (2) have both physical and psychological effects, and (3) may be used to reinforce, modify, or counter existing personal qualities or other elements effects.

ELEMENT ASPECTS

Every element has its own qualities or "aspects," and each aspect has many "varia-

57

tions." These are the designer's means to create any effect possible. A hierarchy could be shown with the element as first order, aspects as second order, and variations as third order. For example, the *element* line has as one *aspect* direction which then has *variations* of vertical, diagonal, or horizontal. The *element* of color has as one *aspect* hue which has *variations* of red, green, yellow, and many more. Some aspects could be further classified. For example, the aspect of hue may be primary, secondary, or tertiary, and each of these has variations. Each element always contains all of its aspects, and each aspect may use one or more variations in a given application. For example, the (element) color (aspect) of hue might use (variations) blue, yellow, and green in the same garment. Aspects and variations define the element's capabilities and provide the designer's repertoire for the visual design of any garment. The following list shows the aspects of each element.

Space. Dimension, enclosure, empty/filled, position.

Line. Path, thickness, evenness, continuity, edge sharpness, edge contour, consistency, length, and direction.

Shape and form. Relative dimensions, size, contour, density.

Light. Wavelength, frequency, photon.

Color. Hue, value, intensity.

Texture. Determinants, surface qualities, hand qualities, light reactions.

Pattern. Source, interpretation, arrangement.

PHYSICAL AND PSYCHOLOGICAL EFFECTS

All elements convey both physical and psychological effects. *Physical visual effects,* including optical illusions, are those that *create apparent physiological changes* of height, weight, or contour of the figure or in color or textural properties. They make the viewer think there is really a difference in the physical characteristic, such as making hair appear lighter than it really is. A mid-range category that applies mostly to color could be called "psychophysical." It combines the physical and psychological as it conveys a *feeling* and an association about a physical property, but does not actually make it look that way. For example, "warm" and "cool" colors convey a "cozy" or "chilly" feeling without necessarily affecting apparent surface temperature.

Psychological effects influence feelings, such as dignity or sophistication, and *moods,* such as youthfulness or happiness. Physical effects are more likely in cultures with some susceptibility to optical illusions. The psychological effects described here are found in most cultures that have experienced Western influence.

These visual effects often come in pairs of opposites, with a line or continuum between extremes. A given effect will range somewhere along that line. For example, in motion effects of color, a "stationary" grey would be at a mid-point between "advancing" white and "receding" black. In mood, a "business" gabardine would range at a point between "sporty" denim and "elegant" chiffon. The following table lists physical, psycho-physical, and psychological effects (types and pairs) and the elements that can contribute to that effect. How each element does that is discussed in that elements chapter. Table II-I shows (1) what physical and psychological effects accompany all elements, and (2) which elements lend themselves to which kinds of effects.

Any element use gives its physical and psychological effects as an inseparable "package." For example, the exciting, passionate *psychological* effects of a brilliant red cannot be separated from its enlarging *physical* effects. Certain element uses tend to pair certain physical and psychological effects, as the following list of examples shows.

	Physical Effects	Accompanying	Psychological Effects
	advancing/enlarging		assertive, bold, dramatic
	receding/reducing		calm, quiet
	heavyweight		serious
	lightweight		carefree
	warm		happy, cozy, cheerful
	cool		calm, serene
	filled, textured		complex, busy
	plain		simple

TABLE II-1   Physical, Psycho-physical, and Psychological Effects of Elements

Effects		Elements					
Types	Pairs	Space	Line	Shape/ Form	Light/ Color	Texture	Pattern
Physical/psycho-physical							
Size (including size and space illusions)	enlarge/reduce	X	X	X	X	X	X
Motion (including size and space illusions)	advance/recede	X	X	X	X	X	X
Density	lightweight/ heavyweight	X	X	X	X	X	X
Distance/extent (including useful geometric illusions)	heighten/shorten lengthen/shorten widen/narrow	X X X	X X X	X X X			
Temperature	warm/cool				X		
Sound	loud/quiet				X		
Moisture	wet/dry				X		
After-image	opposite				X		
Simultaneous contrast	differences				X		
Psychological							
Emotion (partial example list)	assertive/dainty exciting/calm happy/sad stately/casual	X X X X	X X X X	X X X X	X X X X	X X X	X X X X
Action	active/passive stimulating/soothing	X X	X X	X X	X X	X X	X X
Gender	masculine/feminine	X	X	X	X	X	X
Complexity	simple/sophisticated	X	X	X	X	X	X
Drama	dramatic/subtle	X	X	X	X	X	X
Power	strength/delicacy	X	X	X	X	X	X
Age	young/mature	X	X	X	X	X	X

REINFORCING AND COUNTERING

Reinforcing and countering are two techniques of controlling attention. They can be used either for existing figure characteristics or for other elements. For figure characteristics, a *reinforcing* element use would strengthen an existing figure quality, such as using vertical line to strengthen and reinforce figure height. A *countering* technique would minimize, camouflage, or oppose an existing condition, such as straight lines in clothing to counteract too much figure roundness.

To reinforce element interaction, for example, the physically enlarging effects of a bright color would reinforce the enlarging effects of a large scale pattern in the same outfit. Or psychologically, the soft effects of a pastel color reinforce those of a filmy texture in the same garment. On the other hand, the businesslike psychological effect of a tailored style of shapes would counter the mood of a playful fabric pattern. Especially among elements, countering effects can be used successfully, but need great care to be compatible and not clash.

GUIDELINES FOR ALL ELEMENT USAGE

Several guidelines for creating generally desirable effects emerge repeatedly and apply to all elements.

1. The main visual purpose of clothing is to enhance the attractiveness of the wearer. Flattering clothing helps focus attention on the wearer; it does not demand attention to itself. Successful clothing design helps the wearer remain dominant; the person wears the clothes, the clothes do not wear the person.

2. One way to focus positive attention on the wearer is to use elements to draw attention *to* his or her attractive features. In so doing, attention is drawn *away* from culturally less desired features; or they may be camouflaged, allowing attention to go where it is desired and away from where it is not desired. Advancing qualities are best used where attention is desired, and receding ones as background.

3. A guideline for people with extremes of height, coloration, or weight is to use moderate characteristics of elements and avoid extremes of their qualities. Extremes of the element that repeat the personal extreme will accent it by similarity, and extremes of the opposing quality will accent it by contrast. For example, a bulky texture would accent a large person's size by similarity, and a flimsy one would emphasize it by contrast. A medium texture would not accent body size as textural extremes would.

4 *Space*

DEFINITION AND CONCEPT

Space is presented first because it is the element with which the designer starts. It is the empty area or extent, the basic raw material of visual design. It is the "blank" that the designer uses line, shape, color, texture, and pattern to subdivide, fill, break, push, pull, and otherwise manipulate into a composition. Visual design could be defined as organization of space, as it invites manipulation. What artist can resist an "empty" canvas? What designer can ignore a "blank" silhouette?

Space may be two-dimensional emptiness (flat) or three-dimensional void (hollow or having volume). It gives of itself to become shape, form, and pattern, and determines how all elements relate. Draw a line around some space and you have a flat shape. Cover a hollow with a surface and you have a form. Shape and form are simply enclosed space, making an inseparable relationship between space, line, and shape.

Why, then, is space so often ignored in analysis of clothing design? Most reasons result from cultural habits that call attention to enclosed space by naming it "shape." These shapes usually represent objects with meanings, such as "flower," "ball," or "pocket" which further focus attention on the enclosed space. But not giving a corresponding name to *unenclosed* space makes it easy to ignore. Yet shape is enclosed space, and surrounding, unenclosed space separates, defines, locates, and relates the shapes, making a critical complementary relationship. So, far from being "left over" from design, space is its beginning and pervasive element.

Artists often use "paired" terms to describe space/shape relationships:

This area	This area
Enclosed Space	*Unenclosed Space*

Enclosed Space	Unenclosed Space
shape	space
figure	ground
foreground	background
positive	negative
internal	external
	interstitial

"Interstitial space" is the space among unconnected shapes. The pairing of shape/space, figure/ground, positive/negative terms appears in Chapter 3 and throughout art literature. Other paired terms describe whether or not the space inside a shape is subdivided by lines, shapes, or pattern:

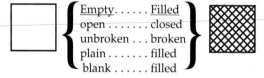

$$\left.\begin{array}{ll} \text{Empty} & \text{Filled} \\ \text{open} & \text{closed} \\ \text{unbroken} & \text{broken} \\ \text{plain} & \text{filled} \\ \text{blank} & \text{filled} \end{array}\right\}$$

These terms help understanding of visual cues that influence our perception of shape and space, and the distinction between them in dress.

CUES INFLUENCING PERCEPTION OF SHAPE AND SPACE

A sense of distinction between shape and space is essential to garment balance, and as we saw in Chapter 3, space can deceive our perceptions. But Figure 4-1 shows cues that help control perception of spatial effects. They include (1) size, (2) overlapping, (3) closeness, (4) density, (5) convexity and concavity, and (6) character of enclosing lines. How these cues are used determines whether we see shape/space and foreground/background spatial divisions as flat or as having a three-dimensional depth and distance. Visual cues that make enclosed space (shape) seem solid or three-dimensional are "advancing cues." They advance, create depth, and increase the apparent distance between foreground and background. Visual cues that reduce apparent distance between foreground and background and minimize a feeling of depth are "flattening cues." They make an area recede, seem hollow, flat, porous, or reduced.

1. Size of Spatial Divisions. Shape sizes that differ from each other and from the background size are more likely to be seen as solid and advancing (Figure 4-1a). Smaller areas are usually perceived as shape and larger areas as space (Figure 3-23). This may result from our everyday experience that a space must be larger for a shape to fit into it. When sizes of subdivisions are similar, the total seems flatter and smoother (Figure 4-1f). In clothing, small shapes like pockets, cuffs, jewelry, buttons, and pattern motifs are perceived as shape and tend to advance; larger areas like skirts or bodices are perceived as background and tend to recede, and the figure/ground distinction is clear (Figure 4-2a). Where sizes of different garment areas are similar, there is confusion as to which is foreground and which is background, and the whole seems flat (Figure 4-2b).

2. Overlapping. Overlapping of shapes so that a complete shape is seen as being in front and a partial shape as behind makes shapes seem to advance and distinguishes foreground from background, as in the flowers overlapping the leaves in Figure 4-1a, and the collar overlapping the bodice in Figure 4-2a. Shapes that are seen completely side by side (Figure 4-1f) seem flat like a picture puzzle, and so have little feeling of depth.

3. Closeness of Shapes. Shapes advance more if they are not touching, are completely surrounded by space, isolated, and floating free, and are seen as being in front of a background (Figure 4-1a). Shapes that are touching suggest that they are on the same surface or plane, hence flat (Figure 4-1f).

Advancing/solid cues | Flattening/hollow cues

Advancing/solid cues

1. Sizes differ (shapes smaller, space larger) (a)

2. Overlapping (a)

3. Shapes not touching (a)

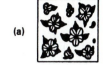
(a)

(f)

Flattening/hollow cues

1. Sizes of areas similar (f)

2. No overlapping (f)

3. Shapes touching (f)

4. Filled (textured or patterned) interior space (b)

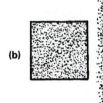
(b)

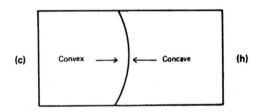
(g)

4. Empty, plain, open space (g)

(c) Convex → ← Concave (h)

5. Convex curves (c) and (d)

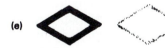
(d) (i)

5. Concave curves (h) and (i)

6. Thick, sharp, solid enclosing lines (e)

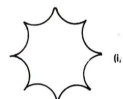
(e) (j)

6. Thin, fuzzy, broken, blurred enclosing lines (j)

For strength of combined advancing effects, note how (a) has differing sized shapes, overlapping petals and leaves, flowers not touching, filled space, convex curves, and thick, sharp enclosing lines. For combined flattening effects, note how (f) has sizes alike, no overlapping, shape edges all touching, porous interior space, no curves, and thin, broken enclosing lines.

FIGURE 4-1 Cues influencing perception of shape and space.

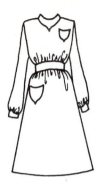

(a) Distinction   (b) Similarity

FIGURE 4-2 Distinguishing among garment parts and their relationships is easier if garment shapes and surrounding spaces are different enough in size to avoid risk of figure/ground reversal illusion and if there is little doubt as to which is foreground shape and which is background space.

4. Density of Spatial Divisions. A subdivided textured, patterned, or filled space is more easily perceived as a solid shape than is a plain area. The latter is easier to see as hollow space or void, or flat and receding. For example, it is easier to see the textured square in Figure 4-1b as a solid shape surrounded by empty space, and the plain square in Figure 4-1g as a hole surrounded by a textured, dense frame. (It is harder to see the empty square as a solid substance and the textured square as a hole.[1]) So filled space advances and enlarges, seems heavier and more solid, while unfilled space seems lighter and recedes (Figure 3-14a). In clothing, patterned or textured areas seem to be in front of plain areas.

An exception occurs when plain pockets are surrounded by a finely patterned fabric. It is clear which is shape and which is background, even though textured or patterned pockets surrounded by plain bodice areas might seem more logical. An-

other variation is eyelet embroidery in which the "shapes" are holes of hollow space surrounded by solid fabric (Figures 2-11h, j, k, l, and m).

5. Convexity and Concavity. Convexity and concavity occur wherever curved lines separate space and shape. The human form is made up mostly of curves. A curved line is convex in the direction toward which it pushes, and concave in the direction that it is being pushed (Figure 4-1c, h). A convexity pushes out as a protrusion, and a concavity "caves in" as an indentation, whether the area is flat or three-dimensional. Areas enclosed by convex lines are easy to see as shapes but difficult to see as holes (Figure 4-1d). It is possible to see an area surrounded by concave lines as a shape, but much easier to see it as a hole surrounded by a frame with convex, scalloped edges (Figure 4-1i).[2]

The above perceptions seem simple enough when all lines are either concave *or* convex, but what happens with areas that have both? If a flat area has touching concave and convex areas of similar size, there is high risk of figure/ground reversal illusions. In Figure 3-25 curves that are convex for the nose and chin become concave for the goblet. Three dimensional convexities and concavities will be discussed shortly.

6. Character of Enclosing Lines. Line variations that are thick, solid, and sharp make the enclosed shape advance, enlarge, and seem more solid and dense and farther from the background (Figure 4-1e). Shapes enclosed by broken, thin, fuzzy, or blurred lines seem flatter, airy, and receding. This is partly because the broken line allows space to flow into and out of the area, suggesting flatness, hollowness, receding, and weakness (Figure 4-1j). Line characteristics are discussed further in Chapter 5.

---

[1]Rudolf Arnheim, *Toward a Psychology of Art* (Berkeley: University of California Press, 1972), p. 248.

[2]Rudolf Arnheim, *Art and Visual Perception* (Berkeley: University of California Press, 1971), p. 225.

SPACE AS GROUND IN A COMPOSITION

Use of perceptual cues to distinguish shape from space invites the question: why is unenclosed space, or background, so vital in visual design?

1. The space around an object gives the object importance, identifies, isolates, defines, and distinguishes it—as in accenting pattern motifs, pockets, or jewelry against a plain background.
2. Space exerts a pressure, which locates and fixates an object at a certain position and distance from other objects, giving stability to a relationship.
3. Space provides distance that determines how shapes, lines, and spatial divisions relate.
4. Space provides rest and relief in a pattern, a visual pause, much as a rest in music or a pause in a sentence provides needed relief from constant sound.
5. Space seems to be behind a shape, pushing it forward and creating depth.
6. Space seems less dense, more airy and hollow than the shapes it surrounds, thus giving these shapes buoyancy.

Thus ground, or interstitial space, is critical "captured space," not just passive, empty distance between other parts, but a tool that gives vitality to relationships of shape.[3] A figure/ground relationship is not simply a static distribution of space, but a highly dynamic interplay of forces in which there is a reciprocal relationship between shape and space, each having equal rights.[4] The designer must have a fine sensitivity to both interstitial space and enclosed space, because the use of each determines the effect of the other. Unenclosed space complements enclosed space, or shape, and shape complements space;[5] both are critical in clothing design.

SPACE AS VOLUME

So far most of our space exploration has been two-dimensional, as flat pictures of garment divisions or fabric pattern. But three-dimensional volume of air space surrounds the body as it moves, walks, runs, or bends, and is critical to functional and structural, as well as visual, design.

Convex and Concave Pressure

We have seen that space enclosed with convex lines seems to have greater density and push out, to want to expand. But open space also pushes in against the enclosed shape. Air pressure is a critical factor of life. An apple in a vacuum will explode from interior pressure; high altitudes with less air pressure may cause swollen feet and legs. A figure of all convex bulges will seem about to explode; one with all concave indentations might suggest imminent collapse (Figure 4-3a, b).

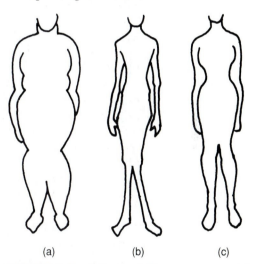

(a) (b) (c)

FIGURE 4-3 A figure of all convex curves (a) with pressure seeming to push out wants to explode. One with all concave curves (b) appears as though too much outside pressure will crush it, and one with both convex and concave curves (c), as in the normal human figure, maintains a feeling of balanced internal and external pressure.

---

[3]Arnheim, *Toward a Psychology*, p. 247.
[4]*Ibid.*, pp. 252, 253.

[5]Graham Collier, *Form, Space, and Vision* (Englewood Cliffs, N.J.: Prentice-Hall, Inc., 1964), p. 36.

Part of the beauty of the human figure is that it is made up of both convexities and concavities (Figure 4-3c). On an average woman's figure the convexities affecting dress are usually the head, shoulder points and shoulder blades, bust, hips, perhaps thighs, buttocks, calves, feet, arms just below the elbow, and hands. The concavities are usually the neck, waist, knees, ankles, and wrists (Figure 4-4a). On a man the major convexities are usually the head, shoulder points, arms just above and below the elbow, hands, buttocks, thighs, calves, and feet, and the concavities are usually the neck area, wrists, knees, ankles, and sometimes elbows (Figure 4-4b).

Knowing the relationships among the location, size, and position of body convexities and concavities is important to the de-signer because: (1) every body concavity helps define a convexity, and (2) every garment depends on the body's convexities for support. A silhouette line comes to rest where the internal pressure of the fleshy shape appears to equal the external pressure of atmospheric space (a pressure sometimes aided by a foundation garment). A designer visually manipulates the play of forces between body and garment convexities and concavities to maintain their complementary relationship and a sense of balance between inward and outward pressures (Figure 4-5).

Space as Hollowness

Although clothing structure is usually analyzed from the outside, it is that hollow space inside a garment that must fit the figure and allow it to move. One might as-

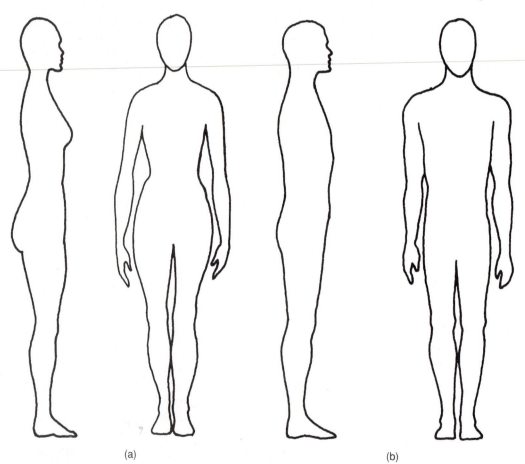

(a)   (b)

FIGURE 4-4 Adult female convexities and concavities (a), and adult male convexities and concavities (b).

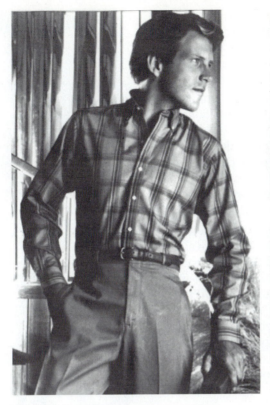 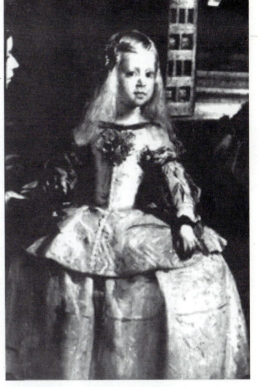

FIGURE 4-5 Body convexities and concavities help keep a balance between inward and outward pressure. Here there is little space between the body and garment, but space is created between pocket layers. Space in the pants is structurally and decoratively "open," and the shirt is structurally "open," but more "filled" or closed decoratively. (Courtesy of Cotton Incorporated.)

FIGURE 4-6 The hollow "trapped" space between the garment and body can insulate and provide space for movement, but if it is extreme it may hinder mobility or entering small spaces. (*The Royal Family "Maids of Honor" and Infanta Dona Margarita* (detail), by Diego Velazquez; 1656; courtesy of Prado Museum, Madrid, Spain.)

sume that interior garment contours are the reverse of exterior ones, and that the exterior and interior must conform to fit.

However, historically, the interiors of garments with padding and boning and petticoats were quite often different from the human form they were meant to enclose (Figure 4-6). Garment interiors were often so rigidly and unnaturally formed that the human figure was grossly squeezed, shoved, distorted, and sometimes injured to fit the garment. And sometimes so much space was trapped between the inside of the garment and the outside of the figure that mobility was affected or sitting in an average-sized chair was difficult

if not impossible (Figures 4-6 and 2-1). Some nineteenth-century hoop-skirts were intended to keep gentlemen at a "proper distance" from the lady. Usually, the more the human figure was distorted, the less functional a garment could be. However, most recent nonceremonial clothing has been designed to be functional, less restrictive, and to have little interior bulk, weight, or rigidity.

Space as hollowness serves four major purposes that affect all three aspects of clothing design. Functional, structural, and decorative design determine how the garment controls its space to meet its four purposes:

1. As seen in Chapter 2, spaces among fabric fibers and yarns provide functional protection, insulating air pockets, ventilation, room for movement, and space for fabric expansion and contraction.

2. Spaces within and among structural garment parts influence their functionality and visual appearance. Space separates the draped folds of a cowl, the pleats or gathers in a skirt, the puffs or flares in a sleeve, or the undulations in a ruffle (Figure 4-7). Space supports the rising stand of a collar (Figure 4-8).

3. Clothing also controls the space between the figure and garment. Either the solid, human exterior and hollow, garment interior contours match closely with little space between body and garment (Figure 4-5), or the garment is less fitted and flows loosely and freely, allowing more space between it and the body (Figure 4-8). Space allows a full sleeve to float free of the arm (Figure 4-6) or to stand out and

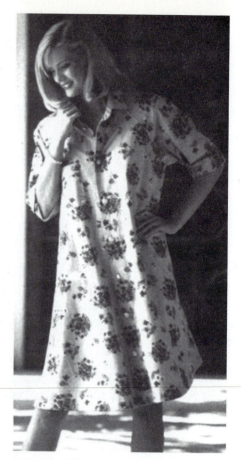

FIGURE 4-8 Volume space helps support the collar and lets the dress float freely from the shoulders. Flat space is decoratively "filled" by flower motifs which are grouped into circular shapes when the distance between each motif is less than the distance between groups. (Courtesy of Mark, Fore & Strike.)

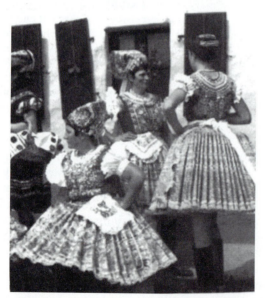

FIGURE 4-7 As volume, space separates the pleats in the skirts of these Czech festival costumes, and helps hold the headdresses and sleeve puffs away from the figure. These skirts are both structurally and decoratively "filled" by pleats and fabric pattern, and appear larger and complex. (Courtesy of Czechoslovak Airlines.)

erect (Figure 4-9). It helps keep position of skirt contours about the figure (Figure 4-9), and provides an area between pocket layers and the figure to place items yet avoid large bulges (Figure 4-5).

4. Clothing also controls the space immediately surrounding the figure. This happens on two levels: (a) with space between layers of clothing that provides air insulation, circulation, and ventilation as well as bulk and room for movement (Figure 4-10), and (b) with space immedi-

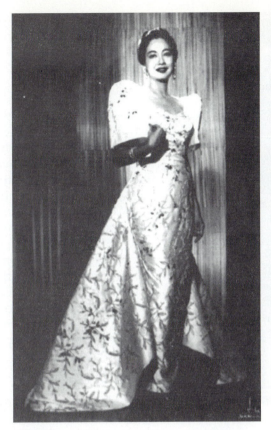

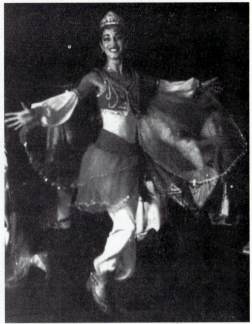

FIGURE 4-10 The sheer cape panels and skirt in this Ciftetelly Turkish dance costume give a layered look between garment layers and increase bulk and command of volume space around the figure as the dancer moves. (Courtesy of the Turkish Government Tourist Office.)

FIGURE 4-9 Space as volume helps support the crisp "butterfly" sleeve on this traditional Philippine *terno* and supports and distributes the flare of its more modern skirt train. The space between the figure and the garment and immediately surrounding it increases a sense of "presence." (Courtesy of the Cultural Center of the Philippines, Manila.)

ately around the entire figure/garment combination. Loose styles such as capes and skirts, which can flare out during movement, create a personal "sphere" allowing body movement and presenting a psychological sense of "presence" and power (Figures 4-9, 4-10, and 4-11).

Figure 4-11 well illustrates all four of these levels: (1) The fuzzy surface texture suggests insulating spaces trapped between fabric fibers and yarns. (2) Space separates each draped fold in the cape, each gather in the skirt, and each layer in the pocket. (3)

The loose styling creates ample space between the figure and the garments to allow freedom of movement. (4) The layering of the flared, draped cape commands space around the figure and creates its own hollow form. The cap captures space near the face, and the surrounding space controlled by the flaring cape extends the figure "presence" well beyond actual figure contours. These functional, structural, and decorative volume space uses also suggest the intimate relationship between space, shape, and texture in achieving garment styles and performance, as we shall see later.

VISUAL EFFECTS OF SPACE USE IN CLOTHING

Illusions in Dress

Space is basic to the useful geometric illusions discussed in Chapter 3. Among car-

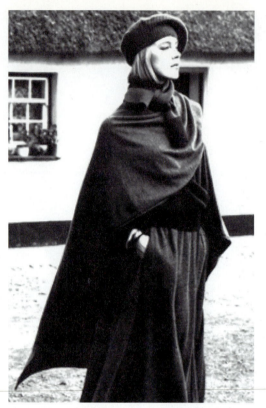

FIGURE 4-11 Space separates each of the soft folds in the cap, draped cape, scarf, and skirt, and provides a dramatic flare of captured space between the figure and skirt, and between skirt and cape. (Photo courtesy of Hoechst Fibers Industries, a division of American Hoechst Corp.)

pentered world illusions, the Sander parallelogram (Figure 3-5a and b) shows that the space and distance through which lines travel, as well as their angles, contribute to misperceptions of their length. In Figure 3-6 it is the spacing between lines of the outer angles and lapels that makes one center section seem larger than the other.

Space is a key element in the size and space geometric illusions that affect apparent figure size. Figures 3-14a and b show how filled space seems larger than empty space, and Figure 3-16 demonstrates the power of spacing between lines to influence apparent total size. In (a) the wider center panel spacing makes the entire bodice appear wider than in (b), where the narrower

center spacing makes the whole bodice seem slimmer. We have also seen how smaller areas are seen as shape and larger areas as space (Figure 3-23).

As space inside shapes is the element that expands or shrinks size, we see its role in the Titchener and Lipps circles of Figure 3-17 in which size differences are exaggerated, and garment styles in which full skirts make fitted bodices seem even smaller and vice versa. These geometric illusions, when deftly used in dress, can be potent tools.

We have seen that spatial cues suggesting depth are most successful in structural design in which features such as collars or pockets are clearly "in front of" larger bodice or skirt areas that are clearly "behind." However, most depth and distance spatial illusions such as figure/ground reversal and spontaneous change of position can become confusing and distracting in dress.

Physical Effects

The above size and spatial illusions influence apparent physical height, weight, size, and proportions subtly but powerfully. Figure 4-12 shows four identical silhouettes, but the size and shape of each seems different because of the differing ways the interior space is subdivided into smaller units of varying proportions. Figure 4-12a shows the empty silhouette as a basis for comparison. Figure 4-12b is subdivided into three long, narrow, "empty" structural shapes that allow a vertically unbroken view from shoulder to hem, and heighten and narrow the figure. Figure 4-12c with the same silhouette breaks the vertical space with hori-

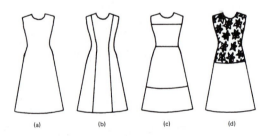

FIGURE 4-12 Varieties of spatial division inside the silhouette.

zontal shapes that shorten and widen the figure. Note that b and c show structural divisions of space. Figure 4-12d, however, uses both structural and decorative spatial divisions with the same silhouette. The dress is divided nearly in half structurally with a dropped waistline; the bodice is further decoratively subdivided by fabric pattern into smaller shapes and spaces. These subdivisions do two things: (1) the small pattern figures surrounded by space seem to advance and enlarge; and (2) the "filled" space of the patterned bodice seems larger than the unfilled space of the skirt (see also Figure 3-14a and b). Thus, spatial divisions create illusions that affect the apparent physical dimensions of the body.

Psychological Effects

Uses of space in clothing can powerfully manipulate feelings. Unbroken space (Figures 4-12b, 4-12c, or 2-2) suggests drama and sophistication and has an uninterrupted loveliness of its own. It may seem strange, but large areas are at the same time bold and serene because they convey a calmness of confidence, the quietness of certainty. The few lines that divide them are firmly committed, and the interstitial spatial role is assured. Many timeless garments of the most elegant simplicity and drama have large, unbroken spaces (Figure 2-2). Unbroken spaces suggest openness, simplicity, and straightforwardness, but can also be frustrating and boring because the eye seeks more complexity, an urge that invites organization of space into new areas and shapes.

Spaces divided somewhat unequally are more intriguing (Figure 4-13a) than those divided equally (Figure 4-13b) or extremely unequally (Figure 4-13c). (This phenomenon is explored further in Chapter 22.)

Small, broken spaces suggest daintiness, delicacy, femininity, intrigue, and invite an analysis of intricate detail. The smaller the motifs and spaces, the stronger the effect (Figure 4-14.) Broken spaces give a more closed-in feeling, a busy-ness, a

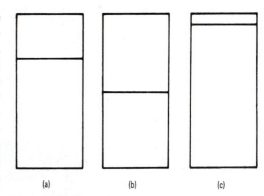

FIGURE 4-13 Somewhat unequal spatial divisions (a) offer more interest than equal (b) or very unequal divisions (c).

complexity, perhaps a tightness. Each detail becomes more dependent on the others.

Grouping also changes effects of shapes and spaces. The outline around a group of shapes may suggest another shape, as with groups of flowers suggesting circles (Figure 4-8.). Neighboring shapes are more likely to be perceived as a group if the spaces among them are (1) narrower than the shapes themselves, and (2) narrower than the space that separates the groups (Figure 4-8).

Close spacing of shapes emphasizes the shapes because the eye has a shorter, easier distance to travel to compare them (see the pants in Figure 4-14). Wider spacing requires the eye to travel farther to compare shapes, so one is more aware of the distance between them (see the blouse in Figure 4-14).

Consistency is the key to strengthening any psychological effect, whether bold or delicate. For bold, assertive effects, use advancing techniques consistently, including shapes smaller than surrounding space; filled shapes edged by solid, thick, sharp lines against plain backgrounds (Figure 4-1a); or large, unbroken spaces (Figure 4-1). For softer, flatter, or more delicate effects, use flattening techniques consistently, including touching shapes of similar sizes edged by thin, broken, or fuzzy lines and small, broken spaces (Figure 4-1f). Combining advancing and flattening techniques on the same surface dilutes the effect, but can also be pleasing and versatile.

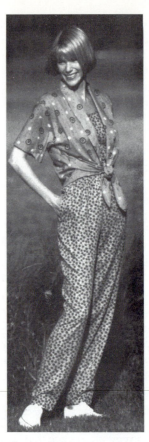

FIGURE 4-14 Small, closely spaced motifs in the pants give a dainty, busy feeling. The closely spaced motifs also emphasize the shapes, whereas the widely spaced motifs in the blouse accent the space and distance among the shapes. The even distribution of motifs gives a regular feeling and does not lend itself to the "grouping" seen in Figure 4-8. (Courtesy of Mark, Fore & Strike.)

Introducing Spatial Effects

Since space plays functional and structural as well as decorative roles in clothing, it can be introduced both structurally and decoratively. As clothing is a hollow form covered by a surface, and is also seen as a flat composition, it contains both two- and three-dimensional space. We have seen functional three-dimensional spaces introduced among fabric fibers, between pleats and gathers, between the body and garment, and between layers of garments. All of these affect functions of insulation, ventilation, and movement as well as visual effects.

Both structural and decorative use of space can create either physical or psychological effects. Structural introductions of space include the visual distance between seams, darts, pleats, gathers, folds, and/or garment edges (Figure 4-12), sizes of garment parts (Figure 4-2), lengths, or width of collars, shirts, pants, skirts—in other words, the amount of unbroken area between structural lines or edges. A "structurally open" use of space in a garment has few seams, darts, pleats, gathers, cuffs, tucks, or folds (Figure 4-12b), and a "structurally filled" or closed use has many (Figure 4-7). Psychologically, a structurally "open" spaced style may appear simple and calm (Figure 4-5), while a structurally "filled" style will seem larger physically and busy (such as the skirts in Figure 4-7).

Decorative means of manipulating space include fabric pattern (Figure 4-8), construction details or applied trims discussed in Chapter 2, and the spaces between them. Both the size (internal space) of motifs or trim and the spaces between them (external or interstitial space) influence apparent figure size. Larger motifs or trim enlarge the body part where they appear; so control is needed for the size effect desired. A "decoratively open" space is plain, or nearly so (Figure 4-12a, b, c); a "decoratively filled" space might be filled by a busy fabric pattern (Figure 4-14) or style features or trims. There may be many degrees between "open" and "filled," and many combinations.

For example, the pants in Figure 4-5 are both structurally and decoratively open, and the shirt is structurally quite open and decoratively more filled. Or, as in the skirts in Figure 4-7, space is both structurally filled by many pleat lines, and decoratively filled by busy fabric pattern and trim. What physical and psychological effects do these different combinations create? What other combinations do you find in Figures 4-8, 4-9, 4-10, and 4-14?

Psychological consistency is usually easier to achieve if advancing techniques (Figures 4-1a to e) are used in structural design because the garment itself is three-dimensional. Flattening techniques (Figures 4-1f to j) are more consistent with the flat fabric, pattern, and trim. Exceptions are possible, but require care.

SUMMARY

Space is area or extent either flat or having volume, the fundamental ingredient of visual design. Enclosed space is usually called "shape," and unenclosed space simply "space," but they are inseparable and have a powerful and complementary relationship. Space-shape relationships can create illusions of depth in which shape is known as figure, foreground, enclosed space, or positive space; and space is called ground, background, negative space, unenclosed space, or interstitial space. Empty space is also called open, unbroken, plain, or blank; and subdivided space is filled, closed, or broken. Cues that influence perception of shape or space include size, overlapping, density, convexity and concavity, and character of enclosing lines. "Advancing" cues increase a feeling of depth between shape and space, whereas "flattening" cues minimize depth.

Space as background defines the shape, advances it, "structures" a location, provides rest, and creates size and shape illusions. Thus, space and shape keep a complementary interplay.

Space as volume inside and surrounding a garment is critical to functional design, insulation, protection, circulation, and body motion. Space captures the areas between fibers and yarns, gathers, under collars, and between layers of garments and the body.

Space conveys physiological effects in illusions of size and depth. Psychologically, unbroken spaces are serene, yet bold, and small, broken spaces suggest delicacy and complexity. Spacing of shapes heightens awareness of shapes when they are close together, and of space when they are far apart.

Clothing uses space both structurally and decoratively. Structural techniques control the distance between structural lines; decorative techniques control distance between motifs, construction details, or trims. Space, as the basic raw element from which visual design is organized, determines space/shape relationships and their effects in dress.

CLASS ACTIVITIES

1. In a fabric pattern, identify the "enclosed" and "unenclosed" spaces. Which occupy the greater area? Which one dominates visually? How does it risk or avoid figure/ground reversal illusion? When you have analyzed the pattern space use, suggest a structural style with which the pattern space would agree. Use as one criteria that the fabric pattern space use must be compatible with garment structural space use and not cause confusion of structural foregrounds and backgrounds (Figure 4-2).

2. Using the visual space cues in Figure 4-1, look for three fabric patterns: (a) using mostly advancing/solid cues, (b) using mostly flattening/hollow cues, (c) using both advancing and flattening cues. Discuss how they differ in character and in physical and psychological effects. Which would work most easily into a garment? Why?

3. In magazines, catalogs, and historic and ethnic costume books, look for garments showing structural and/or decorative examples of the six roles listed under "Space As Ground in a Composition." Discuss why that garment is an example of that role.

4. In magazines, catalogs, or historic costume books, find garment examples demonstrating (a) excessive visual "internal pressure" pushing outward, (b) excessive "external pressure" inward

suggesting collapse, and/or (c) apparent internal/external pressure balance. In each case, discuss the visual cues (Figure 4-1) responsible for the effect.

5. Sitting down, close your eyes and sense where interior surfaces of your clothes touch your body and where there is space between your body and garment. What is that space doing functionally? Is it providing insulation? Air circulation? Allowing for movement? What is it doing decoratively, if anything? Is it supporting a garment style form? Open your eyes and observe the volume spaces between any gathers, pleats, folds, or garment parts or layers. What is that space doing? How is it controlling the space immediately surrounding you? Now stand up and sense how your change of body position changes body/space/garment relationships, asking yourself the same questions, and comparing your responses.

6. Review the size and space illusions in Chapter 3 and Figures 3-14 through 3-18, and find structural clothing examples of them throughout the book, especially in Chapter 6 style diagrams. Discuss their physical size effects and how the illusions contribute to them.

7. In fabric patterns, find examples of (a) widely spaced motifs, (b) closely spaced motifs, (c) evenly spaced motifs, and (d) grouped motifs. Using the descriptions under "Visual Effects of Space Use in Clothing," (a) discuss and compare their visual effects and how they were achieved, and (b) find examples of structural design spaces and styles with which they would agree.

8. In a garment or picture, identify and describe its (a) structurally open areas, (b) structurally filled areas, (c) decoratively open areas, and (d) decoratively filled areas. (Remember that visible structural subdivisions are also decorative.) Discuss (a) their interactions, (b) their physical effects, and (c) their psychological effects. If you were to improve the garment's appearance by using visual space, what would you change? Why?

5 *Line*

DEFINITION AND CONCEPT

Line is an elongated mark, the connection between two points, or the effect made by the edge of an object where there is no actual line on the object itself. Line leads the eye in the direction the line is going, and divides the area through which it passes, thus providing a breaking point in space. Line may enclose space to define a shape or silhouette. As Anderson notes, line may communicate, clarify, symbolize, represent, or interpret.[1] Line usually carries a definiteness that commits it to a specific position; thus, it "makes a statement" about its mood, location, and character.

ASPECTS OF LINE

Every line has nine aspects. These are (1) path, (2) thickness, (3) evenness, (4) continuity, (5) sharpness of edge, (6) contour of edge, (7) consistency, (8) length, and (9) direction. Each aspect has a number of variations. For example, thickness could range from very thin and fine to very thick, or direction could be horizontal, diagonal, or vertical. Figure 5-1 shows the nine aspects of line, several variations, and some physical and psychological effects common in Western cultures, and structural and decorative ways of introducing line in dress.

EFFECTS OF ASPECT VARIATIONS

The many aspect variations of line give it a powerful role in dress. Line manipulates space: line divides it, encloses it, organizes it, pushes and pulls it, separates and contours it. How it does that depends on how each variation of each aspect is used. Here,

---

[1]Donald M. Anderson, *Elements of Design* (New York: Holt, Rinehart and Winston, Inc., 1961), p. 54.

FIGURE 5-1 Line aspects.

Aspect	Variation	Appearance	Physical Effects	Psychological Effects	Ways of Introducing
1) Path	(a) Straight	▬	Emphasizes body angularity, counters rotundity. Straight lines counter body curves and therefore tend to be figure-concealing. Rarely found in nature	Stiff, direct, rigid, precise, dignified, tense, unyielding, sure, masculine, austere	Seams, darts, garment edges, pleats, hems, ribbons, trim, braid, stripes, geometrics, tucks, panels
	(b) Restrained curve		Slightly emphasizes body curves	Soft, gentle, flexible but controlled, graceful, feminine, flowing, passive, subtle, loose. Generally more graceful if slightly irregular, not a geometrically perfect arc	Seams, garment edges and hems, princess lines, linear trims, gathers, draping, fabric pattern
	(c) Full curve	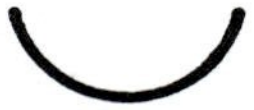	Emphasizes body curves, counters thinness and angularity	Dynamic, feminine, unrestrained, exuberant, youthful, active, forceful, unstable	Seams, garment edges, scalloped edges, pattern
	(d) Bent	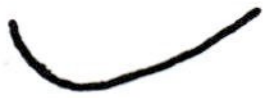	Combines straight and curved effects	This and the restrained curve are the lines most often found in nature: rivers, trees, hills. Can be both forceful and gentle, depending how used	
	(e) Jagged	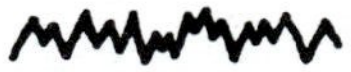	Emphasizes angularity	Abrupt, nervous, jerky, busy, unstable, erratic, spasmodic, excited	Decorative fabric pattern, linear trim
	(f) Looped	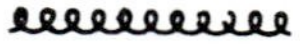	Emphasizes roundness	Swirling, active, soft, feminine, busy, springy, unsure	Decorative fabric pattern, trim
	(g) Wavy	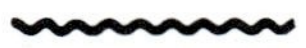	Emphasizes roundness, counters angularity	Feminine, undulating, soft, flowing, graceful, sensuous, flexible, uncertain	Seams and garment edges, fabric pattern, trim
	(h) Scalloped	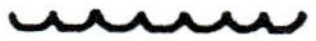	Repeats roundness, counters angularity	Curves provide softness and femininity, sharp points provide crispness and liveliness, youth	Garment edges, pattern, trim

FIGURE 5-1 *Continued*

Aspect	Variation	Appearance	Physical Effects	Psychological Effects	Ways of Introducing
	(i) Zigzag		Emphasizes angularity, counters roundness	Sharp, busy, regular, masculine, jerky, abrupt, intense, stiff	Garment edges, fabric pattern, trim, trim, rick rack
	(j) Crimped		Rough contour	Involved, complex, rough	Lettuce edges, fabric pattern, trim
2) Thickness	(a) Thick		Advances, adds weight	Forceful, aggressive, assertive, sure, masculine	Borders, trims, fabric pattern, cuffs, belts
	(b) Thin		Minimizes weight	Delicate, dainty, feminine, passive, gentle, calm, subtle	Seams, edges, trims, fabric pattern, darts, construction details
3) Evenness	(a) Uneven		Accents bulges	Wobbly, unsure, unsteady, insecure, questioning	Fabric pattern, trim
	(b) Even		Evenness, physical steadiness	Regular, smooth, secure, sure, firm	Seams, edges, pleats, pattern, trim
4) Continuity	(a) Continuous, unbroken		Smooth, reinforces smooth lines, emphasizes bumps and bulges	Consistent, definite, sure, flowing, firm, certain, elegant, smooth. A solid line makes a direct statement of its path	Seams, pleats, gathers, draping patterns, trims, stripes
	(b) Broken		May emphasize irregularities	Less certain, staccato, interrupted, casual, sporty, playful. Any broken line only suggests its path	Insertion, interwoven trims, and belts, topstitching, rows of buttons
	(c) Dotted		May be spotty, varied	Also less certain, staccato,interrupted, playful, suggestive, casual	Sequins, pearls, beading, trims, fabric pattern
	(d) Combinations		Varied	Innumerable combinations of solid and broken lines and dots are possible, and they will tend to convey a busy, "broken" effect. Many combinations can provide a casual crispness.	Lace, edgings, fabric pattern, trim, belts, smocking, quilting, hemstitching
5) Edge/sharpness	(a) Sharp		Emphasizes area as smooth or bumpy	Definite, precise, certain, assertive, incisive, sure, hard	Seams, darts, edges, fabric pattern, ribbon and other trim, stripes
	(b) Fuzzy		Gently increases area size, softens	Soft, uncertain, indefinite, suggestive	Fringe, fur, some braids and trims, fabric pattern, feathers, some translucent fabrics

FIGURE 5-1 *Continued*

Aspect	Variation	Appearance	Physical Effects	Psychological Effects	Ways of Introducing
6) Edge/contour	(a) Smooth	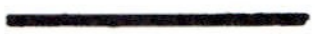	Reinforces smoothness or accents bumps	Suave, smooth, simple, straightforward, sure	Seams, darts, edges, trims, pattern, stripes
	(b) Shaped	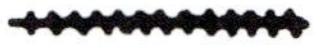	Varied according to kind of shape	Complex, involved, busy, active, devious, intriguing, informal	Lace, fringe, beading, sequins, pearls, pompoms, braids, other trim, fabric pattern
7) Consistency	(a) Solid, sealed, smooth	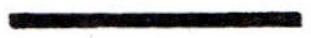	Advances boldly	Smooth, sure, assertive, strong	Stripes, binding, piping, ribbon, rick rack, soutache and middy braid, border trim, belt, sash
	(b) Porous	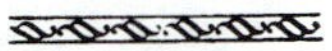	Advances little, may recede	Open, delicate, weak, less certain	Lace edging, eyelet edging and insertion, lace borders, macrame, crocheted bands, rows of drawn work, shirring, open braid belts, gimp, fringe, fabric pattern
8) Length	(a) Long	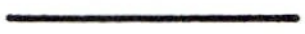	Emphasizes its direction, elongates, smooths	Length of line is usually perceived in relation to other lines or an area. A long line might be a short line for a skirt or dress. Suggests continuity, smooth, graceful flow	Any
	(b) Short		Breaks up spaces, increases busyness	A line perceived as short in relation to others tends to give a more staccato, abrupt effect	Any
9) Direction	(a) Vertical		Heightens, narrows	Dignity, strength, austerity, stability, rigidity, grandeur, alertness, poise	Any
	(b) Horizontal	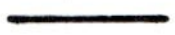	Shortens, widens	Quietness, repose, rest, calmness, passivity, serenity	Any
	(c) Diagonal	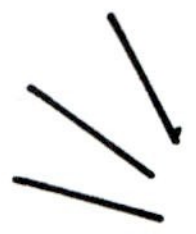	Closer to vertical: lengthens; Closer to horizontal: widens; 45°: Effects more dependence on influence of surrounding lines	Drama, restlessness, instability, activity	Any

descriptions of physical and psychological effects are separated for discussion but, as we have seen, in practice they come as a package.

Physical Effects

As shown in Figure 5-1, *path* variations with straight parts emphasize angularity (Figure 5-2), and those with curved parts accent roundness (Figure 5-3). In *thickness*, a thick line advances and enlarges; a thin line minimizes (Figure 5-4). *Evenness* reinforces smoothness (Figure 5-4), whereas unevenness accents variety (Figure 5-5). *Continuous* lines appear smooth but may accent any bumps (Figure 5-4), while discontinuous lines are broken and less strong (Figure 5-6). Sharp *edges* advance and enlarge (Figure 5-4), while fuzzy, soft edges

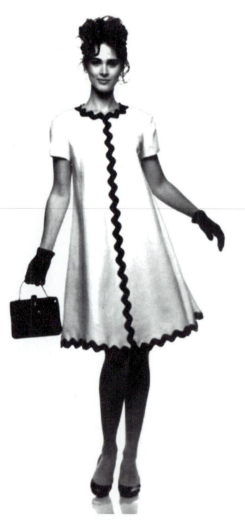

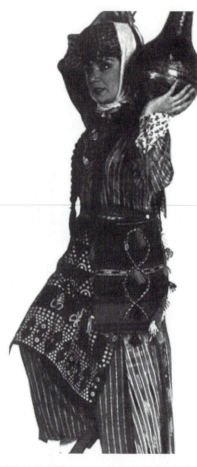

FIGURE 5-2 In this center front zigzag line, physically, the straight lines and parts accent angularity, and the vertical line stresses its direction. Psychologically, the zigzag path seems casual, and the sharp edges are definite and sure. (Courtesy of **McCall Pattern** Company.)

FIGURE 5-3 The wavy line path in the hip pouch has curves that physically reinforce figure curves and psychologically seem soft and feminine. Its uneven thickness and discontinuity seem tentative and less sure. The combination of wavy, thin, broken, uneven variations reinforces a petite, delicate feeling which modifies the effects of the straight, vertical, but thin lines in this Adiyaman dance costume from Turkey. (Courtesy of the Turkish Government Tourist Office.)

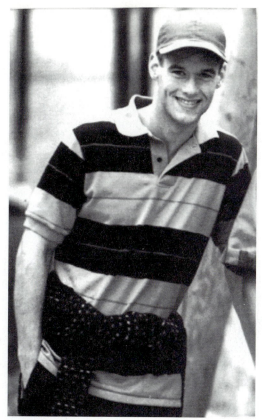

FIGURE 5-4 Physically, the thick, sharp, solid consistency lines advance and enlarge, while they counter the thin lines that minimize. The evenness, continuity, and smooth edge emphasize smoothness but may highlight bumps by contrast. Their horizontal direction widens the shoulders and torso. Psychologically, the straight, thick, smooth, even, sharp, continuous, and solid variations in the same line combine to reinforce each other for a strong, assertive effect. (Courtesy of Pendleton Woolen Mills Menswear.)

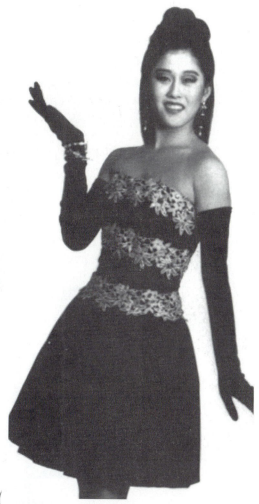

FIGURE 5-5 The straight, horizontal lines of trim give a wide range of effects. In physical effects, the line unevenness made by the shaped edges of the overall straight path counters smoothness, and the lacy consistency seems light and porous and less advancing, although the straightness, thickness, and sharpness are more advancing. Psychologically, the shaped edges seem active and complex, and the lacy consistency seems delicate. But these moods are calmed by the restful horizontal direction. So the "compatible countering" techniques used modify both the mood and the physical effect to create a widening, playful, dressy, and versatile effect. Its width, shaped edges, and porosity require it to be introduced decoratively. (Courtesy of Kristi Yamaguchi and Hoechst Celanese Corporation.)

soften and enlarge less (Figure 5-7). *Edge contour* appears smooth if the edge parallels the center axis (Figure 5-4), and if the edge differs from the path of the line axis, as in a scalloped edge on a straight line path (Figure 5-5).

In *consistency*, a solid, smooth line advances strongly (Figure 5-4), and a porous, lacy line advances less (Figure 5-5). In *length*, a long line elongates more than a

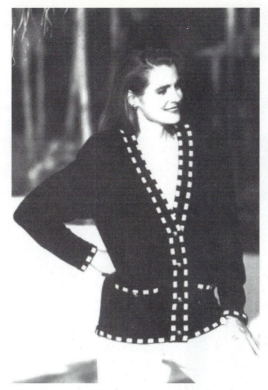

FIGURE 5-6 Physically, the discontinuous edge trim lines appear abrupt and broken, and psychologically less certain and more casual. Each diagonal has its opposing diagonal to maintain balance and stability. When they meet at the center with the point down and the "tails" up, they seem light and young, and help straighten the shoulders. The stronger vertical lines and diagonals lengthen the shoulder-hip area and counter the horizontal trim at the hips. As broken lines, they must be introduced decoratively. (Courtesy of Mark, Fore & Strike.)

short line (Figure 5-2). Of all the aspects, *direction* probably carries the strongest physical effects. Because a line leads the eye in the direction it is going, it physically emphasizes that direction on the body and counters the direction perpendicular to it. So, a horizontal line shortens and widens, and counters height (Figure 5-8 top), whereas a vertical line heightens and narrows, and counters width (Figure 5-8 skirt).

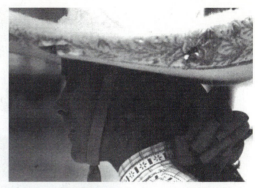

FIGURE 5-7 The furry trim edging the hat brim in this Mexican "Escaramuze" costume shows a fuzzy line edge. Physically, the fuzziness seems fading and receding, and psychologically it seems soft and gentle. The edge softness reinforces the horizontal restfulness. (Courtesy of the Mexican Ministry of Tourism.)

Psychological Effects

Figure 5-1 shows a wide range of psychological effects of *path*. Those with straight components or angles such as straight, jagged, or zigzag seem stiff and masculine (Figure 5-4), and those with curved components such as bent, curved, looped, or wavy seem softer and feminine (Figure 5-3). Complex paths such as jagged and zigzag seem more playful (Figure 5-2). *Thick lines* are assertive (Figure 5-4), and thin lines delicate (Figure 5-8 skirt). *Evenness* seems steady and secure (Figure 5-4), while unevenness seems less secure (Figure 5-3). *Continuous lines* seem sure and flowing (Figure 5-8), whereas broken lines seem less certain and more casual (Figure 5-6). *Sharp edges* are sure and assertive (Figure 5-2); fuzzy edges are soft and gentle (Figure 5-7). *Smooth edges* are sure and simple (Figure 5-4), while shaped edges seem busy and complex (Figure 5-5). In *consistency,* a solid line seems strong (Figure 5-4), and a porous line seems weaker and delicate (Figure 5-5). In *length,* a long line seems stronger and flowing, and a short line seems abrupt (Figure 5-8).

Direction may also have the most powerful psychological effects, most of which spring from everyday associations. Vertical people are usually awake and alert. Vertical trees, candles, utility poles, and buildings defy gravity with their rigidity, firmness, and stability. These qualities are suggested by vertical line in dress (Figure 5-8). Horizontal lines follow the horizon from side to side in a position of rest and yielding to gravity. In dress they convey quiet, repose, rest, passivity, calmness, and serenity (Figure 5-5).

Diagonal lines combine the vertical and horizontal and seem undecided between upright and sideways. So they seem unstable, busy, active, dynamic, restless, and dramatic. Too much diagonal leaning one way may introduce wobbly directional illusions; so diagonals need an opposing diagonal to provide balance (Figure 5-6). If opposing diagonals meets with a downward point (Figures 5-6 and 5-9), the lines seem to lift up, and the effect is lighter, happier, and more youthful. If they meet with an upward point (Figure 5-9) and the lines seem to trail down, the effect is older, heavier, more somber, and droopier. A challenging line, the diagonal often seems sporty, but with masterful use can also convey elegance.

Exceptions can happen with the normal effects of line direction; so guidelines should begin with "usually." For example, the usually lengthening effect of vertical lines (Figure 5-10a) may be lost on a horizontal shape where the shape is wider than the vertical lines are long (Figure 5-10b). The same is true of the widening effects of

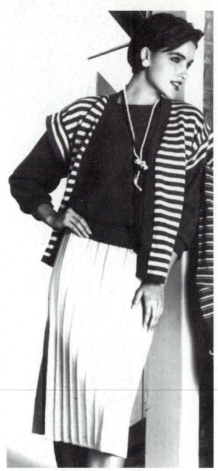

FIGURE 5-8 Although the line paths in the top and skirt are all straight, variations in other line aspects give them very differing effects. Physically, the horizontal direction in the lines of the top shorten and widen, and the vertical lines in the skirt heighten and narrow. Psychologically, in the skirt lines, their thinness seems gentle, their continuity seems smooth, the vertical direction stately and stable, and their long length seems flowing, whereas the short lines in the top seem abrupt. The short horizontal lines in the top are in a long, vertical shape which reduces their widening effect. Conversely, the long, narrow shape of the skirt reinforces the length and direction of vertical skirt lines. The striped top shows how fabric pattern lines are always decoratively introduced, but often command more attention than structural lines. (Courtesy of Cotton Incorporated.)

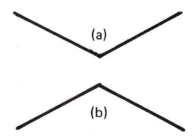

FIGURE 5-9 Meeting diagonals pointing down with ends lifting up are youthful. With point up and ends down, the effect is weighted and older.

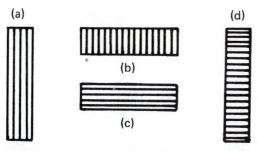

(a)　　　　　　　　　　(d)

(b)

(c)

FIGURE 5-10 The direction of the shape on which lines appear influences their effects.

horizontal lines on vertical shapes (Figures 5-10c and d and 5-8). Similar exceptions occur when lines are repeated in certain patterns, as described in Chapter 11.

COMBINED EFFECTS OF ASPECTS IN ONE LINE

Lines often carry as much expressive power as do words. The two words in Figures 5-11a and b contain the same warning, but the thin, embellished, flowing line of the first completely lacks the impact and urgency of the thick, sharp, straight lines of the second. These differences result from different combinations of line variations. The physical and psychological effects of a line depend on its combinations or "formula."

Innumerable combinations are possible, and each change in the "formula" will change the total effect. For example, all the lines in Figure 5-12 are wavy (path) and solid (continuity), but the variations in thickness, sharpness, and consistency create very different effects. Similarly, although all the lines in Figure 5-13 are

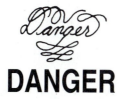

DANGER

FIGURE 5-11 The character of the line conveys as much of a message as the word itself does.

curved and sharp, the variations in thickness and continuity create differing effects.

The power of a mood depends on how line aspects are used. Consistent, reinforcing use of the same mood in all variations is the key to strengthening any mood. For example, to create an assertive mood and advancing effects, each line needs only those aspects that consistently convey that mood: straight, solid, sharp, thick, even, and smooth (Figure 5-4). To convey a soft, delicate mood, each aspect consistently needs those variations and receding effects that suggest that mood: curved, thin, porous, and soft (Figure 5-3). In both cases the effect of one aspect reinforces the effects of others.

More versatility in a line and consequent garment use needs a more modified mood. This can be achieved by combining "compatibly countering" variations rather than all variations conveying and reinforcing the same mood. Not all uses would be advancing and assertive, nor would all be delicate and receding, but there would be some of each which harmonize and modify each other. For example, the straight (path), thick (thickness), continuous (continuity), and sharp (edge sharpness) qualities of the bodice trim in Figure 5-5 are advancing and assertive. But they are modified by the more delicate and receding qualities of being porous (consistency), uneven (evenness), and horizontal (direction). So, consistently selecting variations of aspects to reinforce each other strengthens any mood, and selecting variations that compatibly counter each other produces a moderate and versatile mood.

EFFECTS OF MULTIPLE LINE INTERACTIONS

So far, we have discussed variations and aspects in a single line. However, all garments have many lines, and they all interact to create optical illusions, physical effects, and moods. These effects may reinforce, modify, or counter each other as well as existing figure qualities.

FIGURE 5-12 Though all lines are wavy and continuous, variations in thickness, sharpness, and consistency change effects.

Illusions Using Line and Space in Dress

Geometric and size and space illusions depend on how lines relate to each other in space. Chapter 3 shows how lines, angles, curves, interruptions, and intersections affect each other. The Müller–Lyer illusion lengthens an area more or less depending on the direction of the line "tails" (Figure 3-2a, b, c, d). The horizontal-vertical illusion showed that heightening effects are easier than widening effects because a vertical line appears longer than a horizontal one of the same length (Figure 3-3a, b). A vertical seam or opening seems longer still when, for example, it intersects a horizontal belt or hem (Figure 3-4a, b). The spacing between angles influences their apparent size (Figure 3-6a, b, and c), an illusion which could affect apparent collar width, neck length, and other figure areas. The amount of a circle or sharpness of its curve influences the feeling of roundness a seam or curved edge will convey (Figure 3-7a, b).

In intersecting and interrupted lines, the Poggendorf illusion of displaced interrupted lines shows, for example, how slightly moving a skirt pleat could make it appear to be a continuation of a bodice dart line interrupted by a belt or midriff (Figure 3-8a and b). We have seen that a line pushes hardest where it intersects another at a right angle, or perpendicularly. That "push" may be useful where a single line intersects another, thus countering its direction (Figures 3-3a and b), but risky when combined with other angles that create distortions between fabric patterns and structural design (Figures 3-10, 3-11a, b, and 3-13a, b). Other distracting illusions of line in fabric pattern include directional (Figure 3-19), depth and distance, and autokinetic illusions.

Reinforcing and Countering Effects

We have seen how aspect variations can be used to reinforce or counter each other in a single line, such as using a sharp edge and solid consistency to reinforce the assertiveness of a thick thickness, or using a porous consistency and thinner thickness to reinforce the softness of a wavy path (Figure 5-12). Or casually shaped edges and broken continuity will counter the graceful flow of a curved path (Figure 5-13). When that much potential to reinforce or counter is contained within one line, opportunities are compounded when multiple lines, each with a repertoire of aspects and variations, interact with each other. Reinforcing can build effects to a powerful climax, or "compatible countering" can restrain extreme effects and create a balanced versatility.

In clothing, countering is usually more compatible if it is done within a line rather than among lines. For example, several lines, each containing assertive straight path and vertical direction countered by soft, thin thickness and fuzzy edges would be more compatible than one straight, sharp, thick, enlarging, and assertive line placed next to a wavy, thin, porous, receding, and delicate line in the same outfit.

Some line effects result from clothing lines interacting with each other, and some from the interaction between clothing lines and figure lines. All line aspects are capable of many psychological effects, but those ca-

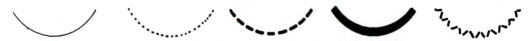

FIGURE 5-13 All lines are curved and sharp, but variations in thickness and continuity change the mood.

pable of the strongest physical effects are path, thickness, and direction.

In direction, line emphasizes the direction it goes on the figure (Figure 5-2) and so should be used in the direction where emphasis or reinforcement is desired. Thus, a vertical line from shoulder to hip lengthens the torso (Figure 5-6); a horizontal line at the shoulder or hips widens them (Figure 5-4). For greatest countering effects, use lines at right angles to an undesired direction, such as a "V" shoulder yoke to widen and straighten round shoulders. In other words, lines parallel to a desired direction reinforce it, and lines perpendicular to an undesired direction counter it.

To reinforce or counter line path effects, curved path garment lines reinforce curved, round shoulder, large bust, or stomach body lines (Figure 5-14c), and counter angular, thin, or bony body lines (Figure 5-14b). Straight path lines and angles reinforce body angularity and boniness (Figure 5-14a), and counter rotundity (Figure 5-14d). Thick lines reinforce larger size (Figure 5-4) and counter small size, but could overwhelm it. Thin lines reinforce

petiteness (Figure 5-3) and counter size, as the thin lines between the thicker lines of Figure 5-4 show.

Introducing Lines in Clothing

Once the kind, direction, and location of lines are established, the designer has many structural and decorative ways to incorporate them (Figure 5-1). Visible structural lines are also decorative unless fuzzy textures or busy fabric patterns conceal them. Any variation of any line aspect may be introduced decoratively, but only certain variations are feasible for structural use. For example, seamlines are by nature thin, continuous, and usually sharp. Thick, broken, or fading variations are not feasible for seams.

Structural techniques for introducing line include:

1. Construction lines, such as seams, darts, fitting tucks, or shirring.
2. Real or perceived edges of garment parts, such as the silhouette or edges of collars, sleeves, belts, hems, pockets, or openings.

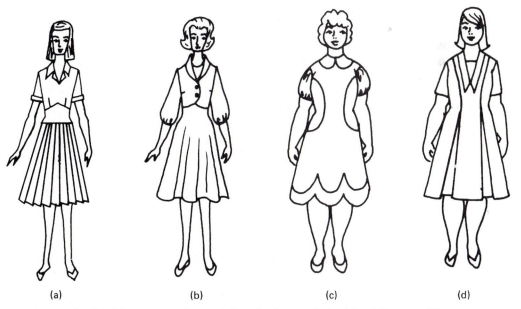

| (a) | (b) | (c) | (d) |

FIGURE 5-14 Straight garment lines reinforce body angularity (a), while curved lines counter, giving softness (b). Curved lines emphasize body roundness (c), while straight lines counter it with smooth control (d).

3. Creases or folds made by pleats, gathers, tucks, or draping.

The shaping and fit of a garment depend on these structural lines, so they are the first to be considered: Will the garment be shaped by darts, seams, draping, pleats, gathers, or a combination of these? Since necessary structural lines (such as seams and edges) are thin, smooth, and continuous, they usually carry the psychological effects of those variations. Their uses and interactions with other lines will greatly influence the total garment mood. Sometimes structural lines may provide all the decoration needed.

Decorative means of introducing line include many linear ones listed under decorative design, and these should agree with structural lines. Such means include braid, rick rack, piping, rows of buttons, insertions, bias binding or strip trims, lace edgings, ribbon, soutache, topstitching, shirring, faggoting, ruffles, fringe, and linear embroidery or beading (Figures 2-10, 2-11). Fabric pattern lines—such as stripes, plaids, herringbones, checks, zigzags, and others—are always decorative (Figure 5-8). Broken, dotted, jagged, looped, porous, and fuzzy lines are almost always decorative because those qualities are not feasible for structural lines (Figures 5-5 and 5-6). They offer opportunity for decorative variety, character, control of mood, and selective emphasis of structural lines.

SUMMARY

Line is an elongated mark connecting two points or defining the edge of a shape. It may be analyzed in its nine aspects according to (1) path, (2) thickness, (3) evenness, (4) continuity, (5) sharpness of edge, (6) contour of edge, (7) consistency, (8) length, and (9) direction. Each aspect has many variations which carry physical and psychological effects and many optical illusions that influence apparent figure size, shape, and dimensions. How these aspects

are used and combined will largely determine a mood and its strength in a garment.

Understanding the effects of single lines contributes to control of their interactions when they are combined, and whether effects are reinforced or countered.

Line may be incorporated structurally and decoratively. Structural techniques include construction lines, garment edges, and creases or folds. Decorative methods include construction details, fabric patterns, or applied linear trims. For some garments, structural lines may provide all necessary decorative appeal. Line establishes the framework of a garment, and command of its use controls the garment's total appearance.

CLASS ACTIVITIES

1. Select a decorative line in a garment. Identify and list the variation used for each of its nine aspects. Then analyze the following points.
   (a) Which variations are advancing/enlarging/assertive?
   (b) Which variations are receding/reducing/delicate?
   (c) Which variation effects reinforce each other?
   (d) Which variation effects counter each other?
   (e) What is the overall physical effect on the figure?
   (f) What is the overall psychological effect on the figure?

2. Select a structural line in a garment and identify and list the variation used for each of its nine aspects. Then analyze the same points (a) through (f).

3. Identify which variations used in the above decorative line (1) would be possible in a structural line; (2) which would not? Compare the overall effects of the structural and decorative lines. Given the limitations imposed by the continuous and thin nature of structural lines, how would you compare the potentials of structural and decorative

lines? Which type of line (structural or decorative) could you depend on for which effects?

4. In a magazine or catalog, select a garment and identify its dominant structural and decorative lines. Then:

   (a) Identify and describe the effects of variations used in each line.

   (b) Analyze how the garment lines interact with each other. How do they reinforce? Counter? Modify?

   (c) Analyze how the garment lines interact with body lines. How do they reinforce? Counter? Modify?

5. In a garment or picture, select and analyze a dominant line as in (1). Assign, choose, or randomly draw from folded labeled paper slips in a container, one of the following effects. As a group, decide changes in variations to shift line effects in the picture to the effect listed on the chosen paper. Which aspect variation changes make the greatest impact? Are you using more reinforcing or countering effects? (Choose from these or other effects: casual, tailored, reserved, advancing, sporty, elegant, heightening, enlarging, businesslike, playful, stately, energetic, minimizing.)

6. In a garment or picture, discuss and compare the effects of structural and decorative lines. Are some structural lines more advancing and apparent than others? How do the decorative lines inside the silhouette interact with the structural silhouette lines? How do they affect the figure?

6 *Shape and Form*

Shape and form accept the invitation issued by space and line. Shape is flat space enclosed by a line, and form is volume space enclosed by a surface, making an inseparable and complementary relationship of space and shape. Shape is an element even though it is composed of space and line because a line completely surrounding a space creates something that a line dividing a space does not, and that creation provides a vast potential that nothing else does.

DEFINITION AND CONCEPT

In art and clothing, shape is defined as a flat, two-dimensional area enclosed by a line. That line creates a silhouette, or outline or edge of an interior area seen as flat. Flat decorative design such as fabric pattern motifs and appliqués, flat garment parts such as collars and pockets, and flat pattern pieces of garment parts such as sleeves before construction, are shapes.

Form is defined as a three-dimensional area enclosed by a surface. If the form is hollow, the interior is seen as volume; if it is solid, the interior is described as mass. For most purposes of art and clothing, the three-dimensional human form is a solid mass bounded by the contours, the protrusions and indentations of the anatomy covered by a surface of skin. Structural clothing parts are hollow forms whose interior volumes relate to and complement the exterior contours of the body, and whose exterior contours usually follow those of the body.

Shape and form as visual design elements are intriguing and challenging because they are so malleable and offer a marvelous potential to express psychological moods and visual illusions.

We have seen how changing any one aspect of line can change its whole effect. And changing or subdividing the space inside a shape can also change its effects. So the powers of shape and form are compounded by the effects of line *plus* those of space. A shape edged by the thin, smooth, continuous line of a curved path and with unbroken interior space (Figure 6-1a), conveys a quite different feeling from one edged by a thicker, porous line of straight path and with subdivided, or "filled," interior space (Figure 6-1b). Thus shapes and forms assume the physical and psychological effects of the lines surrounding them and of the space within and separating them. (Review the effects of each aspect of line and the uses of space to develop combinations. Lines inside a silhouette subdivide the interior space into even smaller shapes, as in Figures 4-12b, c, and d, creating a greater variety of illusions and moods.)

The word "shape" usually suggests geometric shapes, and they and their variations make up both the human figure and clothing. Common, flat geometric shapes with equal sides are the square, circle, equilateral triangle, pentagon, hexagon, and octagon (Figure 6-2). Flat geometric shapes with unequal dimensions include the oval, scalene triangle, isosceles triangle, rectangle, parallelogram, trapezoid, diamond, and "freeforms" (Figure 6-3).

Equally sided three-dimensional forms include the sphere and cube (Figure 6-4). Unequally sided forms include the tube or cylinder, cone, pyramid, box, bell, dome, ovoid or egg, lantern or barrel, hourglass, and trumpet (Figure 6-5). In dress, these geometric shapes or forms are rarely pure, but are close enough to use in clothing analysis. For example, legs seem tubular and a flared skirt is closer to a cone than to any other form; a flower motif may resemble a circle. To master the ways shapes and forms relate, the designer must know their individual attributes.

Attributes of Shape and Form

Shapes project the moods of the lines enclosing them and of the space within them. Rectangles and squares, with their horizontal and vertical sides and firm right angles, seem stable and confident. Shapes with diagonal edges—such as triangles, pentagons, hexagons, octagons, trapezoids, and parallelograms—seem more dynamic but less stable. Curved lines smoothly change direction, so the diagonal effects are softer.

Shape automatically has proportion, the relationship of length to width. Shapes or forms of unequal proportions, such as the cylinder, oval, or cone generally create more visual interest than do those of equal proportions such as the circle, square, sphere, or cube. The inequalities invite comparison of dimensional differences. Unequal proportions in a shape emphasize its dominant direction; the more extreme the proportion the greater the effect. For example, a short, wide midriff yoke shortens and widens. A tall, thin shape, like a long pant leg, heightens and narrows.

How shapes fit together also influences their effects. Some shapes—squares, hexagons, ogives, diamonds, parallelograms, reversed trapezoids, and certain triangles and rectangles—fit tightly together with no spaces in between, giving a sense of security and stability (Figure 6-6). Other shapes leave spaces between them which create new shapes, making up in variety what they lack in snug stability (Figure 6-7). These relationships are important for fabric design, selection, and matching.

(a)    (b)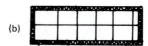

FIGURE 6-1 An unfilled shape edged with a thin, smooth, continuous curved line (a) conveys a feeling much different from that given by a thicker, porous, straight line and "filled" space (b).

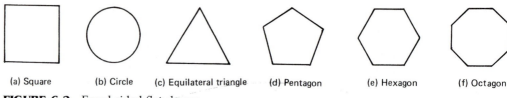

(a) Square   (b) Circle   (c) Equilateral triangle   (d) Pentagon   (e) Hexagon   (f) Octagon

FIGURE 6-2   Equal-sided flat shapes.

Relationships Between Two-Dimensional Shapes and Three-Dimensional Forms

The interplay of actual two- and three-dimensions is a joy reserved for the sculptor, architect, and clothing designer, but denied to the artist confined to a flat surface. A major characteristic of clothing is that it uses both two- and three-dimensional shapes and forms. Although flat pocket and fabric pattern motif shapes stay flat, the flat garment pattern pieces cut in flat fabric are manipulated into three-dimensional style forms that envelope the body. When drawn or photographed on flat paper in magazines, newspapers, or catalogs, the outlines of these style forms create new, flat shapes. These silhouette shapes are often very different from the flat pattern shapes cut into the fabric. The shapes that are actually flat, the style silhouettes seen as flat, and the actual hollow forms continue their distinct identities and roles, but they also create an intimate and ongoing interaction with each other and with the body. Mastering that relationship is essential to good functional, structural, and decorative design. In dress, most actual two-dimensional design is decorative (such as fabric motifs) or structural design perceived as flat (such as pockets or collars). True structural design—that which affects performance and fit—is three-dimensional.

How we perceive shape and form influences how we use and relate them. Arnheim's definition applies either to shape or form: "Shape ... is the external manifestation of the inner forces that produced the object."[1] He notes that the distinctive feature of shape is not its contour, but its structure, as established by a skeletal axis which determines contours. In fact, the same contours may be seen as a different shape when the skeletal axis changes direction, as in seeing a parallelogram as a diamond (Figure 6-8).[2]

Invisible internal forces and skeletal axes suggest contours of flat shapes and three-dimensional forms. The human body is an obvious example as its contours depend on the skeleton and the flesh it sup-

---

[1]Rudolf Arnheim, *Art and Visual Perception* (Berkeley: University of California Press, 1971), p. 52.
[2]Rudolf Arnheim, *Toward a Psychology of Art* (Berkeley: University of California Press, 1972), p. 95.

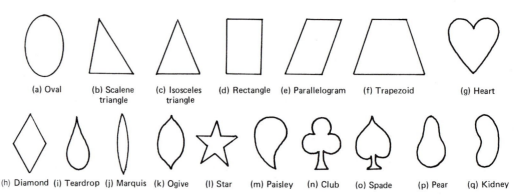

(a) Oval   (b) Scalene triangle   (c) Isosceles triangle   (d) Rectangle   (e) Parallelogram   (f) Trapezoid   (g) Heart

(h) Diamond   (i) Teardrop   (j) Marquis   (k) Ogive   (l) Star   (m) Paisley   (n) Club   (o) Spade   (p) Pear   (q) Kidney

FIGURE 6-3   Unequally sided flat shapes.

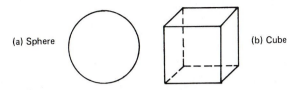

FIGURE 6-4 Equally sided volume forms.

ports. A garment silhouette assumes its major contours from the body structure. Surface contours assume positions because of forces exerted from inside and out.[3] Some skeletal structures are much more apparent than others. For example, it is easier to imagine the skeletal structure determining a leg than that determining a puffed sleeve.

We conceptualize human figures and garments as three-dimensional forms such as cones, spheres, or cylinders. But when they are graphically represented on flat paper, spherical sleeves become circles; cylindrical jackets and sleeves become rectangles; conical skirts and sleeves translate into triangles or trapezoids; and the ovoid head becomes an oval face. We are so accustomed to this flat, graphic interpretation that we switch our perceptions back and forth between two- and three-dimensional concepts almost without realizing it.

What three-dimensional forms might the flat shapes in Figures 6-2 and 6-3 sug-

gest? What flat shapes would be the two-dimensional equivalents of the forms suggested in Figures 6-4 and 6-5?

Although difficult, separating and analyzing the difference between the two- and three-dimensions in a garment are critical. The three-dimensional forms must be functionally practical; they must allow for movement, protection, and comfort. Yet combined, they must also be aesthetically pleasing as both three-dimensional forms and as a flat, pictorial composition with "hanger appeal."

We usually see people from many angles as they move and turn. So we become accustomed to perceiving them as a unit. Looking at the front, we imagine the hidden back as a part of that unit because we remember its presence and appearance. Arnheim notes that knowledge is so wedded to perception that we imagine (subconsciously) the hair on the back of the head when we see someone's face.[4] A "visual

---

[3]Graham Collier, *Form, Space, and Vision* (Englewood Cliffs, N.J.: Prentice-Hall, Inc., 1964), p. 110.

[4]Arnheim, *Art and Visual Perception*, p. 37.

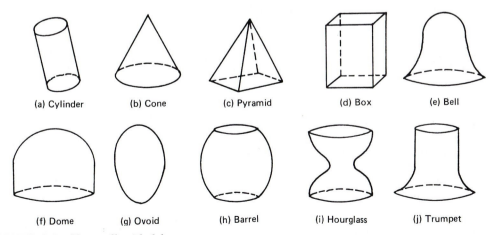

(a) Cylinder (b) Cone (c) Pyramid (d) Box (e) Bell

(f) Dome (g) Ovoid (h) Barrel (i) Hourglass (j) Trumpet

FIGURE 6-5 Unequally sided forms.

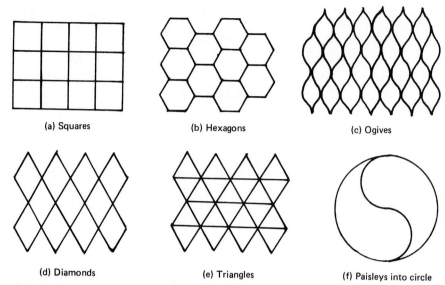

| (a) Squares | (b) Hexagons | (c) Ogives |
| (d) Diamonds | (e) Triangles | (f) Paisleys into circle |

FIGURE 6-6 Some shapes fit snugly together.

concept of solids" allows us to visualize all around a solid body at the same moment.[5] Looking at a garment, we imagine the totality of the form—the conical skirt or tubular pant leg—even though we see only one side at a time. (Designers sometimes take undue advantage of this tendency by designing for front interest only.)

In clothing, a critical two- and three-dimensional relationship is that between the flat shape of the garment pattern piece as it is cut from fabric and the three-dimensional form of the garment part it becomes to enfold the figure (Figures 6-9a and b). The transformation of flat fabric into a three-dimensional garment following the contours and movements of the human figure is the key to structural design. It tells how much extra width is needed for gathers, what

---

[5]*Ibid.*, p. 90.

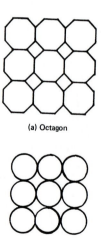

(a) Octagon

(b) Stars

(c) Circle

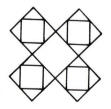

(d) Square or rectangle plus triangle

FIGURE 6-7 Shapes not fitting together create other shapes between them.

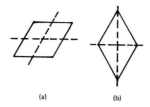

FIGURE 6-8 Identical contours may be perceived as different shapes when the skeletal axis changes direction.

happens to a skirt pattern shape when flare is added, what flat shape is needed for a sleeve cap to curve under the arm and over the shoulder.

The designer must be able to "go in either direction": to look at a flat pattern piece and envision how it will look made up into a hollow garment style, or be able to look at a sketch or an actual garment and visualize the number, shapes, and sizes of flat pattern pieces needed. This skill is critical for estimating yardage, production costs, drafting and sewing time, and level

of difficulty, and for anticipating any matching of the fabric pattern.

Can you envision a finished garment from looking at the pattern pieces in Figure 6-9a? Can you estimate the flat pattern shapes needed for the fit and drape of the bias style by looking at the garment in Figure 6-9b? Check yourself by comparing the two figures.

TWO AND THREE DIMENSIONS IN FIGURES AND FASHIONS

The human figure can be seen as a combination of geometric forms. Throughout history the average adult head has been ovoid; the neck, arms, hands, and legs are dominantly cylindrical. The female torso is usually an hourglass or cylinder. The shoulder, hip, and knee joints, breasts, and buttocks suggest domes or spheres (Figure 6-10). The male torso is dominantly cylindrical, or an inverted, flattened cone if the shoulders are

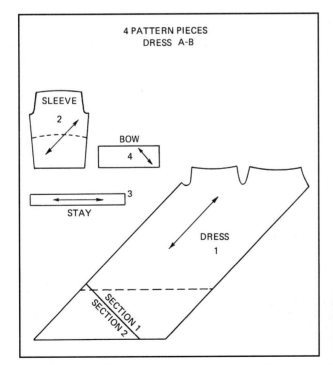

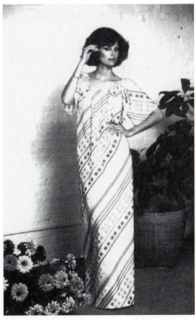

FIGURE 6-9 What kind of three-dimensional form and what garment style would the flat pattern pieces in (a) create when stitched together? Can you see how these pieces would form the fit, drape, and gathers of the dress (b)? (Courtesy **McCall Pattern** Company.)

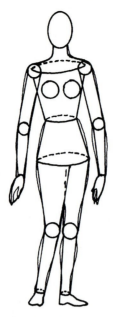

FIGURE 6-10 Dominant geometric forms of females.

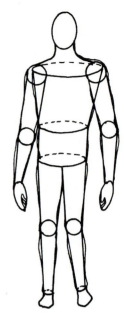

FIGURE 6-11 Dominant geometric forms of males.

much wider than the hips (Figure 6-11). The child's head is predominantly spherical, and body parts cylindrical (Figure 6-12). With age, the torso may become more like a barrel or a pear. When we wish our figures to appear different than they actually are, we don't usually want to change to a totally different sphere, box, or other form. Rather, we want to change apparent proportions of existing forms, to appear taller, shorter, or smaller-waisted, or to have broader shoulders or narrower hips or a longer face.

Personal Analysis

Cultural ideals of beauty determine how we wish to appear to increase our acceptability. The design process and illusions studied earlier use shape and form to achieve desired appearances:

1. (Goal.) Decide how you want to appear overall—for example, generally smaller.
2. (Outside influences.) Analyze your actual figure characteristics, forms, proportions, silhouettes, problems, and strengths. Know where you are to start—for example, round shoulders, large waist, good height.

3. (Criteria.) Decide what effects to create—for example, appear to have wider shoulders, smaller hips, to be taller.
4. (Plan.)
   (a) Decide what illusions will create desired effects—for example, vertical lines to suggest height, widely spaced seams to seem wider, or closely spaced seams to appear narrower. (Review geometric carpentered-world and size and space illusions and physical effects of line and space.)

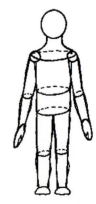

FIGURE 6-12 Dominant body forms of children.

(b) Choose garment part styles that can create the desired illusions.

5. (Carry out plan.) Create or select styles that incorporate the desired illusions.

6. (Evaluate.) Compare the figure appearance in chosen styles with criteria and the previous appearance.

Once your over-all figure appearance goal is set, analyze your present front-view and profile. One way is to stand in front of a mirror, in a body stocking, full slip, or nothing, so as not to break up space or create subdivisions within the silhouette. Another is to stand, wearing only undergarments, against a large piece of plain paper taped to a smooth wall and have someone trace around your figure, front and profile, indicating bust, waist, and hip levels. Or have someone take your vertical and horizontal measurements and record them on the grid and chart in Figure 6-14a.

Visual length or width is the straight vertical or horizontal distance the viewer sees, not allowing for depth. To measure head height, for example, stand against a smooth wall and have someone place a dowel or ruler on the crown going *straight* back to the wall. Repeat at the chin level, shoulder, under the arm, at the bust, waist, hips, and at the knee and ankle. The vertical distance on the wall between each of those points is the visual length of that part. Their total equals total height. This method avoids errors of front-to-back body depth. For "height in heads," divide the head height into total height.

For visual width measures of neck, shoulders, bust/chest, waist, hip, knee, calf, and ankle, have someone place a ruler or dowel along each side of the part *straight* back to the wall, mark and measure the distance. This number is less than half the circumference because it does not include depth or thickness (Figure 6-13).

In the Figure 6-14a grid, one square equals one square inch. Count the squares from the top down the center vertical and mark the vertical measurements. For width, divide the measure in two and count half

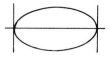

FIGURE 6-13 Visual widths may differ despite similar circumferences because some people are wide from side to side and narrow front to back, while others are thin from side to side and thicker in depth.

on each side of the center vertical at the vertical point of that body part. When all dots are complete, join them, recalling that body lines usually change directions in curves, not sharp angles. Follow the points of measurement faithfully. You may be astonished at the resulting silhouette and think, "Do I look like *that*?" Yes, if you have measured and drawn accurately, you do.

Then study body areas *in relation to each other*. For example, is the waist too wide, too narrow, or pleasing *in relation to* shoulder width and hip width? Is the bust level too high, too low, or pleasing *in relation to* shoulder-bust and bust-waist length? Are legs too long, too short, or pleasing *in relation to* torso length? Study your entire figure, including neck, face, and hands. Remember that similar circumferences may have differing visual widths. For example, of two people with 26-inch waists, one might have a visual width of 9 inches because she is thicker from front to back and narrower from side to side, and the other might have an 11-inch width because she is thinner from front to back and wider across (Figure 6-13).

When you have thoroughly studied your figure to know where you are starting, and have decided what you are satisfied and dissatisfied with, Figure 6-14b will help you identify your desired appearance illusions and select styles to create them. The left-hand column headed "Body Features" lists the various figure components. In the

MEASUREMENTS	S=OK	D=No
Head height	____	____
Neck: chin to base	____	____
Neck base to bust	____	____
Bust to waist	____	____
Waist to hips	____	____
Hip to knee	____	____
Knee to ankle	____	____
Ankle to floor	____	____
Arm: shoulder to wrist	____	____
Wrist to finger tip	____	____
TOTAL HEIGHT	____	____
HEIGHT IN HEADS	____	____
Shoulder width	____	____
Bust circumference	____	____
Visual bust/chest width	____	____
Waist circumference	____	____
Visual waist width	____	____
Hips 9″ below waist circumference	____	____
Hips—fullest circumference	____	____
Visual hip width	____	____
Knee width	____	____
Calf width	____	____
Figure problems:	_____
	_____
	_____

FIGURE 6-14a   Personal measurement analysis.

Body Features (Outside influences)	Desired Appearance* (Criteria)	Styles Helping Create Desired Illusions (Plan)
Over-all weight		
Total height		
General size		
Face		
Chin		
Neck		
Shoulders		
Back		
Chest/rib cage		
Bust		
Waist		
Stomach		
Hips		
Buttocks		
Thighs		
Knees		
Calves		
Ankles		
Feet		
Upper arm		
Elbows		
Forearm		
Wrists		
Hands		
Other (specify)		

*Wider, narrower, longer, shorter, thicker, thinner, straighter, rounder, flatter, sharper, larger, smaller, higher, lower, etc.

FIGURE 6-14b Figure illusions wish list.

second column headed "Desired Appearance," list *in comparative terms* (such as those at the lower asterisk on the chart) by each feature how you would like to appear—for example, taller, shorter, thicker, thinner, smaller. Do not use numbers, such as 5 ft. 6 in. tall, because these do not tell *for you* if this means taller or shorter. If you are satisfied with a body area, enter "satisfied" or "OK" in that column by that body part. This column shows the criteria, effects, and illusions that you want to create. The garment styles that use those forms and shapes are your tools to create illusions.

Current Westernized cultures prize change, but the basic human form does not change. So clothing designers face a constant challenge to create visual variety, while maintaining functional comfort, safety, mobility, and practicality. This requires mastery of the visual, psychological, *and functional* characteristics of clothing styles. These include their three-dimensional functioning forms; their pictorial, flat silhouettes; and how the two- and three-dimensions relate to each other and the body. When you have studied the styles in Figures 6-21 through 6-52, choose the styles for each garment part that meet your criteria.

In Figure 6-14b, enter the names of chosen styles in the column headed "Styles Helping Create Desired Illusions" on the line matching the relevant body part. List as many appropriate styles for each body area as you can to create a style "pool" or repertoire from which to select and combine styles for your personal prescription for any occasion or season. Although you are now using your own figure for practice and experience, as a professional, you may be advising or designing for figure characteristics and desired illusions very different from your own; so you must know the names, visual effects, and functional potentials and risks of *all* styles and garment parts.

Shape and Form in Dress

Figure 6-15 shows examples of flat geometric shapes structurally or decoratively in-corporated in dress. The square, rectangle, triangle, diamond, teardrop, and trapezoid are both decorative and structural (Figure 6-15a, b, c, d, f, and h). The circle, hexagon, oval, ogive, and marquis are primarily decorative (Figure 6-15e, g, i, j, and k). Many shapes can join to create other shapes (Figure 6-7). Almost any shape can find attractive uses in dress.

Three-dimensional, structural geometric forms are most comfortable and attractive when they follow the body part they surround, and most interesting when they have unequal proportions. In Figures 6-16a and b, the equilateral cube and sphere do little to flatter the figure; the other unequal structural forms emphasize a sense of direction (Figure 6-16c to l).

No form or shape works in isolation. Choice must consider how each form will work and look combined with others.

1. The garment form must complement the body, functionally, structurally, and decoratively. For example, tubular pants on tubular legs are more practical than spherical ones could be.

2. Garment parts are generally most attractive when they strike a fine balance of being neither too concealing, too revealing, nor too distorting. In short, they avoid extremes.

3. Avoiding extremes also provides enough variety for balance and interest, but avoids overdone, monotonous repetition on the one hand, and overdone, unrelated variety on the other. In Figure 6-17a the repeated spherical forms further repeat the decorative circles (Figure 6-17d) to create a bulbous garment of overwhelming rotundity (Figure 6-17g), which would make movement awkward, conceal the natural form, and violate a pressure balance by appearing ready to explode.

Figures 6-17b, e, and h go to the other extreme: confusion. Figure 6-17b shows a jumble of forms compounded by a profusion of decorative flat shapes (Figure

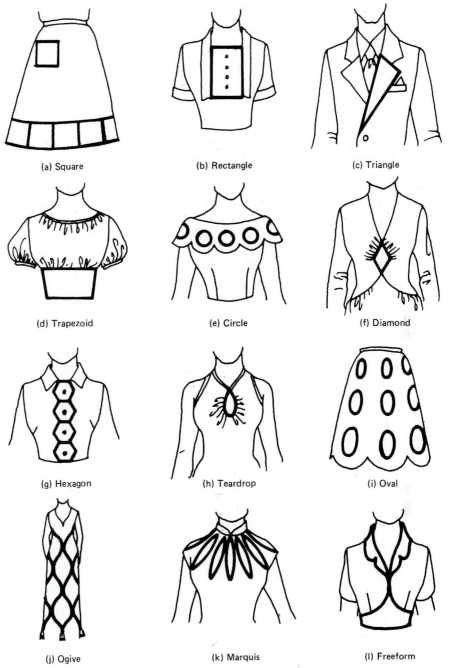

(a) Square   (b) Rectangle   (c) Triangle

(d) Trapezoid   (e) Circle   (f) Diamond

(g) Hexagon   (h) Teardrop   (i) Oval

(j) Ogive   (k) Marquis   (l) Freeform

FIGURE 6-15 Flat, two-dimensional shapes in dress are incorporated in any of three ways: (1) as flat structural garment parts such as pockets (a), insets (b, f), collars (b, c, l), or cut-outs (h); (2) as decorative pattern motif shapes (a, e, g, i, j, k); or (3) as three-dimensional garment part forms whose silhouettes create flat shapes in photographs or pictures (d, l).

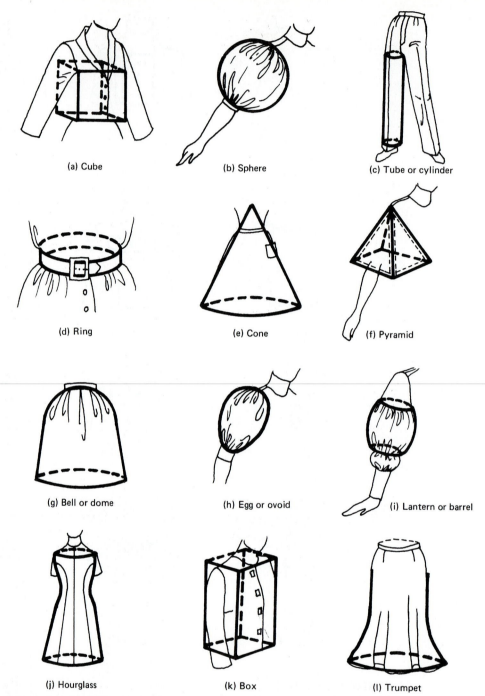

(a) Cube   (b) Sphere   (c) Tube or cylinder

(d) Ring   (e) Cone   (f) Pyramid

(g) Bell or dome   (h) Egg or ovoid   (i) Lantern or barrel

(j) Hourglass   (k) Box   (l) Trumpet

FIGURE 6-16 Three-dimensional forms in dress envelope the figure. Only the cube (a) and sphere (b) are equally sided; all others (c–l) are unequally sided and provide visual variation as well as the basis for garment part fit.

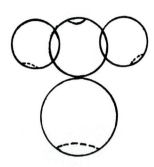

(a) Forms: bodice: sphere, sleeves—sphere, skirt —sphere.

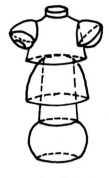

(b) Forms: collar—ring, sleeves—lantern, bodice —cone, skirt—dome, skirt—tube and sphere.

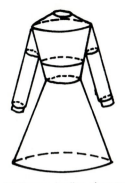

(c) Forms: bodice—inverted cone, skirt—cone, cuff —ring, sleeve—cylinder

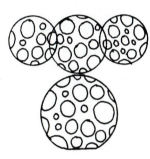

(d) Flat shapes: circles

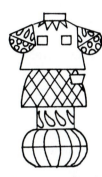

(e) Flat shapes: triangle, teardrop, circle, square, diamond, paisley, rectangle, freeform.

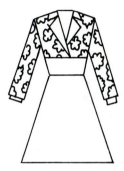

(f) Flat shapes: trapezoid, rectangle, triangle, curvilinear freeforms.

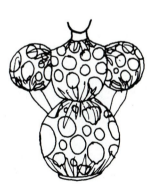

(g) Resulting combination: repetitive sameness, unrelated to figure.

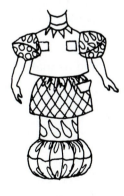

(h) Resulting combination: multiplicity of shapes and forms unrelated to each other or to body forms.

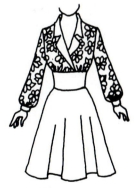

(i) Resulting combination: repetition with variation related to each other and to body forms.

FIGURE 6-17 Three-dimensional forms and two-dimensional shapes must agree with each other and with the human form, and must provide related interest, avoiding either monotony or confusion.

6-17e), resulting in a kaleidoscopic nightmare (Figure 6-17h). It is a cluttered, disorganized concoction with too many different shapes and forms unrelated to each other or to body structure.

Figures 6-17c, f, and i show a balance with a few structural forms well-related to body structure and repeated with enough variation for interest: cone, inverted cone, ring, and cylinder (Figure 6-17c). Seen as flat, these become rectangles, trapezoids, triangles, and free forms (Figure 6-17f). Forms and shapes function well, avoid extremes, and agree with each other and with the human form (Figure 6-17i).

Practice analyzing current and historical garments by their geometric structural forms and decorative shapes. Historical and ethnic garments have the same forms as clothing today, since styles change but the human figure and clothing have the same forms throughout time everywhere. How well do clothing forms relate to the body? To each other? Would they be functional, comfortable, and allow freedom of movement? How well do decorative flat shapes relate to the forms they adorn? What are the flat shape equivalents of the garment forms?

Figure 6-18a shows the flat pattern rectangles that combine to make the classic Japanese kimono, spread flat showing the back, front, and sleeves. Structurally, the garment is combined straight edged and sharply angled rectangles of differing proportions. Yet note how the curvilinear floral fabric pattern especially designed for the kimono flows from one structurally rectangular segment to another, placed to show when the garment envelopes the body. Figure 6-18b shows how the flat rectangles wrap around the figure to become tubes, which in turn become rectangular silhouettes providing a frame and backdrop for an infinite variety of decorative designs. In the figure at the right, note the softening effect of the curved flower motif lines, and their placement on the kimono

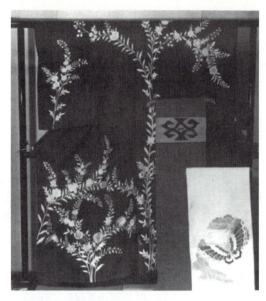

FIGURE 6-18a The traditional Japanese kimono is composed of adjoining rectangular flat shapes of different proportions, giving right angled and straight structural lines, shown here from the back with the front spread open and flat. Their combination provides a "canvas" for decorative design to flow across seam lines for attractive placement on the figure. (Courtesy of Japan National Tourist Organization.)

to show when it is wrapped on the figure. On the seated figures at the left, the overlapping bodices introduce triangles that provide compatible countering through a variety of shapes.

Figure 6-19 shows cone skirt forms, disc-shaped hat brims and dome crowns, and ovoid sleeve sections with tubular cuffs, giving ample variety of forms and corresponding silhouettes. Figure 6-20 shows still different forms and shapes. The skirts are dome formed, the full sleeves are modified spheres or double cones with ring cuffs, and the fitted sleeves and bodices are short tubes. The headdresses combine squares and circles while the trailing ribbons flare into a triangle. In each outfit, how do the forms relate to each other and to the human figure? What flat shapes do their outlines suggest?

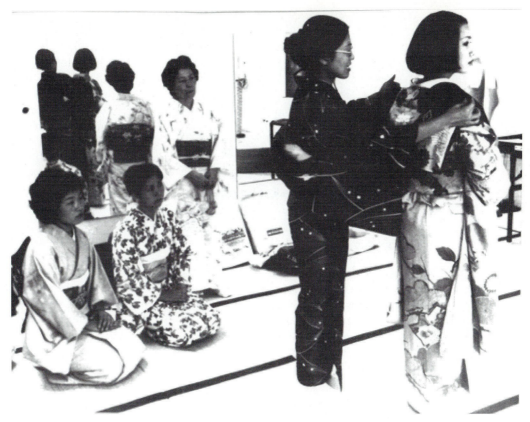

FIGURE 6-18b The flat rectangles of (a) become tubular forms when they envelope the human figure. Though the structural styles are nearly alike, the variety of flat shapes in fabric pattern motifs gives each kimono a unique character. (Courtesy of Japan National Tourist Organization.)

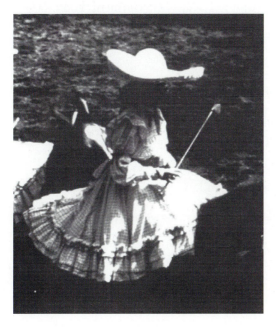

VISUAL EFFECTS IN DRESS

Selecting and combining forms and shapes into effective garments is easier and more efficient if done according to the *characteristics* of a style and the visual effects they create or avoid. The effects described in the following text and in Table 6-1 use characteristics regardless of specific styles or parts of the garment. They alert the designer to the effects to expect, whether they appear

FIGURE 6-19 This Mexican "Escaramuze" costume shows curvilinear forms of cone formed skirt, ovoid sleeves, and dome and disc hat. What geometric flat shape equivalents do their silhouettes suggest? (Courtesy of the Mexican Ministry of Tourism.)

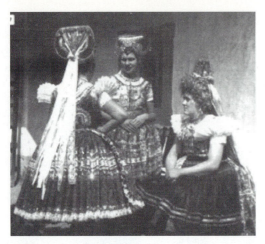

FIGURE 6-20 These traditional Czech festival costumes show a different combination of forms with the dome skirts, tubular bodices and sleeves, and flattened spherical sleeves with ring cuffs, showing still different examples of how various geometric clothing forms relate to the human figure, its appearance, and mobility. (Courtesy of Czechoslovak Airlines.)

in a sleeve, a skirt, a hat, or any other part, and thus provide basic guidelines useful everywhere. This method avoids memorizing many points about one style that might be duplicated in another garment part that in turn would be memorized separately. Learn to recognize characteristics common to different garment parts and styles to master predicting the effects of any one style. Then use an effect only where it is desired, and will not accent an undesired feature. Make these guidelines part of your basic tools in using shape and form in dress. See Table 6-1 for guideline examples applied to different garment parts shown in Figures 6-22 to 6-48.

Practice these analyses with the historical and contemporary styles in the following pages and chapters.

A. Direction/length:
  1. A shape emphasizes its dominant direction, whether the total silhouette or any one part. This effect is especially important in placing seams,

pleats, armscyes, necklines, and waistlines.
  a. A slender, vertical style will heighten and narrow.
  b. A thick or horizontal style will shorten and widen.
  2. Styles with many vertical *and* horizontal subdividing lines offer more opportunities to emphasize either length or width.
  3. Diagonal shapes are more influenced by surrounding lines, shapes, and spaces than are vertical or horizontal lines, and may seem more horizontal or vertical than they really are.
  4. a. The more equally a horizontal line divides an area in half, generally the shorter it will seem.
  b. The closer to one end the division is, the less the shortening effect.

B. Size/bulk:
  5. Snugly fitted styles accent actual body contours, and usually enlarge.
  6. Gently loose styles may seem to add slight weight, or may camouflage extreme thinness or heaviness; it is hard to tell what a loose style conceals.
  7. Shapes extending far away from the body add apparent bulk and weight.

C. Garment/body:
  8. A style may carry its effects to a neighboring part of the body as well as the part it covers.
  9. Hems and edges emphasize the part of the body where they end.
  10. Initial size and shape impressions are of the overall silhouette; then each part is interpreted in relation to the whole.

D. Shape/space effects:
  11. A shape conveys the physical and psychological effects of the lines around it and the filled or empty spacing within it.
  a. Curves reinforce roundness and counter angularity.
  b. Straight lines reinforce each other and counter rotundity.

The effects in Table 6-1 can also be seen in any of the following illustrated hairstyles and garment styles that are grouped according to the part of the body or garment. Descriptions in each garment part section give further examples of effects identified in Table 6-1. They are by no means exhaustive, but they include late-twentieth-century Western styles common and popular long enough to have acquired an accepted name. Many in the adult sections are not repeated in the children's wear where differences are primarily of proportions, not styles. Some may seem old, but in the most current fashion magazines it would be hard to find a style not shown here. Since basic body forms do not change, "fashion" is often simply a new way of interpreting or combining "standard" styles whose forms agree with human body forms.

Facial Shapes and Hairstyles

The face is often the first feature viewed, and the first impression is a lasting one. Many contemporary Westernized cultures regard the oval as an "ideal" shape for a face. Artistically, it is well-proportioned with an interesting width in relation to its length, neither too equal nor too different; so it makes a well-balanced frame and background for the facial features. Second, psychologically it seems stable, but has enough restrained curve for softness. Some people have naturally oval faces; others do not but would like to create that illusion. Still others wish to emphasize facial shapes other than oval. One easy way to discover one's own shape is to pull the hair back and draw the outline of the face on a mirror with lipstick or other removable marker. Then step back and study the resulting shape. Most people have a combination of several geometric shapes usually leaning toward one or two. Dominant face shapes include

Oval—about two-thirds as wide as long, curved chin and forehead, slightly curved cheeks.

Square—short, wide forehead, straight cheeks, and wide, angular chin with prominent jawbones.

Round—short and wide with rounded chin, cheeks, and forehead.

Triangular—wide chin, prominent jawbones, and narrow, pointed forehead.

Inverted triangle—narrow, pointed chin, and wide, low forehead. With a "widow's peak" of hair point at the center forehead, it is also called "heart-shaped."

Diamond—narrow, pointed forehead and chin, and wide, prominent cheekbones.

Rectangular—long, narrow, angular.

The illustrations in Figure 6-21 show straight and Afro hairstyles for men and women, and, for women, plaited. Vertical column a shows various facial shapes compared to their closest geometric shape. Column b superimposes an oval on each geometric shape to compare the two. The difference between the actual shape and the oval provides the key to reveal where to put hair fullness or to avoid it: Since a shape or form extending away from the body adds bulk and weight at that point, to look more oval, put more hair bulk where the actual face shape falls inside the oval (as in columns c, e, g, i, and k) and avoid putting more bulk where the actual shape falls outside the oval. To emphasize the actual shape, put more hair bulk where the actual face shape comes outside the oval and avoid putting any where the shape comes inside the oval (as in columns d, f, h, j, and l). All these styles use this single basic guideline.

Hair covering or exposing parts of the face is also influential. To look oval, use the "countering" technique of a line at right angle to an undesired line direction. For example, a person with a narrow, pointed forehead would avoid a center part and create a horizontal line with bangs (Figure 6-21c, 3 and 5). A diamond face with wide cheeks could cover the edges with flat waves.

			Bodices,			
Guideline	Necklines	Collars	Shirts	Sleeves	Skirts	Pants

TABLE 6-1 Example Styles for Effects by Shape Characteristics

Guideline	Necklines	Collars	Bodices, Shirts	Sleeves	Skirts	Pants
A. *Direction/length:* 1. Dominant direction: a. Vertical shape lengthens.	V, deep square or cowl, U	Chelsea, shawl	princess, surplice, dropped	plain, long fitted, shirt	gored, long dinner, trumpet, pleated, straight fitted	jeans, capri, slacks, ranch
b. Horizontal shape widens, shortens.	bateau, wide square or cowl	bertha, Mandarin, turtleneck	shoulder or midriff yoke	ruffled, puff, cuffs	hip yoke, mini	Jamaica, skort, pedal pushers
2. Many horizontals and verticals offer choice of direction emphasis.	draw-string, sweetheart, square	sailor back, bow, short roll, con-vertible	shoulder yoke, shirt, peasant, western, smock	roll, lantern, virago	tiered, dirndl, hip yoke	jeans, shorts, lederhosen
3. Diagonals influ-enced by neigh-boring lines.	decolette, scoop, V, one-shoulder	Italian, sailor front, Puritan	French dart, surplice, pointed waist	raglan, bell, lantern	handker-chief, draped	jodphurs, diagonal pocket edges
4. Divisions of vertical space: a. Equal shortens more.			camisole, strapless, shoulder yoke	plain, roll, flounce, lantern	midriff yoke, mini, tiered	Bermuda, deck, pedal pushers, culottes
b. Near one end shortens less.			shirt, smock	shirt, long lantern, juliet, epaulet	hip yoke	slacks, Capri, short shorts
B. *Size/bulk:* 1. Snug fit accents, enlarges.	one-shoulder, decolette, scoop		strapless, any snug fit, midriff	long, any snug fit, midriff	snug fitted, trumpet, long dinner	shorts, jeans, any snug fit, leotards
2. Gently loose camouflages.		most flat collars	gently bloused, overblouse, shirt, middy	shirt, roll, bishop, petal	flared, gored, pleated, midi	culottes, gaucho, loose slacks, pant skirt, knickers
3. Extensions add bulk and weight.	cowl, drawstring	ascot, jabot, bow, ruff	full blouse, camisole, smock, peasant	peasant, flounce, leg-o-mutton, cape, puff, virago, ruffled, melon, draped	circular, peasant, pegged, tiered, accordion, some pleats	palazzo, flared, harem

TABLE 6-1 *Continued*

Dresses	*Outerwear*	*Style Features*	*Accessories*	*Men's Shirts, Jackets*	*Men's Coats*	*Men's Accessories*
basic, princess, sheath	polo, Chesterfield, princess, tuxedo	single breasted	fez hat, hood	shawl, dinner, basic, tuxedo	Chesterfield, Ulster	Four-in-hand tie
bouffant, peasant	bolero, Abbe, battle jacket, capelet	peplum, bow, flounce, ruffles	cummerbund, picture hat, pillbox, sailor hat	Mackinaw, shoulder yoke	tailcoat	cummerbund, bow tie, sailor hat, boater
bouffant, pinafore, shirtwaist, jacket, peasant	weskit, battle, blazer, safari, trench	ruffle, bow, peplum, shirring, patch pocket	toque, fedora, derby	Western, Henley, work, safari	Ulster, tailcoat	various ties; hat: Panama, Homburg
princess, pinafore, A-line	Abbe cape, poncho, balmacaan	any used diagonally	cloche hat, toque, any worn at an angle	jacket lapels	balmacaan, cutaway, lapels	vest
dropped waist	safari	any making equal divisions	any making equal divisions	Mackinaw, safari		
mumuu, tunic	balmacaan, coachman	depends on placement	depends how worn	high shoulder yoke	balmacaan	depends on placement
sheath, fitted, princess	snug weskit, any snug fit	most are not snug	tight belts	Western, tapered	tailcoat if snug	any snug fit, vest
A-line, jumper, pinafore, jacket, shirtwaist, granny	cardigan, Chanel, box, blazer, pea jacket, polo, jerkin, balmacaan	varies	varies	sport, work, most jackets	balmacaan, Chesterfield, Ulster	ties
bouffant, peasant, maternity, dashiki, tent	shawl, poncho, capes, swagger	ruffles, peplum, flounce, shirring, bows	head tie, picture hat, sailor, cummerbund	extra-full styles	extra-full styles	varies

| | | | Bodices, | | | |
Guideline	Necklines	Collars	Shirts	Sleeves	Skirts	Pants
C. *Garment/body* 1. Style may affect neighboring figure parts.		tie, bow		flounce, long bell, lantern leg-o-mutton, juliet, melon, ruffled, dolman, puff, cape	dirndl, pegged, circular, hip yoke	any ending above ankle accent leg area exposed
2. Edges emphasize body area.	All garment part edges or hems accent the part of the body where they end, especially if it					
3. Whole is seen first, then parts	First impressions include the entire figure, then each garment and its parts are quickly these perceptions.					
D. *Shape/space:* 1. Shapes convey effects of their lines and space. a. Round reinforces curves, counters angles.	cowl, U, keyhole, scoop, cowl, U, keyhole, scoop	jabot, shawl, bow, ruff, peter pan	princess, surplice, peasant	peasant, leg-o-mutton, juliet, virago, raglan, melon, puff	dirndl pegged, trumpet, draped,	harem, jodphurs, knickers
b. Straight reinforces straight and counters round.	V, square, halter, one-shoulder	Chelsea, sailor, turtle-neck, Mandarin	straight shoulder yoke, shirt, overblouse	straight, fitted, plain, roll	all straight, A-line, gored, pleated, hip yoke	all straight styles

Curved wavy or curled styles can counter straight-edged faces and angular jawbones, cheeks, or noses to give softness (Figure 6-21c, e, g, and i, square, triangular, diamond); or straighter hairstyles can counter extreme roundness.

Plaited styles create more unity if hair ends are brought back to the head, leading the eye back to the face (Figure 6-21k) rather than extending away from it (Figure 6-21l). Curved plaits counter facial angularity, and straight counters round face lines (Figure 6-21k). Most corn-rowing is close to the head and so rarely affects apparent facial shape, but braids and hair part directions can affect the apparent length and depth of the head.

Neck length and thickness also affect apparent facial shape, and hairstyles can affect the appearance of the neck. Generally, shoulder-length styles curled at the ends help a long, thin neck look shorter, and straighter styles may help it look thinner. Shorter hairstyles showing at least the tips of the ears usually help a short or thick neck look longer.

But a hairstyle good for a facial shape may be poor for a certain type of neck, such as a hairstyle that might solve one problem for a square face but create another for a

Dresses	Outerwear	Style Features	Accessories	Men's Shirts, Jackets	Men's Coats	Men's Accessories
TABLE 6-1 *Continued*						
bouffant, peasant, pinafore, muumuu, granny	shawl, poncho	ruffles, peplum, flounce, bows, godets	most hats, belts, and shoes	Western, tapered. Full jackets may accent legs.	cutaway, tailcoat	most hats
is exposed area (neck, face, arms, midriff, or legs) rather than another garment.						
analyzed and then seen in relation to a "rebuilt whole." All styles of all parts will contribute. their characteristics to						
bouffant, peasant, granny	Abbe cape, balmacaan	ruffles, soft bows	any rounded styles	shawl	balmacaan	any rounded style
shirtwaist, shift, tent, flapper, dashiki, caftan, some maternity	battle, box, cardigan, tabard, polo, safari, car coat Chesterfield, tuxedo	any straight-edged style	any straight-edged style	formal, Henley, sport, any straight style	any straight style	any straight-edged style

long, thin neck. Such challenges need individualized solutions which may include consideration of eye, nose, mouth, and chin, as well as the silhouette since the head is viewed in profile as well as from the front. Here, too, choose styles that draw attention to features you wish to emphasize and that camouflage or conceal features you don't.

Necklines

Even though a neckline is a "line," it is included here because it forms the lower edge of the shape created by chin, neck, neckline, and sometimes shoulders. It influences apparent facial shape and neck proportions. Neckline styles (Figure 6-22) are grouped here according to the general effect produced by their dominant direction. Someone wishing to counter a wide face or chin or short neck would choose dominantly vertical or vertically diagonal necklines, such as the shawl, V, U, or halter. Pointed chins or narrow faces would look wider with dominantly horizontal necklines, such as the bateau, wide square, or jewel.

A curved neckline softens angular faces, and straight angled necklines counter a very round face. Necklines also have an important role in the neck and shoulder area. A bony neck probably will

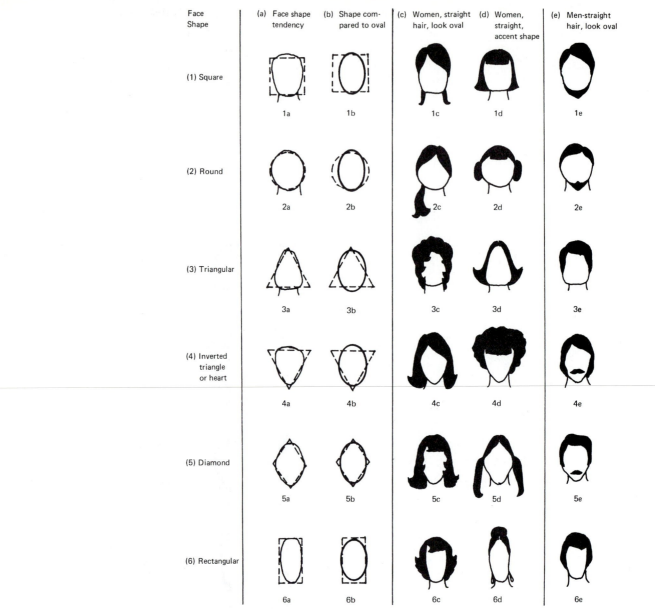

Face Shape	(a) Face shape tendency	(b) Shape compared to oval	(c) Women, straight hair, look oval	(d) Women, straight, accent shape	(e) Men-straight hair, look oval
(1) Square	1a	1b	1c	1d	1e
(2) Round	2a	2b	2c	2d	2e
(3) Triangular	3a	3b	3c	3d	3e
(4) Inverted triangle or heart	4a	4b	4c	4d	4e
(5) Diamond	5a	5b	5c	5d	5e
(6) Rectangular	6a	6b	6c	6d	6e

FIGURE 6-21 Face shapes and hair styles: To look more oval, put fullness where face shape comes inside oval; to accent another shape, place fullness where face shape comes outside oval.

not be flattered by a low-cut neckline. However, the upward thrust of a V could counter round shoulders. Dominantly vertical neck lines may seem to narrow the shoulders, whereas horizontal ones will widen them. A halter neckline may seem to narrow and pull down narrow or round shoulders; but by contrast its centered, vertical diagonals may emphasize very wide shoulders. A high cowl (k) widens shoulders, whereas a deep cowl (a) narrows them.

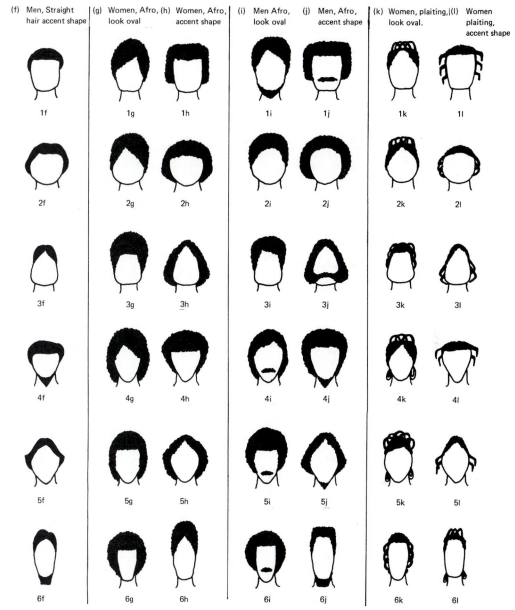

(f) Men, Straight hair accent shape	(g) Women, Afro, look oval	(h) Women, Afro, accent shape	(i) Men Afro, look oval	(j) Men, Afro, accent shape	(k) Women, plaiting, look oval.	(l) Women plaiting, accent shape
1f	1g	1h	1i	1j	1k	1l
2f	2g	2h	2i	2j	2k	2l
3f	3g	3h	3i	3j	3k	3l
4f	4g	4h	4i	4j	4k	4l
5f	5g	5h	5i	5j	5k	5l
6f	6g	6h	6i	6j	6k	6l

FIGURE 6-21 *(continued)*

Collars

Effects of collars (Figure 6-23) are very like those of necklines. However, some styles also include bulk which adds apparent size to the area, such as a long jabot or tie collar adding fullness to a flat chest. Effects of the same style can change if its proportions change. For example, a wide, short sailor collar widens the shoulders, whereas a narrow, long one narrows them.

Bodices

The lower edge of a bodice is stitched to a skirt, whereas a blouse is free at the bottom. Although waistline locations are critical, basic bodice styles can be analyzed in terms of fit or dominant lines (Figure 6-24). Normal fitted (a) and French dart (b) bodices reveal actual body contours, with the normal more lengthening and narrowing because of the vertical waistline darts. It is also used as

Shape and Form   **111**

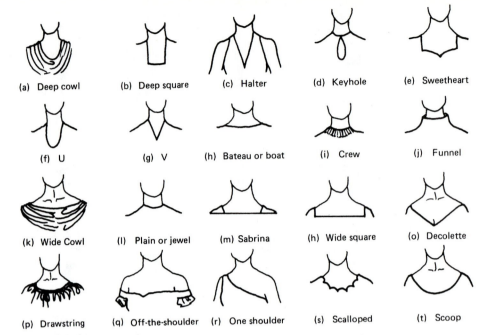

FIGURE 6-22   Neckline styles.

(a) Deep cowl (b) Deep square (c) Halter (d) Keyhole (e) Sweetheart

(f) U (g) V (h) Bateau or boat (i) Crew (j) Funnel

(k) Wide Cowl (l) Plain or jewel (m) Sabrina (h) Wide square (o) Decolette

(p) Drawstring (q) Off-the-shoulder (r) One shoulder (s) Scalloped (t) Scoop

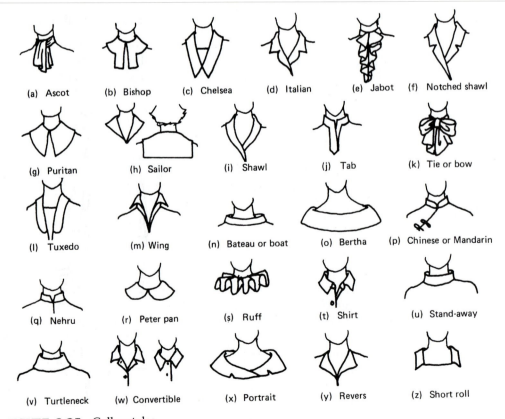

FIGURE 6-23   Collar styles.

(a) Ascot (b) Bishop (c) Chelsea (d) Italian (e) Jabot (f) Notched shawl

(g) Puritan (h) Sailor (i) Shawl (j) Tab (k) Tie or bow

(l) Tuxedo (m) Wing (n) Bateau or boat (o) Bertha (p) Chinese or Mandarin

(q) Nehru (r) Peter pan (s) Ruff (t) Shirt (u) Stand-away

(v) Turtleneck (w) Convertible (x) Portrait (y) Revers (z) Short roll

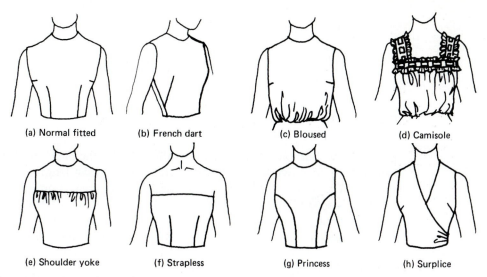

FIGURE 6-24   Bodice styles.

the basic bodice block, sloper, or staple pattern from which all other styles are drafted. Bloused (c) or camisole (d) bodices have extra bulk adding slight apparent weight, or camouflaging thick waists, large busts, or protruding ribs. The horizontal line above the bust on shoulder yoke (e), strapless (f), and camisole (d) bodices shortens the neck-bust length. A princess bodice narrows with vertical segments (g), and the surplice (h),

diagonally overlapping, usually emphasizes actual contours and bust. Except for bust darts, these styles would have similar effects used as back bodices.

Blouses and Shirts

Blouses (Figure 6-25) are usually less fitted than bodices. A smock (a) is full, ending near and emphasizing the hip. It adds ap-

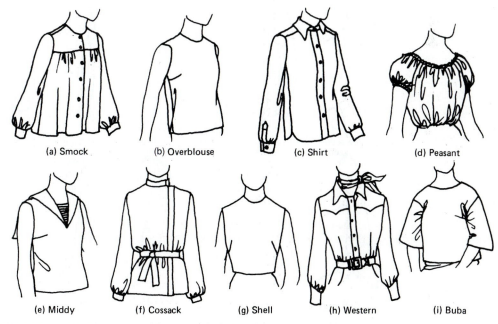

FIGURE 6-25   Blouse, overblouse, and shirt styles.

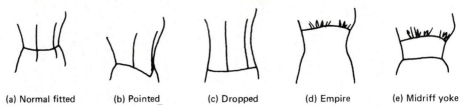

| (a) Normal fitted | (b) Pointed | (c) Dropped | (d) Empire | (e) Midriff yoke |

FIGURE 6-26 Waistline styles.

parent bulk, but can also be a maternity camouflage. The overblouse (b), shirt (c), peasant (d), middy (e), Cossack (f), and buba (i) also add bulk and hide a thick waist or protruding ribs, or lengthen the waist. A shell (g) is more fitted and emphasizes the waist. Blouses intended to be worn tucked in are usually more fitted (h).

Waistlines

Most waistlines are seen in relation to the natural waist (Figure 6-26). The normal, fitted waistline (a) is at the narrowest part of the waist and emphasizes natural contours. The diagonal front-pointed waist (b) gracefully lengthens. The dropped waist (c) lengthens the shoulder-hip area and widens the hip. The empire waistline (d),

under the bust, emphasizes it, shortens the neck-waist length, and lengthens the bust-knee area. Empire and dropped waists some distance from the natural waistline sometimes have a semifitted waist area. The horizontal midriff yoke (e) accents, shortens, and widens the bust-waist area.

Sleeves

Long, Set-In Sleeves. Set-in sleeves have a normal armscye extending from the natural shoulder point to the natural underarm, creating a vertical line which may only slightly narrow the shoulders. Long ones (Figure 6-27) end between the elbow and wrist. The longer and more fitted they are, the more slenderizing (Figure 6-27a–e). A two-piece sleeve (e) is generally used in tailored suit

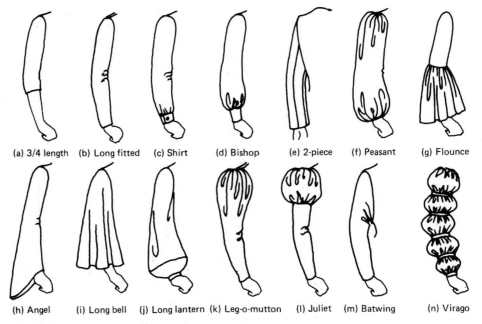

| (a) 3/4 length | (b) Long fitted | (c) Shirt | (d) Bishop | (e) 2-piece | (f) Peasant | (g) Flounce |

| (h) Angel | (i) Long bell | (j) Long lantern | (k) Leg-o-mutton | (l) Juliet | (m) Batwing | (n) Virago |

FIGURE 6-27 Long, set-in sleeve styles.

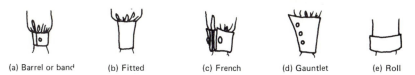

(a) Barrel or band   (b) Fitted   (c) French   (d) Gauntlet   (e) Roll

FIGURE 6-28   Cuff styles.

jackets and coats. Styles such as peasant (f), flounce (g), angel (h), long bell (i), or lantern (j), with fullness between elbow and wrist, add apparent bulk to that area as well as the neighboring waist-hip area. Similarly, those with shoulder fullness, such as leg-o-mutton (k) and juliet (l), may widen and enlarge a narrow shoulder area and emphasize a large or very small bust. Cuffs (Figure 6-28) snug at the wrist may slenderize it, and those extending away add bulk.

Short, Set-In Sleeves. These sleeves (Figure 6-29) have a normal armscye and end above the elbow. The shorter the sleeve, the more the upper arm is emphasized. Short, fitted styles, such as plain (a), cap (b), or petal (c), usually narrow shoulders slightly if the armscye seam is conspicuous, and widen them if it is inconspicuous. Styles bulky at the shoulders, such as puffed (e), ruffled (f), and melon (g), will widen the shoulders and counter round shoulders, but may also emphasize extremes in bust size. The downward slope of short cape (h), bell (i), and lantern (j) may round the shoulders.

Non-Set-In Sleeves. These sleeves (Figure 6-30) have an armscye other than normal. Styles illustrated here are short, but any except the kimono cap could be long, with accompanying effects. The armscye of the

raglan sleeve (a) curves from neck to underarm. It is graceful and allows freedom of movement and room for growth in children, but it emphasizes round shoulders by repeating the downward curve. It can be made with a shoulder dart as shown, or the dart can become a seam, making it two-piece. A split raglan (b), often used in coats and rainwear, is two-piece with a shoulder seam, plain set-in in front and raglan in back. The epaulet (c) is derived from the French military decoration with a horizontal yoke seamline from normal armscye seam near the shoulder to the neck, widening the shoulders. A dolman sleeve (d) is deep-cut under the arm, adding fullness at the underarm-bust area. It is sometimes shown without an armscye seam, like a kimono, but usually with a vertical seam set in on the shoulder toward the neck, narrowing the shoulders. A kimono sleeve (e) cut in one piece with the bodice without the vertical armscye seam widens the shoulders. A longer sleeve needs a gusset (f), which is a diamond or two triangles inserted at the bodice underarm, providing freedom of movement. The gusset shows little when the arm is raised, and disappears when the arm is down; but without it, the strain at the upper seam soon tears the underarm seam. A kimono cap (g) is short

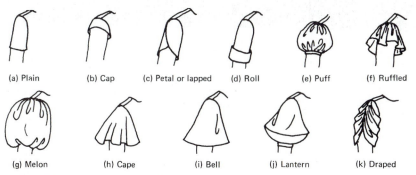

(a) Plain   (b) Cap   (c) Petal or lapped   (d) Roll   (e) Puff   (f) Ruffled

(g) Melon   (h) Cape   (i) Bell   (j) Lantern   (k) Draped

FIGURE 6-29   Short, set-in sleeve styles.

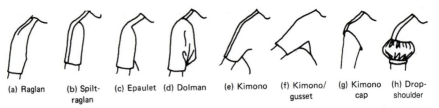

FIGURE 6-30   Non-set-in sleeve styles.

enough to allow freedom of movement, widen the shoulders, and emphasize the upper arm. A drop-shoulder (h) is like a longer kimono cap, widening the shoulder. It can have any of many styles appended to it, each with its own visual effect.

Skirts

More fitted skirts emphasize the actual figure, and more bouffant styles add bulk and weight, but also conceal heavy hips, buttocks, and thighs (Figure 6-31). Generally, the longer they are, the longer the legs will seem; the shorter they are, the more the legs are emphasized. The straight, fitted skirt (a) emphasizes actual figure contours. It serves as the basic pattern from which all other styles are drafted. The A-line (b) is slightly wider at the hem, but not as wide as the flared (c). Gently flared skirts have vertical fold lines that lengthen and narrow, and enough fullness to be functional and camouflage heavy buttocks and thighs. A complete circle skirt is extremely flared (d) which adds fullness in the thigh-knee area. Gored skirts (e) have effects similar to the gently flared, but are usually more lengthening because of the vertical seams. Gores are narrower at the top than at the bottom, creating an illusion of a narrower waist, whereas panels have parallel sides with equal top and bottom widths, and generally widen the waist. A gored skirt may have from four to twenty-four gores, but six, three each in front and back, are shown here. Wrap-around or surplice skirts (f) are distinguished by an overlapping opening from waist to hem.

Gathered, dirndl, peasant, or bouffant skirts are gathered at the waist (g). Those cut on the straight are more bulbous than those cut with slight flare which hangs gracefully. Bouffant skirts add weight while only slightly full ones conceal.

Pleated skirts also provide fullness for walking but lie flatter and more tailored than gathers. They may hang free from the waist or be stitched down to the hipline. All have many strong, narrowing vertical lines, but their arrangements vary considerably. Knife pleats (h) go all in one direction, usually right to left. Box or inverted pleats (i) reverse direction with each pleat and are often unpressed. Accordion or sunburst pleats (j) fan out from the waist, with each crease alternating and no underlay. A kilt (l) combines pleated and overlapped styles.

Pegged skirts (m) and trumpet skirts (n) add greatest bulk and weight where their fullness is greatest and their narrower ends appear smaller. Tiered skirts (o) with each gathered section stitched to the one above, have a flared silhouette. Either the horizontal seams or the vertical gathers can be emphasized.

Mini- (p), midi- (q), and maxiskirts (r) differ mostly in proportions and amount of leg revealed. Midi- and maxiskirts are most lengthening. Miniskirts emphasize the hip-thigh area and lengthen the leg. Other effects depend on leg proportions.

Although floor-length skirts are generally lengthening and narrowing, those with fullness may add some apparent weight and bulk. The long, straight dinner skirt (s) is thinner; the long, gathered skirt (t) is softer. Double wrappers of two pieces (u) add more bulk than single wrappers (v), and the sari, which extends up over one shoulder, is famous for its gracefulness (w).

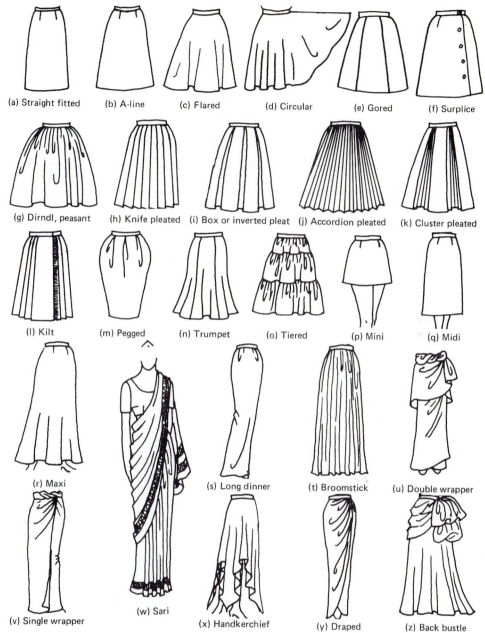

(a) Straight fitted   (b) A-line   (c) Flared   (d) Circular   (e) Gored   (f) Surplice

(g) Dirndl, peasant   (h) Knife pleated   (i) Box or inverted pleat   (j) Accordion pleated   (k) Cluster pleated

(l) Kilt   (m) Pegged   (n) Trumpet   (o) Tiered   (p) Mini   (q) Midi

(r) Maxi   (s) Long dinner   (t) Broomstick   (u) Double wrapper

(v) Single wrapper   (w) Sari   (x) Handkerchief   (y) Draped   (z) Back bustle

FIGURE 6-31   Skirt styles.

Skirt waistlines (Figure 6-32) also range from high to low. The most common is the natural waistline, whether banded (a) or bandless (b). The high-rise (c) and pointed (d) above the waist lengthen the midriff-hip area and emphasize the waist. The dropped or hip-hugger waist (e) lengthens the waist and widens the hips; and the skirt yoke (f) shortens and widens the waist-hip area.

Pants and Other Bifurcated Wear

Bifurcated wear is any two-legged garment, including divided skirts, pants, and some one-piece garments (Figure 6-33). "Skirts" include long, dressy, divided palazzo pants (a), wrap-around pant-skirts (b), flared pants (c), skorts (d), and culottes (j). Skorts, ending above the knee, and culottes com-

Shape and Form   **117**

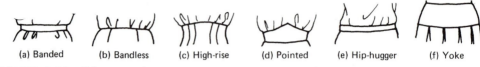

(a) Banded   (b) Bandless   (c) High-rise   (d) Pointed   (e) Hip-hugger   (f) Yoke

FIGURE 6-32   Skirt top styles.

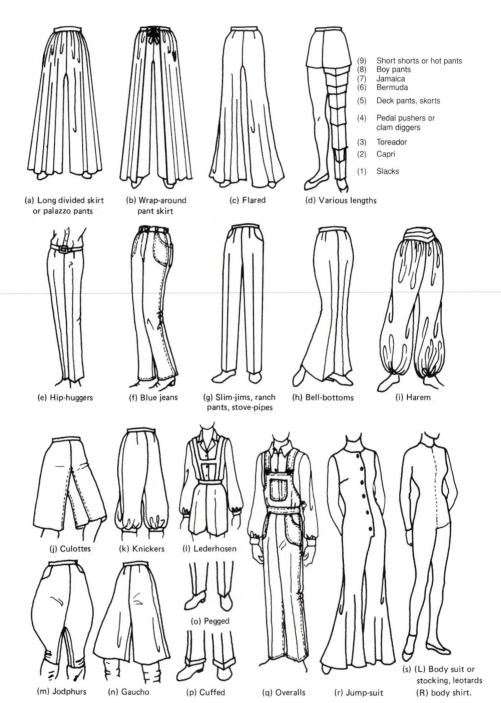

(a) Long divided skirt or palazzo pants   (b) Wrap-around pant skirt   (c) Flared   (d) Various lengths

(9) Short shorts or hot pants
(8) Boy pants
(7) Jamaica
(6) Bermuda
(5) Deck pants, skorts
(4) Pedal pushers or clam diggers
(3) Toreador
(2) Capri
(1) Slacks

(e) Hip-huggers   (f) Blue jeans   (g) Slim-jims, ranch pants, stove-pipes   (h) Bell-bottoms   (i) Harem

(j) Culottes   (k) Knickers   (l) Lederhosen

(o) Pegged

(m) Jodphurs   (n) Gaucho   (p) Cuffed   (q) Overalls   (r) Jump-suit

(s) (L) Body suit or stocking, leotards
(R) body shirt.

FIGURE 6-33   Pants and bifurcated wear styles.

bine skirt and pant characteristics to resemble a skirt when the wearer is standing still, but give freedom of movement.

Pants per se come in a range of lengths, each with its own name and effect (d). Usually, the longer the unbroken vertical area, the longer and narrower the effect; the more evenly it is divided, the shorter it seems. So full-length slacks are usually the most lengthening because of the unbroken space from waist to ankle, then pegged, Capri pants or short-shorts and so on, with deck pants, pedal pushers, and Bermudas the most shortening. Jamaicas generally most shorten thighs because they end near the middle, just as toreador pants most shorten the calf.

The visual effect of pants depends greatly on the figure supporting them, the proportions of exposed leg area, and their generally snug fit which accents every actual contour. Bulky pockets may create undesired bulges.

Hip -huggers (e) with a dropped waist accent the hips. Blue jeans (f) are practical and offer both horizontal and vertical lines for a choice of emphasis. Slim jims, ranch pants, or stove-pipes (g) lengthen and slim the average or thin figure. Bell-bottoms (h) with ankle bulk are feminine on women because the hip-knee-ankle hourglass repeats the female shoulder-waist-hip hourglass silhouette. Harem pants (i) add apparent bulk, but may conceal heavy hips and legs. Knickers (k) gathered below the knee add knee fullness. Lederhosen (l) shorts with suspenders vary in length and are often leather. Full-length jodphurs (m), or riding pants, are worn inside boots below the knee. Above the knee they add bulk to the thighs. Gaucho pants (n) are full and tend to lengthen. Tapered or pegged bottoms (o) narrow in at the ankle and are generally slimming. Cuffed edges (p) on any length or style generally shorten and widen.

Bifurcated garments covering more of the body include overalls or coveralls (q), jumpsuits (r), and body stockings or leotards (s). Jumpsuits come in many variations, usually with front openings and no waistlines. Their dominantly straight lines tend to conceal body curves, while body stockings, on the other hand, reveal every contour.

Dresses

Dresses (Figure 6-34) are normally one-piece garments, street or floor length. Many styles shown here have plain necklines and no sleeves. Basic normal fitted (a) simply combines the basic bodice and skirt, generally emphasizing the torso. Styles without waistlines, such as the shift (b), sheath (c), princess (d), and often the A-line (e), lengthen the figure. The fitted sheath and princess with more verticals narrow average figures, whereas the less fitted shift and A-line with fewer verticals are more concealing. The tunic (f) is shorter and usually worn with a skirt or pants. The bulky bouffant (g) and tent (h) add weight or camouflage actual contours.

Some "dresses" are often worn with other garments: The jumper (i) and pinafore (j) are often worn with blouses; the short sleeved jacket dress (k) accompanies a matching waist-length jacket with longer sleeves that cover upper-arm fleshiness and provide temperature control. The shirtwaist (l), peasant (m), and torso or flapper (n) with many horizontal and vertical lines offer a choice of directional emphasis. Bulky long dresses include the caftan (p), muumuu (q), dashiki (r), or granny (s). The usually narrow, long evening or dinner dress (t) heightens and slims.

Maternity styles must acknowledge the functional needs and contours of the pregnant figure. Choice of focal point depends on both individual preferences and cultural attitudes toward pregnancy. Basic dress styles which allow for expansion and individualization include a loose shift (b) in early pregnancy and tent (h), caftan (p), and loose empire waist or shoulder yoke styles for later pregnancy (o). All may add fullness as well as camouflage contours.

Outerwear

Visual effects of outerwear (Figures 6-35 and 6-36) also depend greatly on their fit, direction, and number of dominant and counter-

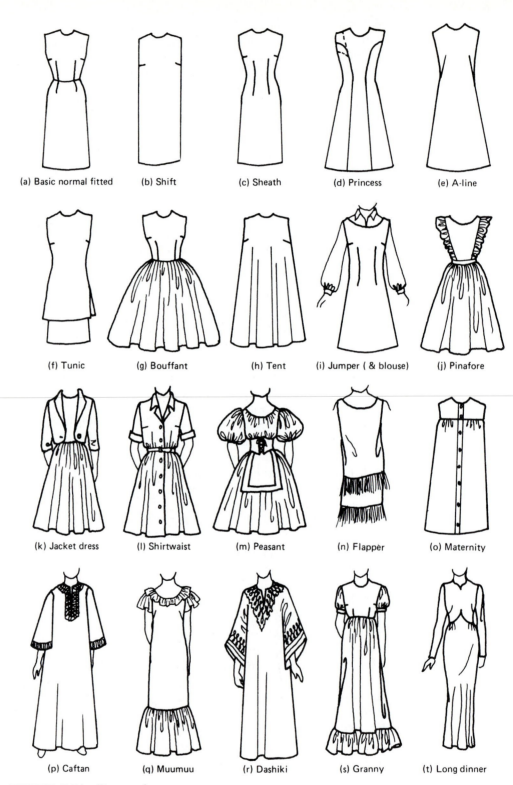

(a) Basic normal fitted   (b) Shift   (c) Sheath   (d) Princess   (e) A-line

(f) Tunic   (g) Bouffant   (h) Tent   (i) Jumper (& blouse)   (j) Pinafore

(k) Jacket dress   (l) Shirtwaist   (m) Peasant   (n) Flapper   (o) Maternity

(p) Caftan   (q) Muumuu   (r) Dashiki   (s) Granny   (t) Long dinner

FIGURE 6-34   Dress styles.

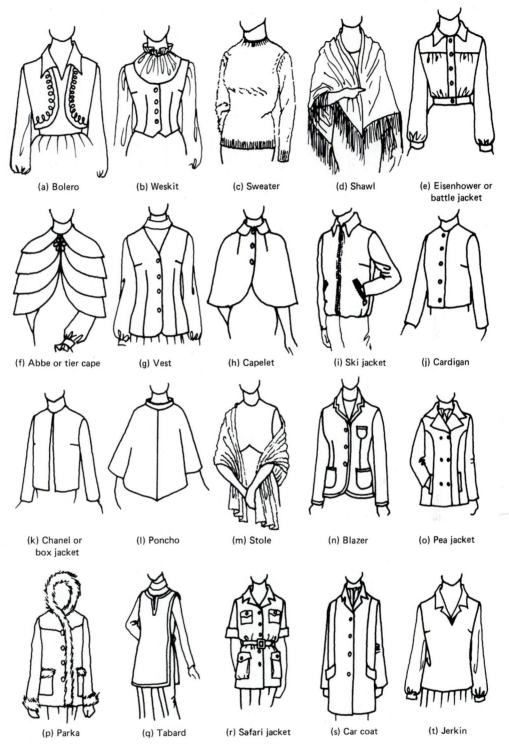

(a) Bolero   (b) Weskit   (c) Sweater   (d) Shawl   (e) Eisenhower or battle jacket

(f) Abbe or tier cape   (g) Vest   (h) Capelet   (i) Ski jacket   (j) Cardigan

(k) Chanel or box jacket   (l) Poncho   (m) Stole   (n) Blazer   (o) Pea jacket

(p) Parka   (q) Tabard   (r) Safari jacket   (s) Car coat   (t) Jerkin

FIGURE 6-35 Short outerwear styles.

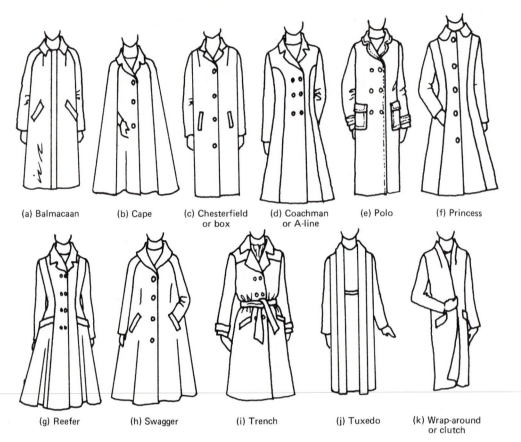

(a) Balmacaan   (b) Cape   (c) Chesterfield or box   (d) Coachman or A-line   (e) Polo   (f) Princess

(g) Reefer   (h) Swagger   (i) Trench   (j) Tuxedo   (k) Wrap-around or clutch

FIGURE 6-36 Long outerwear styles.

ing lines and shapes, and length in relation to width. Outerwear emphasizes the body location at which it ends. Shorter styles ending near the waist—such as the bolero (a), weskit (b), battle jacket (e), capelet (h), and shorter jackets—provide more shortening, horizontal breaking points. Some styles are characterized by general silhouette and others by specific details. For example, although similar in silhouette, a cardigan jacket (j) buttons down the front, whereas a Chanel (k) does not. The upper collar on a Chesterfield (Figure 6-36) is often of black velvet, but as a box coat it matches the rest of the coat. Some sweater styles, such as the polo and cardigan, share names and styles with jackets, shirts, and coats.

Style Features

Figure 6-37 shows popular style features usable in many garment parts. Tabs (a) are strips used as accents. Ruffles (b), peplums (c), and flounces (d) are all stitched at the top and free at the bottom, and may be gathered, pleated, or flared (Figure 2-9b). All shorten, widen, and enlarge their area: ruffles, anywhere; peplums at the hips; and flounces at lower sleeve or skirt edges. Shirring, parallel rows of gathers (e), adds bulk and accents either the direction of the stitching or the perpendicular direction of the gathering folds.

Inset pockets (f) are functional and unobtrusive for flat items, whereas patch pockets (g) accent their shapes and their body location. Welts or flaps (h) may edge pocket openings or merely suggest pockets. The vertical line of single-breasted closings (i) lengthens and narrows, whereas double-breasted closings (j) lead the eye both across and vertically. Godets (k) are wedge-shaped flares inserted at the lower edge of a garment, adding fullness and functional free-

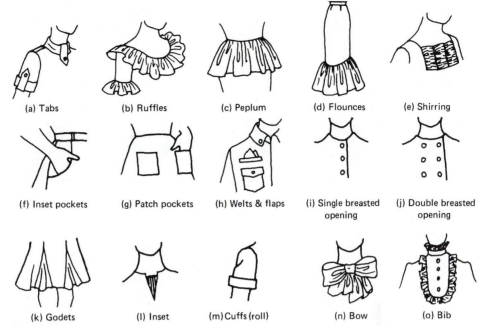

(a) Tabs (b) Ruffles (c) Peplum (d) Flounces (e) Shirring

(f) Inset pockets (g) Patch pockets (h) Welts & flaps (i) Single breasted opening (j) Double breasted opening

(k) Godets (l) Inset (m) Cuffs (roll) (n) Bow (o) Bib

FIGURE 6-37 Style features.

dom of movement, usually at skirt, sleeve, and jacket hems. Insets (l) are usually flat, contrasting accents set into an edge or behind a decorative cutout, emphasizing that area. Cuffs (m) usually shorten and widen, and bows (n) accent their location. Soft bows add bulk and softness, whereas straight-edged bow ties are more tailored. Bibs (o) at the neck front may be stitched down or separate, and fastened at the bottom. Any style feature, whether functional or decorative, draws attention to its location.

Accessories

Accessories are the finishing touch that can make an ensemble exquisite or reduce it to a frumpy concoction. Shapes and forms of hats (Figure 6-38), bags (Figure 6-39), belts (Figure 6-40), gloves (Figure 6-41), and shoes (Figure 6-42) must be functionally and visually compatible, both with other garment parts and with the part of the body where they are used. Shoes visually interact with the shape of the foot and leg and pant or skirt styles, just as hat styles interact with facial shapes, hairstyles, and collars.

Men's Wear

Effects sought in men's and women's wear may be similar but styles to achieve them may differ because of different body proportions and cultural habits. Western women's clothing closes right over left, and men's wear, left over right, but many style names are similar. Men's collar styles (Figure 6-43), shirts (Figure 6-44), and hairstyles can be used to emphasize or counter apparent facial shapes (Figure 6-21). Some men's jacket collars and styles (Figure 6-45), pants (Figure 6-46), outerwear (Figure 6-47), and style features (Figure 6-48) differ from women's, but many are similar, except for proportions and closings, and are not duplicated here. Only those styles that differ appreciably from women's are illustrated here. Men's hats (Figure 6-49) also affect apparent facial shape, and shoes (Figure 6-50) show enough to affect apparent foot proportions.

Children's Wear

Traditionally, children were often dressed as miniature adults in garments grossly un-

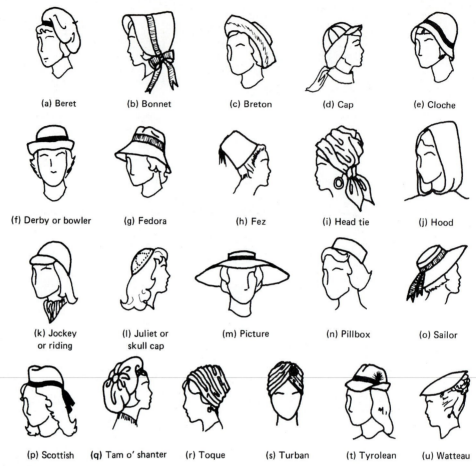

FIGURE 6-38 Head wear styles.

(a) Beret
(b) Bonnet
(c) Breton
(d) Cap
(e) Cloche

(f) Derby or bowler
(g) Fedora
(h) Fez
(i) Head tie
(j) Hood

(k) Jockey or riding
(l) Juliet or skull cap
(m) Picture
(n) Pillbox
(o) Sailor

(p) Scottish
(q) Tam o' shanter
(r) Toque
(s) Turban
(t) Tyrolean
(u) Watteau

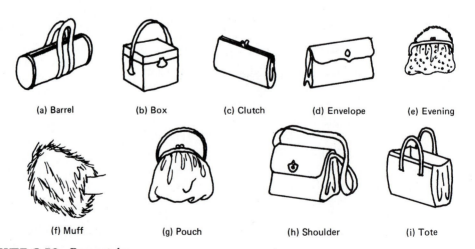

FIGURE 6-39 Purse styles.

(a) Barrel
(b) Box
(c) Clutch
(d) Envelope
(e) Evening

(f) Muff
(g) Pouch
(h) Shoulder
(i) Tote

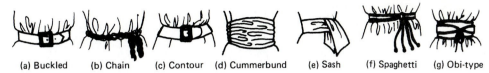

FIGURE 6-40   Belt styles.

(a) Buckled (b) Chain (c) Contour (d) Cummerbund (e) Sash (f) Spaghetti (g) Obi-type

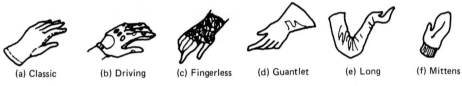

FIGURE 6-41   Glove styles.

(a) Classic (b) Driving (c) Fingerless (d) Guantlet (e) Long (f) Mittens

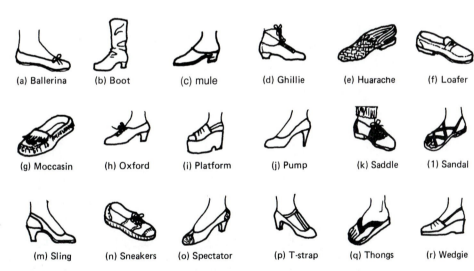

(a) Ballerina (b) Boot (c) mule (d) Ghillie (e) Huarache (f) Loafer

(g) Moccasin (h) Oxford (i) Platform (j) Pump (k) Saddle (l) Sandal

(m) Sling (n) Sneakers (o) Spectator (p) T-strap (q) Thongs (r) Wedgie

FIGURE 6-42   Shoe styles.

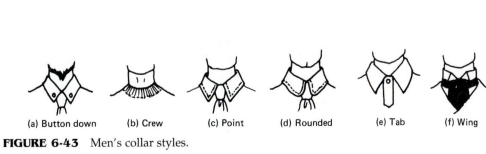

(a) Button down (b) Crew (c) Point (d) Rounded (e) Tab (f) Wing

FIGURE 6-43   Men's collar styles.

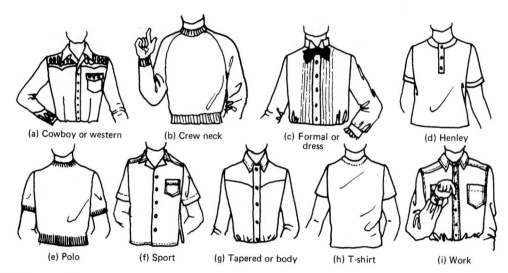

(a) Cowboy or western   (b) Crew neck   (c) Formal or dress   (d) Henley

(e) Polo   (f) Sport   (g) Tapered or body   (h) T-shirt   (i) Work

FIGURE 6-44 Men's shirt styles.

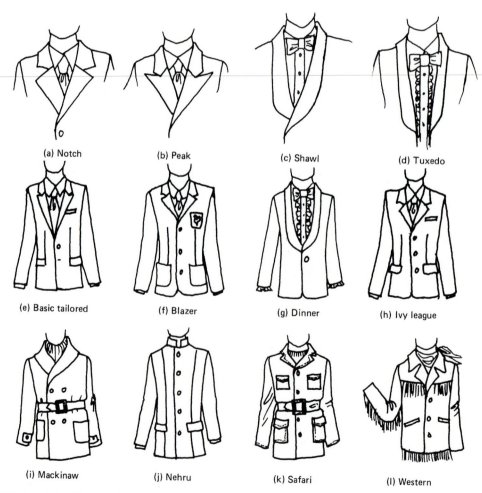

(a) Notch   (b) Peak   (c) Shawl   (d) Tuxedo

(e) Basic tailored   (f) Blazer   (g) Dinner   (h) Ivy league

(i) Mackinaw   (j) Nehru   (k) Safari   (l) Western

FIGURE 6-45 Men's collar and jacket styles.

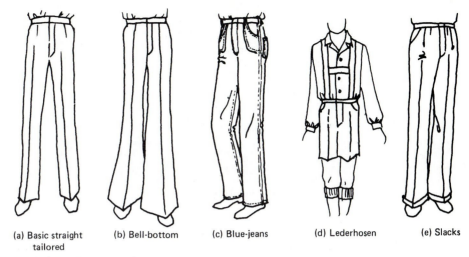

(a) Basic straight tailored   (b) Bell-bottom   (c) Blue-jeans   (d) Lederhosen   (e) Slacks

FIGURE 6-46   Trouser styles.

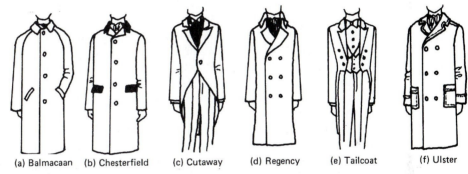

(a) Balmacaan   (b) Chesterfield   (c) Cutaway   (d) Regency   (e) Tailcoat   (f) Ulster

FIGURE 6-47   Men's long outerwear styles.

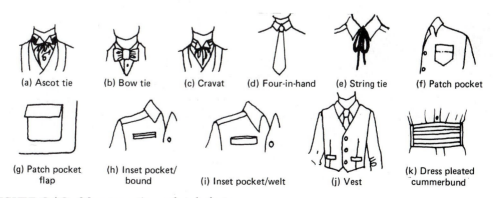

(a) Ascot tie   (b) Bow tie   (c) Cravat   (d) Four-in-hand   (e) String tie   (f) Patch pocket

(g) Patch pocket flap   (h) Inset pocket/bound   (i) Inset pocket/welt   (j) Vest   (k) Dress pleated cummerbund

FIGURE 6-48   Menswear ties and style features.

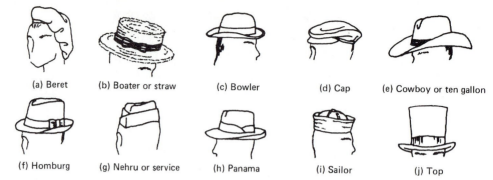

FIGURE 6-49 Men's hat styles.

related to their social and physical needs or motor skills. More recent recognition of their unique needs has stimulated more functional garments.

Visually, the proportions of children's garments are generally shorter, wider, and looser than adult garments. Children's heads are more spherical and larger in relation to the rest of the body than are those of adults. Children's torsos, arms, and legs are dominantly tubular, and the waist is barely defined until puberty. As well as the usual functional roles of clothing, children need styles that allow ample movement, are comfortable, easy to get into and out of, easy to care for, encourage dressing skills, and preferably, can grow with the child. Such features can be incorporated in selected adult styles scaled to children's proportions (Figure 6-51). Front openings, raglan sleeves, pockets or trims to distinguish front from back or right from left, dresses without waistlines, and pants with elasticized waists are simple choices that help both parent and child.

Young children are much more concerned with comfort than appearance, but as they grow, they may welcome a favorite trim or motif. All trims or fasteners must be securely attached, nontoxic, and free of sharp edges. Flammability and long ties are discussed in Chapter 2. Children's feet also need room for growth and extra support, with shoe styles high on the foot and ankle (Figure 6-52).

The preceding analyses are not exhaustive but serve as an introduction to garment and body shapes and forms, their relationships, and their visual effects. Not all the styles illustrated are discussed, and many specialized garments are not illustrated. But the examples given allow the reader to relate the effects listed in Chapter 28 to any style and assess its visual effect on a given figure and with other garments, skills that benefit both the design and consumer.

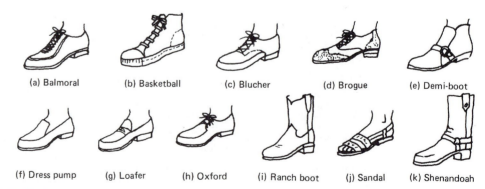

FIGURE 6-50 Men's shoe styles.

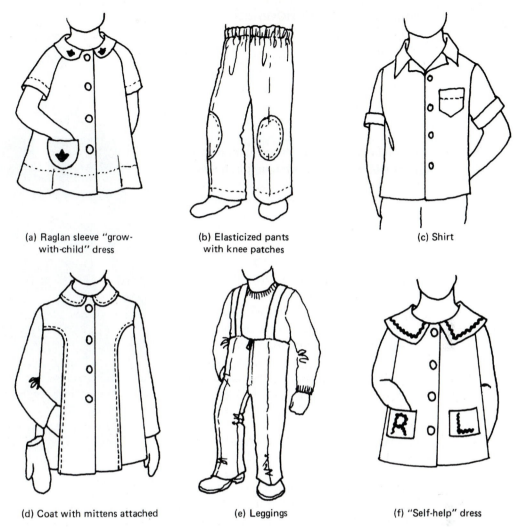

(a) Raglan sleeve "grow-with-child" dress

(b) Elasticized pants with knee patches

(c) Shirt

(d) Coat with mittens attached

(e) Leggings

(f) "Self-help" dress

FIGURE 6-51   Children's wear styles.

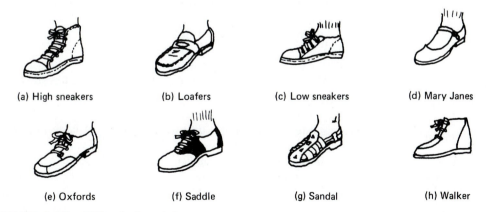

(a) High sneakers

(b) Loafers

(c) Low sneakers

(d) Mary Janes

(e) Oxfords

(f) Saddle

(g) Sandal

(h) Walker

FIGURE 6-52   Chilren's shoe styles.

GUIDELINES FOR CHOOSING AND COMBINING SHAPES AND FORMS IN DRESS

It is easy to develop a personal clothing prescription using the basic effects listed at the beginning of the "Visual Effects in Dress" section and Table 6-1, and matching the effects of different shapes and forms to figure need. Some styles are just one dominant shape or form, such as plain sleeves; but other styles are combinations of forms. When combined forms interact, the dominant directions and shapes may be reinforced, modified, or obscured:

1. Where lines, shapes, forms, and spaces repeat or resemble a form or direction, they reinforce its effects.

2. Where new lines, shapes, and spaces gently counter or vary from the original shape, its effects are modified.

3. Where countering is extreme, or additional lines, spaces, and shapes so different, the original form is lost and its effects destroyed.

Whenever shapes or forms are combined, new ones are created: This is the essence of composition which the designer must know to create pleasing effects.

Likewise, different flat shapes may produce similar three-dimensional forms. For example, the conical skirt in Figure 6-53 is achieved here using skirt godets (Figure 6-37k). However, a similar conical skirt silhouette could be achieved using a flared (Figure 6-31c) or high-flared trumpet (Figure 6-31n) skirt, or a circular flared flounce (Figure 2-9b). Different flat pattern shapes making similar forms will put seam lines, darts, and other structural lines at different places, which will create different shapes as well in the subdivided space inside the silhouette. This interplay of shape into form blends with the other components of the dress in Figure 6-53: the tubular sleeves and the hourglass dress form dramatically edged by the gracefully curved V at the neck. The garment shapes and forms agree

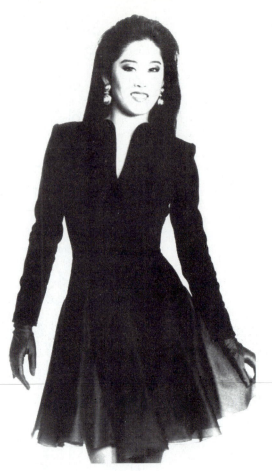

FIGURE 6-53 The triangular skirt godets add fullness for freedom of movement and help make the skirt more conical in the hourglass dress form. The long, tubular sleeves complement and slenderize, as the dominant shapes and forms agree with the figure and provide a variety of forms which interact well and contribute to the whole. (Courtesy of Kristi Yamaguchi and Hoechst Celanese Corporation.)

with the body form and with each other, and offer interesting variety.

Guidelines useful to artists in the past still have merit, but they may have exceptions; so each application needs individual study.

Since the eye tends to perceive wholes before parts, as Morton notes, in clothing, the silhouette "is what we see from a distance before details of structure or decoration are visible, and is responsible for first impressions."[6] Silhouette provides a frame for its parts, which harmonize most if they complement the silhouette. Arnheim notes that relationships among parts depend on the structure of the whole; only when that is established can relationships among parts be analyzed. Then, the more individual a part is, "the more likely it is to contribute some of its own character to the whole."[7] These observations suggest that in clothing the whole is dominant and that subsidiary parts should agree with it in several respects:

1. Parts should agree with the purpose and function of the whole garment.

2. Parts contribute most to wholeness if they vary enough from each other or the silhouette for interest, but are not too different. Major parts follow the general silhouette, and smaller, minor parts afford more variety (Figure 6-53).

3. Geometric and size and space illusions (Chapter 3), and grouping and subdividing of shapes all manipulate apparent sizes, contours, and focus of attention within the silhouette.

4. The human figure generally appears more graceful if some countering of shapes is used.

5. Because the human body moves and is seen from many angles, shapes and forms are regrouped by body movement. As the figure turns or assumes different positions, bending or sitting, what new shape combinations are created? Is the composition of shapes as interesting in profile as from front or back?

The human body offers unique potential for constantly changing compositions of its shapes and forms (Figure 6-54).

---

[6]Grace Margaret Morton, *The Arts of Costume and Personal Appearance*, 3rd ed. (New York: John Wiley & Sons, Inc., 1966), p. 84.

[7]Arnheim, *Art and Visual Perception*, p. 66.

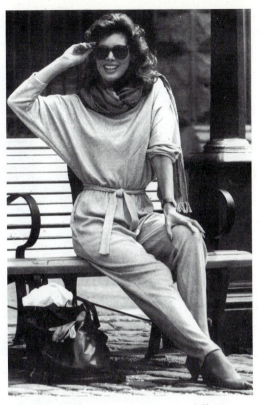

FIGURE 6-54 Garments assume differing forms and silhouettes as the wearer changes positions. Note how the tubular/rectangular sleeve with the arm down becomes a cone/triangle with the arm raised. (Photo courtesy of Jantzen Inc.)

When basic shapes and forms are well chosen to relate to the constant human forms, they often echo across centuries and cultures like variations on a theme. Figures 6-55a and b show traditional and contemporary interpretations of a dramatic banded and notched neckline, tubular bodice, ring belt, tubular pleated skirt, and tubular full bishop sleeves. Yet the variations of fabrics, patterns, proportions, and trim give each its unique stamp of time and place. Look for examples of the variations in each of the figures, then compare the applications to see the timelessness of the guidelines.

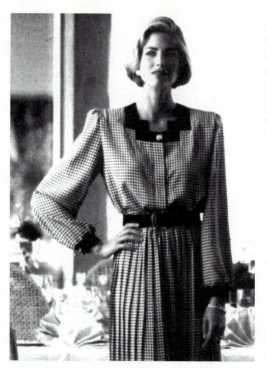

FIGURE 6-55a Tubular forms relate well to the human form functionally, structurally, and decoratively. This contemporary interpretation uses tubes for the bodice, sleeves, and pleated skirt, with ring belt and cuffs and dramatic notched neckline. (Courtesy of Mark, Fore & Strike.)

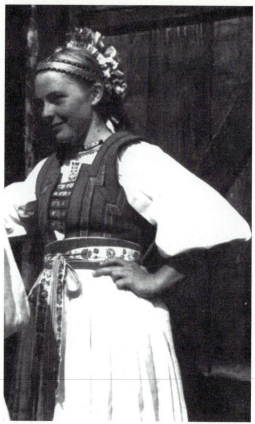

FIGURE 6-55b Another culture uses the same tubular forms for the bodice, full sleeves, and pleated skirt, with ring belt and a similar notched neckline, showing how the same idea may be interpreted different ways and the versatility and different effects possible with similar forms and shapes. (Courtesy of Czechoslovak Airlines.)

SUMMARY

Shape is flat area enclosed by a line, and form is three-dimensional solid or hollow area enclosed by a surface. Their malleability in dress allows various shapes and forms to relate to each other and to the human body. Geometric shapes appear in fabric pattern motifs, in flat structural parts, and as outlines of garment parts shown as flat in pictures. Structural garment and body parts resemble geometric forms. Garment style forms must agree with the body parts they surround. The relationship between flat shapes and three-dimensional forms in clothing is critical. One reason is that the shapes of flat pattern pieces determine the three-dimensional forms of garment styles.

Perception of shapes and forms depends on perception of their apparent internal structure, their axes, their balance of internal and external pressure, and concepts of front and back wholeness.

Developing "prescriptions" for particular effects in dress needs analysis of styles according to their characteristics: similar characteristics produce similar visual effects regardless of garment part. Types of characteristics include direction/length, size/bulk, garment/body relationships, and shape/space effects for styles of necklines, collars, bodices, shirts, waistlines, sleeves, skirts, pants, dresses, outerwear, style features, accessories, men's wear, and children's wear. Combining shapes and forms of garment parts into a whole garment may reinforce, modify, or counter the effects of any one part; so effects depend on the contours chosen and how they are combined to be attractive yet functional.

The successful garment has a comfortable relationship among its parts and between parts and whole. It is beautiful from any angle, at rest or moving, and presents a unified composition of well-combined structural and decorative shapes and forms.

CLASS ACTIVITIES

1. With each person or group selecting a different geometric form, in catalogs or magazines find as many examples of styles using that form as time allows. For how many different garment parts are examples found? How does each use of the geometric form relate to the body part it surrounds? Compare the various styles using the same form for the same garment part. How are they similar? How do they differ?

2. Choose and enlarge a dress style from Figure 6-37. Superimpose various fabric patterns, trims, or other subdivisions on it. How do these subdivision shapes affect apparent style contours and silhouettes?

3. From selected styles in Figures 6-23 to 6-37 or commercial patterns, the instructor may develop sheets showing several style and corresponding main flat pattern piece shapes. Then students can practice matching the flat pattern shapes to the style it creates, looking for cues of gathers, flare, or other features to help relate the flat shape to the three-dimensional style form.

4. Choose a standing, full front view style photo in a fashion magazine. With tracing paper outline each structural part (sleeve, bodice, collar, skirt, pant leg, etc.). What flat geometric shape does each most resemble? Do they appear functionally and decoratively compatible with the human form? With each other? If so, why? If not, why not? How do any pocket, lapel, or fabric pattern motif shapes interact with them?

5. Select a style from Table 6-1.A.2 with many horizontal and vertical structural lines. Design one version of that style emphasizing vertical lines and shapes, and another emphasizing horizontal lines and shapes, and compare the techniques you used and their resulting effects.

6. In the text photographs, magazines, or catalogs, find examples of the guidelines listed in Table 6-1. For each guideline, compare how the same effect may occur in different garment parts and different styles.

7. Analyze styles illustrated in Figures 6-22 to 6-52 by discussing the following questions.
   a. What are the dominant forms of this style—tube, cone, sphere, and so on?
   b. What is the visual effect of this style—lengthening, widening, shortening, narrowing, enlarging?
   c. For what kind of figure asset or "problem" might this style create the desired effect? Why?
   d. How would this style relate to the forms of other garments worn with it? What styles of other parts would you recommend using with it? For what types of figures?
   e. What effect does it have on neighboring parts—emphasizing, concealing, countering?
   f. What psychological mood does the form convey?
   g. What decorative fabric or trim would agree with its structural form—straight-edged, curvilinear, combination?

8. Throughout the text or other sources, compare the use of shapes and forms in current, historic, and ethnic styles. How do changes in length and width change effects of the same form?

9. With the class divided into groups, assign each group one figure problem and up to three geometric forms. The group may choose from these forms and adjust their proportions to create styles for various garment parts that will address the figure problem. Each group could have a different problem, or several groups could have the same problem; then compare their solutions, discussing how they reached them.

7 *Light*

Light is so taken for granted that it is rarely considered as an art medium, especially in clothing. However, without light, there is no visibility and no visual design.

PHYSICAL ASPECTS

Light is the electromagnetic energy making things visible, the radiant energy resulting from vibration of electrons. If the source of energy is the stimulus, then visual perception or sensation is the response.[1] Light provides illumination and color; defines and locates lines, forms, and surfaces; and visually reveals the physical world, including clothing. However, light is an elusive design ele-

ment. One cannot grasp it and control it directly. It must be manipulated indirectly by controlling the surface on which it falls.

Light as Energy

Light forms a tiny portion of the total electromagnetic or radiant energy spectrum (Figure 7-1).[2] The rays in this spectrum are identical in every way except wavelength and frequency.

Wavelength is the distance between the highest point of one wave and the highest point of the next (Figure 7-2). It is measured in nanometers which equal one billionth of a meter (39.37 inches). Wavelengths in the total radiant spectrum range from radio waves kilometers long to cosmic rays so

---

[1]Maitland Graves, *Color Fundamentals* (New York: McGraw-Hill Book Company, Inc., 1952), p. 5; and Ralph M. Haber and Maurice Hershenson, *The Psychology of Visual Perception* (New York: Holt, Rinehart and Winston, Inc., 1973), p. 7.

[2]Graves, *Color Fundamentals*, p. 4; and *The A. F. Encyclopedia of Textiles*, 2nd ed. (Englewood Cliffs, N.J.: Prentice-Hall, Inc., 1972), p. 430.

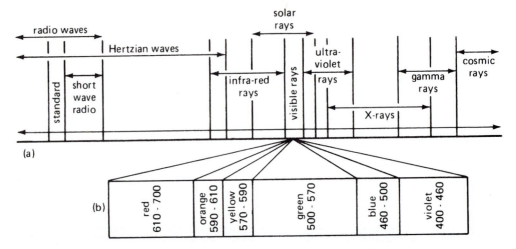

(a)

(b)

red
610 - 700

orange
590 - 610

yellow
570 - 590

green
500 - 570

blue
460 - 500

violet
400 - 460

FIGURE 7-1 The upper part of the chart (a) shows the known radiant or electromagnetic spectrum, and the lower part (b) shows the wavelengths of the major hues in the visible spectrum. The latter comprises only a tiny percentage of the total radiant spectrum. (Upper chart (a): from Maitland Graves, *Color Fundamentals*, p. 4, by permission of the McGraw-Hill Book Company.)

short that millions of them end to end would not equal one meter.[3] Figure 7-1 shows that solar energy rays comprise only a small portion of the total radiant spectrum and only a small percentage of the solar rays are visible light.

Visible light includes those wavelengths between 400 nanometers, or around 63,000 to the inch, and 700 nanometers, or about 33,000 to the inch. Figure 7-1 shows the visible light spectrum divided into colors according to wavelength, with red at the longest end and violet at the shortest:

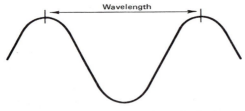

FIGURE 7-2 The distance from the highest point of one wave to the highest point of the next is a wavelength.

1. red = 700–610 nanometers (slowest frequency)

2. orange = 610–590 nanometers

3. yellow = 590–570 nanometers

4. green = 570–500 nanometers

5. blue = 500–460 nanometers

6. violet = 460–400 nanometers (fastest frequency)[4]

Frequency is the number of wavelengths passing a point per second. Frequencies for the visible portion of the spectrum are too fast for real human comprehension. The longest visible wavelength, red, has the slowest frequency; and the shortest wavelength, violet, has the fastest or highest frequency. Likewise, the longer wavelength colors in between have the slower frequencies, and the shorter wavelengths the faster. The wavelength times its frequency equals the speed of light, so all the hues with dif-

---

[3]Haber and Hershenson, *Psychology of Visual Perception*, p. 7.

[4]Frederick W. Clulow, *Colour: Its Principles and Their Applications* (Dobbs Ferry, N.Y.: Morgan and Morgan, Inc., Publishers, 1972), p. 63; and "Color and the Human Being," *A. F. Encyclopedia of Textiles*, p. 427.

ferent wavelengths and frequencies travel at the same speed.

Level of illumination, or *brightness,* depends on the amount of energy radiated—the more energy, the brighter the light which comes "packaged" in units called photons. Thus, the brighter the light, the higher the number of photons per second.[5] So the visual effects of light rays depend on three factors: wavelength, frequency, and level of illumination.

Visual Perception of Light

Light radiates out from a source in all directions and reflects from surfaces in all directions; so the eye receives enough light from all possible directions to stimulate vision.[6] Thus, "the eye is a highly specialized instrument 'tuned' to receive and respond only to" the wavelengths and frequencies of light waves, just as the ear is tuned to receive and respond to the longer wavelengths of sound waves.[7] We experience light in two ways: direct and reflected. We perceive direct rays in the air coming from a natural source, such as the sun, stars, or firelight; or an artificial source such as light bulbs. Everything else we see is light reflected from a surface, and that comprises about 95 percent of our visual experience.

Unlike the architect or interior designer, the clothing designer has little opportunity to control light sources. Clothing is seen as reflected light. So, the designer must anticipate the kind of light in which a garment will be worn, and then control the surfaces on which light will fall to create desired effects. Just as the "appearance of an object is affected by the light which makes it visible,"[8] the surface also influences the effect of the light. A designer can choose surfaces better by knowing how light affects them.

---

[5]Haber and Hershenson, *Psychology of Visual Perception,* p. 7.

[6]*Ibid.,* p. 8.

[7]Graves, *Color Fundamentals,* p. 5.

[8]Ray Faulkner and Sarah Faulkner, *Inside Today's Home,* 3rd ed. (New York: Holt, Rinehart and Winston, Inc., 1968), p. 124.

PSYCHOLOGICAL EFFECTS OF LIGHT RAYS

Lightness and darkness have inspired beliefs, superstitions, and moods throughout history. We always react—sometimes subconsciously, sometimes differently from one culture to another, but we do respond. Discussion here addresses only the lightness and darkness of the anticipated lighting in which a garment will be worn. For example, daylight or lighted classroom or office use might suggest casual styles. However, evening or dim lighting might suggest a sophisticated, quiet style. Psychological effects of color are discussed in Chapter 8.

Lightness

Lightness in most cultures is stimulating and lifting; it suggests openness and clarity. Light reveals and informs us about our surroundings and allows us to see what we are doing. Expressions about light have evolved through history, such as "seeing the light" or the "age of enlightenment," suggesting awareness and knowledge.

However, too much light is tiring, whether it is too bright, too shiny, or too large. For example, a wall covered with shiny white satin would induce visual fatigue.

Darkness

Darkness, or absence of light, in many cultures suggests gloom, mystery, seriousness, threat, or fear of the unknown, such as going into a dark cave. The terms "Dark Ages" and "being in the dark" imply ignorance.

Darkness can also suggest age, sophistication, experience, and quietness. Theatre lobby and restaurant lights are often dimmed because people are usually quieter in dim light. Darkness may also suggest sadness or mourning.

PHYSICAL EFFECTS OF LIGHT RAYS

The physical effects of light depend on the nature of its source and of the objects it strikes. Light rays define object contours, distance, location, position, surface texture, and colors; therefore, effects will differ according to source sharpness, brightness, and angle. A change in the light source can change and manipulate figure and garment contours.

Effects by Source: Sharp or Diffuse

Light from a small, sharp source—such as certain spotlights or pinpoint lights—gives bright highlights and sharp, dark shadows. These accent three-dimensional contours and heighten drama (Figures 7-3 and 7-7).

However, light from a diffused source (such as the sun), or from multiple sources (such as rows of fluorescent lights) strikes more surfaces from more angles, thus minimizing shadows and highlights, flattening contours, and smoothing texture surfaces[9] (Figure 7-4). Sometimes lighting is arranged to eliminate shadows that might interfere with work.

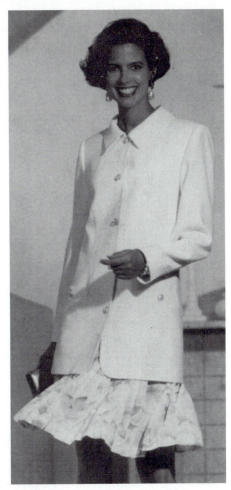

FIGURE 7-4 Light from multiple overhead or diffused sources such as the sun strikes many contours at many angles, reducing highlights and shadows, and smoothing contours and textures. Light coming from both sides of the model lessens the shadows and seems to smooth the jacket and nearly eliminate shadows in the skirt pleats, making it appear more flared. (Courtesy of Pendleton Woolen Mills.)

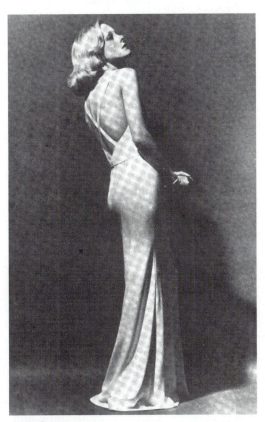

FIGURE 7-3 Light from a sharp source plays on a figure emphasizing its three-dimensional qualities and creating highlights and shadows from draping, folds, gathers, or various textures. (Photo courtesy of Du Pont.)

[9]*Ibid.*, p. 124.

Effects by Source: Angle and Amount

The angle of the light source determines the angle of reflection and how much is absorbed or reflected. For example, a sharp light striking a fabric from a low or side angle (Figure 7-5a) will bounce off, also at a low angle. However, more light striking a fabric from a high or perpendicular angle (Figure 7-5b) will be absorbed, resulting in brighter colors.

Generally, the higher the level of illumination, the more light will be reflected. But if a source provides more light than a surface can absorb, the excess is all reflected, dulling the surface colors. More light is reflected if a fabric surface is shiny, and more is absorbed if the surface is dull.

Some fabrics in dim light seem solid and opaque, but in brighter light seem more sheer. Fabrics that seem opaque with light coming from the front may become translucent when lighted from behind (Figure 7-6).

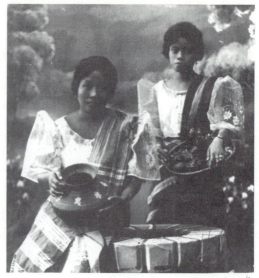

FIGURE 7-6 The light from the left falling on the outside of the sleeves at the left makes them appear more opaque. The sleeves at the right with more light from behind appear more sheer in these traditional "traje de mestiza" from the Philippines. (Courtesy of the Cultural Center of the Philippines, Manila.)

Form Definition: Stationary and Moving

Form seems to gain vitality from light. In Figures 7-3 and 7-7 the play of light accents the three-dimensional convexities and concavities and gives character to both figure and garment. Light distinguishes form from space and protrusions from indentations, defines the roundness of a cylinder, the volume and angles of a box, and shows their interactions. Highlights and shadows made by draping, gathers, pleats, or shirring create their own lines and shapes on the larger forms of which they are a part.

The play of light on a moving figure creates constantly changing highlights and shadows among shifting garment tensions, positions, and folds. Shadows may become highlights or vice versa as a figure changes position. Light also reveals figure turning, reminding one to make a garment visually interesting from the back and side as well as the front.

Light and Surface Textures

Textures can react to light in three ways: they may reflect, absorb, and/or admit it. Which happens depends on the (1) sharpness or diffusion, angle, and amount emitted by a light source; and (2) surface qualities and thickness of the texture. The designer and consumer control light by controlling the surface on which it falls.

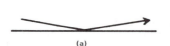
(a)

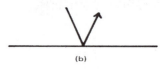
(b)

FIGURE 7-5 More light bounces off a shiny surface if it strikes from a low, side angle (a). More is absorbed, or reflected at a higher angle, if the light strikes from a higher angle (b).

Light reflected from a smooth or shiny fabric, such as satin, chintz, or lamé, is sharp and bright. However, light reflected from a rough or dull surface, such as flannel, many knits, cotton, or wool, is more diffuse and even. Thus, brightness is determined by the source, amount, and angle of the light and by the reflecting ability of the surface it strikes.

Fabrics and other textures can have a magnificent range of reflecting and absorbing abilities, from nearly total reflection from polished metal, the shimmer of satin, the sparkle of sequins, or the flash of jewels, to the deep, rich, almost total absorption in velvet (Figure 7-7). The silhouette effect of light admitted through sheer or translucent sleeves or overskirts may be lovely and intentional, but a lighted doorway may reveal the need for an overlooked lining or slip.

Each fabric has its own personality which may change with a change of lighting. Chapter 9 will show how different fibers and fabric structures react differently. Even the right and wrong side of the same fabric may react differently to light. So the designer observes the play of light both on individual textures, and to see how reflecting, absorbing, or admitting surfaces complement each other.

Light and Temperature

Light literally affects the temperature of a surface it strikes. More light bounces off a light-colored surface, and the reverse side of that surface stays cooler. That is why light colors are literally cooler for summer or tropical clothing, houses are usually white or pastel, and light-colored cars stay cooler inside in hot climates. Dark-colored surfaces absorb more light rays which are transformed into heat. So winter coats in cold climates are often dark to help absorb any sunlight that reaches them. A dull, dark surface absorbs more heat than a shiny, dark surface. Sunbathing in a black bathing suit will be hotter than in a lighter colored suit, and an unlined suit of contrasting dark and light colors may yield a patterned suntan. Mannequins dressed in black and white printed fabrics in early atomic bomb tests were burned in the dark areas but not in the white areas. Light skin in the sun reflects more light rays but has less melanin pigmentation to protect it from the rays it does absorb. Darker skin has more protective melanin but also absorbs more heat; so dark skin can also be subject to the effects of sun and heat rays.

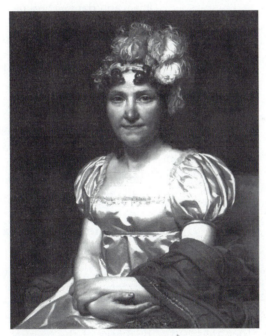

FIGURE 7-7 The light accents the spherical roundness of the puffed sleeves and hat, as shadows show concavities at the neck and under the bust. Highlights and shadows create dramatic lines in the sleeve gathers, and light reveals a rich variety of textures: shiny satin, soft, dull, wrap with its sparkling border; smooth skin, curly hair, and feathery hat. (*Madame David*, by Jacques-Louis David; 1813; National Gallery of Art, Washington; Samuel H. Kress Collection.)

Color: White and Colored Light and Selective Absorption

People often think that color is in or on an object, but all color is *light*. Without light

there is *no* visual perception at all. The colors we see depend on (1) the colors in the light rays themselves, and (2) the pigmentation of a surface to absorb or reflect light rays.

"White" light appears white because it contains all the colors of the visible spectrum. A "balanced" white light contains almost equal amounts of all visible wavelengths. A white light striking a surface can react in two ways: First, it can bounce off as unchanged white light, as in highlights reflected from shiny metals, mirrors, lustrous satin, or shimmering water.

Second, the white light may slightly penetrate a surface. The surface pigment then *absorbs all the color wavelengths except one which is reflected to the eye. The color of that reflected wavelength is the color we see*. So we see the only color or wavelength *not* absorbed in the pigment. For example, if white light falls on a "red" cloth, that cloth pigment or dye absorbs all the wavelengths except red which it cannot absorb. So that wavelength is reflected; we see it as red and thus see the cloth as red. This process is known as "selective absorption," and every color we see is the result of it.[10]

If balanced white light strikes a surface with no pigmentation to absorb wavelengths, then *all* wavelengths are reflected, and we see the surface as white. If a surface contains pigments to absorb all wavelengths, then few are reflected, and the surface appears black. Thus, the color seen in a fabric depends on which light wavelengths are absorbed and which are reflected.

"Unbalanced" white light has all the wavelengths, but in uneven amounts. As a result, colors of the stronger wavelengths appear brighter, and those of the weaker wavelengths seem duller. For example, unbalanced white light such as mercury street lights and fluorescent lights contain more short green and blue wavelengths; so green or blue fabrics appear brighter. These lights contain less red, orange, or yellow; so colors derived from them such as lipstick, skin,

and hair look dull. These lights are sometimes called "cool" whites. "Warm" whites contain more red, orange, and yellow, such as light coming from sodium fog and street lights, incandescent light bulbs, sunlight, firelight, and candlelight (Table 7-1). They intensify yellows, oranges, and reds, giving a warm glow to skin and hair colors which are derived from red-oranges, oranges, and yellow-oranges for all races. However, green and blue fabrics seem duller in "warm" white light.

Because the same color looks different under different "white" lighting, it is critical to choose a fabric color in the lighting in which it will most likely be worn. A flattering color in candlelight may look disastrous under fluorescent lights. Much interior lighting is fluorescent, but even some tubes labeled "daylight" are usually a cooler color than sunlight or incandescent light (Table 7-2). Many fabric stores have mirrors by outside windows for customers to see how a fabric will look either in fluorescent light or daylight, and a fabric color should be checked before it is used.

Colored lights contain only one or a few colors or wavelengths. *A surface pigment can reflect only the colors in the light wave-*

TABLE 7-1 Effects of Varied Lighting on Colors

Color in Daylight	As Seen under Sodium Vapor	As Seen under Mercury Vapor
Blue	dark brown or black	deep violet
White	light yellow	bluish white
Green	brownish yellow	deeper green
Yellow	yellow	greenish yellow
Black	black	black
Orange	brown	brown
Light red	yellowish brown	brown
Brown	brown	grey
Red	brown	dark brown or black

Chart courtesy of Research Association for the Paper and Board, Printing and Packaging Industries (P.I.R.A), Surrey, England.

---
[10]Walter Sargent, *The Enjoyment and Use of Color* (New York: Dover Publications, Inc., 1964), pp. 29–30.

TABLE 7-2 Effects of Fluorescent Lighting on Colors

Color Samples	Daylight	Standard Cool White	Deluxe Cool White	White	Standard Warm White	Deluxe Warm White	Soft White
Pink	fair	fair	good	fair	good	good	enhanced
Red	fair	dulled	good	dulled	good	good	fair
Maroon	dulled	dulled	fair	dulled	fair	enhanced	dulled
Rust	dulled	fair	fair	fair	fair	enhanced	fair
Orange	dulled	dulled	fair	fair	fair	enhanced	fair
Brown	dulled	fair	good	good	fair	good	good
Tan	dulled	fair	good	good	fair	good	good
Gold	dulled	fair	good	fair	good	good	fair
Yellow	dulled	fair	fair	good	good	fair	good
Chartreuse	good	good	good	good	fair	dulled	good
Olive	good	fair	fair	fair	dulled	dulled	fair
Light green	good	good	fair	good	dulled	dulled	dulled
Dark green	enhanced	good	fair	good	dulled	dulled	dulled
Turquoise	enhanced	fair	fair	dulled	dulled	dulled	dulled
Peacock blue	enhanced	good	fair	dulled	dulled	dulled	dulled
Light blue	enhanced	fair	fair	dulled	dulled	dulled	dulled
Royal blue	enhanced	fair	fair	dulled	dulled	dulled	dulled
Purple	enhanced	fair	fair	dulled	good	fair	dulled
Lavender	good	good	fair	dulled	good	fair	dulled
Magenta	good	good	good	fair	enhanced	good	dulled
Grey	good	good	fair	fair	fair	fair	fair
White	gray	white	dull-white	tan-white	yellow-white	dull-white	pink-white

*Dulled: subdued from original color.
 Fair: color less bright than under daylight of equal intensity.
 Good: appearance as good as under daylight of equal intensity.
 Enhanced: richer in appearance; color appears brighter than under daylight of equal intensity.
 Chart courtesy of *American Fabrics Encyclopedia of Textiles,* 3rd ed. (1980), p. 427.

lengths that strike it and that it cannot absorb. If red light falls on a "red" cloth, it reflects red. But what happens if a fabric pigment cannot reflect the only color in the light rays striking it? If only green wavelengths fall on a cloth pigmented to reflect only red, it will look black because the fabric receives no red to reflect and it is absorbing the green it receives. Table 7-3 shows the effects of major colored lights on colored surfaces. Watch especially for their effects on orange surfaces, since skin and hair are variations of orange. Other subtle colors like turquoise would widen the range of effects. These effects help show why most restaurant and theatre lights tend toward reds and oranges, rather than green, blue, or violet lighting.

When colored light strikes a white surface, there is no pigment to absorb light rays; so the white reflects whatever light rays it receives. So blue light striking a white surface appears blue; blue light striking a black surface will be absorbed, and the surface will appear nearly black. We see that blue light striking blue pigment appears blue, and blue light striking a white surface also appears blue. So if blue light strikes a blue and white patterned surface, both will appear blue, and the pattern will seem to evaporate.[11] This technique used on the stage can make the same costume look plain or patterned simply by a change of lighting.

---

[11]Graves, *Color Fundamentals,* p. 47.

TABLE 7-3 Effects of Colored Light on Colored Surfaces

Surface Color	Red Light	Orange Light	Yellow Light	Green Light	Blue Light	Violet Light
Red	bright red	red-orange	orange	grey	black	black
Orange	light red-orange	orange	yellow-orange	dull brown	grey	grey or black
Yellow	red-orange	orange	bright yellow	yellow-green	greyish	dull yellow or grey
Green	black	dull green or grey	yellow-green	bright green	greyish or blue-green	grey or black
Blue	grey, black	grey or black	grey	blue-green	bright blue	blue-violet
Violet	red-violet	rusty red	dull violet or grey	grey	blue-violet	bright violet

The chart provides a guide but exceptions and variations caused by chemicals in the dye, fabric, or finish may interact with light rays, causing distortions in effect. This gives even more reason to see a fabric under the lighting in which it is most likely to be worn.

Level of Illumination and Color

The level of illumination influences color perception in three ways: brightness of surface colors, lightness and darkness of a color, and color distortion. Very bright lights may seem to dull fabrics because the level of illumination may be more than the fabric can absorb; so more white light is reflected, mixing with and dulling the perceived color. A garment in a bright spotlight may seem drab and harshly glaring, but it will brighten in a softer light.[12]

The level of illumination also affects the light or dark appearance of a color in the "Purkinje effect."[13] As light dims, some colors darken more quickly than others. Blues and violets, with shorter wavelengths, retain reflecting ability better and appear relatively lighter in dimmer lights. Reds and oranges, with longer wavelengths, lose their reflecting ability quicker and look darker faster.

The level of illumination also affects perception of a color according to its position in the spectrum (Figure 7-1). In bright white lights, colors lean toward yellow and seem warmer; yellow looks almost white. In low lights, colors leans toward blue and seem cooler; green slides toward blue, and orange toward violet.[14] For example, to enrich a red in dim light, the fabric color might lean toward orange to compensate for the weak light that pushes it toward violet. Or to cool a green in bright sunlight, it might lean toward blue to compensate for the brilliance that pushes it toward yellow. For any such effects, color can be selected according to the anticipated level of lighting.

SUMMARY

Light is an elusive element caused by a small percentage of the wavelengths near the middle of the radiant energy spectrum. Any light we see depends on wavelength, frequency, and the amount radiated. We experience light as either radiating directly from a source or reflected from a surface; most visual experience is caused by reflected light. A clothing designer must control light indirectly by controlling the surfaces it strikes.

One must anticipate the lighting in which a garment will probably be worn—its sharpness or diffusion, source location, balance, color, and level of illumination—

---

[12]Sargent, *Enjoyment and Use of Color,* p. 78.

[13]M. Luckiesh, *Visual Illusions: Their Causes, Characteristics, and Applications* (New York: Dover Publications, Inc., 1965), p. 139.

[14]Sargent, *Enjoyment and Use of Color,* p. 83.

and then control the surface on which light falls by selecting style, shapes, textures, and colors to reflect the desired effects. The sharpness and angle of the light source play on gathers, draping, and pleats to create highlights and shadows. Texture can absorb, reflect, or admit light according to the qualities of the light source and texture surface qualities and density. Dark surfaces absorb more light and transform it into heat; light surfaces reflect more light rays, staying cooler.

Color perception depends on the colors in the light rays and a surface pigment. The pigment absorbs all wavelengths but one, which it reflects and we see. This phenomenon is known as "selective absorption." Unbalanced, "white" light will brighten those colors of its strongest wavelengths, dulling the others. In dim lights, shorter wavelengths look lighter, longer wavelengths look darker. Colors lean toward yellow in bright lights and toward blue in dim lights.

Thus, the designer can manipulate light indirectly by anticipating the kind of lighting in which a garment will be worn and by controlling the contours, textures, and colors of the surfaces on which it falls. Knowing the nature of light allows success in choosing surfaces.

CLASS ACTIVITIES

These activities require a room that can be darkened, that can accommodate a small, overhead spotlight, and that has a slide projector with red, green, and blue slides or filters; a screen; an outside window; and overhead lighting.

1. Compare the smoothing and flattening effects of diffuse overhead lighting or daylight with the sharp highlights and deeper shadows of overhead spotlight on (a) figure and garment contours, convexities and concavities, (b) light and shadow lines created by gathers,

pleats, shirring, or tucks (see how the light changes the lines as the wearer moves), and (c) fabric surfaces (preferably plain white): satin (right and wrong sides), velvet (with nap at different angles), corduroy, fleece or other rough-surfaced texture, matelassé, seersucker, broadcloth, organdy, chiffon, crepe, and others.

2. Repeat the preceding steps, comparing effects of the overhead angle of the spotlight with the side angle of the projector light beam, using fabrics draped on a figure.

3. Using the slide projector beam shining on a screen, hold a sheer fabric such as organdy or chiffon in front of the projector to show increased opacity with the light source on the same side of the fabric as the viewer, and then behind the projector but in front of students to show increased transparency in "backlighting."

4. Hold a small prism in the projector white light beam and turn it slowly until it breaks into the spectrum of hues, showing that all hues are in white light.

5. Compare different plain fabric colors, especially greens, turquoises, blues, violets, and magentas under incandescent, fluorescent, and daylight to show differing effects of balanced and unbalanced white light on fabric colors. If possible, include mercury, sodium, or other unbalanced white lights. Observe reds and oranges brighter in daylight and incandescent light and duller in fluorescent lighting, and blues and purples brighter in fluorescent light and duller in incandescent or candlelight.

6. Using solid color red, then blue, then green slides or filters in the projector, compare their effects on plain, differently colored fabrics, including black and white, to demonstrate selective absorption.

7. Using a blue and white print fabric, show the fabric pattern in the projector

white light beam and its disappearance in a blue light. (Or use green and white with green light, or red/pink and white with red light.) Then try the blue or green print in the red light, or red print in green light and observe and compare the results through selective absorption.

8. Invite students to bring or wear a garment from their closets to see its color changes under balanced and unbalanced white light and under differently colored lights. Ask students to predict effects according to selective absorption before putting the fabrics under the lights.

8 Color

DEFINITION AND CONCEPT

Color is that magnificent aura that envelops us with endless, subtle nuances, elating, depressing, soothing. We respond to it physically and psychologically, consciously and unconsciously. Even before style it is color that makes us notice a particular garment on a store rack. Color helps distinguish and identify objects, it changes apparent size or shape, and it provides key sales appeal. Those sensitive to its infinite variations and influences know it as the most powerful design element.

Color has so intrigued mankind throughout history that a whole literature and symbolism have developed around it. But since color is light, its mastery can be equally elusive. How do you catch a rainbow? Words do not capture the essence of color, yet mastering color effects in dress requires a color sense that comes from knowing its language and theories, reveling in, and experimenting with it. Words introduce a framework to experience color's physical properties, psychological effects, symbolism, and uses.

Color is basically two things: an external occurrence and an internal sensation. Surfaces appear colored because they reflect certain light waves which stimulate brain receptors. So a surface appears colored when an external event and an internal event combine into an experience.[1] Birren notes that "there is a vast difference between the world of color as a physical and scientific phenomenon and the world of color as personally experienced in human sensation."[2] He sees the former as

---

[1]William Charles Libby, *Color and the Structural Sense* (Englewood Cliffs, N.J.: Prentice-Hall, Inc., 1974), p. 25.

[2]Faber Birren, *Principles of Color, A Review of Past Traditions and Modern Theories of Color Harmony* (New York: Van Nostrand Reinhold Company, 1969), p. 49.

146

FIGURE 8-18. Personal skin and hair hue, value and intensity color analysis.

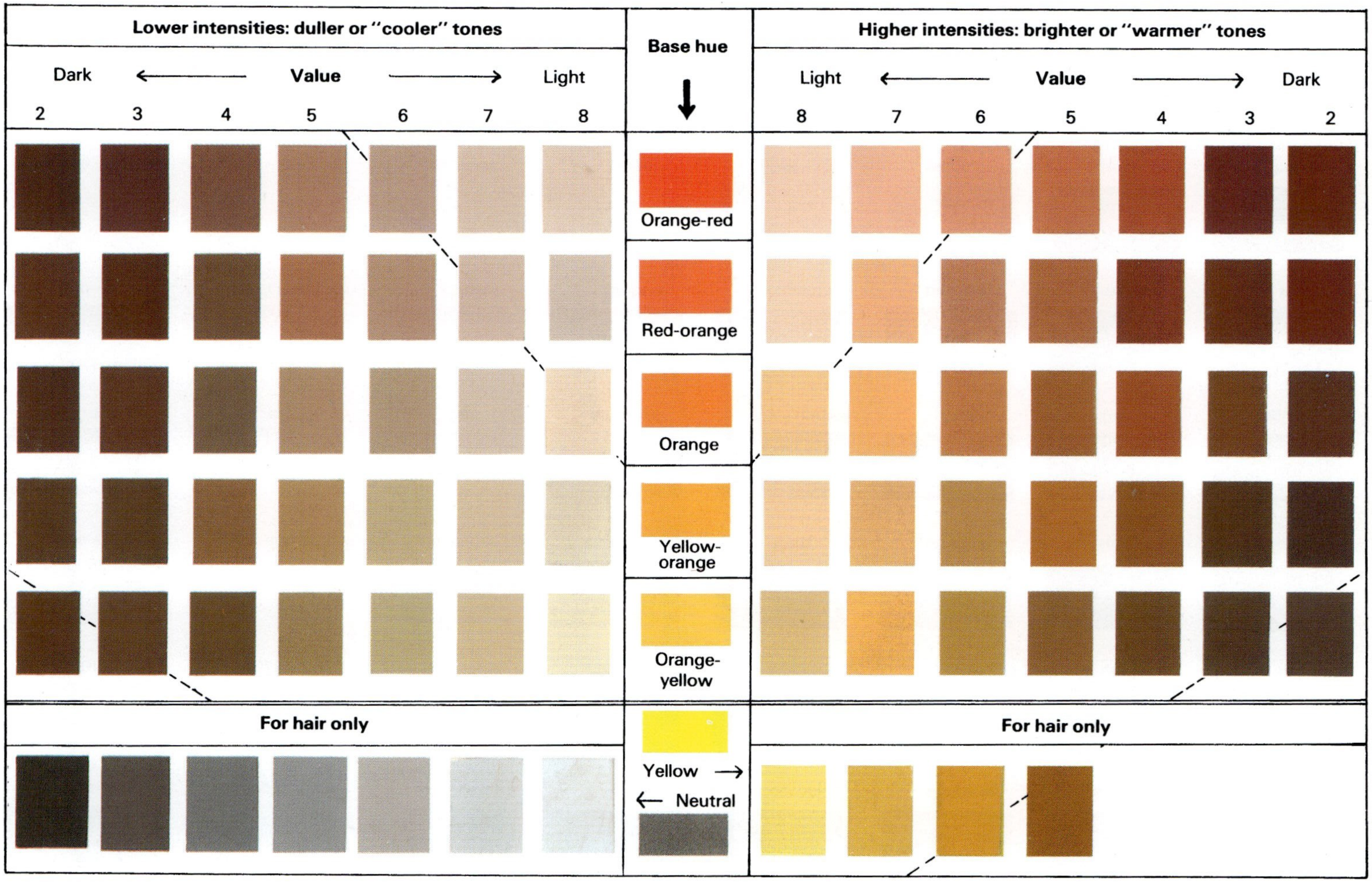

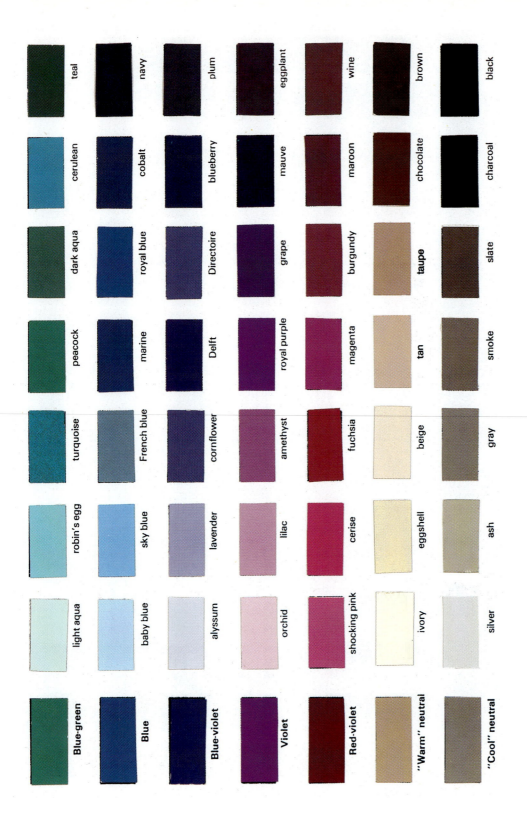

teal	navy	plum	eggplant	wine	brown	black	
cerulean	cobalt	blueberry	mauve	maroon	chocolate	charcoal	
dark aqua	royal blue	Directoire	grape	burgundy	**taupe**	slate	
peacock	marine	Delft	royal purple	magenta	**tan**	smoke	
turquoise	French blue	cornflower	amethyst	fuchsia	beige	gray	
robin's egg	sky blue	lavender	lilac	cerise	eggshell	ash	
light aqua	baby blue	alyssum	orchid	shocking pink	ivory	silver	
Blue-green	**Blue**	**Blue-violet**	**Violet**	**Red-violet**	**"Warm" neutral**	**"Cool" neutral**	

FIGURE 8-17. Common names of common colors.

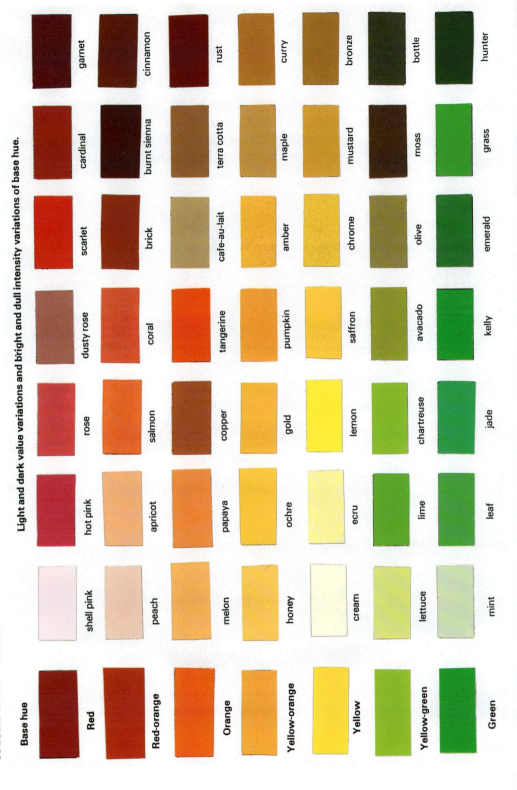

Light and dark value variations and bright and dull intensity variations of base hue.

Base hue							
Red	shell pink	hot pink	rose	dusty rose	scarlet	cardinal	garnet
Red-orange	peach	apricot	salmon	coral	brick	burnt sienna	cinnamon
Orange	melon	papaya	copper	tangerine	cafe-au-lait	terra cotta	rust
Yellow-orange	honey	ochre	gold	pumpkin	amber	maple	curry
Yellow	cream	ecru	lemon	saffron	chrome	mustard	bronze
Yellow-green	lettuce	lime	chartreuse	avacado	olive	moss	bottle
Green	mint	leaf	jade	kelly	emerald	grass	hunter

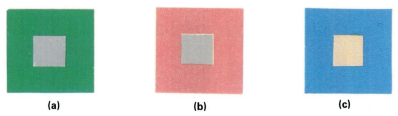

(a) (b) (c)

FIGURE 8-11. Hues bring out the effect of their complements in neutrals and very dulled colors. Green (a) makes its gray center seem pinkish; pink (b) its center greenish; and aqua (c) its beige center brighter.

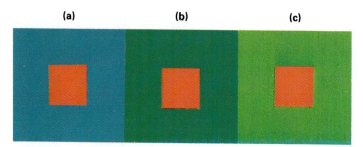

(a) (b) (c)

FIGURE 8-12. Simultaneous contrast: Differing hues can look alike. Differing center reds look more alike because differing backgrounds push centers toward the complement of the background.

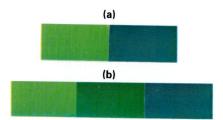

(a)

(b)

FIGURE 8-13. Contrast and adaptation: Similar hues push each other apart (a), but adding the intermediate hue emphasizes their similarities (b).

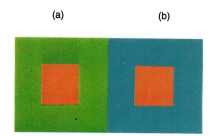

(a) (b)

FIGURE 8-14. Simultaneous contrast; Identical hues can appear different with different backgrounds. The green in (a) pushes its center toward red, and the blue-green in (b) pushes its toward red-orange.

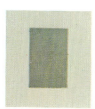

(a) (b)

FIGURE 8-15. Differing values can look alike: Lighter gray in (a) darkens center gray; darker gray in (b) lightens its center, making them appear alike. Yet (a) center is lighter than (b).

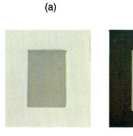

(a) (b)

FIGURE 8-16. Identical values can seem different on different backgrounds: Background (a) darkens its center as (b) lightens its center.

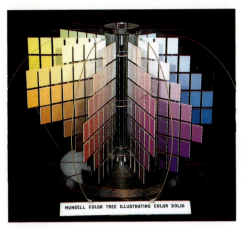

FIGURE 8-6. Munsell Color Tree showing hue, value, and chroma progressions in three dimensions. (Courtesy of Munsell Color, Baltimore, MD 21218.)

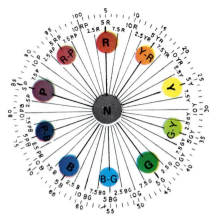

FIGURE 8-7. Munsell related hue symbols arranged on 100 hue circuit. (Courtesy of Munsell Color, Baltimore, MD 21218.)

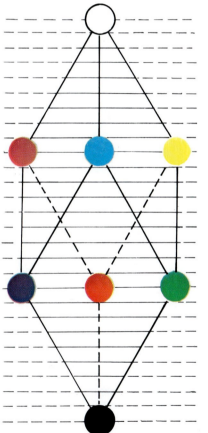

FIGURE 8-8. Küppers rhombohedron with light primaries around lower points and secondaries, or graphic primaries around upper points, 27 steps on pole from white to black. (From **Color Origin, System, Uses** by Harald Küppers © 1973 by Litton Educational Publishing, Inc. Reprinted by permission of Van Nostrand Reinhold Company.)

FIGURE 8-9. Ostwald hue "page" with neutrals along vertical pole and pure hue at the point.

FIGURE 8-10. Ostwald double cone.

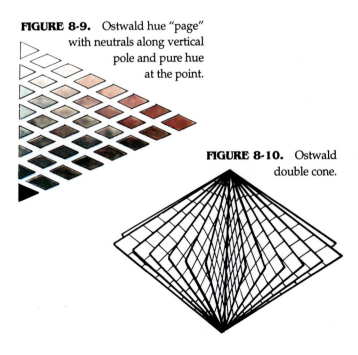

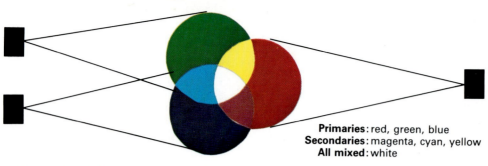

Primaries: red, green, blue
Secondaries: magenta, cyan, yellow
All mixed: white

FIGURE 8-1.   Light or physics color theory.

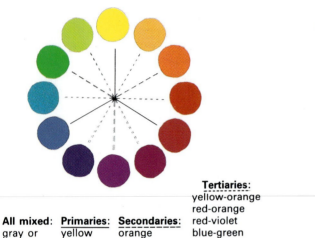

All mixed:	**Primaries:**	**Secondaries:**	**Tertiaries:**
gray or	yellow	orange	yellow-orange
black	red	violet	red-orange
	blue	green	red-violet
			blue-green
			blue-violet
			yellow-green

FIGURE 8-2.   Prang hue wheel.

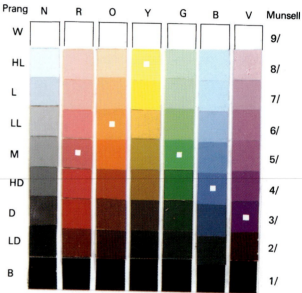

Tiny white squares show pure hue at home value.

FIGURE 8-3.   Value chart.

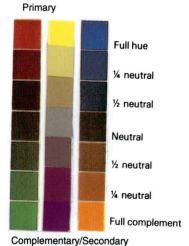

Primary

Full hue
¼ neutral
½ neutral
Neutral
½ neutral
¼ neutral
Full complement

Complementary/Secondary

FIGURE 8-4.   Prang intensities.

FIGURE 8-5.
Munsell hue, value, and chroma scales arranged in color space. Value is on vertical pole; hues, the spokes around the pole; and chroma, distance out from the pole. (Courtesy of Munsell Color, Baltimore, MD 21218.)

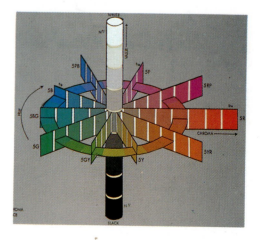

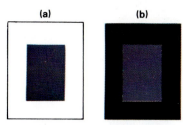

FIGURE 8-19. Extreme value contrasts overwhelm hue perceptions (a) while close values may accent hues (b).

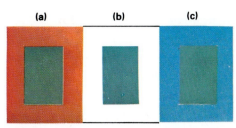

FIGURE 8-20. Differing intensities may appear similar. Dull blue-green against red-orange (a) seems like the medium in (b) and brighter in (c).

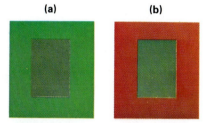

FIGURE 8-21. Identical intensities may look different: The same color seems duller against brighter intensities of the same hue (a) and brighter against complements (b).

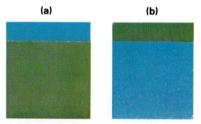

FIGURE 8-22. Small areas of bright intensity balance larger areas of dull intensity (a) while large areas of brightness overpower small dull areas (b).

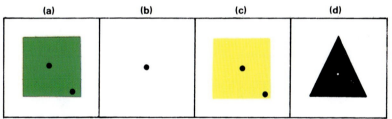

FIGURE 8-23. Hue and value after-images: Look at the center dot in green (a) for twenty seconds, then at the dot in (b). What color appears? Stare at (a), glance away and back to (a), and it seems dulled. Look at (d) awhile, then at (c). What happens? Look at (d), then at (b). What happens?

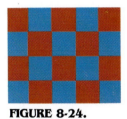

FIGURE 8-24. Long wavelength reds with short wavelength blues require constant eye refocusing, so colors clash.

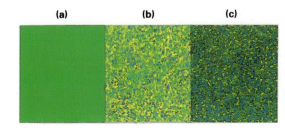

FIGURE 8-25. The flat green mixture (a) is smooth, while the pointillism of blue and yellow dots in (b) and analogous greens in (c), seen from a distance, create a visually mixed, rich green.

Effects of principles applied to color

FIGURE 8-26. Repetition of color: Using colors more than once helps unify patterned and plain areas and requires care as colors accent direction of repeats.

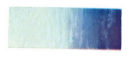

FIGURE 8-27. Sequence of color: Each color appears in a certain order of succession, keeps the same position in each repeat, and leads the eye in the direction of progression.

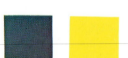 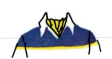

FIGURE 8-28. Alternation of color: Two colors changing back and forth in the same order lead the eye in the direction of the regular exchange.

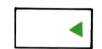

For **gradation of color,** see Figures 8-2 and 8-7 for steady, distinct progression of hues, 8-3 and 8-9 for light to dark value steps, and 8-4 and 8-9 for intensity.

FIGURE 8-29. Transition of color: Hues can slide smoothly from one to another, while value fades from dark to light and intensity melts from bright to dull.

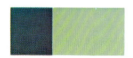

FIGURE 8-30. Contrast of color: Advancing and receding hues counter each other, light and dark values show powerful opposition, and bright and dull intensities accent unlikeliness.

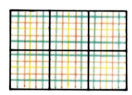 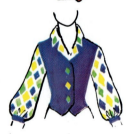

FIGURE 8-31. Emphasis of color: Advancing qualities of hue, value and intensity highlight a location against receding qualities.

FIGURE 8-32. Proportion of color: How do areas of one hue compare to areas of others? Light in relation to dark areas? Bright compared to dull? Is there variety to avoid equality or extremes?

FIGURE 8-33. Balance of color: Variety of hue, light and dark values, and bright and dull intensities all help to balance color schemes. Intermingling helps balance distribution of colors among each other, and garment placement according to color weight helps overall steadiness. (See also Figure 8-22).

FIGURE 8-34. Harmony of color: Agreement of feeling is easier when advancing or receding qualities of hues, values and intensities convey similar moods, giving enough variety for interest but avoiding boredom or conflict. The sweater colors consistently convey a bold, assertive mood.

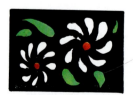 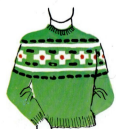

infinite but the latter as simple because the brain tends to group and organize similar perceptions. The external-internal distinction is important because each sometimes operates differently and may seem inconsistent, though science doesn't yet know why.

Color as external phenomenon is the visible light spectrum of wavelengths radiating from a light source or reflecting surface. It concerns the physicist, who measures and analyzes the qualities and interactions of those wavelengths, and the chemist and colorist, who manipulate pigments to reflect them.

Color as internal experience is the sensation from eye perception and brain interpretation of wavelengths that reach the eye. It concerns the physiologist, who studies the body's physical reaction to light stimulus, and the psychologist, who studies emotional and psychological reactions. The clothing designer must control the external color stimulus to elicit the desired internal response.

This internal sensation is often illusory compared to the objective, external color. Several colors can be made to look like one, or one like several. Albers observed, "In order to use color effectively, it is necessary to recognize that color deceives continually."[3] No one, however artistically sophisticated, is immune from color deception. Everyone with normal vision is susceptible to its physiologically based illusions. We can control effects of color by understanding its external properties and our internal reactions to them.

"EXTERNAL" COLOR

Exploring paint stores supports Libby's estimate that there are at least 30,000 different colors.[4] Lovibond, a stained glass pioneer, devised filters that could combine into 9 million colors.[5] The sensation we loosely call "color" is a combination of three aspects or dimensions: hue, value, and intensity. *Every color has all three.* Difference in colors results from differences in those three dimensions, each of which plays a distinct role, interacting with others according to certain, named relationships.

Dimensions of Color

Hue is a particular group of wavelengths such as red or blue coming from the light spectrum or their corresponding sensation reflected from a pigment color wheel. Hue is light wavelength, whether from a direct source or reflected from a pigmented surface. A pure hue is on the color wheel or spectrum with nothing added. It is the basic quality of color (Figures 8-1, 8-2, 8-7).

Hues next to each other on a color wheel are *analogous*, or *adjacent*. Hues opposite each other across the wheel are *complementary* because together they complete the spectrum, each containing primaries the other lacks (Figures 8-2, 8-7).

Figures 8-1 and 8-2 show how some hues play unique roles and determine relationships with other hues. *Primary* hues can mix to create all other hues, but no other hues can combine to create primaries. Different color theories have different hues as primary; each set of primaries agrees with the way that theory applies. Equal mixtures of two primaries are *secondary,* or binary, hues. Any mixture of a primary and one neighboring secondary gives a *tertiary,* or intermediate hue. Any mixtures between two primaries give pure hue secondaries and tertiaries, but if a mixture extends beyond the second primary and includes any of the third, any resulting colors will be dulled because that third primary is included. The complement of a primary is always a secondary, which is made from the two remaining primaries. The complement of a

---

[3]Josef Albers, *Interaction of Color,* rev. pocket ed. (New Haven, Conn.: Yale University Press, 1975), p. 1.
[4]Libby, *Color and Structural Sense,* p. 6.

[5]*Colour,* Marshall Editions Limited (London: Grange Books, 1991), p. 10.

secondary is always the third primary. Complements of tertiaries are opposite tertiaries, which together contain all three primaries and complete the color circle.

Value is the lightness or darkness of a hue. A pure hue with white added is a *tint* and described as a *high value*, and a pure hue with black added is a *shade*, a *low value*.

Every pure hue on a color wheel has its own level of lightness or darkness called *normal*, or *home value*. Yellow, the lightest hue, has the highest home value. Orange is next, then red, green, blue, and violet lowest, with the darkest home value. Tints of dark hues such as violet can be darker than shades of hues with light home values (Figure 8-3). Light hues such as yellow or orange change less in value from the pure hue to white and more to black. Dark hues such as blue change more toward white and less toward black. Black paint darkens a hue faster than white lightens it; so relatively more white and less black is needed to change it.

We never experience pure white or pure black from a colored surface because even the whitest surface absorbs some light, and the blackest velvet reflects some.[6] Fabric can approach but never achieve absolute blackness or whiteness; effects depend on the fabric texture. A shiny, black satin or dull broadcloth appears lighter than a rich, black velvet. Black and white can provide crisp accents or rich backgrounds.

Some lightened hues seem clear; darkened they seem sumptuous; but adding black or white also changes them. For example, black darkens yellow and pushes it toward green; red with black seems violet; some light violets seem pink. Shadows are rarely simply blacker, they often seem to change hue depending on fabric color, texture, and the light source.[7]

_____

[6]Frederick W. Clulow, *Colour: Its Principles and Their Applications* (Dobbs Ferry, N.Y.: Morgan and Morgan, Inc., Publishers, 1972), p. 19.

[7]Birren, *Principles of Color*, p. 60; and Walter Sargent, *The Enjoyment and Use of Color* (New York: Dover Publications, Inc., 1964), p. 67.

Blacks, greys, and whites are true neutrals because they betray no hue. Greys mixed from hues are so evenly balanced they cancel, or neutralize, each other. Balanced pigment mixtures of all hues result in greys because no hue in any mixture is as light as white or as dark as black.

Intensity is the brightness or dullness of a hue and is sometimes called saturation, chroma, purity, or vividness. Bright colors have high, and dull colors low, intensity. A pure hue in the light spectrum or color wheel has maximum possible intensity; and black, grey, or white have maximum dullness as neutrals. A hue is brightest only at its home value; so adding any black, white, or contrasting hue will dull it. For example, a darkened yellow is dull, just as a pale violet is dull, and pure red is brighter than a pale pink or deep wine.[8] Some hues can be brighter than others. Red has the greatest brightness capability, then orange, yellow, green, blue, and violet the least.

Adding the complement, the hue opposite on the color wheel, dulls a hue. The more of a complement used, the duller a hue becomes, until equal strengths of two complements neutralize each other to grey so that the hues cannot be traced. Mixing "equal strengths" rather than "equal amounts" is necessary to produce grey because pigment concentrations vary. Mixing equal amounts of bright red and quiet green gives dull red, not grey which needs stronger green.

Colorful Language

Knowing the language of color helps us use color. Hue is the basic property of all colors. Value modifies hue to be lighter or darker. Intensity modifies hue to be brighter or duller. So value and intensity describe variations of any given hue. We say "light blue" (not a blue lightness), or a "dull red" (not a red dullness). Hue is the beginning of all color. Every possible color starts from a

_____

[8]Libby, *Color and Structural Sense*, p. 16.

"base" or "core" pure hue that either remains pure or is lightened, darkened, and/or dulled to any variation we call a color. So the three dimensions of color have a special relationship: *Value and intensity modify hue.*

Neutral black, grey, and white are often described as colors, but have no identifiable hue. Neutrals, colorless glass, and mirrors are *achromatic,* or without hue. Surfaces or lights with identifiable hue are *chromatic,* with color. A substance that produces color is a *colorant.* Pigment, dye, or ink are colorants for surfaces like fabric and skin that reflect light rays.

"INTERNAL" COLOR

Color Perception

The evening sky sliding from blue high above to peach at the horizon, the brilliant edge of a grey cloud floating past the sun, the green of grass different in the shadow and sun are but a few examples of the vast array of colors to which we are sensitive. A person of normal vision can discriminate among over 10,000 colors,[9] including 160 pure hues, 200 grey values, and up to 20 levels of brightness.[10]

We can make these distinctions because of the delicate structure of the eye and its relationship with the brain. On the retina in the back of the eye are rods and cones. Rods cover a large area, allow peripheral and light and dark vision, but not color—this is why our night vision has little color. The cones are sensitive to color and are concentrated toward the center of the retina. At the center of this cone concentration is the fovea, near the blind spot, where the optic nerve goes to the brain, carrying the visual impulses which the brain translates and interprets as sight.

Color perception is still not thoroughly understood, but several theories agree that there are three types of cones, each type sensitive to red, green, or blue wavelengths. The eye is considered most sensitive to green. We perceive violet, for example, because a surface reflecting that wavelength calls both red- and blue-sensitive cones into action, mixing them in our perception only.

We do not actually "see" light rays in the air, only their reflections from surfaces or dust particles. Kueppers notes that light "rays are not colors; instead they cause the visual system to produce color sensations," and notes further that "there are no fixed correlations between color stimuli and color reception."[11] All of these factors help make human color experience highly subjective and individual, and contribute to the "deceptiveness" of color mentioned earlier.

The eye focuses longer wavelength colors, such as red, behind the retina making them seem to advance. Shorter wavelength colors, blue and violet, focus in front of the retina and seem to recede. When both long and short wavelength colors are seen on a flat fabric surface, they are more comfortable to look at if they are subdued and the pattern puts the reds or oranges in front of a blue or violet background. Bright red and bright blue used together in a pattern force constant eye refocusing, causing a clashing vibration called "chromatic aberration," that can literally hurt to look at for more than a few seconds (Figure 8-24).

Distortions of Color Perception

Several types of color perception distortions are common. Color blindness is thought to be a deficiency in one or more of the three types of a cone which prevents perception of "its" hue and other hues made from it. The cones that usually are most affected cor-

[9]Harold Küppers, *Color: Origin, System, Uses* (London: Van Nostrand Reinhold Ltd., 1973), p. 15.

[10]Rudolf Arnheim, *Art and Visual Perception* (Berkeley: University of California Press, 1971), p. 339.

[11]Harald Kueppers, *The Basic Law of Color Theory,* 1st U.S. ed., trans. Roger Marcinik, Barron's Educational Series (Woodbury, N.Y.: Barron's, 1982), pp. 10, 27.

respond to red-green color blindness which is a heredity most common in men.

Noninherited visual defects may be caused by liver, eye, or other diseases, industrial toxins, or excessive alcohol or nicotine use. Defective color vision is highest, 1:16, in urban areas of developed countries and lowest, 1:50, in tropical rain forests and the Arctic.[12]

Age is also a factor as the lens of the eye tends to yellow with age, distorting color perceptions toward yellow. Clothing colors might appear more yellowish to an elderly person than to a younger viewer.

Physiologists traditionally believed that everyone with normal vision perceives color identically; a green was presumed to look like the same green to everyone viewing it at the same time in the same light. But recent research suggests that cone spectral sensitivities can vary among individuals, causing slight differences in color perception.[13] A color seen in different lighting also appears different. Since color is not in a surface, but in the light that strikes it, a change in the light source changes the appearance of a surface color. "We do not see surfaces because light reveals color, but because surfaces reveal the color in the light,"[14] which the eye perceives and the brain interprets.

Surface colors are also subject to constant change of lighting, but the visual system is extremely adaptable to different lighting.[15] Such adaptability allows perceptual "color constancy" in which the "perceived color of a surface tends to remain constant despite changes in illumination."[16] Like learned geometric illusions, when we have often seen a surface color under various lighting and developed an "image" of it, we may then "see" that color as constant regardless of lighting changes. Color constancy may also be affected by colors in one area of the visual field being influenced by colors elsewhere.[17]

Color vocabulary among different cultures shows both consistencies and discrepancies. The absence of words for green or blue in some cultures was attributed to a simple level of sociotechnological development or to cultural values in which those colors were unimportant. Some recent studies, however, suggest perceptual differences in the tropics where more ultraviolet rays penetrate the atmosphere. In some cultures, names of objects that are a particular color are used for that color word, like "sky" for "blue." Other research has shown a global pattern of "universal" color terms in which 98 languages had at least terms for black and white, and additional terms almost always appeared in the same order cross-culturally: next red, then green and/or yellow, then blue, then brown.[18] So both consistency and variations appear in human color vision, awareness, and description.

Mystery still shrouds many processes that cause color sensation or distortion; but the interactions among pigment, light, eye, and brain show the intimate relationship between external and internal color. Mankind's long efforts to reconcile external and internal color have led to color theories intended to identify, analyze, explain, organize, and show how color works.

THEORIES OF COLOR

Theories of color show it in a structured way; they are maps for exploring color[19] and aids in understanding why colors interact and deceive as they do.

[12]*Colour*, pp. 36–37.
[13]Gordon E. Legge and Fergus W. Campbell, *Vision of Color and Pattern*, J.J. Head ed. (Burlington, N.C.: Carolina Biological Supply Company, 1987), p. 8.
[14]Libby, *Color and Structural Sense*, p. 10.
[15]Kueppers, *The Basic Law of Color Theory*, p. 9; and Legge and Campbell, *Vision of Color and Pattern*, p. 9.
[16]Jacob Beck, *Surface Color Perception* (Ithaca, N.Y.: Cornell University Press, 1972), p. 1.

[17]Legge and Campbell, *Vision of Color and Pattern*, p. 10; and E. H. Land, "The Retinex Theory of Color Vision," *Scientific American*, 237 (1977), pp. 108–128.
[18]*Colour*, pp. 50–51; and Brent Berlin and Paul Kay, *Basic Colour Terms: Their Universality and Evolution* (Berkeley: University of California Press, 1969).
[19]Libby, *Color and Structural Sense*, pp. 18, 23.

In the 1600's Isaac Newton beamed a white light through a glass prism, breaking the beam into the hues of the visible spectrum, and thus launched many efforts to explain and organize color. Colorists have tried to visualize their theories by structuring them into geometric models which multiplied as fast as the ideas they represented.

Newton bent his spectral band into a circle, joining the red and violet ends into an early color wheel. Some theorists used a square, triangle, or six-pointed star. Adding more hues brought any shape closer to a wheel, which has remained the dominant flat model.

Including value and intensity related the three dimensions of color to the three dimensions of space and created three-dimensional models. Most of these are based on a ball or globe with a vertical central pole for value, with black at the "south pole" to white at the "north." Since the value pole is also neutral, intensity goes from dullest at the central pole outward horizontally to brightest furthest from the pole. Hues ring around the "equator," so that slicing the sphere across the "equator" would show the hue wheel.

There are three types of color theories: (1) physical or light, (2) pigment, artist's, or graphic, and (3) psychological or visual. Of these, only the physical, or light, theory is scientifically provable, as wavelengths interact consistently, independent of human perception or intervention. Pigment and psychological theories deal with human perception of color as light reflected from pigmented surfaces.

Why light and pigment theories have different behaviors and primaries is not entirely understood, but knowledge of each helps understanding of the other. They do have in common that as long as only two primaries are mixed, the intervening hues are pure and bright.[20]

However, light and pigment theories differ as more hues are mixed together.

Adding more hues in the light spectrum lightens values and resulting colors. Combining all light primaries "adds up to" white; so the light theory is called *additive*. Mixing more pigment hues together absorbs or "subtracts" more light waves; so fewer waves are reflected and the color appears darker. So pigment theories are called *subtractive*. In light theory, white is the presence of all color because all wavelengths are present, and black is the absence because no wavelengths are present. In pigment theories, white is the absence of all color because there is no pigment to absorb wavelengths, and black is the presence of all color because pigment is absorbing all wavelengths.

To understand color interactions in body and dress, discussion here considers both types of theories; for physics the light, or physical, theory; and for pigment theories the Prang and Munsell, Ostwald's psychological theory and Küppers' combined light and pigment model.

Light Theory

Newton's prism bent, or refracted, the white light beam into its component hues at different angles, separating the hues of the visible spectrum. Longer wavelength red and orange bent less, and shorter wavelength blue and violet bent more (Figure 7-1). Others later identified the light primaries as *red, green,* and *blue,* a finding verified by physicists ever since. The light primary red leans toward orange, and the blue toward violet. As primaries, these cannot be produced by any other light combinations, but they create all other hues in light rays. Red plus green creates yellow, red plus blue gives magenta, and blue plus green gives a greenish-blue, or cyan (Figure 8-1). (Why yellow is not a light primary is not really known.) Thus, light secondaries are magenta, cyan, and yellow, and are nearly the same as pigment or graphic primaries (Figure 8-2). Light primary and secondary complements are red and cyan, blue and yellow, and green and magenta.

---

[20]Albers, *Interaction of Color,* p. 29.

Combining complements, or all light primaries, yields white (Figure 8-1). Just as Newton separated hues from a white beam, so they can recombine into white light.

Pigment Theory: Prang or Brewster

By 1831 Brewster laid the groundwork for what has become known as the Prang theory. Its structure is simple, straightforward, and practical. While Prang primaries of red, yellow, and blue spun on a disk appear orange-grey, not a true grey, they do give the best distribution of long and short wavelengths. Reds, oranges, and yellows cover nearly 40 percent of the light spectrum (Figure 7-1)[21] and are critical in clothing selection because all human skin and hair coloration is derived from those hues, so all clothing colors interact with some version of them. In this book, analysis of interactions of skin and clothing color uses the Prang theory.

Since 1731, users have experienced first-hand the "primary nature of red, yellow, and blue in pigment."[22] No other pigment hues combine to make red, yellow, and blue; but these mix well to make all other hues. (The light secondaries of magenta, cyan, and yellow, sometimes called graphic primaries, also work in certain media.)

For Prang secondaries, red and yellow make orange, blue and yellow make green, and red and blue make violet, so orange, green, and violet are the secondaries. The tertiary hues between primaries and secondaries on a standard 12-hue wheel are red-orange, yellow-orange, yellow-green, blue-green, blue-violet, and red-violet (Figure 8-2), making 3 primaries, 3 secondaries, and 6 tertiaries. A wheel can be divided into many finer distinctions with more tertiaries, but the primary, secondary, and complementary relationships remain the same.

Prang values have nine steps from white to black, indicated by initial letters:

W (white), HL (high light), L (light), LL (low light), M (medium), HD (high dark), D (dark), LD (low dark), and B (black) (Figure 8-3). The white squares show primary and secondary hue home value levels, and their tints and shades.

For intensity, Prang showed the subtractive nature of pigment, and the ability of complements to neutralize each other. Intensity charts show seven steps from a full primary at the top to its full complement secondary at the bottom (Figure 8-4).

Each step down with more complementary secondary dulls the primary until equal strengths are neutral at the center. Then from pure secondary at the bottom, each step up with more primary complement is again dulled to neutral at the center. These steps show that the more complement is added, the duller the hue. He labeled these as full hue, ¼ neutral, ½ neutral, neutral, ½ neutral, ¼ neutral, and full (complementary) hue. Each secondary complement contains the other two primaries, so primary-secondary complementary pairings (red-green, blue-orange, or yellow-violet) complete the spectrum, as do complementary tertiaries.

Prang theory does not analyze all three color dimensions in one model and is imprecise, but the flat wheel and charts work easily and well.

Pigment Theory: Munsell

Color identification at the turn of the century depended on inconsistent terms and unreliable memory. Munsell compared color names to vague musical notes of "lark, canary, cockatoo, and cat."[23] He sought to measure and label each dimension of color consistently and to relate all three with a formula that would always mean the same color. This meant that a particular pink with a Munsell formula label or "notation" in New York could be exactly matched by

---

[21]Libby, *Color and Structural Sense*, p. 54.
[22]Birren, *Principles of Color*, p. 11.

[23]Albert H. Munsell, *A Color Notation*, 5th ed. (New York: Munsell Color Company, 1919), p. 10.

its notation in Paris. Such notations eliminated the guesswork of slippery terms like "butterfly pink," and standardized a common language of color.

Munsell used a spherical model to visualize his theory. The vertical central pole is value, intensity brightens horizontally from the dull central pole outward, and hues ring the equator (Figures 8-5, 8-6). Thus any given location in the sphere had a specific hue, value, and intensity.

Munsell hue structure is based on visual, not pigment, mixtures. He correctly avoided the terms "primary" and "secondary" since not all of his hues are primary. Although Prang primaries of red, yellow, and blue pigments mix well, they appear orange-grey, not grey, when spun together on a disc. To spin a true grey and minimize the orange, Munsell reduced the reds through yellows from their nearly 40 percent of the light spectrum to only 25 percent of his hue wheel. This allowed spinning a neutral grey using five hues: red, yellow, green, blue, and purple, which Munsell called "principal" hues. Two neighboring principal hues mix to form an "intermediate" or "compound" hue between every two principal hues.

Hues progress clockwise around the wheel so that each intermediate hue begins with the name of the next clockwise principal hue. They are identified with initial letter labels: red (R), yellow-red (YR), yellow (Y), green-yellow (GY), green (G), blue-green (BG), blue (B), purple-blue (PB), purple (P), and red-purple (RP) (Figure 8-7). These five principal and five intermediate hues give a wheel of ten "major" hues.

Figure 8-7 shows how Munsell identified up to one hundred finer hue distinctions from his ten major hues. He put a number between 1 and 10 in front of the major hue initial letters to show how the hue "leaned." The number 5 is centered on the pure major hue, numbers toward 1 lean toward the next counterclockwise (left) major hue, and numbers between 5 and 10 lean toward the next clockwise (right) major hue. Number 10 shows the half-way

point between major hues before the next clockwise hue becomes dominant. So a 2.5R leans toward red-purple (RP), a 5R is pure red, a 7.5R leans toward yellow-red (YR), and a 10R is half way to YR. Then the 1 to 10 numbers begin again for those hue refinements dominated by YR, giving a total of a 100-hue wheel. In the sphere model, each hue has a vertical page showing its value and intensity variations.

For value, Figure 8-5 shows how Munsell used the central north-south pole with numbered steps, with black at 1 at the lower end, 5 at a mid-range grey, and white at 9. The darker or lower the value, the lower the notation number; the lighter or higher the value, the higher the number. Thus lighter and darker versions of a hue can be labeled precisely. A pink would have a high value number, and dark wine a low one. Figure 8-3 shows that each pure hue has a home value (with white squares) and corresponding numbers at the right. Yellow is lightest and highest at 8, then yellow-red at 6, green and red at 5, blue at 4, and purple at 3.

Munsell called intensity "chroma," from the Latin word for color. Since the value pole is also neutral, dull colors are near the center pole, and they brighten horizontally outward. While hues are brightest at their home value, Munsell also realized that some pure hues are capable of greater brightness than others, and so could extend out further horizontally from the neutral pole. These differences created "bulges" in the sphere so that yellow extends out furthest at its high home value, and blue and purple extend out furthest at their lower home values (Figure 8-6). Most horizontal lines at the white or black ends of the pole are short because extremely lightened or darkened hues are also duller. Munsell numbered chroma levels with low numbers for low chroma or dull and higher numbers for higher chroma or bright. Red could extend up to 14; yellow-red and yellow 12; purple-blue 9; green-yellow and green 8; blue, purple, and red-purple 6; and blue-green 5. (These levels may increase as brighter pigments are developed.)

To show the three color dimensions in one notation formula, Munsell used the pattern HV/C: H (hue number and letter initial), V (value number) followed by a slash, and C (chroma number). So 5R5/14 indicates a pure red at home value and brightest chroma. A 2.5R7/3 shows a purplish-red (hue) that is light (value) and dull (chroma). So each color has its own formula or notation. This notation system for consistent and exact identification of each dimension of any color, and his sphere, which showed relative hue, value, and intensity positions, were perhaps Munsell's greatest contributions. They standardized color identification with concise formulas that transcended language barriers and slippery memory, and have been adopted by many industries, the Inter-Society Color Council, and the U.S. National Bureau of Standards.

Psychological Theory: Ostwald

In 1870 Hering suggested "psychologically primary" hues that "perceptually … have no visual resemblance to each other."[24] By 1916 Ostwald based his system on black, white, and four psychologically distinct major hues: red, green, yellow, and blue. He subdivided the wheel into twenty-four hues, with five intermediate hues between any two major hues, and red as complement of green, and blue of yellow.

Every hue had its own triangular "page," with white at the upper point, black at the lower point, and pure hue at the outer point (Figure 8-9). Each edge had eight steps: vertical value from black to white, from white to pure hue, from black to pure hue, and from median grey to pure hue, making twenty-eight variations of value and intensity on each hue page. Multiplied by twenty-four hues, this gave 672 colors, plus eight neutrals made 680. Joining all the triangles along their vertical value edge created a double cone, with a central, vertical value pole and pure hues around the sharp "equator" (Figure 8-10).

Ostwald saw little difference between intensity and value; he discussed dulled hues by their grey content, and devised his own terminology: tints were "saturation"; shades, "brightness"; and intensity, "tone." Every hue was numbered, with yellow at 1. Two letters showed value levels with a letter earlier in the alphabet showing the amount of white added to the hue, and a later letter showing the amount of black. Thus every color was given a formula. A "1ec" is a light, dull yellow, and "13ne" a darker, bright blue. Ostwald also sought fool-proof color harmonies, but his major contribution may be a system recognizing human perception of psychologically distinct hues.

Combined Theories: Küppers

The puzzling differences between light and pigment theories have inspired efforts to reconcile them. The similarities of the light secondaries and pigment primaries (red/magenta, yellow, and blue/cyan), and the light primaries and pigment secondaries (orangish red/orange, purplish blue/violet, and green), suggest a consistent relationship between light and pigment theories. Küppers' system combines light and graphic pigment primaries on one rhombohedron model[25] which he regarded as a "geometric illustration of the law of vision" because regular interconnections between color origin, uses, and sensation can be derived from it.[26]

A rhombohedron is a diagonally stretched cube with six diamond-shaped surfaces (Figure 8-8). Of its eight points, or corners, the base is black with twenty-seven steps up a central vertical value pole to the top white. The three upper points are the graphic primaries: magenta, yellow, and cyan; the three lower points are light pri-

---

[24]Birren, *Principles of Color*, p. 20.

[25]Küppers, *Color*, p. 19.
[26]Kueppers, *Basic Law*, p. 69.

maries: red, blue, and green, making the primaries of each theory serve as secondaries for the other. Küppers assigned ten intervening colors from one primary to the next, and from a primary to its nearest black or white point, making each surface a color grid. Future applications of this model may increase understanding of light and pigment theory interaction in color use.

COMMON NAMES OF COMMON COLORS

Color theories and formulas are essential to the professional and the industry but hold little meaning or imagery for the buying public. Advertising a dress in "Munsell's 2.5GY7/5" would probably sell few garments.

However, nature's palette provides a brilliant range of understood terms that strike a useful balance between technical formulas and fleeting, uninformative fashion names such as "elephant's breath," "glowworm," and "passion."[27] Most common color names describe familiar, unchanging colors in nature or are traditionally associated with certain colors. Some colorists use French words to describe their chosen colors, such as *cerise* for cherry red, *aubergine* for eggplant, or *cafe-au-lait* for coffee with cream. Popular colors reemerge periodically; so the professional must be able to visualize colors instantly when asked, for example, "How will a fuchsia and chartreuse skirt look with a teal top and a mauve and ochre scarf?"

Figure 8-17 shows fourteen rows of colors derived from the twelve basic Prang hues, "warm" and "cool" fashion neutrals, and their common names. The left-hand column is the pure "base hue," and the colors to its right are its lightened, darkened, and/or dulled variations (and the pure hue if it also has a popular name). Since only

[27]Faber Birren, *Color: A Survey in Words and Pictures* (New York: University Books, 1963), p. 116.

black, white, and greys are true neutrals, the row of browns and beiges labeled "warm neutrals" refers only to popular fashion terminology, not to color theory terminology. These are not true neutrals because they can be traced to a hue: orange.

Because nontechnical language is imprecise and not scientific, these common color names must be regarded as approximate. The chart shows base hues and common color variations of value and intensity. Some may regard a particular color as slightly different from the chart, but it does distinguish colors and encourages color sensitivity.

Fashion professionals must be able to project or trace color deviations to create well-balanced color schemes and predict color interactions and illusions. What can be done with a pure hue? It may be lightened, darkened, and/or dulled into many variations. Or one may first see a final color and "work backward" to identify its base hue and then determine what black, white, and/or complement was added to change its value and/or intensity. For example, "dusty rose," a dulled tint of red could be made by adding white and black, or white and green, the complement of red. Similarly, pink is simply a tint of red, and brown a shade of orange. A final color may be lighter, darker, or duller, but not brighter than its pure base hue. The more a final color differs from its base hue—extremely darkened, lightened, or dulled—the harder its derivation is to trace. For example, a pale melon might seem to derive from either orange or red-orange. Playing with color sharpens tracing ability.

PERSONAL COLORATION

Pigments react to light essentially the same way whether they are natural (in plants, rock, flowers, human or animal skins, or hair) or artificial (in paint, cosmetics, inks, fabric dye, food coloring, or elsewhere). That means that they can be analyzed similarly as variations of hues. A landscape artist mixes blue and yellow to make various greens, the dominant base hue of most plants. A portrait painter mixes red and yellow to make various *oranges, the dominant base hue family of human skin and hair coloration.* Then the artist lightens with white, and/or darkens with black, and/or dulls with the complement to suggest skin or hair variations. So as every possible color is a combination *of a base hue at a particular value and intensity level, so is all human coloration,* and it can be analyzed on that basis to predict effects of clothing colors.

Skin Color

Skin colors are the background against which clothing colors are perceived. Most people like a skin color that makes them look healthy, as health and illness are often described in terms of color: "rosy glow," "ruddy complexion," "in the pink of health," or "sallow or ashen," "so sick he looked green," or "yellow jaundice." Value is not seen as an indication of health, although in some Western societies light-skinned people associate "a good tan" with good health, but this is a cultural and historical association. However, hue and intensity are usually associated with health. Base hues leaning toward red suggest good health, and abnormally yellow hues, poorer health; brighter intensity skin suggests good health, and duller intensities, frail or delicate health or sickness. These associations appear to be cross-cultural and cross-racial.

Base *hues* that dominate all human skin coloration, regardless of race, are in the orange-red to orange-yellow hue range. Despite social labels of "red" or "yellow" races, the value chart (Figure 8-3) shows that no human has a pure red or pure yellow skin base hue (although some albinos are near a tint of pure red). Some African, European, and North American groups lean more toward red, and some Asian and Mediterranean groups lean more toward yellow. No human group has dominantly green, blue, or violet skin. Figure 8-18 shows the orange-yellow to orange-red range of base hues of human skin and hair on the central vertical column.

Values in Figure 8-18 extend horizontally on each side of the central vertical hue column. More steps are possible, but these seven show a range from the darkest value, numbered 2, at the outer edges, and lightening and increasing to 8 at the center. Most people racially labeled "white" are actually in the beige ranges, and people labeled "black" are in a wide range of browns.

Intensity is shown here flattened and simplified since our Figure 8-18 is a flat page. It shows duller intensities on the left half of the page and brighter intensities on the right half, with the hue scale down the center. We see that the brighter the orange-based pigment (less complementary pigmentation), the brighter the skin intensity, and the duller the pigment (more complementary pigmentation), the duller the skin tone for the same reason that complements dull each other. So the dulled, wide range of beige and brown skin variations of oranges depend on the intensity levels of our pigmentation. Skin described as "bright" is flattering in most cultures, whereas "dull" is not; so the term "warm" is used here for brighter intensity, and "cool" or "delicate" for duller intensity.

People of one group sometimes stereotype all those who differ from them as being one color, and thus fail to perceive the vast and rich range of human coloration and the subtle changes within it. However, those who work with clothing colors, which are always interacting with personal coloration, need a keen appreciation of human color ranges.

The chart in Figure 8-18 is simplified, but everyone is closer to one of its colors than to any other. To pinpoint your own base hue, value, and intensity levels, under balanced white light or daylight, find the color that most nearly matches your forehead and cheeks, since they cover the largest areas. Does your skin hue on the chart lean toward the yellow or the red? What number on the value range is it? Is it on the higher or lower intensity side of the chart?

Keep in mind that most people have uneven coloring, perhaps dark circles under the eyes or shadows or freckles. Those who tan may be darker in summer than in winter. All these factors influence color effects of clothing; so understanding your own and others' coloration is a necessary professional sensitivity.

Hair Color

Hair color uses the same chart and method of analysis as skin color since hair color is also in the red to yellow hue range. But hair color does include pure yellow and greys (shown on the bottom row of Figure 8-18, with yellows on the brighter intensity side and greys on the duller). The more yellow the hue base, the lighter the value (blonde), and the closer to red, the darker the value (pink or blackened yellow hair is rare). Figure 8-18 shows natural hair colors between the broken V lines from lower center to top outer corners. Hair color may darken in winter and lighten with summer sun exposure. Hair is usually darker than skin, but exceptions are the white-haired/dark-skinned person, or a blonde with a deep tan. Traditional combined analyses of skin and hair color created stereotypes: Irish, Mediterranean, and the like. (More recently, clocks and seasons and other irrelevant labels have been used to stereotype.) However, with ease of changing hair color, traditional "types" fade, and choice of whether to emphasize skin, hair, or eye color emerges.

Eye Color

Eye color usually serves as an accent since it is so tiny. It usually has two base hue ranges: red-orange to yellow-orange, usually darker value brown and hazel; and blue-violet to blue-green, usually lighter value and almost grey to bright blue.

Composite Human Coloration

Skin, hair, and eye color are the "background" influenced by clothing colors.

How can you use clothing colors to make a dull skin appear brighter? To bring out red highlights in hair? To make eyes look bluer? To make skin look healthier? To make skin and/or hair look lighter or darker? To create subtle color effects between person and dress? What if a color that brightens your skin dulls your hair? Each of us is unique: just as billions of snowflakes are similar but not identical, so is human coloration. Differences may be slight, but enough to negate stereotypes and give each of us a unique potential for clothing color effects that no one else in the world has. These differences make color selection highly individual, not type cast.

PHYSICAL EFFECTS OF COLOR

Here we come literally face to face with the powerful effects of color that enlarge, reduce, lighten, darken, brighten, dull, advance, recede, shift hue, or cause other phenomena. When colors are seen next to or touching each other in garments or with skin and hair, they are "juxtaposed," and cannot escape mutual influence and illusions.

Any given color is an inseparable "package" of hue, value, and intensity. Although we see only the combination, we must isolate them to study and understand effects of each dimension to control effects of the combination. The major illusions that use color were introduced in Chapter 3. Here we shall explore how each type of illusion manipulates each dimension of color and its impact on personal and clothing color interactions. Illusions giving physical effects include simultaneous contrast, after-image, irradiation, and visual mixtures.

As you study the effects and their clothing examples here, also study Tables 8-1, 8-2, and 8-3. In physical effects of color, Tables 8-1 and 8-2 show effects according to hue families and value and intensity levels. Part A in Table 8-1 charts predictable simultaneous contrast and after-image effects for hue, value, and intensity across the top row. With those predictions you can move to

TABLE 8-1 Hue, Value, and Intensity Effects

	HUE		VALUE		INTENSITY	
A. PHYSICAL EFFECT	*Red, Orange, Yellow*	*Green, Blue, Violet*	*Light*	*Dark*	*Bright*	*Dull*
Simultaneous contrast	Complements: green, blue, violet	Complements: red, orange, yellow	Dark	Light	Dulls same hue, brightens complement	Brightens
After-image	Complements	Complements	Dark	Light	Pastel complement	Little or none
B. PSYCHOPHYSICAL EFFECT						
Temperature	Warm	Cool	Cool	Warm	Warm	Cool
Motion	Advancing	Receding	Advancing	Receding	Advancing	Receding
Size	Enlarging	Reducing	Enlarging	Reducing	Enlarging	Same
Density	Heavy	Lightweight	Lightweight	Heavy	Heavy	Lightweight
Sound	Loud	Quiet	Loud	Quiet	Loud	Quiet
Moisture	Dry	Wet	Dry	Wet	Dry	Wet
C. PSYCHOLOGICAL EFFECT						
Emotion	Courage, excitement	Calmness, dignity	Innocence, delicacy	Formality, mystery	Exuberance, intensity	Meditation, serenity
Action	Stimulating	Soothing	Stimulating	Soothing	Stimulating	Soothing
Gender	Feminine	Masculine	Feminine	Masculine	Masculine	Feminine
Drama	Dramatic	Subtle	Extreme contrast: dramatic Close contrast: subtle		Dramatic	Subtle
Sophistication	Simple	Sophisticated	Simple	Sophisticated	Simple	Sophisticated
Age	Young	Mature	Young	Mature	Young	Mature
Season	Summer, fall	Winter, spring	Spring	Fall, winter	Summer, fall	Winter, spring

TABLE 8-2	General Guide to Choosing Effective Colors		
TO LOOK:	CHOOSE:		
A. Physical (Skin and Hair Colors)	Hue Base	Value	Intensity
1. More red-based	1. Greens		
2. More red-orange-based	2. Blue-greens		Lower intensity
3. Orange-based	3. Blues	Varies	than actual
4. Yellow-orange-based	4. Blue-violets		skin or hair color
5. Blond (yellow) (hair)	5. Violets		
6. Darker		6. Light	
7. Lighter		7. Dark	
8. Brighter			8. Lower (duller) than skin or hair
9. Duller or "cooler"			9. Higher (brighter) than skin or hair
B. Psychophysical:			
1. Warm	1. Red, orange, or yellow base	1. Medium and dark	1. Bright
2. Cool	2. Green, blue, or violet base	2. Light	2. Dull
3. Advancing, active	3. Warm	3. Light	3. Bright
4. Receding, passive	4. Cool	4. Medium and dark	4. Medium and dull
5. Larger	5. Warm	5. Light	5. Bright
6. Smaller	6. Cool	6. Dark	6. Dull
7. Heavier, denser	7. Warm	7. Dark	7. Bright
8. Lighter weight	8. Cool	8. Light	8. Dull
9. Loud	9. Warm	9. Medium and light	9. Bright
10. Quiet	10. Cool	10. Dark	10. Dull
C. Psychological:			
1. Exciting	1. Warm	1. Medium and light	1. Bright
2. Calm	2. Cool	2. Dark	2. Dull
3. Masculine	3. Cool	3. Medium and dark	3. Bright
4. Feminine	4. Warm	4. Light	4. Medium, soft/dull
5. Assertive	5. Warm	5. Medium	5. Bright
6. Delicate	6. Cool	6. Light	6. Dull
7. Dramatic	7. Warm	7. Strong contrast	7. Bright
8. Subtle	8. Cool	8. Close contrast	8. Medium and dull
9. Young	9. Warm	9. Light	9. Bright
10. Mature	10. Cool	10. Dark	10. Dull

Table 8-2. The top section A, Column 1 under "To Look" lists personal skin and hair color effects, and Columns 2, 3, and 4 under "Choose" show what kinds of hues, values, and intensities will create those personal color effects. Table 8-3 goes the next step, listing specific clothing colors in the left column, and their physical simultaneous contrast and after-image effects on skin and hair colors in Column A. Studying all three tables in order will help you practice verifying the effects described here and illustrated in the color figures.

Simultaneous Contrast

"Simultaneous contrast" in color means that any actual differences in touching colors seem exaggerated while being viewed. Each property increases apparent differences from the other. The "dominating" color usually covers a larger area and influ-

TABLE 8-3 Selected Color Effect Profile Chart

Color	A. PHYSICAL		B. PSYCHOPHYSICAL							C. PSYCHOLOGICAL			
	Hue Simultaneous Contrast	After-image	Temperature	Motion	Size	Density	Sound	Emotion	Action	Gender	Drama	Sophistication	Age
Shell pink	light greens	faint, if any	medium	medium-advance	enlarge	light	medium-quiet	soft	medium	feminine	delicate	simple	young
Dusty rose	pale greens	faint greens	medium-warm	medium-advance	medium-enlarge	medium	medium-quiet	pleasant	medium	feminine	gentle	medium	medium
Scarlet	greens	greens	hot	advance	enlarge	heavy	loud	exciting	active	feminine	dramatic	straight-forward	medium-young
Apricot	light blue-greens	faint blue-greens	medium-warm	medium-advance	enlarge	medium	medium	soft	medium	feminine	gentle	fresh	young
Orange	blues	blues	hot	advance	enlarge	medium-heavy	loud	stimulating	active	feminine	assertive	simple	young
Rust	blues	faint blues	warm	medium	medium	medium-heavy	medium	spirited	active	feminine	intrigue	sophisticated	medium
Gold	pale blue-violets	pale blue-violets	warm	advance	enlarge	medium	medium-loud	happy	active	feminine	medium-dramatic	medium-fresh	young
Yellow	violets	orchids	hot	advance	enlarge	medium-heavy	loud	cheery	active	feminine	medium	simple	young
Chartreuse	red-violets	pale pinks	warm	advance	enlarge	medium-heavy	loud	fresh, new	active	medium	dramatic	medium	young
Olive	soft red-violets	faint pinks	medium-warm	medium	medium	medium	medium	friendly	medium	medium	soft-firm	medium	medium-young
Mint green	pinks	pinks	cool	advance	enlarge	light	medium-quiet	fresh-soft	medium-quiet	medium-feminine	subtle	simple	young
Kelly green	reds	pinks	medium-cool	advance	enlarge	medium-heavy	loud	lively	active	medium-masculine	dramatic	simple	young
Hunter green	soft reds	faint pinks	cool	recede	reduce	heavy	quiet	restful	quiet	masculine	subtle	simple	mature

TABLE 8-3 *Continued*

Color	A. PHYSICAL		B. PSYCHOPHYSICAL					C. PSYCHOLOGICAL					
	Hue Simultaneous Contrast	After-image	Temperature	Motion	Size	Density	Sound	Emotion	Action	Gender	Drama	Sophistication	Age
Light aqua	pale red-oranges	faint, if any	cool	medium-advance	enlarge	light	quiet	refreshing	medium-active	medium	medium	sophisticated	medium-young
Turquoise	red-oranges	pale red-oranges	medium-cool	advance	enlarge	medium-heavy	loud	smooth	active	medium-masculine	dramatic	sophisticated	medium-young
Teal	red-oranges	red-oranges	cool	recede	reduce	medium-heavy	medium-soft	soothing	medium-quiet	medium-masculine	subtle	sophisticated	medium
Baby blue	oranges	faint, if any	cool	advance	enlarge	light	soft	peaceful	quiet	masculine	subtle	simple	young
Royal blue	oranges	oranges	medium-cool	medium-advance	medium-enlarge	medium-heavy	medium-loud	calm	medium-active	masculine	bold	simple	medium-mature
Navy	oranges	oranges	cool	recede	reduce	heavy	soft	serene	quiet	masculine	subtle	simple	mature
Orchid	soft yellows	faint, if any	cool	medium-advance	enlarge	medium-light	soft	tranquil	quiet	medium-feminine	subtle	sophisticated	mature
Royal purple	yellows	yellows	medium-cool	advance	medium-enlarge	medium-heavy	medium-loud	stately	medium-quiet	medium-masculine	dramatic	sophisticated	mature
Fuchsia	yellow-greens	yellow-greens	warm	advance	enlarge	medium-heavy	medium-loud	playful	active	medium-feminine	dramatic	sophisticated	mature
Wine	yellow-greens	faint yellow-greens	warm	recede	reduce	heavy	quiet	enigma	quiet	feminine	subtle	sophisticated	mature
Beige	faint blues	faint, if any	medium-warm	advance	enlarge	light	quiet	casual	medium-quiet	medium-masculine	subtle	simple	medium-young
Brown	soft blues	faint, if any	warm	recede	reduce	heavy	quiet	natural	quiet	medium-masculine	subtle	simple	mature
Black	lightens	white	warm	recede	reduce	heavy	quiet	dignified	quiet	masculine	dramatic	sophisticated	mature
White	darkens	black	cool	advance	enlarge	light	medium	joy	active	feminine	dramatic	simple	young

ences colors of smaller areas; so in Figures 8-11 to 8-16 and 8-19 to 8-22, the background frames "push" the central color, making smaller identical colors appear different, differing colors appear alike, or exaggerating actual differences. Simultaneous contrast is perhaps the most powerful and useful illusion in the color magician's repertoire, with many applications. In clothing use, garment colors usually "push" skin and hair colors, making the wearer look lighter, darker, brighter, duller, or like a particular hue. Since many hue effects either seem to push analogous hues apart or strengthen complementary effects, keep Prang wheel (Figure 8-2) hue relationships in mind, and verify them on the wheel as you explore. Sometimes differing side effects tag along with main effects, and sometimes more than one illusion may be operating in the same area. Some clothing examples may be desired; others avoided.

I. **Hue. Effects of differing hues push each other apart on the wheel *toward* the complement of the dominating hue,** but do not necessarily look *like* it.

   A. **Effect: A hue gives the effect of its complement to a very dulled color or neutral** (Figure 8-11). The green of (a) makes the center grey seem pinkish; the pink of (b) makes the same grey seem greenish; and the blue-green of (c) brightens the red-orange hint in the dull beige.

   Clothing example: *This is one of the most important effects in clothing color use.* The secret is to *choose the hue effect desired, then wear its complement.* The dulled oranges of skin and hair are very subject to clothing color complementary effect—the duller the skin or hair, the more susceptible. The right blue-green or blue enriches skin oranges. Avoid strong complements of hues that make you appear unhealthy. Red may give skin or hair a greenish tinge; the right green will make it more rosy. Violet brightens blond hair, but may

make skin more sallow. Exceptions do occur when a clothing color reflects up into the face, and it picks up that color, but the complementary effect is far more common.

   B. **Effect: Touching complements intensify each other.** Look only at Figure 8-12b and see how the red energizes the green and vice versa. Each seems more brilliant than if it were alone.

   Clothing example: A violet bodice brightens blond hair, a green top intensifies a red sunburn, and blue brightens orange-based skin.

   C. **Effect: Contrasting hues seem nearly complementary** (Figures 8-12a and c). The blue-green of 8-12a pushes its center bluish-red toward its red-orange complement. The yellow-green of 8-12c pushes its center red-orange toward its red-violet complement. Each dominating hue pushes toward its complement.

   Clothing example: A blue top pushes "red" hair toward orange, a blue-violet one makes blond hair more golden, and green pushes red-orange skin toward red. All dominating hues are pushing *toward* their complements.

   D. **Effect: Closely related (analogous) hues push each other apart** (Figure 8-13a). The blue-green makes the yellow-green seem more yellow, and the yellow-green pushes the blue-green toward blue, accenting their differences. However, inserting the missing intervening green ties the related greens together, emphasizing their similarities, an effect Arnheim calls "adaptation"[28] (Figure 8-13b).

   Clothing example: Pure red pushes red-orange hair toward orange; yellow-orange will push it toward red. Fuchsia may make pink skin seem

_____

[28]Arnheim, *Art and Visual Perception,* p. 354.

orange; red-orange pushes an orange skin toward yellow. Orange may push pale blond hair to look yellow-greenish, while a yellow-green may help it seem more golden.

E. **Effect: Identical hues may look different** (Figure 8-14). The yellow-green background of 8-14a pushes its red toward red-violet (y-g complement), while the blue-green of (b) pushes its red toward red-orange (b-g complement), making the reds appear different, even though they are alike.

   Clothing example: Contrasting collar and sleeve hues might make identical face and arm colors appear different.

F. **Effect: Differing hues may appear alike** (Figure 8-12). The blue-green background of 8-12a pushes its bluish red center toward red-orange (complement of b-g) to look like the red in (b), the yellow-green background of (c) pushes its orangish-red center toward red-violet (complement of y-g), again appearing like the (b) red. Yet a white mask with a hole over each red shows each red to be different.

   Clothing example: Slightly differing lipstick and nail polish colors could appear alike against slightly different face and hand skin colors.

II. **Value. Value contrast is the most powerful effect on human perception; light and dark are the first noticed visual distinctions, and are easily exaggerated. Effects of differing values push each other apart, increasing apparent differences.** Light values make darker ones appear even darker, and darker values lighten lighter ones. As with hue, differing values can be made to seem alike, and identical ones different.

A. **Effect: Light values darken darker ones further; and darker values lighten lighter ones** (Figures 8-15, 8-16). The light frame of Figure 8-15a makes its lighter center seem darker, and the dark frame of (b) makes its darker center lighter, making both centers appear identical. However, the center of (a) is lighter and (b) darker. The light frame of Figure 8-16a pushes its center darker, and the frame in (b) makes its center seem lighter than the center in (a). However, the centers are identical.

   Clothing example: Very dark values next to the face will lighten skin and hair; very light values darken skin and hair.

B. **Effect: Extreme value contrasts overwhelm hue perceptions; close values accent hue differences** (Figure 8-19). Value contrast is powerful and must be handled with care. The initial impact of Figure 8-19a is dark against light; awareness of the dark as a violet hue comes later. However in (b), where values are both dark, the violet hue is noticed sooner and seems lighter and brighter. Similar values make hue differences more apparent.

   Clothing examples: People need some value contrast for interest. Too extreme contrast seems stark and draining; too little is bland and boring. The secret is to *use enough value contrast for interest but not enough to overwhelm.* Absolute white against very dark skin or hair blackens them and overwhelms skin or hair hues. Stark black against very light skin or hair drains the skin and pales the hair. An ecru against the dark, or navy against the light keeps dramatic contrast, but with a softer touch; so off-white or contrasting collars or scarves between bodice and face may be flattering.

   Many people have natural, "built-in" value contrast: lighter skin/darker hair, or the reverse, and needn't depend on clothing to provide value contrast. Those with little natural value contrast (light skin/light hair or dark skin/dark hair), must depend on clothing to provide it. Certain close value relationships can be subtle, since they heighten hue distinctions, but may be risky if they invite unintended comparisons. Pure white may make teeth appear dingy or eyes bloodshot, or nearly white hair dirty. Pure black may make nearly black hair seem reddish, brown, or dull. Very light or dark clothes accent the figure against our daily multicolored background, while moderate values blend less conspicuously.

III. **Intensity. Differing intensities push each other apart, increasing apparent differences,** whether in the same or a different hue. They are powerful since intensity influences how healthy or ill we look.

   A. **Effect: In the same hue, a bright intensity makes a dull one seem duller; dull intensity further brightens brighter ones** (Figures 8-20 and 8-21). The bright blue-green background of 8-20c further dulls its center blue-green, and its dull center brightens the frame. Similarly, the bright green frame of 8-21a dulls its center further, and the dull center further brightens the frame.

   Clothing example: The secret is that *the duller the skin or hair intensity, the more subject it is to dulling by brighter colors; the brighter the personal coloration, the brighter the clothing colors it can sustain without being dulled.* Because skin colors are dulled versions of oranges, bright oranges usually further dull and drain low-intensity skin and hair browns and beiges. Conversely, just the right paled beige, sand, or soft brown, duller than skin or hair, may brighten it because the duller clothing color may brighten the skin or hair color. This effect is highly individualized because it depends upon each person's skin and hair intensity levels.

   B. **Effect: Complements intensify each other** (Figures 8-12b, 8-20, and 8-21). Hue simultaneous contrast showed that complements also intensify each other (Figure 8-12b). Here the intensity dimension shows that contrasting hues are critical in brightening duller intensities or making differing intensities appear alike or identical ones different. In Figure 8-20 the three center intensities of blue-green look alike, but the center of (a) is dullest, (b) brighter, and (c) brightest. They appear alike because the complementary frame of (a) brightens its center, and the bright frame of (c) dulls its same-hue center. Conversely, the centers in Figure 8-21 are identical, but the center in (a) is dulled by the brighter frame of the same hue. The (b) center appears brighter because its complementary frame brightens it. So complements can help brighten a dulled color.

   Clothing example: Since complementary hues brighten dull colors, one would wear the complement of the skin or hair color one wishes to brighten. An additional intensity factor subdues the complement to enliven the skin or hair color even more. A bright blue complement might overwhelm a pale beige skin, but a soft sky blue could give it new life. Royal purple could drain pale blond hair, but quiet amethyst might enrich it. A gentle jade green could brighten pink skin, and aqua could warm a cool brown skin. Rich, bright skin or hair can use brighter clothing colors without being drained than low-intensity skin or hair can. Individual variations of intensity make clothing color selections very individual.

After-Image

After-images or "successive contrast" occur *after* extended exposure, not during it (as in "simultaneous contrast"), unless we view something for a long time. Color after-images are negative: we see the opposite quality of the stimulus. They apply mostly to hue and value, and generally reinforce the effects of simultaneous contrasts because they also increase apparent opposites. The A parts in Tables' 8-1, 8-2, and 8-3 after-image column show that after-image hue and intensity effects are also complementary, and value effects create opposites. Bright colors usually give pale after-images, but they are visible enough to affect apparent personal or clothing color. Pale, medium value, dull intensities give weak, if any, after-images. For each experiment in Figure 8-23, stare at the stimulus color for about twenty seconds. After-images in clothing use need deft handling for intended effects because, whether it is plain or patterned, the after-image follows wherever you look until it fades.

I. **Hue. Negative hue after-images create complementary effects.**
   A. **Effect: A hue stimulates the after-image of its complement against white** (Figure 8-23a and b). Hue after-images appear as pigment theory complements of the stimulus hue. Stare at the center dot of the green in Figure 8-23a, then at the dot in (b), and a pink square emerges.
   Clothing example: A bright green jacket makes its white trim look pinkish; a purple skirt might make a white blouse look yellowish.
   B. **Effect: An after-image hue mixes visually with any surface hue, giving a color that is a combination of the two** (Figure 8-23a and c). Stare at the center dot in the green (a), then at the dot in the yellow of (c). An orangish after-image emerges as an overlay because the pink after-image of green is mixing visually with the yellow surface to give yellow-orange. (If you are unsure, look at the lower right dot in (c), and the overlapping after-image is part yellow-orange and part pink.) Reverse

that by staring at yellow (c), then at green (a), and the orchid after-image of yellow gives a bluish tinge to the green. Look at the lower right dot in (a) to see the overlap difference.
   Clothing example: Clothing after-images are usually seen against skin or a clothing color; so remember the complement of any bright hue worn. The orange after-image of a blue top brightens skin and hair, but the blue after-image of a bright orange is dulling.
   C. **Effect: With extended viewing, a complementary after-image dulls the stimulus hue** (Figure 8-23). As the eye tires, the complementary after-image develops as an overlay, dulling the original hue. Stare at the dot in green (a) of Figure 8-23, then at (b) till the pink appears, then back at (a) to see the green dull. Use the lower right dot in (a) to check the difference.
   Clothing example: Prolonged viewing of a bright garment will dull the color. To control the effect, break up bright colors in a print, or confine bright colors to small areas and use quiet colors for larger areas.

II. **Value. Negative value after-images create effects opposite the stimulus.** Mid-range values rarely produce after-images.
   A. **Effect: An extreme value (dark or light) creates the after-image of its opposite** (Figure 8-23b and d). Stare at the white dot in (d), then at the dot in (b). A triangle appears, whiter than the paper. A white triangle would produce a black one.
   Clothing example: The white after-image of a black skirt could further lighten white clothes or skin or hair; the black after-image of a white shirt could blacken dark hair or skin.
   B. **Effect: Negative value after-images mix with other surface colors** (Figure 8-23c and d). Stare at the white dot in (d), then at the dot in

yellow (c). The part of the yellow square covered by the triangle seems lighter from the white after-image of the black.

Clothing example: Dark after-images of white garments darken and dull skin, hair, and other clothing colors; white after-images of black lighten and dull them. To control the illusion, control the size of extreme value areas, or modify the values.

III. **Intensity. Negative after-images influence color intensity** (Figure 8-23). Negative after-images occur with bright hues and extreme values, rarely with dull colors or moderate values.

A. **Effect: Complementary hue after-images dull the hue being viewed and brighten its complement.** The pink after-image of green in Figure 8-23a dulls a green, but brightens a red. Large areas of bright color become visually tiring and create complementary after-images which dilute the surface color.

Clothing example: The orange after-image of a bright blue sweater brightens the skin, but may dull the blue sweater itself.

B. **Effect: Negative value after-images may dull a color** (Figure 8-23). The overlay of black or white after-images would dull, as well as darken or lighten, a color.

Clothing example: Black or white after-images could dull the skin or hair, or another clothing color.

Irradiation

I. **Value. Value irradiation occurs when perception of light areas spills over into darker areas.**

A. **Effect: Light values advance and enlarge; dark values recede and reduce** (Figure 3-31). Light colors seem to expand their object and bring it closer; dark colors shrink it and make it seem more distant.

Clothing example: Light colors will enlarge the figure areas they cover; dark colors will shrink the areas they cover, making hips look smaller or minimizing a heavy bust. A light yoke may enlarge shoulders. Similar values on each side of the figure keep one shoulder, hip, or half of the bust from appearing larger than the other.

B. **Effect: Shadows emerge at cross-points of a white grid on a black background** (Figure 3-33). No dark value to "spill into" at cross-points makes distracting compensatory shadows emerge.

Clothing example: This disturbing illusion is most likely in fabric pattern; so study a pattern before selection.

Visual Mixtures

While paint mixtures give a smooth, flat color, visual mixtures result when the eye and brain mix tiny, intermingled dots of colors yielding a vibrant, "textured" color. Artists called this "pointillism," because "points" of color mixed visually into new colors. The main clothing use for such mixtures is in textured or tweedy fabric pattern backgrounds for accents of component colors. The larger and more contrasting the "points," the greater the distance needed for mixing; they should be small enough to mix at a normal conversing distance. Colors mix visually by pigment theory, so the results are predictable.

I. **Hue. Primaries visually mix into secondaries and tertiaries; analogous or related hues merge into their intervening hue** (Figure 8-25). Compare the smooth, flat, mixed pigment green of (a) with the pointillistic blue and yellow primaries mixture of (b) and the related yellow-green and blue-green mixture of (c). How do their qualities differ? How far away from you do they merge?

II. **Value: Extreme value contrast needs greater viewing distance or smaller points to produce a visual mixture.** Very light and dark colors alone are harder to mix visually than if intervening values are included.

III. **Intensity: Complements, mixtures that include all three primaries, or black and white yield dulled visual mixtures** (as well as dulled pigment mixtures). Combining brighter and duller intensities usually dulls the dominating brighter color.

Visual mixtures can be subtle or dramatic, but careful use is needed to keep control.

PSYCHOPHYSICAL EFFECTS OF COLOR

The following color effects are often called "psychological," since they seem to affect feelings. However, since they also influence apparent physical properties, such as heat, motion, physical dimensions, and density, they appear here as "psychophysical"; and those that affect only moods, emotions, or temperament are called psychological. They arise from our associations of color with daily experiences which have become an automatic part of us so we react subconsciously.

The Psychophysical Effects of Table 8-1B show which hues, values, and intensities produce which psychophysical effects of temperature, motion, size, density, sound, and moisture. Part B of Table 8-2 (columns 2, 3, and 4) match the hue, value, or intensity quality to choose to create the specific psychophysical effects in column 1. Part B of Table 8-3 lists the psychophysical effects of twenty-seven specific common colors. These tables can help match color property choices to desired effects.

Temperature

Our experience with warm sunlight, a hot fire, or molten metals shows that most hot things are reds, oranges, and yellows. The blue of the sky, shadows in a glacier, the blue-green splash of the ocean, the violet of distant mountain peaks and mists, or the green of a forest suggest that violets, blues, and greens are cool hues. The versatility of green is a subtle glory of nature as it is composed of warm yellow and cool blue; so with more yellow it is warmer; with more blue it seems cooler. Violet also contains a warm red, and a cool blue, so a violet leaning toward red is warmer and toward blue is cooler.

Warm hues have similar effects, as do cool hues; so many of the following analyses group hues as "warm" and "cool" to avoid naming each hue every time. A warm hue complements a cool hue on the color wheel, and their effects balance each other in use. Because skin and hair colors are derived from warm oranges, warm coloration is always a part of clothing and personal appearance.

Value and intensity also suggest temperature: light values cooler and dark values warmer. They literally are, since light colors reflect light rays and dark colors absorb heat. Bright intensities also seem warmer, and dull intensities seem cooler. The chill of pale blue walls and icy mirrors of a fur salon beguiles customer interest in the warmth of fur, just as the warm reds and oranges of store walls help sell air conditioners.

Motion

Illusions of motion are most likely in fabric pattern but can occur in whole garments. Some are distracting, and some can be very effective with careful use.

I. **Hue. Certain hues or edges of adjoining hues shift distance, size, or sharpness.**
   A. **Effect: Warm hues advance; cool hues recede.** Warm hues seem to come closer; cool hues seem to drift away.
   Clothing example: Warmly hued garments or patterns seem to come forward; cool-hued ones retreat.

B. **Effect: Warm hues and white spread and merge; cool hues and black shrink and separate.** Reds, oranges, and yellows merge with each other and with white, but stand out against black; green, blue, and violet merge with each other and with black, but stand out and separate against white.[29]

Clothing example: In fabric pattern, warm hues and whites work easily into a soft blended effect. Warm hues against black or cool hues on white will look distinct.

C. **Effect: Juxtaposed bright long and short wavelength hues clash and vibrate** (Figure 8-24). Long wavelength reds focus behind the retina, short wavelength blues and violets focus in front. Bright intensities of these together clash because the lens of the eye must constantly refocus, creating a disturbing vibration known as "chromatic aberration."

Clothing example: Such fabric patterns become physically uncomfortable to view, a sensation avoidable by dulling intensities of one or more of the colors involved.

D. **Effect: Edges fade between adjacent hues of like value and intensity.** Albers calls this "vanishing boundaries."[30] The edge between pink and orchid clouds would disappear.

Clothing example: Fabric pattern adjacent hues of similar values and intensity can blend into soft, flowing effects.

II. **Value. Light values advance; dark values recede.** As with irradiation, light values seem to move forward and dark ones move away. In clothing, they can make the figure seem closer or further away.

III. **Intensity. The brighter the intensity, the more it stands out.** Although Arnheim notes that "distinctness of color depends more upon brightness than upon hue,"[31] hue is brightest only when pure, and hues have varying brightness capabilities. (See Munsell chroma.)

A. **Effect: Bright intensities advance and enlarge, dull intensities recede.** Bright intensities fly at the viewer, seeming to bring the object along and thus enlarging it. Dull intensities retreat backward.

Clothing example: To look larger, use bright intensities; to look smaller, avoid them. Intensity also has social uses. A bright garment accents the wearer in a subdued environment, a dull one is inconspicuous. Stage costumes are often bright, but a hostess dressing to blend with her decor allows attention on the guest of honor. As Küppers notes, neutrals make the wearer inconspicuous, allowing the role to dominate.[32] So store personnel in black allow focus on customers and merchandise, the grey flannel suit allows attention to business. In most Western cultures women dress in brighter colors than men (the reverse of the animal world), but fashion cycles change and eras of brighter male attire may emerge.

B. **Effect: Small areas of brightness balance larger areas of dull intensities** (Figure 8-22). Since brightness advances and dullness recedes, a small, bright area commands as much attention as a large, dull area (Figure 8-22a). Conversely, a small dull area is lost against a large bright area (Figure 8-22b).

Clothing example: Dull intensities as backgrounds and large areas balance small, advancing, bright areas, creating intensity balance. Duller in-

[29]Calvin Harlan, *Vision and Invention, A Course in Art Fundamentals* (Englewood Cliffs, N.J.: Prentice-Hall, Inc., 1970), pp. 100, 104–105.

[30]Albers, *Interaction of Color,* p. 63.

[31]Arnheim, *Art and Visual Perception,* p. 354.

[32]Küppers, *Color,* p. 12.

tensities harmonize well with more colors than do bright ones, and so are practical, versatile, and economical for major purchases like coats and suits and as background for bright accents to dress "up" or "down" an ensemble. Duller colors also lessen the risk of bright colors overwhelming lower-intensity, smaller areas of skin and hair.

Size

Size seems related to motion since colors that advance also enlarge. Nearness suggests largeness and distance smallness. Warm hues, light values, and bright intensities seem to enlarge the wearer, while cool hues and dark values seem to reduce, but dull intensities do not necessarily reduce. Birren suggests that yellow is most enlarging, then white, red, green, blue, and black most reducing.[33]

Density

Density refers to weight per volume, *regardless of size*. Dark values suggest greater density; so of two cubes the same size, a dark one seems heavier than a light one. Everyday associations of light sky above and heavy dark earth and rocks below make cool hues, light tints, and dull intensities seem light and airy; and warm hues, dark values, and bright intensities seem heavy and solid. In dress, density seems more comfortable with lighter colors higher and heavier colors lower. Large areas of heavy colors above light colors risk looking top-heavy, but small areas of a heavy color can balance larger areas of an airy color.

Sound

Orange or bright pink assail us with a loud shout, but a dark blue or grey is soft, showing our link between sight and sound. We can control "noise levels" by choosing color according to the impression desired or the occasion. Warm hues, light values, and bright intensities seem loud; cool hues, dark values, and dull intensities seem quiet and soothing. Clothing for gala and sporty events invite noisy colors, and sedate occasions quiet ones.

Moisture

Albers suggests wet-dry effects of color, with yellow-greens through blue-green as wet, and violet through red to orange as dry. Experience associates watery and misty green, blue-green, and blue with moisture, whereas red, orange, beige, and yellow easily suggest dry desert or canyons.[34] Dark values and dull intensities seem more humid; light values and bright intensities seem drier.

PSYCHOLOGICAL EFFECTS OF COLOR

Some people choose bright clothes to counter the mood of rainy, dreary weather; others choose dull colors to agree with a sullen sky. Color profoundly affects our moods, a power the sensitive designer uses to influence the mood of a garment, its wearer, and viewer. Much is written about the psychology and symbolism of color: Some works claim to assess personality traits according to color preferences; others relate color symbolism and behavior. Many such associations are culture-bound, for different colors "mean" different things in different societies as agreed by its users. No color has any inherent, intrinsic "meaning." In many Western cultures white is the bridal color, symbolizing purity; in India, red is the bridal color. Westerners use black for mourning, whereas some cultures use white. The following sections generally describe Western reactions to color.

---

[33]Birren, *Principles of Color*, p. 77.

[34]Albers, *Interaction of Color*, p. 60.

Part C of Table 8-1 shows the psychological effects of emotion, action, gender, drama, sophistication, age, and season produced by different hues, values, and intensities. Part C of Table 8-2 shows types of hues, values, and intensities to choose when creating exciting, calm, masculine, feminine, assertive, delicate, dramatic, subtle, young, or mature effects. Part C of Table 8-3 profiles these effects for selected specific colors. Using these tables in order focuses from relating general psychological effects to color qualities, to relating specific moods to specific colors.

Emotion

The full color spectrum has been orchestrated for the range of human emotions: We speak of being puce with rage or green with envy, of having the blues, of being a yellow coward. The following hue associations appear frequently.

Red. Love, passion, power, courage, primitiveness, excitement, danger, sin, sacrifice, vitality.

Red-orange. Spirit, energy, gaiety, impetuousness, strength, boldness, action.

Orange. Warmth, cheer, youthfulness, exuberance, vigor, excitement, extremism.

Yellow-orange. Happiness, prosperity, gaiety, hospitality, optimism, openness.

Yellow. Brightness, wisdom, enlightenment, happiness, cowardice, treachery, ill health, warmth.

Yellow-green. Friendship, sparkle, youth, warmth, restlessness, newness.

Green. Youth, inexperience, growth, envy, wealth, refreshment, rest, calmness.

Blue-green. Quietness, reserve, relaxation, smoothness, faithfulness.

Blue. Peace, loyalty, restraint, sincerity, conservatism, passivity, honor, serenity, gentleness.

Blue-violet. Tranquility, spiritualism, modesty, reflection, somberness, maturity, aloofness, dignity, fatigue.

Violet. Stateliness, royalty, drama, dominance, mystery, formality, melancholy, quietness.

Red-violet. Drama, perplexity, enigma, intrigue, remoteness, tension.

Brown. Casualness, warmth, tranquillity, naturalness, friendliness, humility, earthiness.

Black. Dignity, mourning, formality, death, sophistication, gloom, uncertainty, sorrow, ominousness, mystery.

Grey. Calmness, serenity, resignation, dignity, versatility, penitence.

White. Joy, hope, purity, innocence, cleanliness, spiritualism, forgiveness, love, enlightenment.

In general, cool hues, dark values, and low intensities seem calm; warm hues, light values, and bright intensities seem more outgoing.

Action

Colors evoke powerful feelings of action or passivity ranging from stimulating to relaxing. Birren reports research findings that color affects heartbeat, respiration, brain activity, and blood pressure.[35] Warm, light, and bright colors are more stimulating; cool, dark, and dull colors more relaxing. In dress, color can express an active or a quiet personality or occasion.

Gender

Color also expresses gender. Warm hues, light values, and soft intensities seem soft and feminine; cool hues, dark values, and bright intensities seem strong and masculine. Bright colors in sports uniforms are often seen as masculine. Western cultures consider pink as feminine and blue as masculine, Oriental *yin-yang* considers light colors masculine and dark colors feminine; so associations often depend on culture.

Drama

Some colors shout for attention; others beguile with subtle distinctions. Warm hues, bright intensities, and extreme contrasts of

---

[35]Birren, *Color: A Survey,* pp. 177–78.

hue, value, or intensity command attention, riveted dramatically on color and wearer. Cool hues, dull intensities, and subtle combinations of closely related hues, values, and intensities offer gentle but intriguing nuances.

Sophistication

Technologically developed societies often equate sophistication with technical complexity and primitiveness with simplicity, a tendency which can include psychological reactions to colors. Most preindustrial, natural vegetable and animal dyes gave warm colors which became known as "primitive," or "earth," colors. Fast colors in cool hues were rare, and became common only with later synthetic dyes. The technological complexity associated with them may have suggested sophistication to early users. Thus, warm hues suggested simplicity, and cooler hues sophistication.

Researchers see the Ostwald psychological primaries of pure red, yellow, green, and blue as the first colors young children notice. With more color experience people notice secondaries, and later the tertiaries. Thus, the primaries suggest simplicity, and the more complex tertiaries suggest sophistication.

Some people see bright hues as straightforward and duller colors as subtle, so bright colors seem simple, and duller intensities seem sophisticated. Light values seem "untouched" and innocent, so are often used for children's wear. Dark values and black suggest mystery, sophistication, and experience.

Age

Sophistication relates closely to age; so warm hues seem young and carefree; cool hues seem suave, experienced, and mature. Tints seem pure, young, and naive; shades seem older, smoother, and mellow. Bright intensities seem young and vivacious; dull intensities and neutrals seem subtle, serene, and mature. Children rarely wear dark, dull colors, and the elderly seldom wear bright tints. Colors that convey the exuberance of youth cannot also convey the quietness of age, but the range of color moods in between is as vast as the number of years between young and old.

Seasons

The idea of seasons echoes age and temperature. The colors of nature's stages of growth, ripening, and decay portray seasonal rise and decline. Goldstein takes the seasons through the hue spectrum, waking from cold winter blue into budding spring of blue-green and green; to the unfolding summer of green, yellow-green through yellow-orange, to the maturing autumn of orange, to red-violet, and back to the slumbering winter violet to blue.[36] In values and intensities, pastel tints suggest the freshness of spring, bright normal values the ripening of summer, and duller shades the repose of fall and winter. Spring clothing fashions are often pastels, summer colors are lively and happy, and fall fashions are dark and rich.

COLOR SCHEMES

Color schemes call upon everything you have learned so far about color aspects, names, theories, personal coloration, and effects because they combine all of them. Color schemes are structured guidelines to experiment with color harmonies, but they are not automatic guarantees of beauty that assume the artist's role or deny flexibility. None are foolproof; too many other factors enter in, such as texture, lighting, and amount and intermingling of each color. Artists are wary of rules that may usurp creativity; art without creative thinking is seldom art. But color schemes can provide a foundation for creative use of color.

[36]Harriet Goldstein and Vetta Goldstein, *Art in Everyday Life*, 4th ed. (New York: Macmillan Publishing Co., Inc., 1969), p. 176.

Formulas

Color scheme formulas show the number and wheel relationship of hues in a scheme. Schemes can be based on one to five or more hues, but several different kinds of schemes might have the same number of hues. So the formula tells both how many hues are in the scheme format and how they relate on the hue wheel. Then even one formula can create many schemes by choosing different hue combinations that fit the same pattern or formula. Figure 8-35 shows formulas and examples for nine types of color schemes using the Prang wheel.

Hues involved in any formula depend on two things: the theory used and the number of colors on the wheel. Different theories arrange hues differently. For example, the Prang complements yellow and violet (Figure 8-2) would be yellow-green and purple or yellow and purple-blue on a Munsell wheel (Figure 8-7). The following analyses use the Prang wheel (Figure 8-2), and the reader is invited to apply formulas to the Munsell wheel (Figure 8-7).

Complements stay as opposites regardless of how finely the color wheel is divided, but other formulas use different hues if there are different numbers of hues on a wheel. For example, 3 analogous hues on a 12-hue wheel might include yellow, yellow-green, and green; but on a 24- or 100-hue wheel, 3 analogous hues might include only yellow and 2 finer variations of yellow-green.

There are traditionally two types of color schemes: related and contrasting. Related color schemes use hues close to each other on the color wheel and include monochromatic and analogous types (Figure 8-35a, b); all others are contrasting, using opposing hues (Figure 8-35c–i).

A *monochromatic* color scheme uses one hue—*mono* or "one" and *chromatic* or "containing color." Such a scheme contains only value and intensity variations of one hue (Figure 8-35a). For example, a scheme based only on orange might include bright orange, beige, brown, and melon.

Analogous color schemes use two to four hues next to each other on the color wheel (Figure 8-35b). Some suggest that all hues contain the same primary; others do not. While at least two hues are needed, formulas of more than four hues on a 12-hue wheel involve contrasting hues. Despite simultaneous contrast "pushing," analogous schemes retain softening similarities.

A *complementary* color scheme uses two hues opposite each other on the color wheel (Figure 8-35c). The opposite warm and cool hues intensify each other. Several of the following color schemes are simply variations of the complementary formula.

Double complementary schemes use two adjacent hues and their complements, giving a four-hue format of two adjacent pairs of complements (Figure 8-35d). A Prang example would be yellow and yellow-green and their complements, violet and red-violet. This wording of the formula avoids the error that might result from hues adjacent to two complements not being complementary.

Adjacent complementary schemes contain two complements and one hue next to one of the complements, giving a three-hue format (Figure 8-35e). So in a yellow and violet example, the adjacent hues could be any one of four: blue-violet, red-violet, yellow-orange, or yellow-green.

Single-split complementary schemes use three hues: one hue and the hue on each side of its complement (Figure 8-35f). It begins with two complements, omits one, and takes the hue on each side of it. So starting with red-orange and blue-green, omit the red-orange and take the hue on each side—red and orange—for a three-hue format of blue-green, red, and orange.

Double-split complementary schemes have four hues: one hue on each side of two complements (Figure 8-35g). It begins with two complements, such as red and green, then blocks out both. On each side of the omitted red it uses red-orange and red-violet; on each side of the omitted green it uses blue-green and yellow-green. The resulting scheme is also two separated pairs of complements.

(a)

Type: Monochromatic
Format: 1-hue format
Formula: Variations of value and intensity of one hue

(b)

Type: Analogous
Format: 2-4-hue format
Formula: Two or more hues next to each other on the color wheel

(c)

Type: Complementary
Format: 2-hue format
Formula: Two hues opposite each other on the color wheel

Contrasting schemes

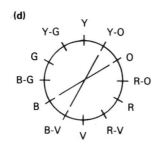

(d)

Type: Double complementary
Format: 4-hue format
Formula: Two adjacent hues and their complements

(e)

Type: Adjacent complementary
Format: 3-hue format
Formula: Two complements and one hue next to one

(f)

Type: Single split complementary
Format: 3-hue format
Formula: One hue and the hue on each side of its complement

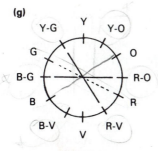

(g)

Type: Double split complementary
Format: 4-hue format
Formula: Hue on each side of two complements

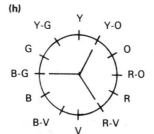

(h)

Type: Triad
Format: 3-hue format
Formula: Three hues equidistant from each other on the color wheel

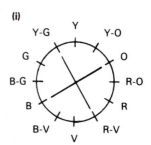

(i)

Type: Tetrad
Format: 4-hue format
Formula: Four hues equidistant from each other on the color wheel

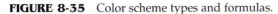

FIGURE 8-35 Color scheme types and formulas.

Triad color schemes use three hues equally spaced on the color wheel, a three-hue format (Figure 8-35h). Prang primaries make a triad color scheme, as do the secondaries. Other combinations are all tertiaries.

Tetrad schemes use four hues equally spaced on the color wheel, a four-hue format (Figure 8-35i). On a 12-hue Prang wheel this makes two equally separated pairs of complements: a primary and secondary and two complementary tertiaries.

Figure 8-35 and the preceding descriptions show that while analogous schemes can have varying numbers of base hues, monochromatic is based on one hue; complementary is based on two; adjacent complementary, single split complementary, and triad are based on three hues; and double complementary, double split complementary, and tetrad are based on four. These are the simpler but by no means all the possible color scheme formulas. Some popular ones are not found in any of these.

Color Scheme Development

Choosing the formula and a set of pure hues that fit that formula is the first step in developing a color scheme. But leaving those base hues all pure at home value and full intensity in a scheme can be overwhelming, loud, tiring, and risk vibration, and does not allow the range of illusions, psychophysical effects, and moods that color can produce (Table 8-3). The second step is to create that range of effects by varying the values and intensities of those hues to make some lighter, some darker, some duller, and some brighter. That means that a scheme may have more final "colors" than the number of hues in the scheme, because variations of those hues have been added. For example, a complementary scheme *based* on the two hues red and green might be developed into a final scheme of shell pink, garnet, mint, leaf, and hunter green, giving value and intensity variety (Figure 8-17). And these *five final colors are based on the two pure complements;* so they all *still fit the formula,* yet give a harmonious

distribution of attention and a balance of advancing and receding effects. The horizontal rows in Figure 8-17 show some value and intensity variations of the base hues in the left column. Playing with these in color schemes sharpens and shows the need for ability to trace colors to their original base hue and to make variations from that hue.

Color schemes with value and intensity variations are described as "natural order" or "inverted order" harmonies. "Natural order" harmonies use hues with light home values, such as orange, as light colors in a scheme and hues of darker home values, such as blue, as darker colors, for example melon and navy (Figure 8-17). "Inverted order" harmonies use hues with light home values as dark colors, and those with dark home values as light colors, such as dark brown and baby blue from the orange and blue-based hues.

Black, grey, and white can be included in a color scheme without distorting its formula because they are true neutrals, but the "fashion neutrals" of beige and brown add orange to the formula. A color scheme of black, grey, and white variations of neutrals is called monochromatic even though no hue is involved. Both black and white make striking accents.

Munsell and others devised mathematical formulas recommending how bright, dull, light, or dark one color should be in relation to another, and how much area each should cover. For clothing use, the key is balance. In general, larger areas of darker or duller colors balance smaller areas of lighter or brighter colors. More refined experiments can begin from that guideline.

A harmonious color scheme needs well-balanced value and intensity contrast for both physical and psychological effects; the more contrast, the more enlarging physically and the more severe psychologically. Combinations of similar values and intensities require great care and skill; successful ones may be exquisite, but failures are disastrously bland, dirty, or crass.

Several options patterned after Munsell's models for scheme color similarities and contrasts follow; some aspects are held constant and others change.

One Dimension Similar, Two Contrasting:

1. Similar hues, contrasting values and intensities
2. Similar values, contrasting hues and intensities
3. Similar intensities, contrasting hues and values

Two Dimensions Similar, One Contrasting:

4. Similar hues and values, contrasting intensities
5. Similar hues and intensities, contrasting values
6. Similar values and intensities, contrasting hues

All Dimensions Similar:

7. Similar hues, values, and intensities

All Dimensions Contrasting:

8. Contrasting hues, values, and intensities

Possibilities with contrasts and combinations of hues, values, and intensities are infinite. We have studied them separately, but they cannot be applied separately in dress; other factors such as amount and location also demand attention. For example, will one solid color cover a large skirt where its effect is isolated and distinct? Or will colors be scattered among each other, as in a print?

Rigid formulas provide no automatic solutions because fabric, garment style, and the wearer also influence color scheme use in clothing. But formulas do give ideas for using color derivations, illusions, and interactions for effective use of color in dress.

COLOR IN DRESS

Color in clothing is an individual matter for two reasons: (1) Your personal combination of skin, hair, eye, and lip coloration, and the consequent reaction of clothing colors to it, is unique to you; and (2) your personal goals—exactly *how* light, dark, bright, delicate, large, small, exciting, or calm you wish the effects to be—are also unique to you. This means that a particular combination of hue, value, and intensity into a final clothing color that is just right for you is also unique. Have you ever admired a color on a friend with skin and hair colors similar to yours, but when you held the color up to your face, you looked drab? Color is so subtle and powerful that *only a slight change in actual colors can bring tremendous changes in the effects of their interactions.* This is why clothing color choice is so delightfully, and necessarily, individual. It is also why attempts to apply exact colors from a predetermined "prescription" list to a stereotyped group of people often fail. The person who understands the color aspects, theory, illusions, and effects commands knowledge to find the most flattering hue at the right value and intensity: a becoming final color. The person who knows *how color works* and how to use it has no need for preformed lists of color prescriptions aimed at artificially stereotyped group labels; they are no substitute for color facts.

Two key steps are essential to success in using color in dress: (1) Know basic color facts and effects, and (2) apply design process in using them. The preceding material on color aspects, theories, and effects sets a solid stage for the individual use of color in dress. You begin design process when you select which effects to have as your goals: To look: More red? Orange? Lighter? Darker? Brighter? Warmer? Cooler? Larger? Smaller? Exciting? Calm? Once you have (1) decided your goal effects; (2) analyzed your own skin and hair hue, value, and intensity qualities (outside influences); (3) established criteria of specific effects to be achieved; and (4) identified the general characteristics of your chosen color(s), then experiment to refine the exact combination of hue, value, and intensity levels that makes you sparkle. Tables 8-1, 8-2, and 8-3 help narrow your choices. Then fabric swatches, a mirror, and the lighting in which you expect to wear the color will help you. As you experiment, ask yourself:

1. Will lighting be the same?
2. Will your skin be dark, light, suntanned, or pale?
3. Will your hair be sun-bleached, tinted, or otherwise different?
4. Will make-up be the same, different, or absent?
5. Will the color be used near the face or elsewhere on the figure?
6. Will it be used as dominant or accent?
7. Will it be used in a solid area, or broken up among other colors in a fabric pattern?

Changes in any one of these factors will dramatically influence the impact of a color, so try to make your experimental conditions as close to the anticipated reality as possible.

Some hold that most people can wear nearly any hue. This may be true *if* it has just the right value and intensity levels to flatter their personal coloration and is used in the right place and amount. Remember that any color is an inseparable package of hue, value, and intensity which brings along *all* of its effects: physical, psychophysical, and psychological. The strength of those effects depends on how much and where the color is used. Color can create surprises. Color the garments of the same style in Figures 8-36a–e and see the strikingly different effects produced by color differences alone. If a hue makes you look cool, but too calm, you might adjust its value for more liveliness. That is a wonderful potential of color: it can be "orchestrated" by controlling its hue, value, and intensity levels. But once the color "package" is chosen, to accept its physical effect on skin or hair color is also to accept its temperature, motion, size, weight, and moods.

Table 8-3 and Figure 8-17 can help you decide on your "color package." Although not exhaustive, the sampling suggests the variety of effects possible and can help you gain confidence in using color personally or professionally. But imprecise words are no substitute for actual colors; experiment as much as possible.

The dominant color usually occupies the largest area, and generally determines the physical and psychological effects, so it must be chosen and placed carefully. Sub-

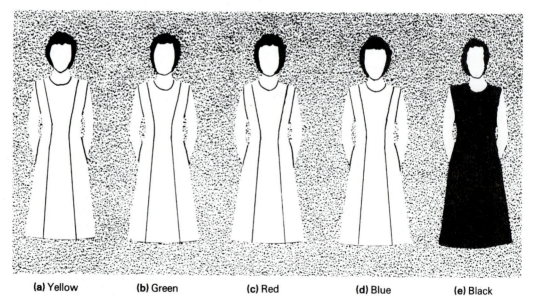

(a) Yellow   (b) Green   (c) Red   (d) Blue   (e) Black

FIGURE 8-36 Color in the garments above to see the difference color alone can make in apparent size, weight, motion, temperature, or mood.

dued colors have proven their economy and versatility.

Against the dominant color, it is usually an accent color that (1) highlights physical and psychological effects, (2) draws attention where we wish it, and (3) blends well with the dominant colors. Unity is generally easier to achieve with a few colors than with many. All colors—dominant, subordinate, and accent—must harmonize.

Different goals and criteria invite different kinds of color prescriptions. For example, a person wishing to look smaller in the hips, larger in the shoulders, to brighten the skin and look cool might choose an analogous color scheme of green, blue-green, and blue and develop it into a scheme of a navy blue skirt, a light aqua top, emerald green accessories with white accent, and a printed scarf including navy, light aqua, emerald green, and teal—four colors from three analogous base hues (Figures 8-2 and 8-17). The base hues are all cool, and complementary to skin orange; there is variation in value and intensity; the slimming dark, dull navy is below the enlarging, lighter values on top. The brighter intensities are small accents that balance the larger, duller areas and direct attention where it is desired. See how Table 8-4 summarizes this in the design process.

One of the joys of playing with color in dress is the freedom of color choice. Arnheim notes that usually the "appearance and expression of color are modified by subject matter," and are "perceived in relation to the 'normal' color of the object."[37] But since clothing has no "normal" or "abnormal" color, we are free to revel in the whole spectrum.

SUMMARY

Color is external event and internal sensation, the perception and interpretation of visible light wavelengths from red through the spectrum to violet, as they come from a light source or reflect from a surface. All color has three aspects: *hue,* the position in the spectrum or on a color wheel; *value,* the lightness or darkness of a hue; and *intensity,* the brightness or dullness of a hue. Black, greys, and white are true neutrals. Primary hues are those from which all other hues may be mixed; secondary hues are equal mixtures of two primaries; tertiaries, or intermediate hues, are those between primaries and secondaries. Analogous, or adjacent, hues are next to each other on a wheel, and complements are opposite each other. We perceive different colors because

TABLE 8-4 *Summary Design Process Chart for Color Example*

1. General color goal:	Woman's cool, flattering summer outfit
2. Relevant outside influences:	Dull complexion, large hips, narrow shoulders, warm season
3. Criteria:	Brighten complexion, reduce hips, enlarge shoulders, appear cool

4. Plan: *Color selection*
    and placement   *Reason*

- Analogous color scheme: green, blue-green, blue
  Variations: emerald green, light aqua, teal,
  navy, white accents
	- Cool hues for summer, flattering to personal
	  coloration

- Navy skirt	- Dark value to reduce hips
- Light aqua top	- Light value to enlarge shoulder area, low-intensity blue-green complement of skin to brighten it

- Small accessories and scarf of aqua, teal, navy,
  and white
	- Cool, to give variety, direct attention where
	  desired

---

[37]Arnheim, *Art and Visual Perception*, p. 337.

of the functions of rods and cones in the eye responding to different wavelengths and levels of illumination.

There are many theories concerning color. The light, or physical, theory is additive, because adding primaries together adds more wavelengths and results in white light. Its primaries are red, green, and blue. Pigment theories are subtractive, because combining primaries allows more light waves to be absorbed, or subtracted out, in the pigment, and the result is grey or black. Primaries in the Prang theory are red, yellow, and blue; Munsell's principal hues are red, yellow, green, blue, and purple. The Ostwald or psychological theory deals mostly with how color is perceived; its major hues are red, green, blue, and yellow. Küppers' rhombohedron combines the light and pigment theories. Human coloration of skin and hair ranges in variations of red-oranges to yellow-oranges.

Physical effects of color include simultaneous contrast, motion, after-images, irradiation, chromatic aberration, adaptation, and visual mixtures from pointillism. Psychophysical effects include temperature, motion, size, density, sound, and moisture. Psychological effects include emotion, action or relaxation, gender, drama, sophistication, age, and seasons.

Color schemes suggest various combinations. Related color scheme formulas are monochromatic and analogous; contrasting color schemes include complementary, double complementary, adjacent complementary, single-split complementary, double-split complementary, triad, and tetrad. Well-balanced schemes need some hues lightened, others darkened, or some dulled, giving attractive variety. Color, well used, is a powerful and beautiful design element that enriches all clothing.

CLASS ACTIVITIES

1. If the class has not had previous systematic color experience, the instructor may demonstrate and then help students do a (a) Prang 12-hue wheel from 3 primaries (3 primaries, r, y, b; 3 secondaries, o, g, v; 6 tertiaries); (b) value scale; (c) intensity scale from primary through neutral to secondary complement. Use an easy, water-based paint, and make all step differences equal. Figures 8-2, 8-3, and 8-4 can guide chart structure, but do not try to match colors; make them consistent for the kind of paint used.

2. Choose a pure hue, one tint, one shade, and one dulled intensity of it, and note their Munsell notations. Look in magazines and newspaper ads and other "popular" writing to see how many different word names are attributed to that color. For the buying public, which is the most informative? Why?

3. Choose a color from the left column of Table 8-3. Choose one physical, psychophysical, or psychological effect that you would like to change. Keeping the same base hue, how would you change the value and/or intensity to create the desired effect? How might you change value and/or intensity to create the opposite effect?

4. Have a partner identify and analyze the hue, and the value and intensity levels of your skin and hair. If Munsell charts for that purpose are available, use those. Or use Figure 8-18 to find the closest color to your skin or hair. Then see where that color is positioned on the chart according to the center hue column, horizontal value rows, and high (right) or lower (left) intensity sides. Then make your own formula: y-o to o-r for base hue, number 2 (dark, at outer edges) to 8 (light, near center) for value, and H for higher (right side) or L for lower (left side) intensity. Are you satisfied being that color? Or would you rather look more reddish? Yellowish? Lighter? Darker? Brighter? Duller? Identifying your personal color location gives you a clue to deciding and achieving your desired effect. Will you choose clothing colors that are complementary

or analogous to your own base hue? Lighter to make you look darker? Or vice versa? Duller to look brighter? Or vice versa? Knowing your own color(s) gives a basis to explore clothing colors.

5. Using Tables 8-1 and 8-2; your knowledge of physical, psychophysical, and psychological effects; knowledge of your own coloration; ½ yard each of plain, nonshiny fabrics in various colors; and various kinds of lighting; hold each fabric under your chin to experiment with various colors to identify and analyze their effects on your skin, hair, and eyes.

6. With students of varying skin, hair, and eye coloration, use the previous exercise to demonstrate differing hue, value, and intensity simultaneous contrast, afterimage, and irradiation effects.

7. Choose a color that is flattering for your skin, but poor for your hair (or vice versa). How might you modify the color to be attractive with both skin and hair? Or to accent one and downplay the other? Experiment with other techniques such as creating a break with an off-white at the neckline. What happens? Why?

8. With the class in groups, assign each group a color scheme formula. Provide about 5 by 8 inch paper color swatches in a variety of values and intensities in each of the twelve Prang hue families. When the groups have developed a well-balanced (light/dark, bright/dull) color scheme based on hues fitting that formula, invite other groups to trace the derivations of those colors to their base hues and identify the type of scheme used.

9. Compare the Prang and Munsell wheels for complements and analogous hues (Figures 8-2, 8-7). Using different standard color scheme formulas (Figure 8-35), compare the actual hues involved for Prang and Munsell theories.

10. With a fabric pattern sample, identify the colors in it. Trace those final color de-

rivations to their base hues, and identify and look at their relationship on the Prang wheel to identify and analyze their color scheme formula. Using the same formula but different hues, create a new color scheme.

11. Develop the boldest (or most subtle) color scheme you can. What makes it so? Select other moods and develop other color schemes to create them.

12. Select hues that do not fit any of the color scheme formulas in Figure 8-35, and create a well-balanced color scheme from them. What makes it successful?

13. Using ½ yard fabric samples, choose two analogous or contrasting colors. Begin with a sample of each in solid color. Then, with fabric patterns using those colors broken into progressively smaller units in each fabric, analyze the changes in effects and color units. What happens when they reach pointillism?

14. Select and develop a color scheme for one or more of the following clients. Indicate the area/amount and figure location of each color, why you chose it, and what effects you predict.

    a. Man with dark brown skin, thin figure wishes to look dark, heavier, and shorter, in garment for casual youthful, summer occasion.

    b. Elderly woman with sallow skin, grey hair, narrow shoulders, largish hips, wishes to look livelier, younger, with wider shoulders, and smaller hips in garment for summer casual wear.

    c. Tall, thin teenager with acne and red hair wishes to direct attention away from skin and to hair, to look shorter but not heavier in outfit for winter school wear.

    d. Dress firm caters to half-size matrons' wear; personal coloration of potential customers unknown; it can be assumed customers wish to look taller and slimmer.

9 *Texture*

DEFINITION AND CONCEPT

Texture is the visible and tangible structure of a surface or substance. It has three aspects: (1) the tactile qualities of a surface, (2) the tactile qualities of a manipulated three-dimensional substance, and (3) the visual qualities of surface and substance.

Texture is the very medium, the tangible substance from which clothing is made; and it appeals to three of our senses: touch, sight, and hearing. These reasons make alertness to *functional* design especially important in the study of texture.

A baby putting a shoe in its mouth is discovering by trial and error which sense organs are appropriate for examining which kinds of substances. He or she will learn that shoes are to be felt and seen but not tasted. We learn about texture by everything we touch from infancy on. With experience we develop a tactile memory: merely seeing a familiar surface or substance stimulates a memory of its feel. So we describe something as "velvety" because it looks as though it would feel like velvet. But reliability of tactile memory dwindles as new fibers imitate familiar fabrics, and new textures emerge. What looks like linen or suede may be a synthetic with a very different feel, so fabric users must educate their fingertips as well as their eyes and minds.

Most studies of textiles focus on fabric composition and characteristics; however, this study focuses on aesthetic and performance qualities of texture as they work into a garment structure. This means knowing surface qualities, hand, light reactions, and their four determinants, upon which thousands of qualities depend.

DETERMINANTS OF TEXTURE

All fabric texture variations from sheer chiffon to bulky fleece to sturdy canvas depend on only four factors: fiber content, yarn structure, fabric structure, and finishes. Each affects the visual, tactile, and performance qualities of a texture.

Fiber Content

Fiber is the *chemical substance* from which yarn and fabrics are made. Fiber length, shape, chemical composition, and performance properties influence final fabric resilience, absorbency, heat conductivity, shrinkage control, washability and resistance to insects, heat and fire, acids and alkalis, and mold or mildew, and how they perform in a garment. Natural fibers include cotton, linen, wool, silk, ramie, alpaca, and other minor fibers; man-made and synthetic fibers include rayon, acetate, nylon, polyester, acrylics, fiberglas, olefin, and others. Long fibers, such as silk and synthetics, are *filaments* and give a shiny, smooth, cool touch, and sometimes stronger fabrics. Short fibers, such as cotton, wool, and cut synthetics, are *staples* and give a relatively dull, rough, fuzzy, warm touch, and sometimes weaker fabrics. Extremely fine polyester "microfibers" are finer than many natural fibers, yet can be very strong, durable, and bright in fabrics.[1] Some fibers or combinations of fibers contribute to static electricity, which makes fabrics cling.

Yarn Structure

Yarns are spun fibers, the next step in creating a fabric. Very different fibers may look similar given the same yarn structure; or the same fiber may look and perform very differently given different yarn structures. A very long, or filament, fiber yarn is generally smoother and more slippery than a fuzzy one of very short, or staple, fibers. Staple fibers laid parallel to each other before being twisted, as in worsted wool, are smoother than those left crimped and more

random, as in wool flannel. Whether one or a blend of several kinds of fibers are in a yarn also influences final texture.

Yarn twist also influences surface and hand. High twist yarns such as crepe give a pebbly surface and wrinkle resistance, or a hard-surfaced, smooth, strong, and somewhat elastic fabric. Low twist creates a shiny texture from lustrous filament fibers and a soft-surfaced fabric from fuzzy staple fibers. The S or Z direction of the twist and whether all yarns twist in the same direction or some twist S and some Z, as in crepes, influences surface and hand of a texture.

The number of ply, or strands a yarn has twisted together, influences textural thickness and strength. Generally the higher the ply, the stronger the yarn. The thickness of a yarn influences how many yarns can be worked into an inch, and consequently the fineness or coarseness of a texture.

Novelty yarns create interesting surface contours, such as the random bulging ribs produced by slub yarns. Yarns of more than one type of strand, ply, thickness, and/or degree or direction of twist such as bouclé, nub, flake, spiral, or ratiné, create a variety of bumpy, curly, or fuzzy surfaces and insulating air pockets in the fabric itself. Such surfaces are visually interesting, but often functionally vulnerable because uneven twist and thickness make uneven strength, and loops are easy to snag. Elasticized yarns allow stretchy fabrics. Compare the appearances of the yarns in Figures 9-1 and 9-2.

Fabric Structure

Types of Structures. Fabric structure is the interlocking of fibrous yarns into a flat fabric. Fabric structure provides the most easily seen differences in texture. Structures could be film, felt (fibers adhering directly to each other without first being spun), lace, net, braid, crochet, macramé, knit, or woven (Figures 9-1, 9-2). Knits could be single, double, weft, warp, or pile knits. Woven structure could be plain, twill, satin, dobby, leno, Jacquard, loop pile, cut pile, double, or other.

---

[1]"Fabric Innovations: The New Microfibers," *Vogue Patterns*, January/February 1991, p. 30.

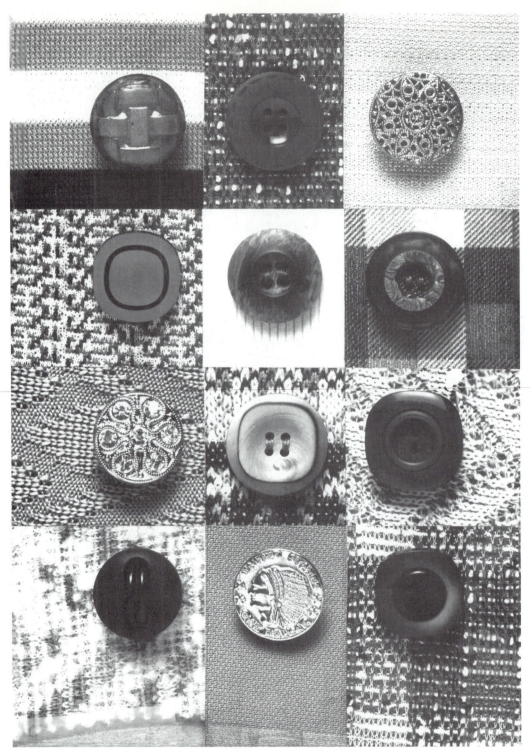

FIGURE 9-1. Different fabric structures, notions, and trims can give a magnificent range of surface contours, "textured" effects, and light reactions. Which fabrics are woven and which are knitted? Which appear "textured," and which appear "patterned"? (Courtesy of La Mode buttons by B. Blumenthal & Company.)

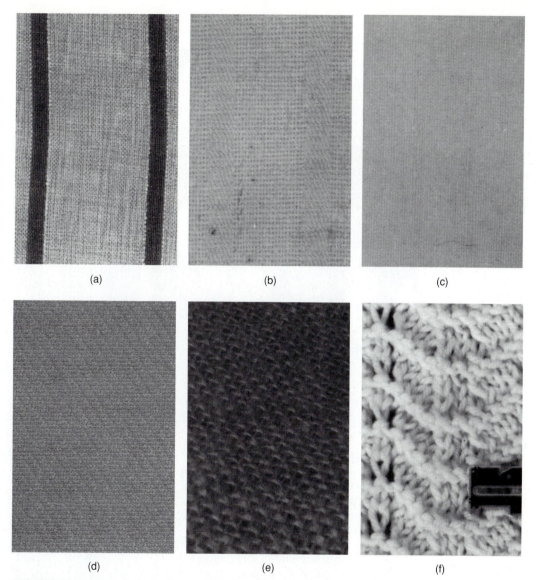

(a)   (b)   (c)

(d)   (e)   (f)

FIGURE 9-2. Density depends on both the fineness or coarseness of the yarn and the openness or compactness of the fabric structure. (a) Fine yarn, medium weave. (b) Medium yarn, tight and loose weave. (c) Fine yarn, fine weave. (d) Medium yarn, fine knit. (Photos courtesy of Celanese Fibers Marketing Company.) (e) Coarse yarn, loose weave, burlap. (f) Coarse yarn, coarse knit. (Photos courtesy of Belding Lily Company, subsidiary Belding Heminway Company, Inc., Box B, Shelby, N.C.)

Weaving generally gives the strongest and most stable fabric structure and least stretch. The warp, or lengthwise yarns, can withstand the most tension. Weft (woof, or filling), the crosswise yarns, can take less strain than warp. "Balanced" fabrics have similar numbers of warp and weft yarns per square inch and are stronger than unbalanced weaves. Their stability necessi-

tates darts, seams, and other construction techniques to shape the flat fabric to the body's contours (Figures 9-3, 9-4).

Knitted fabrics are more flexible, wrinkle resistant, and stretchy, qualities which allow conforming to body contours with few seams or darts (Figures 9-3, 9-4). Knitted fabrics will stretch, some horizontally or vertically, some both, but their stable,

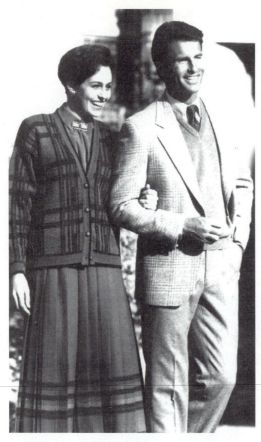

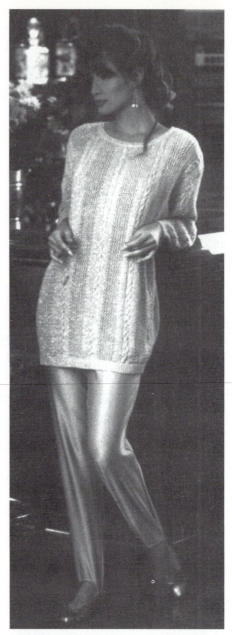

FIGURE 9-3. Woven fabric is stable and needs garment pieces cut in shapes with seams and darts to conform to body contours and hold the style. Wiry, firm textures make good tailored wear as they retain sharp edges and shape, as in the man's jacket; and hold sharp creases, as in his pants and her skirt pleats. The knitted fabric structure gives a softer, more flexible texture as in both sweaters. (Courtesy of Pendleton Woolen Mills.)

stitched seams may break. Some knits may stretch and sag or bag, and so may need seams or linings for stability in skirt seats and pants. Nonwoven fabrics like knits generally can withstand less stress. Lace, net, crochet, and other fragile structures with yarns constantly changing directions have little tensile strength (Figure 9-5).

Grain. The direction of the yarns, or "grain," is critical to the way a fabric works into a garment. Both nonwoven and woven fabrics

FIGURE 9-4. Knitted fabric structures are flexible and stretchy, allowing them to conform to figure contours with fewer structural garment seams or darts. Knit pants of elasticized yarns are stretchy and figure conforming. Knit weights may vary from fine yarns and thin density, as in the pants, to thick yarns and bulky structure, as in the sweater. Here synthetic filament fibers contribute a lustrous shine light reaction. (Courtesy of Mark, Fore & Strike.)

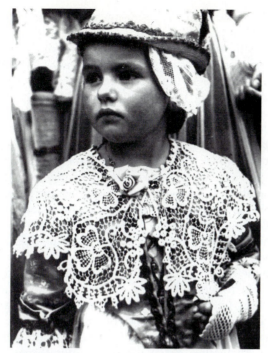

FIGURE 9-5. The porous lace cape and net mesh gloves in this child's traditional costume from Valais-aeria in Switzerland gives a delicate effect. The lace and mesh lend themselves to ceremonial uses because their yarns of constantly changing direction have little tensile strength and cannot withstand stretching, and the open structure could snag easily. Their delicacy makes them ideal for dressy, non-stressful occasions. (Courtesy of the Swiss National Tourist Office.)

have "grain" as they behave differently when used at different angles. Woven fabric warp is strongest and should go in the direction that receives the greatest stress in a garment, usually vertical: the lengthwise pull of a skirt when seated, of pants when knees bend, of sleeves when elbows bend, and of bodices when shoulders reach or stretch. Fabrics on the bias—the diagonal between lengthwise and crosswise yarns—are more flexible and drapable, allowing soft, elegant effects, but require care to avoid sagging hemlines or droopiness. Woven fabrics "on grain," with lengthwise and crosswise yarns straight and interwoven at right angles, net,

lace, and felt lack this flexibility of grain, but hold crisp styles better.

For a smooth, even hang, grain should enter a seam or dart at the same or similar angle on each side (Figure 9-6a). If one side is more bias than the other, the bias side may pucker or flop toward itself because it has less stability (Figure 9-6b). The straight of the grain is usually at the center of any garment piece so each edge is equally off grain, and seam angles are even. Grain use is critical to shaping and draped effects.

Combinations of Fabric Structures. These create new textural potentials but need caution. Two fabrics bonded or laminated together produce a thicker, firmer texture; but their joining must be permanent and on-grain and their care and performance qualities compatible. They rarely serve well for stress uses. Tufting, embroidery, shirring, and swivel weave motifs add surface interest but reduce resistance to surface friction.

Finishes

Finishes are chemical or mechanical treatments which use heat, pressure, and/or chemicals to affect the fabric surface or penetrate the fibers. Some finishes are primarily for appearance: Bleaching whitens a fabric, embossing produces raised patterns, and flocking creates a fuzzy surface. Ciréing, glazing, schreinering, and calendering all increase the sheen of a surface. Moiréing gives a lus-

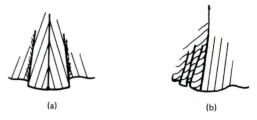

FIGURE 9-6. Grain entering a seam at the same angle on both sides helps a flare hang evenly (a); grain entering at uneven angles makes the seam and flare fall toward the side of greater bias (b).

trous pattern resembling water ripples, and dye adds color.

Other finishes affect both visual and tactile qualities: Singeing increases surface smoothness, and tentering keeps the fabric even and on-grain. Napping provides a soft fuzziness, and shearing gives an even surface to cut-pile fabrics. Puckering may result from embossing or chemicals. Sizing increases stiffness and sometimes shine.

Functional finishes include soil release, wash and wear, mercerizing, permanent press, weighting, heat reflecting, antiseptic, antistatic, absorbency, and resistance to wrinkles, shrinking, slippage, water, moths, mildew, and flame. "Polytherm" chemical finish attached to fibers and triggered by body heat can either warm or cool the wearer.[2] Fulling, crabbing, and decating primarily improve the texture and performance of wool. With their advantages, finishes may create some undesired side effects, which the industry works to reduce.

Combining Determinants

A given fiber spun into a given yarn interlocked into a given fabric structure treated with a given finish creates a given, specific, final fabric with a given name that usually reflects its fiber content and fabric structure such as "nylon chiffon," "polyester double knit," or "wool gabardine." Changing any one determinant creates a totally different final fabric texture, even though the other three determinants are held constant. For example, keeping the fiber, yarn, and finish the same in three fabrics, but changing fabric structure could yield final textures as different as a firm, woven denim; a stretchy knit jersey; or a porous lace. So cotton *fiber* can be made into *fabrics* of broadcloth, chambray, chiffon, organdy, plissé, voile, dimity, velveteen, corduroy, piqué, poplin, canvas, lace, net, jersey, gabardine, chintz, terry cloth, sateen, denim, and many more

---

[2]Amy West, "Hot/Cold Threads," *Popular Science,* February 1988, pp. 73–75, 116.

simply by varying yarn structure, fabric structure, and/or finishes. How does each of these fabrics differ from the others even though they are all made of cotton fiber? Conversely, a satin woven *fabric structure* could be made from silk, rayon, nylon, acetate, or polyester *fibers,* and even though they all have the same yarn and fabric structure, each will have a slightly different feel and drape because of the differing fiber content. Varying more than one determinant multiplies the possible effects greatly; so there are thousands of ways various aspects of these four determinants can be combined in a texture. Since some fabrics are imitations of others, and labeling laws require that the fiber content be given on the fabric bolt, store fabric departments should include fiber and fabric names and/or structures on their display signs.

Visual and tactile substance or structural textural interest may be added to fabric before or during garment construction. A flat, smooth fabric invites textural manipulation into smocking, shirring, gathers, pleats, puckers, quilting, ruffles, piping, embroidery, appliqué, or trapunto (Figures 9-7, 9-8, and 2-5 to 2-9). Natural or imitation nonfabric textures—leather, suede, bone, glass, plastic, metal, wood, pearls, shells, raffia, straw, paper, ceramics, beading, sequins, rhinestones, studs, bangles, and others—add character. Buttons alone show many nonfabric clothing textures available (Figures 9-1, 2-13).

Trims add yet another textural dimension: ribbon woven in and out of lace insertion, rick rack, braid, embroidered leather or net make creative textural combinations, but must have compatible mood, performance, and care qualities to function as one texture in use (Figures 2-10 to 2-19).

ASPECTS OF TEXTURE AND THEIR USES IN DRESS

The above four determinants of fiber content, yarn structure, fabric structure, and finishes create a vast array of fabric surface

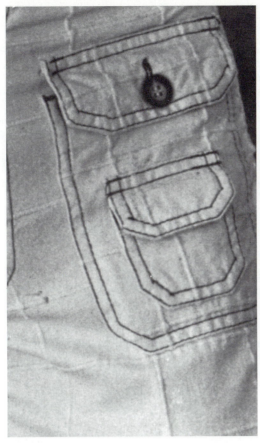

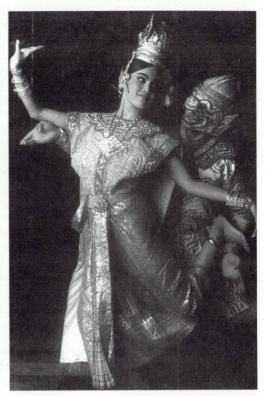

FIGURE 9-7. The fine tucks in the fabric were added before construction, and the pocket topstitching during construction, both giving textural and pattern interest to the garment. (By Campus, courtesy of Men's Fashion Association.)

FIGURE 9-8. The trapunto-like raised surfaces on the bodice and collar add textural interest as well as pattern, and the hand of the bodice fabric is stiff enough to hold its style independently of the figure in this Thai dancer's costume. The sheen of all the textures moves with her motions, emphasizing her dancing. (Courtesy of Thai Airways International Limited.)

and hand qualities and light reactions which, in turn, influence how a texture will look and perform in a garment. As you explore these qualities, relate each to its determinants. Table 9-1 lists qualities of surface and hand. Each of these can range along a continuum from low to high as shown on Table 9-2. Some ranges could have hundreds of possible steps between low and high. Surface is the introduction to a texture; so we shall begin with surface qualities and then examine properties of a total thickness.

Surface Characteristics

Surface quality is mainly two-dimensional and flat: those properties perceived by sliding the fingertips over the surface of a fabric lying flat. On the ASTM chart (Table 9-1), they are the last three qualities: surface contour, surface friction, and thermal character.

Surface contour, or divergence from planeness, refers to deviations from absolute smoothness and ranges from smooth to rough: satiny, ribbed, fleece, or other surfaces (Figure 9-1). Smoother surfaces are likely from smooth, filament *fibers* like silk and synthetics; low twist, combed, or even *yarns;* plain or satin weaves or smooth knit *fabric structures;* and glazed or singed *finishes.* Rougher surfaces are likely from fuzzy, crimped, staple *fibers* like cotton and wool; slub, ratiné, or other novelty or uncombed

TABLE 9-1. List of Terms Relating to the Hand of Fabrics*

Physical Property	Explanatory Phase	Terms to Be Used in Describing Range of Corresponding Component of Hand
Flexibility	Ease of bending	Pliable (high) to stiff (low).
Compressibility	Ease of squeezing	Soft (high) to hard (low).
Extensibility	Ease of stretching	Stretchy (high) to nonstretchy (low).
Resilience	Ability to recover from deformation	Springy (high) to limp (low). Resilience may be flexural, compressional, extensional, or torsional.
Density	Weight per unit volume (based on measurement of thickness† and fabric weight)	Compact (high) to open (low).
Surface Contour	Divergence of the surface from planeness	Rough (high) to smooth (low).
Surface Friction	Resistance to slipping offered by the surface	Harsh (high) to slippery (low).
Thermal Character	Apparent difference in temperature of the fabric and the skin of the observer touching it	Cool (high) to warm (low).

*Methods of test for evaluating properties relating to the hand of fabrics were published as information by Committee D-13 on Textiles, the latest publication being in *1965 Book of ASTM Standards,* Part 24.

†Measurements of thickness and weight are made in accordance with the procedures described in the ASTM methods for specific fabrics.

Reprinted by permission of the American Society of Testing and Materials from *ASTM Standards on Textile Materials,* Vol 7.01, Table 7, Standard D-123, Copyright 1982, p. 98.

TABLE 9-2. Ranges of Texture Surfaces, Hand, and Light Reactions

Texture Qualities:	Ranges:		
Surface Qualities:	*Low*	*to*	*High*
Surface Contour:	smooth ⟵————————⟶		rough
Surface Friction:	slippery ⟵————————⟶		harsh
Thermal Character:	warm ⟵————————⟶		cool
Qualities of Hand:			
Flexibility:	rigid ⟵————————⟶		supple
Compressibility:	hard ⟵————————⟶		soft
Extensibility:	nonstretchy ⟵————————⟶		stretchy
Resilience:	limp ⟵————————⟶		resilient
Density: yarn:	fine ⟵————————⟶		coarse
structure:	open ⟵————————⟶		compact
thickness:	thin ⟵————————⟶		thick
Light Reaction:			
Luster:	dull ⟵————————⟶		shiny
Opacity:	transparent ⟵————————⟶		opaque

yarns; "textured," novelty, coarse, or uneven pile *fabric structures;* or *finishes* such as brushing or embossing.

Functionally, a firm, tight, smooth surface generally wears better in garments likely to receive hard wear. Fuzzy surfaces catch and hold more soil but show it less. Pile surfaces are soft, but soon show wear with continued pressure or friction, or flatten to a dull white. Surfaces with floating yarns or open loops (such as satin, lace, net, and some knits) and some novelty fabrics (such as lamé and sequined fabrics) are vulnerable to snagging and friction. In general, the more yarns floating free, or the rougher or more open a surface, the more fragile the fabric. Such fabrics are usually reserved for dressy occasions where friction is less likely.

Visually, a fuzzy, rough, or coarse surface enlarges the figure and softens its silhouette where a smooth or fine surface looks hard and creates a sharp silhouette. A "textured" surface with tiny pattern filled space seems larger than a smooth, plain one with empty space. Seams may disappear in rough surfaces, giving a structurally unbroken but decoratively busy spatial effect. Table 9-3 column E compares surface contours for specific fabrics.

Surface friction refers to how surfaces slide over or catch each other with traction, and range from slippery to harsh. The fiber, yarn, structure, and finishing properties that give a texture smooth surface also contribute to slipperiness, and those that make it rough may also give it more traction and harshness. Slipperiness is necessary to slips or linings intended to slide by other garments, but slippery ski wear can be fatal to fallen skiers who slide off a cliff because their clothing has no traction on the snow.[3] Leather has more traction than cloth, a good quality for gloves.

Most textures have a right (outside) and wrong (inside) side. The inside surface of a garment is critical to its comfort and function; one that feels scratchy, sticky, rough, or "unbreathing" usually hangs in a closet. So the smoother, softer, more slippery side is usually worn next to the skin. Some garments with harsh outer surfaces use facings with the "wrong" soft side next to the skin, yet invisible outside. Table 9-3 Column F shows surface friction levels for example fabrics.

Thermal character is the apparent, independent fabric temperature compared with skin temperature. A texture "warm" to the touch has a low thermal character because of the *low difference* between fabric and skin temperature, and a "cool" texture has a high thermal character because of the high difference between fabric and skin temperature. While fuzzy yarns and rougher fabric structure determinants usually link with warm touch, and smooth yarns and fabric structures with cooler touch, the fiber content property of absorbency is a major determinant. More absorbent fibers, such as cotton and wool, are warmer to the touch, while many less absorbent synthetics, such as nylon, feel cool, even clammy, especially when moisture evaporates from their less absorbent surface. Thermal character also elicits psychological reactions such as warm coziness or cold formality. Table 9-3 Column G shows a range of thermal characters in listed fabrics.

The following are but a few of the terms that could refer to fabric surface quality:

* airy	flakey	* nubby	* scaly
* blistered	* flocked	* pebbly	scratchy
* bristly	* furrowed	* pitted	* shaggy
* bubbly	* furry	* pleated	* shirred
* bumpy	* fuzzy	* porous	silky
cool	* glassy	prickly	sleek
* corrugated	* glazed	* puckered	* slick
* cracked	* grainy	* quilted	* slippery
crepy	granular	raspy	* smooth
curly	gritty	* ribbed	* undulating
delicate	* grooved	* ridged	* uneven
downy	* hairy	* rippled	* velvety
* embossed	harsh	* rough	warm
* feathery	* leathery	* sandy	waxy
* fine	* metallic	* satiny	* woolly

*These qualities are also visible and involve light reactions.

---

[3]Susan M. Watkins, "Designing Functional Clothing," *Journal of Home Economics*, Vol. 66, No. 7 (Nov. 1974), p. 36.

Hand

Hand means the tactile qualities of a manipulable three-dimensional substance. Not just a flat surface touch, hand involves the whole fabric as it is bent, crushed, stretched, twisted, folded, squeezed, or otherwise manipulated; and as it interacts with body contours and air space, or assumes its own three-dimensional style forms.[4] Fabric hand powerfully influences apparent figure size by how it behaves in the space surrounding the body: how it hangs, gathers, drapes, pleats, or folds; how heavy, fine, or bulky it is. It includes the first five properties on the ASTM chart (Table 9-1), and its ranges are shown on Table 9-2.

Flexibility tells how supple or rigid a fabric is, and whether it will drape softly or retain a bouffant style. A crisp, stiff texture independently holds styles that will droop in a pliable jersey. A supple texture depends on body contours for support and invites gathers, draping, shirring, smocking, and soft styles that hang in graceful, fluid folds and flowing silhouettes (Figure 7-3). Wiry, firm textures hold tailored shapes, sharp edges, pressed pleats, and style contours better and are generally good for smooth styles whose shaping comes from seams and darts (Figure 9-3). Stiff or crisp textures need little support from the figure. Standing out from the body, they create bouffant silhouettes in puff or peasant sleeves, and full skirts or ruffles (Figures 6-20, 9-8).

Functionally, the very flexibility of supple textures that makes them collapse against the figure also allows body movement, and the very stiffness of rigid textures that holds independent styles also makes it necessary to allow space between the garment and body for body movement. Visually, stiff textures add volume and enlarge heavy figures even more, but may overpower small, thin figures, while thin, supple textures cling to the figure, revealing every bump or bone beneath them.

Any determinant can create a wide range of flexibilities, but woven, net, and lace fabric structures are generally more crisp, and knits are more flexible; sizing, glazed, and embossed finishes increase crispness. Table 9-3 Column H compares flexibility of listed fabrics. Review Figures 6-22 to 6-52 to see which styles need which kinds of textures to hold their shapes.

Compressibility is the way a fabric responds to squeezing. It influences whether or not a fabric will feel comfortable at body points that bend or fold, such as the elbow, hip, or knee. Cotton, silk, wool, rayon, and acrylic fibers can be very squeezable, as can knit structures and softening finishes. Jute, fiberglas, and some other synthetics are usually less squeezable, as are felt, lace, net, and some woven fabric structures, and glazed, sized, embossed, ciréd, and certain performance finishes such as wrinkle and soil resistance. Table 9-3 Column I shows which listed fabrics are more and less compressible.

Extensibility or stretchability greatly influences structural design need for shaping by seams or darts; a stretchy fabric will conform to body contours and need fewer shaping seams (Figure 9-4) than a nonstretchy one (Figure 9-3). Wool fibers, crimped and elastic yarns, and knit fabric structures have the greatest extensibility. Linen and most synthetic filament fibers and even yarns have little stretch. Woven fabric structures have some only on the bias, but felt, braid, lace, and net have little without tearing. Table 9-3 Column J compares extensibility among the example fabrics.

Resilience is the ability to spring back from squeezing, twisting, or stretching to previous form. It depends primarily on fiber content and fabric structure. Wool, nylon, and polyester are resilient fibers, and knit a resilient fabric structure. Cotton, linen, and rayon fibers in woven structures have little resilience; so they hold wrinkles. Today's busy consumer usually wants fabrics that return to their original forms, so resilience is an important functional quality.

---

[4]See Debbie Ann Gioello, *Profiling Fabrics: Properties, Performance & Construction Techniques,* Language of Fashion Series. (New York: Fairchld Publications, 1981), throughout.

Blending resilient fibers such as polyester with nonresilient fibers such as cotton in a yarn, or using wrinkle-resistant finishes helps prevent wrinkles. Table 9-3 Column K compares resilience of specific fabrics.

Density is the weight per volume of a texture. Table 9-2 shows its three components of fine to coarse yarn, open to compact fabric structure, and thin to thick thickness. These three components may be mixed into hundreds of density variations. A fine yarn could make a compact fabric, such as percale, an open fabric, such as tulle, a thin one such as organdy, or a thick one such as terry cloth. A coarse yarn could make a tight fabric, such as canvas, or an open fabric, such as burlap. The number of ply in the yarn, its smoothness or bumpiness and finishes such as fulling also influence the bulk, fineness, and density of a fabric. Density is associated with weight although fabric is more air by volume and more fiber by weight. So bulky fabrics with tiny air pockets trapped between fibers and yarns may be lightweight as density influences the functional insulating or ventilating properties of a texture (Figure 9-2f).

Fine, smooth, filament fibers such as silk and most synthetics give a lower density. Low ply, even, smooth yarns, and open, thin fabric structures (such as lace, net, or loose plain weaves or knits) also contribute to lower density. Crimped, fuzzy staple fibers such as cotton or wool add higher density. High ply, low twist, or uneven novelty yarns such as slub or ratiné, and thick, compact fabric structures such as heavy knits, fleece, and pile or double weaves, and bulking finishes such as fulling and beetling each contribute to higher density. Table 9-3 Columns L, M, and N show yarn, compactness, and thickness for density of example fabrics.

Textural density and structural design must complement each other. For example, a gathered skirt with enough fullness to look graceful in a medium density jersey would look puffy in a heavy wool and skimpy in a thin chiffon. Clothing manufacturers can make their patterns for their planned textures, but pattern companies can only recommend textures for given styles. Study Figures 6-22 to 6-51 asking which styles need which kinds of density.

Functionally, lower density textures are generally light in weight, take little space, and dry quickly, but are more fragile. Higher density textures are usually more sturdy, but also heavier, bulkier, and slower drying. Medium densities give the most versatility.

Visually, thick, heavy, stiff, and bulky textures add the most size and weight and conceal figure contours the most, but the basic guideline still holds: to avoid emphasizing extreme figure heaviness or thinness, avoid extremes of textures.

Density greatly influences the construction techniques needed to work a texture into a garment. Thin, sheer textures generally need narrow French seams and rolled hems to be inconspicuous, or full hems to hang well. Fine, compact fabrics lend themselves to more intricate structural designs. Lining a thin fabric with a firmer one increases its potential uses. Fabrics of medium weight and thickness are versatile, often pleat well, and are firm enough to hold styles away from or close to the body (Figure 9-3). Bulky, thick textures need simple, smooth structural designs with few seams (Figure 9-4 sweater). Gathers, tucks, pleats, and other three-dimensional treatments that add bulk may be good for fine or medium textures, but too bulky for already heavy textures.

Terms describing three-dimensional qualities of hand might include:

* airy	firm	nonstretchy	* smocked
brittle	flexible	* open	soft
bulky	flimsy	papery	* solid
* coarse	fluffy	* perforated	spongy
compact	foamy	* pierced	springy
crepy	* furry	* pleated	stiff
* crinkly	hard	pliable	stretchy
crisp	harsh	* porous	supple
* crumply	kinky	* quilted	thick
* delicate	* lacy	* ridged	thin
dense	* leathery	rigid	tough
even	limp	rubbery	uneven
* filmy	* lumpy	* shirred	unyielding
* fine	* meshy	* silky	wiry

*These qualities are also visible and involve light reactions.

TABLE 9-3. Textural Determinant, Surface, Hand, and Light Reaction Qualities of Selected Fabrics

A. Fabric Name	B. Common Fiber Content	C. Common Fabric Structure	D. Special Finishes	E. Surface Contour	F. Surface Friction	G. Thermal Character	H. Flexibility
Broadcloth	cotton/ polyester	plain weave	calendering mercerizing	smooth	medium-slippery	warm	medium-high
Brocade	cotton silk	jacquard weave	calendering mercerizing	medium-high	medium	warm	firm
Burlap	jute	plain weave		medium-rough	harsh	medium-warm	medium-firm
Chiffon	silk nylon polyester	plain weave	calendering	smooth	medium-slippery	medium	supple
Chintz	cotton	plain weave	glazing	smooth	slippery	medium-warm	crisp
Corduroy	cotton	cut pile weave	napping	ribbed	medium	warm	medium
Denim	cotton polyester	twill weave	mercerizing	medium-smooth	medium	warm	firm
Double knit	polyester	weft knit	heat-set	medium-smooth	medium	medium	medium-high
Flannel	cotton	plain weave	brushing	fuzzy	medium	warm	medium-high
	wool	twill weave	fulling				
Fleece	wool nylon	pile knit	napping	fleecy	medium	medium-warm	medium-high
Gabardine	wool, cotton	twill weave	calendering decating	medium-smooth	medium	warm	firm
Jersey	cotton, polyester, nylon, acrylic	single knit	varies	smooth	medium-slippery	varies with fiber content	supple
Lace	silk, linen, cotton, nylon, rayon, polyester	lace	varies	medium-rough	medium-harsh	medium	medium to crisp
Net	nylon, polyester	knit	varies	medium-rough	medium-harsh	cool	stiff
Organdy	cotton	plain weave	calendering glazing	medium-smooth	medium	medium-warm	stiff, crisp
Satin	silk, acetate, polyester	satin weave	varies	smooth	slippery	cool	supple
Taffeta	silk, nylon, acetate, polyester	ribbed plain weave	calendering	medium-smooth	medium-slippery	cool	crisp
Terry cloth	cotton	loop pile weave, knit	brushing	rough	soft/ harsh	warm	pliable
Velvet	silk, rayon, nylon, polyester	warp pile weave	brushing	smooth pile	low with nap, higher against	warm	supple

I. Compressi- bility	J. Extensi- bility	K. Resil- ience	L. Density: Yarn	M. Density: Compactness	N. Density: Thickness	O. Opacity (front light)	P. Luster	Q. Dura- bility
medium-soft	low	medium	fine	compact	medium-thin	opaque	soft shine	medium-high
medium-low	low	medium	medium	compact	medium-thick	opaque	soft shine	medium-high
medium-low	low	low	coarse	medium-open	medium	medium-opaque	dull	medium
high	low	medium-high	fine	open	thin	sheer	medium-dull	fragile
low	low	low	medium-fine	compact	thin	opaque	shiny	medium
medium	low	medium	medium	compact	medium	opaque	medium-dull	medium-high
medium-low	low	low	medium	compact	medium	opaque	dull	high
medium-high	medium	high	medium-fine	compact	medium	opaque	dull	high
medium-high	low	medium-high	medium	compact	medium	opaque	dull	high
medium-high	medium	high	medium	compact	thick	opaque	dull	medium
medium-low	low	medium-high	medium	compact	medium	opaque	medium	high
high	high	medium-high	medium-fine	medium-compact	medium-thin	medium-opaque	varies with fiber content	medium
medium-low	low	low	fine	open	thin	trans-parent	usually dull	fragile
low	low	low	fine	open	thin	trans-parent	dull	fragile
low	low	low	fine	open	thin	sheer	medium-dull	medium-low
medium	low	medium	fine	compact	medium	opaque	shiny	fragile
low	low	medium-low	fine	compact	thin	medium-opaque	lustrous	medium-low
high	low, medium	high	medium	compact	thick	opaque	dull	medium-high
medium	low	medium-low	medium-fine	compact	medium-thick	opaque	dull, medium	medium

Visual Reaction to Light

Surface and Hand. Textures can react to light in three ways: admit, absorb, or reflect. Most textures react in at least two ways, and some in all three at the same time. A *transparent* texture admits the most light, and one can clearly distinguish objects and details through it. A *translucent* texture admits enough light to show vague silhouettes behind it but not details. Translucent textures absorb or reflect about as much light as they admit. *Opaque* textures admit little or no light; they either absorb or reflect it.

A texture totally admitting light would be invisible, as some clear plastic films nearly are. Even "transparent" lace and net yarns reflect enough light to make them visible. Some fabrics seeming opaque become translucent if strong light shines from behind (Figure 7-6), an interesting effect in sleeves and overskirts but not base skirts. Translucency changes with the location of the light source, explaining "shadow panels" or double layers in slips. Table 9-3 Column O compares opacity of selected fabrics.

In an opaque fabric, light interacts only with the surface contours. Opaque textures that reflect more light are shiny; if they absorb more light they are dull. Many surfaces tantalize the eye by doing both. Figure 9-4 shows many varieties of textural surface and substance reactions to light.

Filament fibers (such as silk or nylon), smooth, low-twist yarns, and smooth, satin weave fabric structures with long floats create shiny surfaces and brilliant highlights. Finishes such as glazing, calendering, ciréing, or beetling add luster. Fuzzy, crimped staple fibers (such as cotton or wool), uncombed, uneven novelty yarns (such as slub, bouclé, or ratiné) in a plain weave or knit give a dull matte surface. Their tiny, separate fibers reflect and scatter light in many directions, leaving few shadows and creating a soft, flat effect. Nubby fabrics with slub yarns or tufted, pebbly surfaces with stronger and more distinct bumps create shadows (Figure 9-1).

Cut piles usually have a nap in which the pile fibers lie in one direction. Viewed from that direction, the surface looks lighter because the sides of the fibers are reflecting the light; but looking into the pile gives a darker, richer effect because more light is being absorbed in between the fibers (Figure 9-9a and b). Aspiring seamstresses with velvet or corduroy skirts of light and dark gores have learned sadly to lay all pattern pieces in the same direction on a napped texture. Table 9-3 Column P shows luster of specific fabrics.

Textural light reactions can spotlight or camouflage a person. Shiny textures advance and enlarge and highlight the body area where used; dull textures seem to recede and allow attention to go elsewhere (Figure 9-10). A shine moves with the body and so rivets attention on the motion; so only a small shiny accent area can balance a larger area of dull surface. Sheer fabrics suggest a lightness and airiness which opaque fabrics cannot achieve (Figure 9-10), while they call attention to what is underneath. Simultaneous contrast also accents differences between shiny and dull, rough and smooth, sheer and opaque, coarse and fine.

The descriptions marked with an asterisk on the surface quality and hand lists are also visible. They show that most visible

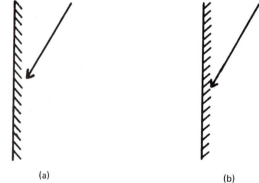

(a)   (b)

FIGURE 9-9 Light striking the sides of fibers bounces off, making the fabric look lighter and duller (a). Light penetrating down among the fibers is absorbed, giving the pile a rich depth (b).

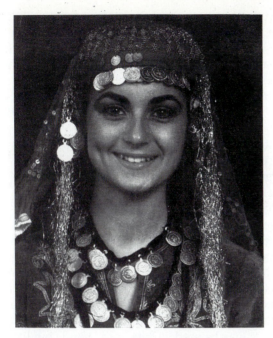

FIGURE 9-10 The shiny and dull, soft and hard, and wispy hair and smooth skin personal textures complement each other as they interact with the sheer veil, opaque and dull bodice, and shiny coins and tinsel of this Turkish folk dance costume, repeating the shine and sparkle or contrasting the opaque, dull surfaces. (Courtesy of the Turkish Government Tourist Office.)

textural qualities are varieties of surface contours or densities. Exclusively visual light reactions are listed below.

brassy	golden	patina	silvery
coppery	iridescent	pearly	sparkly
crystalline	lustrous	polished	translucent
dull	matte	sheer	transparent
enameled	mottled	shimmery	unpolished
glossy	opaque	shiny	

When tiny flecks of different visible properties are combined in a fabric it is often described as "textured" rather than "patterned" (Figure 9-1 top center and right). What distinguishes the two? Arnheim notes that we perceive surfaces as textured when our perception shifts from seeing units as individual, such as motifs in a pattern, to relating overall tiny constants throughout a field. We see these tiny units as rather evenly dispersed; they do not regroup themselves into larger, meaningful shapes. So visible texture "emerges from an inspection of the whole," without real movement or motif, but a "kind of molecular milling everywhere."[5] This "milling" often makes a good background for accents.

Seeing a surface as either texture or pattern also depends on the distance from which the fabric is seen. Seen closely, textural units may seem like distinct shapes; but farther away, they merge and blend into a dispersion over a whole surface (Figure 9-1). Given the tiny size of textile fibers and yarns, most units merge into a textural perception before we reach the distance from which we usually speak to a person (Figure 9-3).

Texture and Color. Smooth, flat, rough, or shadowy textural reactions to light have a profound influence on color perception. The same color looks totally different reflected from different surfaces. For example, a red might look dull pink "with" the nap on a pile fabric, but a rich, deep red viewed "into" the nap. A transparent fabric takes on tones of a color behind it: a sheer yellow may look orange in front of an opaque red. Colors generally seem lighter on a shiny surface than a dull one; a smooth green in satin will seem smoother and will change as highlights and shadows change. Colors from "textured" and wrinkled fabrics seem darker because of more shadows,[6] and colors on fuzzy surfaces mix with fiber highlights and shadows, dulling them slightly. Colors on firm, smooth surfaces seem flat.

Some yarns and fabric structures yield intriguing iridescent effects of color. Plain weaves using one color for lengthwise warp and another color for cross-wise weft make colors shift back and forth, depending on whether more warp or weft is show-

---

[5]Rudolf Arnheim, *Toward a Psychology of Art* (Berkeley: University of California Press, 1972), p. 172.

[6]Patricia Lambert, Barbara Staepelaere, and Mary G. Fry, *Color and Fiber* (West Chester, Pa.: Schiffer Publishing Ltd., 1986), p. 61.

ing. With dull-surfaced yarns like cotton, the colors undulate, as in chambray. With smooth, shiny yarns, the effect is a shimmering radiance. Pointillistic visual mixing of colors results either when different colors of fibers are spun together or yarns are woven together.[7]

Colors change when fabrics become wet, an important point for bathing suits and rainwear. Whites and pastels especially become transparent; so they need heavier textures or linings to prevent unexpected revelations. Legal actions have resulted from surprised swimmers emerging from the water to find themselves involuntarily immodest. Heavier textures are also needed for light-colored outerwear to prevent inside seams and facings from showing if worn over dark colors. Thus color effects should be checked in both the lighting *and* the textural conditions in which they may be used.

COMBINING QUALITIES OF HAND, SURFACE, AND LIGHT REACTION

Experience develops a "feel" for textures that helps to analyze all aspects of hand instantly and simultaneously, individually and combined, and when it is still or moving.

Textural Hand and Body Motion

The designer must know how textures respond to body movement. Does a texture stretch and flex as the wearer bends and reaches? Does it undulate softly about the body, swing loosely, or cling? Does it jut out stiffly or fold softly? How does the texture influence the way a style moves with the figure? Is it comfortable to move in? Does it stay in place and move with the body, or does it slip and ride into an uncomfortable location? DeLong describes this interaction as the "kinesthetic qualities" of a texture.[8] What is responsible for

which property? Flexibility? Extensibility? Density? Surface contour? Are these qualities in turn most determined by fiber content, yarn, fabric structure, or finish? A good texture for any garment will both look and feel right whether the wearer is moving or sitting still. Being able to link this result with its determinant causes increases power of choice.

Textural Combination and Garment Function

Rarely is a garment of a single texture; so textural combinations need attention on two functional points: performance characteristics and care requirements.

Performance characteristics determine how textures will act alone or together. They require compatibility on all the surface and hand qualities. Otherwise, a stretchy texture stitched to a nonstretchy one, or a thick, heavy texture seamed to a thin, flimsy one will probably pucker or tear. Fuzzy textures leave lint on fabrics like velvet, and fleecy linings may leave deposits on clothes worn underneath. A stiff, crisp texture sewn with a supple one may complicate draping, a note not only to combine compatible textural qualities, but to use appropriate construction techniques in doing so.

We often think of textural combinations as the outer surface, or "face fabric." But inside textures of interfacing, seam binding, twill tape, stays, reinforcements, zipper tapes, linings, or shadow panels must agree with the face fabric for a smooth, successful garment (Figure 2-4a, b, c).

Care requirements of any joined textures should be the same or compatible, or an incompatible texture should be removable, and labeled to clearly state that removal is necessary for cleaning. Permanently joined textures or trims all should be either washable or dry cleanable. Upset customers lament buttons or trims that fade or bleed into the garment. Leather or suede collars on washable garments soon meet their doom, and trouble lurks for

[7]*Ibid.*, pp. 49, 162–63.
[8]Marilyn Revell DeLong, *The Way We Look* (Ames, Io.: Iowa State University Press, 1987), pp. 69–70.

vinyl trims which may dissolve in dry-cleaning solutions. Sequins, lamé, and beading also need special care. Sharply edged buttons or trims are a hazard both to the wearer and to fibers. Any face fabric or interior linings or tape stays likely to shrink should all be preshrunk before cutting. High heat means trouble for synthetics stitched to heat-resistant fabrics. Knowing the determinant characteristics helps in combining and caring for textures.

Textural Combinations in Ensembles

Not only are a variety of textural qualities combined in one garment, but multiplied when garments are combined into outfits. For example, the outfit in Figure 9-11

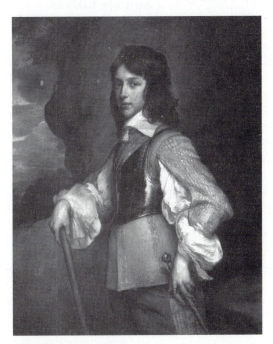

FIGURE 9-11 This costume of a soft shirt, sparkling braid, firm tunic and trousers, and smooth shine of the hard metal vest make a rich, yet compatible combination of surface and hand qualities, light reactions, and performance characteristics. (*Henry, Duke of Gloucester,* by Adriaen Hanneman; c. 1653; National Gallery of Art, Washington; Andrew W. Mellon Collection.)

shows a compatible variety of textural qualities. The white shirt appears soft, thin, compressible, and fine (hand); smooth (surface); opaque, and dull (light reaction). The braid of the sleeved tunic looks rough, harsh, and cool, and the fabric smooth (surface). The fabric seems firm, compact, non-stretchy, and fairly thin (hand); and opaque and dull while the braid is shiny (light reaction). The metal armor vest is smooth, slippery, and cold (surface); rigid, non-stretchy, and thick (hand); opaque and shiny (light reaction). Each texture is chosen for its function, to relate well to the body part it covers, and for compatibility with the other textures. The shirt provides warmth and softness and easy movement; the tunic gives warmth and padding; the rigid metal vest protects vital organs, avoids body areas that bend, and looks assertive. So all textural qualities complement each other.

CLOTHING AND PERSONAL TEXTURES

The human body has its own textures that invite comparison with each other and with clothing. Figure 9-10 shows how the sheen of hair, sparkle of eyes, and gloss of lips and teeth offer a pleasing balance of textures with each other. It also compares personal textures with clothing: the hard sparkle of the coins and tinsel complement the soft, dull skin while they accent the eyes and teeth, and the sheer veil contrasts the opaque underlying textures of fabric, skin, and hair. Clothing textures very similar to or very different from personal textures will emphasize personal textures. Satin flatters a fine, smooth skin but makes a porous or wrinkled one look even more irregular; poodle-cloth would repeat very curly hair, and be more interesting with wavy or straight hair. Flocked surfaces might emphasize blemished skin. Opaque, medium-surface-contour, firm textures show less comparison to skin texture.

PSYCHOLOGICAL EFFECTS OF TEXTURE IN DRESS

Texture can dignify, soothe, or enliven the mood of a garment. One structural style duplicated in three different textures conveys three different psychological moods. For example, a shirtwaist dress in denim seems sporty; in gabardine, brisk and businesslike; and in silk crepe, soft and graceful. Many styles depend on texture as much as on structural design, color, or fabric pattern to convey mood. Some simple structural styles gain stately elegance merely from the textures (Figure 7-7). The viewer sees only visual qualities but the wearer experiences both tactile and visual sensations.

Tactile Effects

Only the wearer feels a texture on the skin from both the inside and outside of a garment, a sensation which suggests a particular mood. Soft, warm cotton flannel in children's nightwear suggests a cozy comfort that helps relaxation and sleep. People may feel more "businesslike" in crisp, firm textures (Figure 9-3), or slinky and sensuous in smooth, supple, or silky fabrics (Figure 7-3). Firm but pliable active sportswear textures give security of durability, and ease of motion. Constricting textures as in girdles may also impose psychological restraint. Thus, the interior touch of textures is as critical as the outside touch.

Visual Effects

Textures can suggest age, sophistication, occasion, and character. Rarely is a child dressed for everyday in satin or lace in Western cultures; these fabrics suggest a sophistication reserved for the more experienced.

Concepts of textural formality or casualness often spring from experience with durability. Fragile textures assume a delicate mood, and sturdy textures seem sporty because of their durability. Medium textures are versatile because they avoid mood extremes and can be dressed "up" or "down."

Table 9-4 lists general psychological associations common in Western cultures, showing that a texture can project the mood of both the wearer and the occasion. How might you add to such a list?

Audible Effects

The rustle of taffeta and the soft swish of satin seem elegant and sumptuous. The crackle of leather seems sporty and earthy, and the clatter of wooden beads, the jangle of metal bracelets or trim, or the rubbing of corduroy all seem casual. So textures project moods by their sounds as well as their touch and appearance.

Combinations

Textural popularity swings with the styles, the times, and availability of new textures.

TABLE 9-4

Mood	Surface Qualities	Hand	Light Reaction	Possible Fabrics
Sporty	semi-smooth, warm	firm, compact, flexible, sturdy, resilient	opaque, dull	gabardine, denim, poplin, shark-skin
Youthful	semi-smooth, warm varying	crisp or soft, pliable, firm	opaque, dull, translucent, transparent	gingham, organdy, seersucker, batiste, eyelet, taffeta
Sophisticated, dressy	smooth, slippery, cool, certain rough ones	supple, thin, fine, resilient, flexible or sumptuous	shiny or dull, translucent, transparent	satin, crepe, lamé, chiffon, velvet
Businesslike	semi-smooth, semi-warm	crisp, firm, compact, sturdy	opaque, dull	gabardine, double knit, worsted, broadcloth
Casual	semi-rough, warm, semi-harsh	soft but firm, medium-coarse, flexible	opaque, dull, translucent	corduroy, flannel, knit felt, broadcloth

Double knits inspired styles impossible with woven fabrics. The crisp, bouffant styles of the late 1950s and early 1960s gave way to the 1970s droopy look and the loose, padded looks of the 1980s and 1990s.

Yet some people may wish to project a personal psychological image regardless of a prevailing fashion. The sturdy person might choose softer textures to project more grace; the thin, lanky person might choose firm textures to project stability. So some textural moods may change with fashion, and others will change only with the wearer's self-image.

Combining textures for psychological as well as physical compatibility requires harmony. Combinations with visual and tactile variety but consistent mood are usually most satisfying. Crepe with satin or plissé with broadcloth are similar in mood and care requirements but compatibly different in surface contour and light reactions. Many psychologically successful combinations involve similarities in mood, age, care requirements, and performance characteristics; and contrast in light reaction, thermal character, surface friction, and surface contour.

Textures may support each other in a structural style. For example, a supple chiffon alone could never hold the shape of a melon sleeve; but over taffeta, it could seem crisply bouffant. Combined textures usually increase stiffness and bulk (and their corresponding psychological effects) rather than suppleness and airiness. Changing any one textural determinant can shift the whole mood of a fabric, giving the designer and consumer rich and versatile textural repertoires to project the subtlest of moods or the fieriest of personalities.

SUMMARY

Texture holds a special role as a design element because it is the very stuff from which the garment is made and because it appeals to three senses: touch, sight, and hearing. Fabric texture depends on its fiber content, yarn structure, fabric structure, and finishes. A change in any single aspect may greatly alter the entire texture, thus making possible a vast range of qualities.

Texture is analyzed in three aspects: the tactile qualities of a surface, the tactile qualities of a manipulated three-dimensional substance, and the visual qualities of surface and substance. Surface qualities include surface contour, surface friction, and thermal character. Hand refers to flexibility, compressibility, extensibility, resilience, and density. Light may be admitted, absorbed, and/or reflected.

Clothing textures interact visually with each other, with personal textures, and with body contours and structural styles, creating illusions or accenting reality. Textures interact functionally in their surface and hand qualities; so they need compatible qualities of hand, strength, and use of grain. Hand is critical to how well a style holds its shape and moves with the body. Textures combined in a garment must be compatible in performance characteristics and care methods. Textures must be as comfortable on the inside as they are practical and attractive on the outside, whether the body is still or in motion.

Psychological effects of textural touch, sight, and sound greatly affect the mood of a garment, even one with the same structural design. Soft textures generally suggest formality or relaxation, and firmer textures seem businesslike or sporty. The rich varieties of surface, hand, light reaction, sounds, and moods make texture a powerful and beautiful medium in clothing design.

CLASS ACTIVITIES

1. Follow design process for personal texture choices: (a) Set the goal of an appropriate textural choice for (1) fall class use, (2) dressy occasion, or (3) tailored business wear; (b) list influencing outside factors of (1) personal skin touch and textural appearance, (2) personal hair touch and textural appearance, and

(3) personal preferences; (c) list functional, structural, and decorative criteria according to the goal chosen and personal influencing factors; (d) on a list of ASTM surface and hand qualities and light reactions, select a level of each quality; (e) from a selection of labeled swatches, choose the fabric that most nearly matches the combination of qualities you have selected. For the fabric, list fiber content, yarn structure, fabric structure, and finishes if known.

2. With the class divided into groups, give each group a collection of four different fabric textures labeled A, B, C, and D. On a form listing the ASTM surface and hand qualities and light reactions vertically, rank the textures from 4-high to 1-low for each quality across, entering the sample letter under its rank number. Then circle and connect all the As (or others) to see and compare textural profiles.

3. Select one of the profiled fabrics from Activity 2 and on the basis of its qualities and appearance, recommend a structural style and occasion.

4. List a range of construction techniques: pressed pleats, unpressed pleats, gathers, tucks, smocking, draping, flares, smooth style, sharp edges, crisp cuffs, or others. By each, list the surface, hand, and light reactions that technique needs, and suggest fabrics with the best combination of qualities.

5. Identify the psychological mood of a given texture and the selection of determinants that contribute to it. Then select a different mood and choose *one* determinant that you would change to change the mood. How would you change it? Why?

6. Assume that you work for a pattern company and are responsible for the listing of recommended fabrics on the pattern envelope of each style. With given styles selected from Figures 6-22 to 6-37 or a pattern book, select a specific fabric, listing name and fiber content, and justify your choice according to how surface, hand, and light reaction qualities will work into the structural style.

7. Choose one fabric in different fiber contents and compare their properties. Then suggest different styles and/or uses suggested by the differences in fiber content.

10 *Pattern*

DEFINITION AND CONCEPT

Pattern is an arrangement of lines, spaces, or shapes with color on or in a fabric. (In this book the term *pattern* will mean fabric pattern, not garment pattern, unless so specified.) Technically it is not a basic design element because it can be broken down into its component elements, but in practice it is treated as an element because it is a medium, an ingredient that can be manipulated with its own visual effects.

Pattern marshalls the collective physical and psychological effects of line, space, and shape. The way each is used strengthens, weakens, or makes the overall effect of a pattern more subtle or versatile. It seems to have an independent life, giving or withholding psychological and physical effects that one of its component elements alone cannot, the total effect being greater than the sum of its parts as it powerfully influences apparent size, weight, delicacy,

grandeur, restfulness, or activity, contributing a versatile range of character to the fabrics and garments it adorns.

Arnheim notes that what distinguishes pattern from a "textured" effect may be that "units...fit into...comprehensive shapes."[1] Separate units may group themselves together in "upward complexity" into a perceptible shape or may subdivide in "downward" complexity.[2] Using few units helps their shapes, sizes, colors, and positions keep units distinct.[3] So pattern uses an artistic hierarchy of dominant and subordinate areas and a rhythm resulting from their relative positions.[4] In this hierarchy, the structure of the whole determines the place and

---

[1]Rudolf Arnheim, *Toward a Psychology of Art* (Berkeley: University of California Press, 1972), p. 172.

[2]Rudolf Arnheim, *Art and Visual Perception* (Berkeley: University of California Press, 1971) p. 70.

[3]Arnheim, *Toward a Psychology*, p. 172.

[4]*Ibid.*, pp. 98, 174.

201

function of each part and is in turn determined by its parts[5] (Figure 10-1). What, then, are the parts and aspects of pattern?

ASPECTS OF PATTERN

We usually see the colored lines, spaces, and shapes of a pattern as groups of motifs. But what distinguishes their parts? Every pattern contains each of three aspects: source, interpretation, and arrangement.

Source

Every pattern motif comes from one of four major sources, although the last three are really subcategories of man-made sources, and each source could have finer divisions.

Natural objects are the most frequent source for motifs (Figure 10-1). Most natural objects lend themselves to pattern use, the most popular being flowers, which provide infinite variety; interesting shapes, proportions, and colors; and calm, pleasant psychological associations. They rarely disturb us and so do not detract attention from the wearer. Other favorites from nature, such as leaves, fern, ivy, animals, waves, snowflakes, seashells, wood grain, and marble are pleasant and have proportions that translate well into patterns.

Man-made objects have inspired an endless variety of pattern motifs such as teapots, toys, wheels, buildings, maps, clocks, bricks, keys, and others (Figure 10-2). Although many have neutral associations, they are more likely than natural motifs to evoke specific memories, thus narrowing the range of occasions for which they might be appropriate.

Imagination releases creativity from material object sources. For example, a cross-sensory interpretation of an idea may

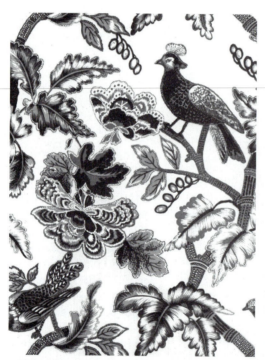

FIGURE 10-1 Line, shapes, and spaces fit into meaningful patterns of flowers, leaves, and birds, easily distinguished, yet easily related. They have a hierarchy that projects an overall impression or invites detailed analysis. (Courtesy of and design copyright by Boussac of France, Inc.)

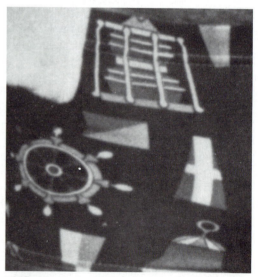

FIGURE 10-2 The ship's wheel, bell, and boxes in the fabric pattern portray objects made by man. (Courtesy of Men's Fashion Association, by Catalina.)

[5]*Ibid.*, p. 230.

arise from a nonvisual source—a scent or sound—and suggest lines or shapes that are not images of any object (Figure 10-3). Except for circles and occasional straight lines, perfect geometric forms in nature are rarely visible to the naked eye. They are most often imagined.

Symbolism is a special type of imagination. It is a way of initially visualizing and identifying in a small space something which could not usually otherwise be seen, such as an idea, political movement, religion, organization, or commercial firm. For example, the peace symbol, traffic signs, logos, or national flags are all visualizations of invisible concepts (Figure 10-4). Letters stand for sounds, words stand for ideas, numbers stand for quantities. Chemical symbols stand for physical elements, musical notes stand for sounds, statistical symbols stand for procedures and results.

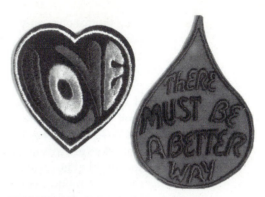

FIGURE 10-4 Symbols are visual images standing for something else, which is usually intangible. These letters and words stand for sounds and ideas. Such symbols often make attractive fabric patterns if properly used. (Courtesy of Best Emblem and Insignia Co., Inc.)

Some groups have assigned symbolic meanings to natural or man-made objects, but those sources are still the natural or man-made objects, such as the donkey and elephant used for American political parties or the cross, a man-made object used for Christianity. A truly symbolic source is an originally created image, like a word or number signifying something independent of its shape or lines.

The designer must be sensitive to symbolic sources as pattern motifs. Symbols no longer in use or some, such as the yin and yang symbol (Figure 27-1), may not evoke concern when used decoratively. But the decorative use of many symbols, such as religious, political, commercial, and military or copyrighted symbols, may be considered disrespectful or even illegal. Stars and stripes may be used together in a pattern, but the American flag itself may not be made into a garment, and similar restrictions apply to flags of other nations. It is wise to check relevant authorities before using symbols for decorative purposes.

Interpretation

Every source must somehow be visually presented or interpreted. Some sources

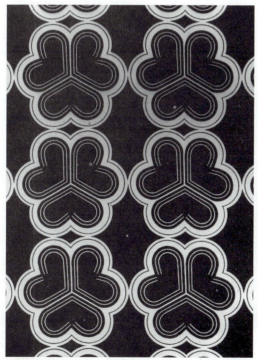

FIGURE 10-3 Man's creativity is unfettered in its design of imaginary motifs. (Courtesy of and design by Boussac of France, Inc.)

lend themselves only to some interpretations. A pattern may contain motifs from more than one source, and may contain more than one interpretation.

Realistic interpretation portrays natural and man-made objects since imagination itself is invisible, and only visible objects can be seen. Objects appear as they actually are; colors are true as in a color photograph; and highlights, shadows, and overlapping show depth and perspective. There are no black lines defining edges, nor blue leaves or purple cows.

Realistic interpretations require great skill to create exquisite patterns. If the object portrayed actually is flat, the interpretation may work well (Figure 10-5). But if the object is three-dimensional, it should be portrayed as flat on flat fabric. Otherwise,

problems may arise when a motif trying to look three-dimensional on a flat fabric surface is then formed into three-dimensional garment gathers, flares, and pleats. The probable result is conflict and confusion between pattern and structural design because the motif interpretation is not true to its flat medium.

Stylized, or conventionalized, interpretations also portray natural or man-made objects that have been changed in color, simplified, flattened, distorted in shape, edged with lines, or given other deviations from reality, but the objects they represent can still be recognized (Figures 10-1 and 10-2). Stylization allows distortion of shape to fill fabric space regardless of actual motif shape.

Flattened stylized motifs are in keeping with the flat medium. So when the flat motif *and* fabric are made into a three-dimensional garment, the fabric carries the motif along easily into its contours.

Abstract interpretations visualize man's imagination as free forms, hazy shadows, wispy trails, or simply interesting shapes or lines (Figure 10-6). They are nonrepresentational and do not portray any visible object, natural or man-made. Some objects stylized beyond recognition as nebulous, abstract shapes like clouds or inkblots vaguely suggest "things." Many pleasing abstracts simply suggest nothing more than a mood.

Geometric interpretations are a special kind of abstract because they also stem from the imagination and portray no objects. Yet they are good for flat fabrics and suggest no distracting object or occasion (Figure 10-7). The may seem casual, tailored, sporty, or elegant. Islamic craftsmen were masters of intricate, geometric patterns based on mathematical formulas. Stripes, plaids, checks, tweeds, dots, chevrons, and even "stars" are geometric interpretations of imagination (since our own sun is a star and is round). Geometric lines and shapes carry the psychological effects of their edges. Straight-edged stripes, plaids, or shapes adapt well to straight structural lines of pleats, cuffs, and belts (Figure 10-10).

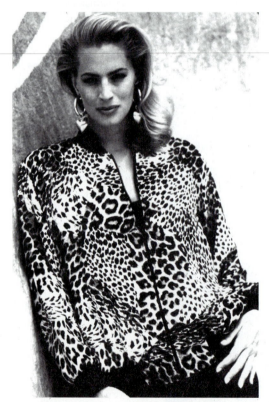

FIGURE 10-5 A realistic interpretation shows the depth, natural coloration, and absence of outline; it is like a color photograph, true to reality. (Courtesy of **McCall Pattern** Company.)

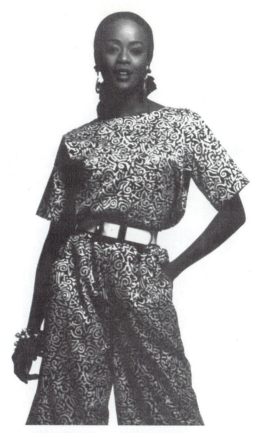

FIGURE 10-6 Abstract interpretations from human imagination, itself invisible, do not portray any objects. They are simply lines, shapes, and colors without meaning. Busy patterns can complement simple structural styles and claim attention from silhouette lines. (Courtesy of **McCall Pattern** Company.)

Arrangement

Every motif must be arranged or distributed in some way on the fabric. Any matching and fabric width must be anticipated to plan how much fabric is needed and to estimate production costs. More fabric and cost are required with patterns that need matching or have large motifs or repeats.

A repeat is the distance from where a pattern begins until it begins again (Figure 10-8). A roller print warp repeat is equivalent to the circumference of the roller until it rolls again to its starting point. Repeats of stencil, block, or screen prints equal the

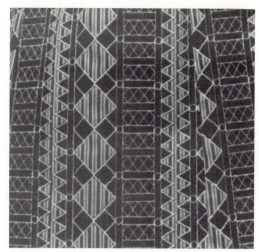

FIGURE 10-7 Geometric interpretations of imagination have an order, a precision, and a rigidity not conveyed by freeform abstracts. Here, embroidered squares, triangles, and straight lines suggest mathematical exactness. (Courtesy of Schiffli Embroidery Manufacturers Promotion Fund.)

width of the applying tool, unless these repeats are part of a larger composition.

A motif interpretation can generally be used in any of six arrangements: all-over, four-way, two-way, one-way, border, or spaced. Each arrangement creates unique effects.

All-over arrangements give the same effect from any angle: warp, weft, bias, or any other (Figure 10-9). Motifs may be closely or widely space. A directional effect may be present in details, but barely apparent from the distance a person is usually recognized. These are among the easiest patterns to use because they usually require little matching and the least amount of fab-

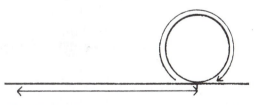

FIGURE 10-8 The circumference of the roller equals the length of a repeat in roller prints.

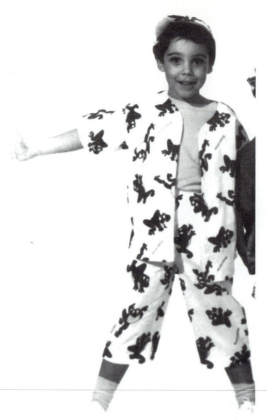

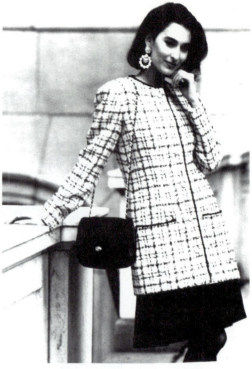

FIGURE 10-9 All-over arrangements give the same effect from any angle, and are economical because they seldom need matching and use less fabric. Motifs should agree with the wearer's age and size. (Courtesy of **McCall Pattern** Company.)

ric. Well-designed all-over patterns lead the eye easily around the surface.

Four-way arrangements give the same effect with each 90° or quarter turn in both directions of warp *and* weft (Figure 10-10). These include polka dots in rows, ginghams, and balanced checks and plaids. (A "balanced" check or plaid is equal on all four sides.) Any motif arranged in any rows is directional, even if it appears over all of the fabric. Four-way arrangements often require matching either on warp or weft, grain permitting. If lines run with the grain, they may be used in any of those four warp and weft directions, but give a totally different diagonal effect on the bias.

Two-way arrangements give the same effect when turned at 180° angles. Vertical stripes appear vertical again only at a 180° turn, completely upside down. The same thing must be happening on each side of each set of stripes (Figure 10-11a). Rectangular ginghams, plaids, and other geometric patterns are often two-way arrangements (Figure 10-11b). Patterns designed so that motifs reverse direction make it possible to lay pattern pieces in either warp direction and reduce yardage cost, and matching needs (Figure 10-11c).

One-way arrangements give the same effect at only one angle. Turned any other way, they seem lopsided, sideways, or upside down. They include motifs that have a "right side up," such as trees, people, words, or numbers (Figure 10-4). Many geometric stripes or plaids at first glance seem two- or four-way, but matching attempts

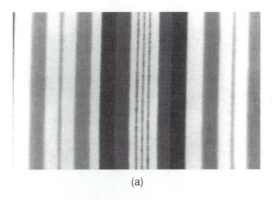

(a)

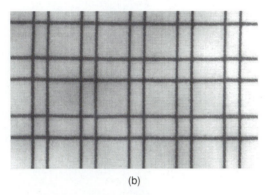

(b)

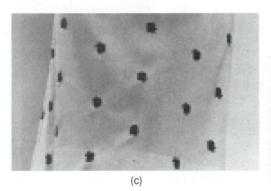

(c)

FIGURE 10-11 (a) Two-way arrangements give the same effect at a 180° turn. With stripes, the same thing must be happening on each side of each unit of stripes. (Photo courtesy of Celanese Fibers Marketing Company, fabric in Arnel and nylon.) (b) Rectangular plaids are two-way rather than four-way arrangements. (Photo courtesy of Celanese Fibers Marketing Company, fabric in Fortrel polyester.) (c) The placing of any motifs in rows creates a directional arrangement; here the alternating direction of stems becomes a two-way pattern in the embroidered skirt. (Courtesy of Schiffli Embroidery Manufacturers Promotion Fund.)

bring disaster. When different things happen on each side of a set of stripes (Figure 3-14b), unbalanced plaids (Figure 10-12), or checks, all garment pieces must lay in the same direction. For certain matching, the parts may be laid to reverse each other, but this needs careful planning and usually more fabric, resulting in higher cost. One-way arrangements demand skill and care, but well-matched patterns often indicate better quality in other construction.

Border arrangements place the main motifs along one or both selvages, or woven fabric edges (Figure 10-13). If both selvages are used, one usually dominates. Subordinate motifs may be scattered throughout the body of the fabric, with size and placement related to the border which emphasizes the selvage direction. Borders are ideal to reinforce the direction of the structural lines along edges of hems, collars, jackets, sleeves, pockets, and pants.

Spaced arrangements are usually self-contained compositions so named for their singular relationship to the fabric space

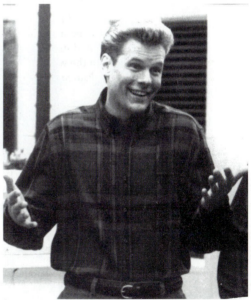

FIGURE 10-12 This plaid is one-way because the order of the horizontal lines in each group appears the same from only one angle. (Courtesy of Pendleton Woolen Mills Menswear.)

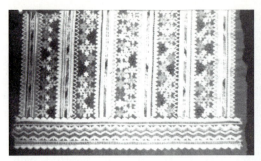

FIGURE 10-13 Border arrangements feature major motifs along one edge of the embroidered net, and supporting motifs throughout the body. (Tunisian embroidery, author's collection.)

they occupy. Three variations are most common: (1) those that accent a place on the figure (Figure 10-14a); (2) those that follow the shape of a structural garment part (Figures 10-14b and 2-20); or (3) those that fill a length of fabric such as a scarf, tablecloth, or rug in one complete composition completely framing a large, central motif among smaller, subordinate ones (Figure 10-14c) which may be repeated in sub-

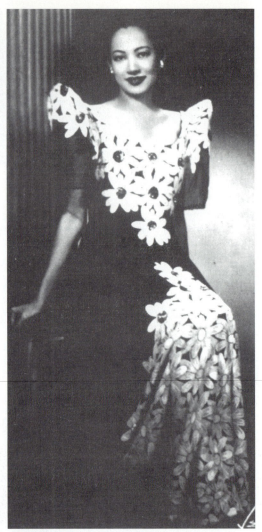

FIGURE 10-14b The flowers follow the structural areas of the sleeve caps, bodice, and skirt front of this traditional Philippine "terno." The large motifs enlarge the figure, and their stylized flatness agrees with the flat fabric. (Courtesy of the Cultural Center of the Philippines, Manila.)

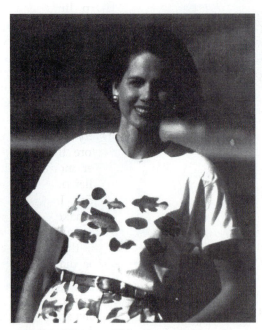

FIGURE 10-14a This singularly placed group of fish accents the bust. (Courtesy of Mark, Fore & Strike.)

groups large enough to follow structural design in different garment parts (Figure 10-14d). Any repeats of the whole are often large, up to two yards, yet stand complete, distinct, and unified, allowing challenges and opportunities to relate pattern to structural design rarely possible with all-over or directional arrangements.

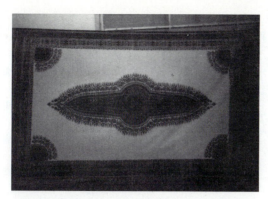

FIGURE 10-14c The framed large motif relates to open space and submotifs. (Java "Dutch wax" print, author's collection.)

PATTERN QUALITY

Pattern motifs may have only one or several sources or interpretations within one pattern; so combinations need careful planning.

Although concepts of beauty are culturally conditioned and subjective, criteria for pattern quality do emerge to guide composition and appropriateness of pattern to texture and fabrication process.

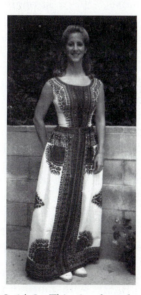

FIGURE 10-14d This simple style uses a complete repeat of the framed, spaced pattern in (c) for the skirt and the large central motif for the bodice to relate pattern to structural design. (Garment author's collection, photo courtesy of Deborah Christiansen.)

Composition

The effectiveness of a pattern usually depends on the individual motifs and their relationships to each other. The following guidelines often work well into pattern design.

A. *Individual motifs are the basic components of any pattern.*
   1. *Interesting motif shapes and proportions* may already exist or be created by stylizing or abstraction (Figures 10-1, 10-14c).
   2. *Flattened motifs* agree better with fabric flatness, although some overlapping depth illusion can be successful (Figure 10-14b).
   3. The more *self-contained* a motif is, the more it may give its own character to the whole.[6]
   4. *Consistent mood* among design elements in motifs is the key to consistent effects in pattern, since line, space, and shape carry their own psychological effects into a pattern. For example, bright colors reinforce sharp lines and forceful shapes; whereas wispy shapes, curved lines, and soft colors complement each other.
   5. *A well-balanced scheme* that includes contrast in hue, value, and intensity helps distinguish different parts of a pattern.
   6. *Variety in motif size* invites the eye to explore throughout the pattern as larger motifs gently dominate and smaller ones are supportive (Figure 10-15a). Too great a size difference may make a large motif seem out of place against tiny ones (Figure 10-15b); those identical in size and shape may be monotonous (Figure 10-15c).

B. *Organization of individual motifs produces interaction* among them, creates character, and inspires an overall impression

---

[6]Arnheim, *Art and Visual Perception,* p. 66.

Pattern   **209**

(a)　　　　　　　　　　(b)　　　　　　　　　　(c)

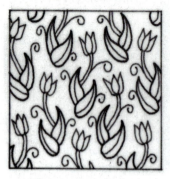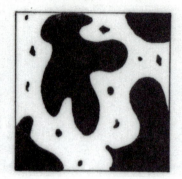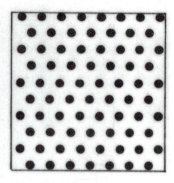

FIGURE 10-15 Pleasing variety of motif sizes (a) helps coordinate an interesting pattern. With extreme size discrepancies (b), there is no one distance from which the entire pattern seems pleasing; motifs either overpower or disappear. However, identical sizes (c) soon become uninteresting.

that Arnheim describes as the idea of similarity. This means that the degree to which parts of a pattern resemble each other determines the degree to which they seem to belong together.[7] Further, the relationships among parts depend on the structure of the whole,[8] meaning that a pattern needs a sense of total organization to structure interaction of interesting spaces, sizes, shapes, and lines.

1. *Spacing* slightly larger than the size of the motif helps distinguish shape from space, since a larger area is usually seen as space and the smaller as shape. Too much space between motifs may look spotty; too little may look crowded. The right spacing helps integrate space and shape into pattern.

2. *Size distinction* between figure and ground is essential to avoid distracting illusions of figure-ground reversal or spontaneous change of position. Review the carpentered-world, size and space, and depth and distance illusions, and line and space effects in Chapters 3, 4, and 5 to see their effects in pattern.

3. The *organization of motifs* into a pleasing and interesting arrangement of any type is a challenge, and a well-designed pattern shows it. Even apparently random, all-over patterns require skill.

4. A *gentle movement*, a *sense* of direction and rhythm, flows from a well-designed all-over arrangement, not strongly enough to make it directional; but seeming to move easily throughout. Directional arrangements have more explicit directional movement.

5. *Interesting size, position, and composition of repeats* determine much of the movement and character of a pattern.

6. *The degree of detail* helps determine mood. Elegant patterns may have more refined detail and restraint; simpler, flatter, casual patterns have less detail and more exuberance.

Pattern, Texture, and Fabrication Process

Patterns harmonize better if they agree with fabric texture, especially its density, surface contour, and reaction to light. Heavy, bold patterns may contradict the character of fine, sheer fabrics. Similarly, a finely detailed pattern would be impossible on a fleecy surface. Detailed patterns need

---

[7]*Ibid.*, p. 67.
[8]*Ibid.*, p. 66.

smooth surfaces; rough surfaces need simpler, flatter patterns. A busy pattern on satin would compete with its moving shine, a busy one on velvet might obliterate the richness of the pile. The fabric designer must decide whether pattern, surface contour, or light reaction is to dominate.

A pattern true to the process of its creation is psychologically satisfying; it seems to belong. Tie-dyeing creates softly fading edges; batik or stencil create sharply defined contours. Lace suits the delicacy of flower motifs, and plaids and stripes suit the weaving process; spaced patterns of irregularly flowing lines lend themselves to hand painting. So a fabric seems more honest if its pattern agrees with the technique of its creation; and a versatile repertoire of techniques is available.

INTRODUCING PATTERN TO FABRIC

There are two basic ways to introduce pattern to fabric: in the fabric itself during fabrication, applied on the surface of the completed fabric, or a combination of these methods.

Patterns in Fabric

Patterns created during fabrication allow confidence that such patterns are on-grain when the fabric is. Indeed, in many such fabrics the pattern *is* the grain.

Woven patterns result from different-colored yarns or different weaves. In yarn-dyed patterns, the warp and/or weft use several colors of yarn to create stripes and plaids that automatically go with fabric grain (Figure 10-16a). A traditional hand-woven variation of this method, called "ikats," uses yarns individually tied and dyed along different lengths of each yarn to create a pattern when it is untied and woven, requiring great skill and tension control for matching (Figure 10-16b). Other woven patterns use differing numbers of weft and warp yarns floating over each other for differing distances. These

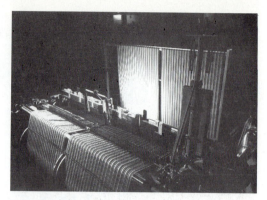

FIGURE 10-16a Yarn-dyed warp and/or weft produce straight-edged woven stripes and plaid automatically on grain as the fabric is woven. (Courtesy Avondale Mills.)

may be one color, as in damasks, or several colors, as in brocades or other jacquards, tapestry, or swivel weaves (Figures 10-17a and b). Combined loop and cut pile, "sculptured" pile cut to varying heights, or pile weave motifs on flat weave backgrounds can create patterns on some terry

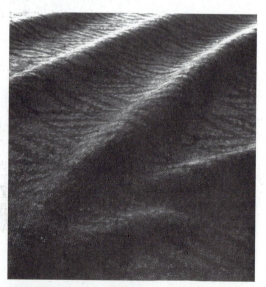

FIGURE 10-16b Where the pattern is light, warp yarns have been tied along different places, dyed, then untied, and carefully arranged in order on the loom so each yarn is in its proper pattern position to make this traditional hand woven warp "ikat" from Thailand. (Courtesy of Thai Airways International Limited.)

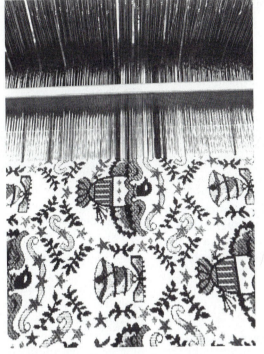

FIGURE 10-17a Jacquard and other weaves of varying colored yarns and float lengths can create interesting curvilinear woven patterns. (Courtesy American Textile Manufacturers Institute.)

cloths and velvets. Double weaves give flat motifs of various colors or puckered patterns, such as in matelassé.

Nonwoven patterns result from variations of yarn color or fabric surface. Knitted-in patterns can result from the same stitch in different colors at different places (Figure 10-18), or from ribbing, cables, or other raised areas all in the same color (Figure 9-4). With lace, crochet, and macramé, the pattern *is* the fabric (Figure 10-19).

Patterns Applied to Fabric Surface

In an already fabricated textile, most patterns result from printing on the fabric surface or from added decorative yarns.

Printing takes three major forms: direct, discharge, and resist. Direct printing from engraved rollers or wooden blocks carved in relief usually has motifs with sharp edges (Figure 10-20). Thermachrome transfer and photo printing can have softer edges. Discharge prints usually have small, light-colored motifs where dye has been removed, or "discharged," from dark backgrounds.

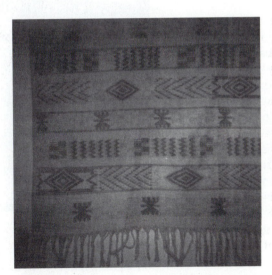

FIGURE 10-17b Swivel and inlay weaves create geometric or straight-edged patterns with the fabric grain. (Handwoven Nigerian Akwete cloth, author's collection.)

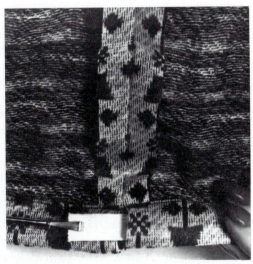

FIGURE 10-18 Different colored yarns in the same stitch make a knitted-in pattern. (Courtesy Belding Lily Company, subsidiary Belding Heminway Company, Inc., Box B, Shelby, North Carolina.)

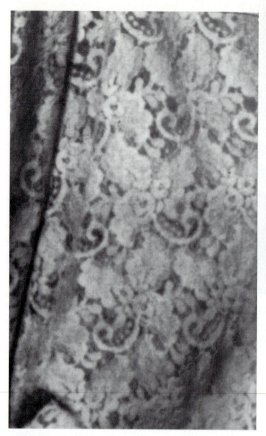

FIGURE 10-19 In lace, the fabric structure *is* the pattern. (Photo courtesy American Enka Co.)

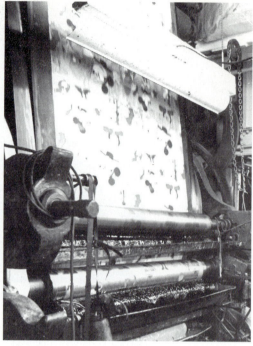

FIGURE 10-20 Roller prints are among the most frequent surface applications and usually have sharply edged motifs. (Courtesy American Textile Manufacturers Institute.)

Resist patterns are usually sharply edged. A resist medium on the fabric surface prevents dye from reaching the fabric; so color penetrates only the openings in the medium. Resist media include paste (applied directly or through a stencil) (Figure 10-21), batik (which uses wax), stencil (a flat plate with holes in it), and screen printing (a cut-out adhered to a fine fabric screen). Rotary screen printing uses a finely perforated drum (Figure 10-22). In these resist techniques, sharp edges give little opportunity for shading, except in some photo and rotary screen prints. Tie-dyeing squeezes the fabric into tightly compressed gathers, pleats, tucks, or puckers which give softly edged abstracts when the ties are released after dyeing (Figure 10-23).

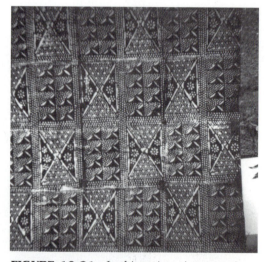

FIGURE 10-21 In this resist print, paste is forced through a stencil which is lifted so the paste resists the dye. After dyeing, pasted areas remain white when the paste is washed out. (Nigerian Adire cloth, author's collection.)

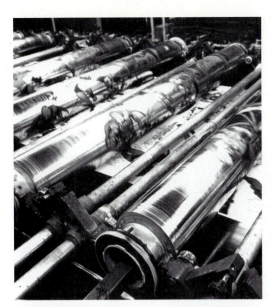

FIGURE 10-22 Rotary screen printing offers a variety of edge and character options as dye is forced through tiny holes in a cylindrical screen. (Courtesy American Textile Manufacturers Institute.)

In warp printing only warp yarns are printed and then woven with a single-colored weft, giving a soft, shadowy motif.

Other dye applications include brush or spray painting. Edges are sharp, soft, or fading with spray.

Other substances can also create patterns. Paste motifs are flat and sharply edged, and flocking has slightly fuzzy edges.

Patterns from threads or yarns applied to or through a surface include embroidery, eyelet, needlepoint, quilting, trapunto, or patchwork (Figures 2-5 and 2-6). Their flat, sharply edged motifs carry a wide range of physical and psychological effects, especially from unusual combinations, such as embroidery on net (Figure 10-13), which gives a delicate, lacy air.

Airiness also emerges from drawn work in which certain yarns are drawn together and caught with another thread, making tiny holes which form transparent motifs (Figure 10-24). A shimmering water effect emerges from moiré; other patterns may be embossed in thin fabrics.

Some techniques combined on the same fabric can be beautiful but need careful handling. Small woven patterns may blend well (Figure 10-25); and drawn-work with embroidery is a delicate combination (Figure 10-24). But some combinations, such as printing on eyelet embroidery, may be distracting.

Ways of incorporating pattern on fabric range from centuries old, traditional, labo-

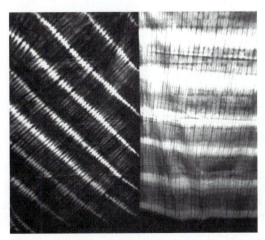

FIGURE 10-23 Tie-dyeing produces softly edged shapes or lines, here pleated and then tied at regular intervals. (Nigerian tie-dye, Abeokuta, author's collection.)

FIGURE 10-24 Drawn-work and padded embroidery combine beautifully on this Philippine abaca *jusi*. (Author's collection.)

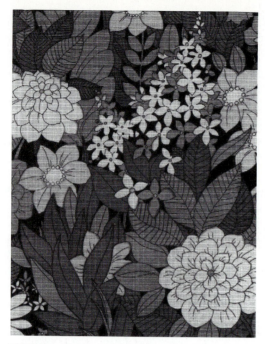

FIGURE 10-25 The ribbed woven plaid on this floral print is muted enough to combine well as a woven-printed pattern. (Courtesy of and design copyright by Boussac of France, Inc.)

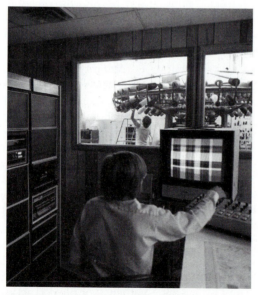

FIGURE 10-26 Computers speed production as a pattern is programmed on a computer which controls the rear knitting machine to create the pattern seen on the screen. (Courtesy American Textile Manufacturers Institute.)

rious hand techniques to modern, computer-programmed patterns (Figure 10-26). The way a pattern is introduced greatly influences its edge, depth or flatness, level of detail, or personality, and with source, interpretation, and arrangement, it can determine visual effects.

VISUAL EFFECTS

Pattern commands attention as a plain fabric cannot, often even before structural lines do. Because pattern is composed of line, space, shape, and color, it combines their physical and psychological effects to create its own impressions which may either reinforce, modify, or counter the effects of individual elements.

Physical Effects

Review geometric, size and space, and depth and distance illusions and the physical effects of line, space, and shape and their influence on apparent body size, directional effects, and focal points. Many of these appear in pattern in the following points.

1. Pattern accents and enlarges the body part where used (Figure 10-15).

2. The larger the motif, the more enlarging the pattern, though tiny patterns do not reduce (Figure 10-14b).

3. Extremes of pattern size emphasize extremes of figure size. Large motifs on a heavy person accent size by repetition; a tiny pattern accents by contrast. A tiny motif on a small person reinforces petiteness; a large motif is overpowering (Figure 23-1).

4. Directional patterns emphasize that direction on the body (Figure 10-11a).

5. Extreme contrasts of color and line enlarge; gentle contrasts do so less (Figure 10-5).

6. Pattern adds visual interest to plain textures that might otherwise be boring (Figure 10-10).

7. Pattern attracts attention away from the silhouette and so can camouflage body contours (Figure 10-5).

8. Pattern can complement simple structural styling (Figure 10-6).

9. Sharply edged motifs are more emphatic and enlarging than fuzzy-edged motifs, and make figure-ground distinction easier (Figure 10-9).

10. Patterns subject to directional, figure-ground reversal, spontaneous change of position, or autokinetic illusions are distracting (Figures 3-9, 3-27, 3-33, and 3-35).

Psychological Effects

One structural style can assume many temperaments just by changing fabric pattern, thus bringing in the psychological effects of its uses of line, space, shape, and color. The following are some of the psychological effects of pattern common in Westernized cultures:

1. Pattern combines the psychological effects of the lines, directions, sizes, shapes, and spaces comprising it. Similar uses reinforce effects; opposing uses modify them (Figure 10-3).

2. Closely spaced motifs may seem crowded, widely spaced motifs may seem spotty (Figures 10-21 and 10-11c).

3. Flattened motifs suggest simplicity (Figure 10-9). Motifs suggesting depth seem more complex and sophisticated (Figure 10-1).

4. Plant and flower motifs, and flowing or shadowy abstracts, may seem "feminine" (Figure 10-1); animal, certain man-made objects, and geometric motifs have more "masculine" associations (Figure 10-5).

5. Motifs such as spice jars or gardening tools suggest specific things or events and limit the use of a garment because of that psychological association (Figure 10-9). Non-representational motifs do not suggest such specifics and so are more versatile (Figure 10-21).

6. Large motifs and spacing are vigorous and bold; tiny motifs are dainty (Figures 10-3, 10-13).

7. All-over arrangements seem steady (Figure 10-6), whereas directional ones carry the effects of their dominant direction (Figure 10-11).

8. Certain object motifs suggest age and are most satisfying if they agree with the age of the wearer (Figure 10-9). Toys seem good for a toddler's dress, but not for a business suit.

Choice and combination of these effects helps determine the overall mood and character of a pattern. How well a pattern contributes to a beautiful garment depends on how well it complements the structural design.

PATTERN IN CLOTHING

Pattern and Structural Design

Pattern as decorative design agrees with and is subordinate to structural design: it follows structural lines, is compatible, moves beautifully, and is well placed, well sized, and practical.

Pattern that follows structural lines agrees most easily and logically with a structural design. Borders that follow hems, stripes that follow pleats, and plaids that match all help reinforce straight structural lines (Figure 10-27).

A complex structural design with many seams or darts needs a small, simple pattern, or none. Conversely, a large or busy pattern needs few, simple structural lines and smooth garment contours (Figure 10-14b). Otherwise, the structural lines are obscured or the pattern is sliced up by seams and its effect destroyed. Shirred, smocked, gathered, or pleated styles need tiny, simple patterns if any.

Garment and pattern compatibility allows harmony. Sharp pattern edges and commanding arrangements agree with dramatic structural styles (Figure 10-14b). Small,

soft patterns may be more versatile (Figure 10-16b). The bolder a pattern, the more difficult it is to blend with a garment style.

Beauty in motion is also a unique contribution of pattern. Pleated skirts have been designed of striped fabric that appeared all one color when the wearer stood still but revealed a colorful whirl in motion (Figure 10-28). Some Japanese kimonos have been exquisitely designed so that different parts of the pattern are revealed as the wearer moves into different positions (Figure 10-29).

Location of motifs, especially large ones, is critical to their effect. For example, few people would likely place a large motif directly on the buttocks, abdomen, or bust. Large motifs call for skill to control attention.

The size of the motif should agree with the size of the wearer and the garment part. A large motif on a small sleeve may be lost. One motif so large that the wearer must turn for all of it to be seen leaves an incompleteness frustrating to the viewer.

Motif sized should also depend on the distance from which it will be seen. Stage costumes may use larger motifs for distance and for dramatic impact, but smaller motifs are needed in everyday life where visual interaction occurs at a normal speaking range of a few feet. Only part of a large motif might show on a toddler's dress and would overwhelm the child's size. A size that

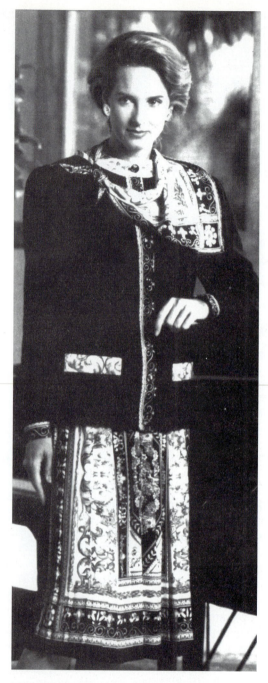

FIGURE 10-27 This framed, spaced arrangement follows structural design in the scarf and again in the skirt as it follows straight lines of the pleats and the hem. Sub-motifs follow the cuff and center front edges and enliven the pocket and neck edges. (Courtesy of Mark, Fore & Strike.)

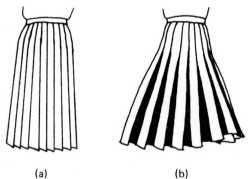

(a)   (b)

FIGURE 10-28 Pleated skirts may appear plain when the wearer is standing still (a), but motion reveals striped pattern dramatically (b).

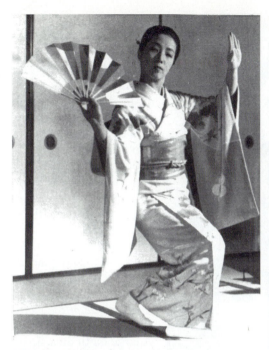

FIGURE 10-29 Japanese kimonos are examples of garments designed so that different parts of fabric pattern and their relationships show as the wearer changes positions. (Courtesy of Japan National Tourist Organization.)

gives a pleasing impression from the maximum distance at which a person's face is recognized usually works well.

Pattern practicality is important to garment care. Small, all-over patterns show soil less than plain fabrics and are handy for clothing receiving hard wear. But they should not be used to hide poor structural design or workmanship.

The combination of patterned and plain areas in an outfit creates its own simultaneous contrast. Plain areas accent patterned busyness, and patterned areas accent plain spaces and edges. Small, even patterns are generally easier for such use (Figure 10-30).

Matching needs depend on arrangement and size of the motifs and repeats. Small motifs in all-over patterns rarely need matching. Directional, one-way, border, spaced, and submotifs often do, thus increasing garment cost.

On-grain patterns are critical to relating pattern to garment. Patterns in the fabric

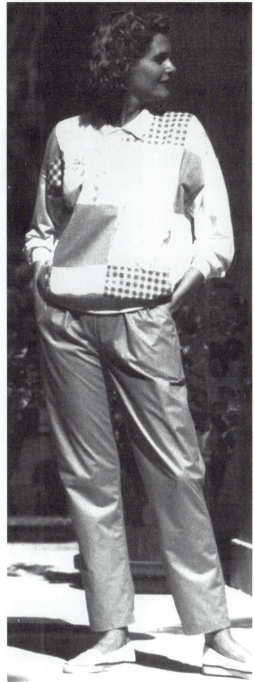

FIGURE 10-30 Several patterns combined in one outfit need several things in common: similarity of colors, small sizes, level of detail, and spacing; and compatibility of motifs, moods, and appropriate age and occasion. Including plain areas accents edges and pattern busyness. (Courtesy of Mark, Fore & Strike.)

are more reliable than those on its surface. Off-grain fabric usually returns to being on-grain with use, and a woven or knitted-in pattern automatically returns to it. Directional patterns printed slightly off-grain will be nothing but trouble: A garment cut and constructed off-grain to match the pattern will not fit as the grain returns to normal, or if fabric is straightened and on-grain before cutting, then the pattern will not match. Printed directional patterns must be scrutinized and off-grain ones avoided. Patterns on bonded or laminated fabrics also need inspection, even woven-in ones, since the face fabric may be pulled off-grain when layers are adhered.

Combining Patterns

There are times when combining patterns in the same garment or outfit may enrich the overall effect. This is most likely when:

1. Motifs are compatible in subject, and with the occasion and wearer's age (Figure 10-30).

2. Motifs have similar, small size and close spacing, since the use of several patterns means smaller structural areas for each (Figure 10-30).

3. If several arrangements are used, they are compatible and interchangeable (Figure 2-20).

4. Interpretations have comparable levels of detail (Figure 10-30). One is not a flat, simplified silhouette and another minutely detailed.

5. Patterns have at least one color in common, or the same pattern in different color schemes.

6. Color use is compatible in all patterns, with similar degrees of value and intensity contrasts.

SUMMARY

Pattern is an arrangement of lines, spaces, and shapes with color, in or on a fabric. It has its own character and effects beyond those of its component parts. Every pattern has a source, an interpretation, and an arrangement. Sources include nature, man-made objects, man's imagination, and symbolism. Interpretations include realistic, stylized, abstract, and geometric. Arrangements can be all-over, four-way, two-way, one-way, border, or spaced.

Pattern composition and appropriateness greatly influence its effectiveness. Well-proportioned individual motifs work easily into patterns. Compatibility in size, spacing, organization, sense of movement, size of repeats, and character all influence the overall quality of a pattern. A pattern compatible with the texture it adorns harmonizes better.

Pattern may be incorporated either in or on a fabric. Patterns in fabric may be woven or nonwoven. Surface techniques include printing, painting, and others such as quilting, embroidery, or open work.

Visual effects of pattern enlarge, command attention, and emphasize or camouflage figure characteristics. Psychological effects follow those of the other elements in the pattern.

Pattern is most effective if it follows a garment's structural lines and shapes. Effects are increased when attention is devoted to the size and location of major motifs, their effects when the body is in motion, matching needs, grain, and practicality. Patterns may combine successfully if motif size, interpretation, colors, and character are similar.

CLASS ACTIVITIES

1. In chapter figures illustrating sources, if example is large enough, identify interpretation and arrangement; identify sources and arrangement in interpretation illustrations; and identify sources and interpretations in arrangement illustrations. In each case, analyze how the three aspects interact, whether or not they seem appropriate for each other and why. Other illustrations

throughout the book or elsewhere may also be used.

2. With each class group assigned a criterion for pattern motif or organization and an allotted time, from a collection of pattern examples each group should select a good and a poor example of that criterion and analyze why it succeeds or fails.

3. On a given simple structural style (such as a slightly gathered skirt or shirtwaist dress), compare the effects of all-over, one-way, two-way, four-way, border, and spaced pattern arrangements. Which is the easiest, hardest, and most effective to relate to the structural design? Why?

4. To practice pattern evaluation, for a given pattern: *Identify* on a form listing (a) elements and their aspects down the left; and (b) (1) dominant (since there may be more than one) variation used, (2) physical effects, and (3) psychological effects heading three columns across the top. Put blanks below each for each element aspect and complete the form, giving a profile of that pattern's use of elements and their effects. *Analyze* in discussion: (a) Which element uses reinforce each other's effects and how? (b) Which ones counter each other and how? (c) What, if any, optical illusions does the pattern create? Are they flattering or distracting? Why? (d) For what (1) ages, (2) styles, and (3) occasions is this pattern appropriate and why? (e) Is the pattern appropriate to the texture in/on which it is used? Why or why not?

5. With a selection of various textures in white or plain colors and a selection of color pictures of printed surface patterns (such as roller print, silk screen, stencil, tie-dye, or sprayed), match each

pattern to its most appropriate texture and justify your choices.

6. With a flat-looking stylized pattern and a realistic pattern showing depth and distance, drape both of them into the same gathered, draped, or other style and compare the effects of the two interpretations as flat fabric assumes the three-dimensional style forms.

7. Choose patterns introduced to fabrics in various ways (woven, knitted, lace, printed, embossed, or embroidered) and match them to appropriate structural styles selected from Chapter 6, pattern books, or catalogs. Justify your choices according to pattern and textural implications for the structural style.

8. Compare the psychological moods of patterns introduced in various ways (woven, knitted, lace, printed, embossed, or embroidered) and suggest appropriate occasion uses for each, justifying your choices.

9. Find examples of patterns illustrating each point under "physical effects" and "psychological effects" and show why a given pattern exemplifies that point.

10. Using Chapter 6 (Figures 6-23 to 6-37, 6-44 to 6-46, and 6-51), pattern books, or catalogs, and a selection of patterns, match appropriate patterns to structural styles and justify your choices according to "Pattern in Clothing" guidelines.

11. Compare care requirements of patterns introduced in various ways, discussing the implications of snagging, fading, off-grain, crocking, or other risks relating pattern and texture.

12. Using the guidelines under "Combining Patterns" and a selection of patterns, choose several that would be compatible in one outfit, and explain your choices according to the guidelines.

III *Principles*

A visual design principle is the guideline or method for manipulating an element to create a specific visual effect. The action and the result share the same name, as in applying the technique of balance to achieve the effect of balance. Table III-1 shows each principle, the elements it can use, the other principles it contains or which may contribute to it, and other principles in which it is inherent or to which it may contribute. The table shows emerging patterns of relationships. Parallelism, radiation, rhythm, concentricity, proportion, and scale can use only the elements of space, line, shape, and pattern. All of the other principles can use all of the elements including color and texture. Repetition and contrast emerge as fundamental principles inherent in or contributing to many others, as they reflect our responsiveness to the two phenomena of similarities and differences. One sees the many complex principles listed in which the simpler, linear principles are inherent or contributors. Then

the list dwindles as it progresses toward unity to which all other principles may contribute as the culmination.

Principles are more flexible than recipes or formulas, almost infinite in their applications and relationships. Although each is distinct in theory, in practice it may be difficult and often unnecessary to pinpoint where one stops and another starts or to itemize their interactions. However, as loose as these guidelines are, there are limits beyond which a violation becomes clumsily apparent.

Even if it is short and simple, each principle is given its own chapter for purposes of clarity, organization, and quick reference. The designer needs to know what type of principle it is, its level of power, its degree of complexity, to what elements it can apply, and its potential in dress. Usually those principles that can apply to most elements are more powerful, and those that can apply to fewer are less powerful, but there can be exceptions.

TABLE III-1 Principle Interactions with Elements and Other Principles

PRINCIPLE	USABLE ELEMENTS	OTHER PRINCIPLES			
		Inherent In It	Which May Contribute to It	In Which It Is Inherent	To Which It May Contribute
Repetition	all	contrast		parallelism, alternation, concentricity, gradation, radiation	sequence, rhythm, emphasis, balance, proportion, scale, harmony, unity
Parallelism	space, shape, line, pattern	repetition			concentricity, proportion, gradation, rhythm, balance, harmony, unity
Sequence	all	contrast	repetition	alternation, radiation, concentricity, gradation	rhythm, emphasis, balance, proportion, scale, harmony, unity
Alternation	all	repetition, sequence, contrast	parallelism		rhythm, emphasis, balance, harmony, unity
Gradation	all	repetition, sequence, contrast			balance, scale, harmony, unity, rhythm, emphasis, proportion
Transition	all	contrast		radiation	rhythm, balance, proportion, harmony, unity
Radiation	space, shape, line, pattern	repetition, gradation, transition, sequence, contrast			rhythm, emphasis, proportion, scale, balance, harmony, unity
Rhythm	space, shape, line, pattern		repetition, contrast, gradation, concentricity, parallelism, transition, alternation, sequence, radiation		emphasis, balance, proportion, harmony, unity
Concentricity	space, shape, line, pattern	repetition, sequence	parallelism		rhythm, emphasis, proportion, scale, balance, harmony, unity
Contrast	all			sequence, alternation, gradation, transition, radiation, proportion, emphasis, balance, scale, harmony, unity, rhythm	

Emphasis	all	repetition or contrast	sequence, radiation, concentricity	harmony, unity	balance
Proportion	space, shape, line, pattern		all linear and highlighting	balance, harmony, unity	scale
Scale	space, shape, line, pattern		radiation, repetition, gradation, sequence, alternation		rhythm, proportion, balance, emphasis, harmony, unity
Balance	all		all above	harmony, unity	
Harmony	all	proportion, balance	all above	unity	
Unity	all	proportion, balance, harmony	all above		

There are three general types of principles: linear (or directional), highlighting, and synthesizing. A linear principle leads the eye from one place to another or builds to a climax, emphasizing the direction it develops on the figure. Highlighting principles occur at a given point, focusing attention on that part of the body. Synthesizing principles lead the eye around the composition of the garment, relating and integrating its parts.

Directional Principles	Highlighting Principles	Synthesizing Principles
repetition	concentricity	proportion
parallelism	contrast	scale
sequence	emphasis	balance
alternation		harmony
gradation		unity
transition		
radiation		
rhythm		

The directional principles are generally the simplest, the highlighting principles more involved, and the synthesizing principles the most complex. Hence our study begins with repetition, the simplest of the directional principles, and progresses to unity, the most complex of the synthesizing principles and the goal of visual design.

All principles can be used either structurally or decoratively, although some are used more often decoratively. The way principles are used influences the functional as well as the structural and decorative success of a garment, a recognition underlining all their applications. To help students visualize the application of a principle to a particular element, line drawings show a "pure" application and one applied to dress.

Each principle is defined at the beginning of its chapter, and all were defined for comparison at the end of Chapter 3.

11 *Repetition*

DEFINITION

Repetition is use of the same thing more than once, arranged in different places. It is the simplest, most fundamental principle; so is a building block for many of the others.

EFFECTS

Our human tendency to seek similarities is answered in the principle of repetition. Repeating any element use or principle underscores its importance, reinforces its effects, and controls the direction of attention.

In repetition, the eye moves from one use of an element to its repeat, emphasizing the direction on the figure the eye must travel to reach the repeat and making repetition a directional principle. For example, a patch pocket on each hip leads the eye horizontally across the hips, widening them. A color repeated in collar and belt helps vertical emphasis. A repeat should go in a direction to be emphasized.

Regular repetition spaces all repeats identically. The regularity of the spacing between repeats strengthens the direction of the repeats. *Irregular* repetition varies the spacing between repeats, weakening the direction of the repetition. This happens especially with line, when the direction of the line is perpendicular to the direction of the repeats. For example, regular vertical spacing of horizontal lines strengthens the vertical effect and thereby reduces the widening effect of the horizontal line (Figure 11-1a). But irregularly spaced horizontal lines retain more of their widening effect because regularity of vertical spacing is missing (Figure 11-1b).

Psychologically, some regular repetition may be reassuring, but too much may be boring. Irregular repetition suggests relatedness, but with more subtlety.

225

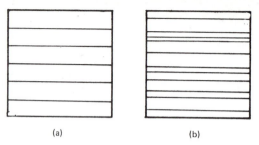

(a)   (b)

FIGURE 11-1 Regularly repeated vertical spacing between horizontal lines weakens their widening effect (a), but irregularity of the vertical spacing loses the vertical invitation (b).

Repeats occurring in several directions will urge the eye to relate them and minimize effects in any one direction. Such repeats can help unify a composition if they are well-related, close to each other and to the desired focal point, and lead the eye so smoothly that they seem to belong in that relationship. Widely scattered repeats may look spotty if they seem unrelated.

REPETITION AND THE ELEMENTS

Repetition can apply to every aspect of every element: each of the nine aspects of line, each possible space or shape, each light reaction, each dimension of color, each surface or hand quality of texture, each pattern motif or placement. This versatility increases the power of repetition and creates opportunities to either reinforce or modify the strength of an element's visual and psychological effects. The gentle gracefulness of a thin, continuous, curved line is reinforced by repetition (Figure 11-2a). Or, repeating opposing curved and straight lines further modifies the moods of fluidity and rigidity (Figure 11-2b)

Repeated horizontal spacing between vertical pleats (Figure 11-2c) uses space to counter the vertical direction of the pleats. Human symmetry leads to horizontal repetition of structural forms, such as sleeves and pant legs, which strengthens a horizon-

tal direction (Figure 11-2d). Shapes in a pattern are usually repeated and lead the eye in several directions (Figure 11-2f).

Repeating color is one of the most powerful ways to unify an ensemble. A pattern color repeated in accessories or trims ties an outfit together, but must be used carefully when the repeated colors suggest a broken line that emphasizes a direction (Figure 8-26). Repeating textural light reactions, surface contours, or hand all reinforce feelings of weight, volume, or flexibility (Figure 11-2e). Repeating whole patterns in different parts of a garment is another powerful way to unite an outfit (Figures 11-2f and 11-4).

REPETITION AND OTHER PRINCIPLES

Repetition is the simplest principle, with only contrast inherent in it; it is difficult to achieve without contrast. The "again" of repetition suggests a break to distinguish between the first and second use of the element. Without such contrast there would be continuity (Figures 11-3a and b); so there must be variety even in repetition.

Repetition is inherent in several other principles—parallelism, alternation, gradation, radiation, and concentricity; and a contributor to emphasis, balance, proportion, scale, harmony, and unity. Often another principle is itself repeated, reinforcing its effect. For example, contrast of filled pattern space and empty space might be repeated over and over (Figure 11-4). Also, because repetition leads attention compellingly from one usage to another, it is critical to achieving emphasis and unity. Some principles, like rhythm, are possible to achieve without repetition but much easier with it.

INTRODUCING REPETITION

Structurally, a center vertical line may make each garment side a mirror, or reversed repetition, of the other. Forms,

11-2(a) Line: Repetition of line path, thickness, continuity, consistency, edge, direction reinforces effects.

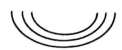

11-2(b) Line: Repetition of opposing line paths modifies effects.

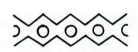

11-2(c) Space: Horizontal repetition of spacing between lines invites the eye across.

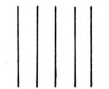

11-2(d) Shape and form: More than one of the same shape emphasizes the direction of the repeat.

  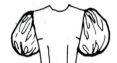

See Figure 8-26 for color repetition effects.

11-2(e) Texture: Several directions of repeats of texture help unify the bodice.

  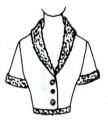

11-2(f) Pattern: Periodic repeats of arrangement as well as use in several garment parts here lead the eye vertically.

  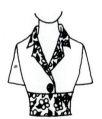

FIGURE 11-2 Repetition and the elements.

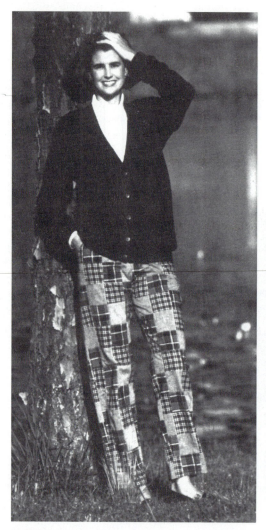

── ── ──   ──────

(a)   (b)

FIGURE 11-3 The break between lines suggests something different between them. This results in repetition (a), rather than continuity (b).

FIGURE 11-4 The two pant legs and sleeves each provide horizontal repetition of forms, and the repeated round shape of the buttons leads the eye vertically. The line motifs are repeated within each pattern, the large and small plaid patterns themselves are repeated, and the pattern-filled squares and empty-space squares are all repeated, helping to unify the pants. (Courtesy of Mark, Fore & Strike.).

sleeves, collars, lapels, pant legs, and bodice and skirt halves duplicate each other horizontally (Figure 11-4). Shapes, seams, or darts might be repeated in many places, and structural techniques of pleats, gathers, or draping carefully repeated could help unify a garment.

Decoratively, all types of motifs and patterns, applied trim lines and shapes, colors, texture surfaces, light reactions, and decorative spacing can be repeated to control the direction, distance, and strength with which the gaze will be directed (Figures 11-4, 11-5).

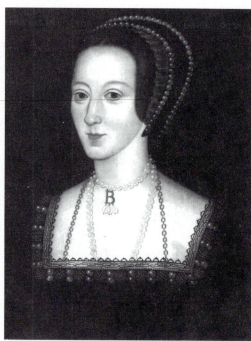

FIGURE 11-5 The repeated, spherical pearl forms outlining the headdress frame and accent the face, yet find a unifying echo in the necklace and the neckline trim. The repeated crease lines of the pleated ruffle edging the headdress reinforce the repetition of the pearls. The repeated linear motifs in the trim edging the neckline lead the eye in the same direction, reinforcing the structural line. (*Anne Boleyn;* courtesy of the National Portrait Gallery, London.)

SUMMARY

Repetition is the simplest and most basic of all principles. Its directional effect leads the eye from one use of an element to its repeat, emphasizing that direction on the body and reinforcing the element's effect. It can apply to every facet of every element, making it a powerful principle. It is inherent in several other linear and highlighting principles, and a major contributor to the synthesizing principles. It lends itself well to both structural and decorative uses, emphasizing a direction or pulling a composition together.

CLASS ACTIVITIES

1. With the class in groups, assign each group an element. Allow two minutes for the groups to look around the class and find someone wearing an example of repetition of "their" element. Then for each group, ask the "model" of their element to stand while the group analyzes (a) what makes this use an example of repetition of their element, (b) its physical effects, and (c) whether it is introduced structurally and/or decoratively.

2. To add interest to Activity 1, invite all students to wear an example of repetition of an element of their choice. If they are not chosen by the group analyzing that element, when the group has completed its chosen analysis, the group and/or the entire class may be invited to analyze the student volunteers' use of repetition.

3. In magazines or catalogs, find an example of repetition and identify (a) all of its uses in that outfit and all of the elements it is using, (b) why each is an example of repetition, (c) the direction each use emphasizes on the figure, and (d) how the respective uses of repetition applied to different elements interact in the garment and on the figure. For example, do the repeats of color reinforce the direction of the repetition of line or shape? Or does the direction of repetition of one element counter the direction of repetition of another element? If so, is there a dominant direction emphasized? Or does their interaction help unify the outfit?

12 *Parallelism*

DEFINITION

Parallelism is the use of lines lying on the same plane, equidistant at all points and never meeting. It is a useful but not a strong principle.

EFFECTS

Parallelism is also a directional, or linear, principle as it leads the eye from one parallel line to the next. The equidistant spacing of the lines means that the parallelism develops at right angles to the direction of the lines themselves. The more parallel lines, the weaker the directional effect of each line; the fewer parallel lines, the stronger the directional effect of each line. Many short parallel lines emphasize the direction of the parallelism; a few long parallel lines emphasize the line direction (Figure 5-10a, d). In Figure 12-1a, the line direction is vertical, whereas the parallelism progresses horizontally; so each modifies the effect of the

other. Parallelism will not bring strong directional effects to body appearance, but psychologically it reinforces the effects of the line aspects of path, thickness, and others (Figure 5-1).

PARALLELISM AND THE ELEMENTS

Parallelism applies only to line, space, shape, and their combination in pattern, and so its potential is limited. Usually expected with straight lines, parallelism also applies to curved lines. For example, parallel railroad tracks curve around mountains, and parallel lines in dress curve around collars or pocket flaps (Figure 12-1b). The space between any two parallel lines must be even, but the space between sets of parallel lines might vary, as in irregularly repeated stripes (Figure 11-1b). Parallel rows of shapes show a direction, but the shape angles dilute the directional impact of the row and the parallelism (Figure 12-1c).

230

12-1(a) Line: Stripes are the same distance
apart at all points.

12-1(b) Line and space: Lines parallel
edge path.

12-1(c) Shape and space: Rows of shape
stay same distance apart.

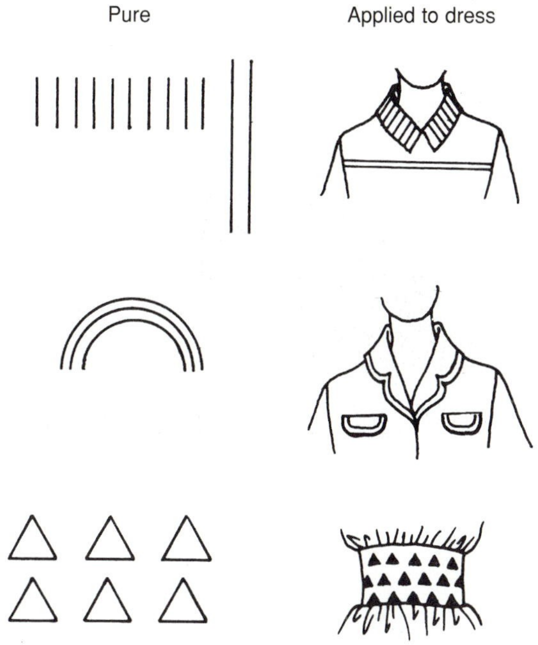

FIGURE 12-1   Parallelism and the elements.

PARALLELISM AND OTHER PRINCIPLES

Parallelism has repetition because it must have at least two lines. Identical spacing between lines brings further repetition. Parallelism is intrinsic to concentricity, and may contribute to gradation, rhythm, balance, proportion, harmony, and unity.

INTRODUCING PARALLELISM

Structurally, parallelism is easiest in shirring (Figures 12-2a, 12-4), pleats (Figures 12-2b and 12-3) that must be the same distance apart at each end, and straight belts, cuffs, and pockets (Figure 12-5).

Parallelism is most often used decoratively, as in patterns of stripes, plaids, chevrons, ginghams, checks, tweeds, and may other geometrics (Figures 10-11a, b, 12-2c, and 12-5). Applied linear trims such as ribbon and rick rack often parallel the edges of necklines, sleeves, waistlines, and hems (Figure 12-2d). Binding or topstitching parallel to seams or edges reinforces structural lines and may functionally hold in place facings, interfacings, or seam allowances (Figures 12-1b and 12-5). Tucks (Figure 12-2e) are also functional if they can be released for fit.

SUMMARY

Parallelism is a rather weak, directional principle using lines spaced equidistant at all points. It strengthens the direction the parallelism is developing, countering the effects of the direction of the lines. It has repetition and contributes to several of the more complex principles. In dress it lends itself structurally to pleats, shirring, and garment edges. Decoratively it is popular in striped and other linear patterns and rows of applied trim.

CLASS ACTIVITIES

1. In magazines, catalogs, or student dress, find examples of (a) a few long, vertical lines with short, horizontal parallelism, (b) short, vertical lines with long, hori-

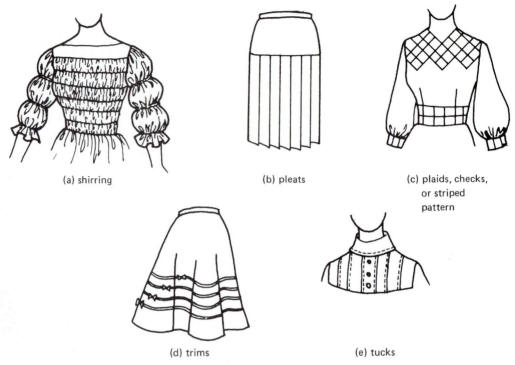

(a) shirring   (b) pleats   (c) plaids, checks, or striped pattern

(d) trims   (e) tucks

FIGURE 12-2 Ways of introducing parallelism.

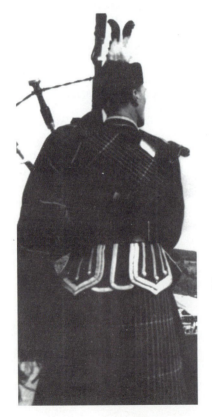

zontal parallelism. Compare their directional effects on each figure. Do the same with horizontal lines and vertical parallelism, and compare their effects with the vertical lines and horizontal parallelism.

2. Find examples of pleats in several skirts and compare the effects of parallel and nonparallel pleats.

3. Compare examples of structural and decorative parallelism. Which is more likely to involve long lines and less parallelism, and which shorter lines and more parallelism? Which is usually more obvious in garments? Compare the effects.

FIGURE 12-3 Not all pleats are parallel, but these structural kilt pleats are parallel where they hang free. The light, horizontal, decorative plaid lines in the kilt parallel each other and the hem, and in the sash. The applied trim braids edging the lappets hanging from the waist parallel the structural edges in this traditional Scottish kilt ensemble in Grampian, Scotland. (Courtesy of the British Tourist Authority.)

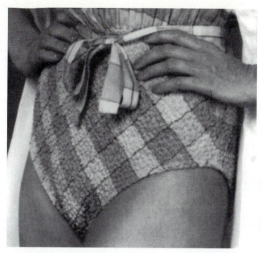

FIGURE 12-4 The structural, parallel elastic shirring provides fit, and the perpendicular sets of intersecting parallels provide decorative pattern in this bathing suit. (Photo courtesy of Sun Club by Catalina.)

4. In fabric patterns or matched garment pieces in which parallel stripes are made to intersect, what geometric carpentered-world illusions may be created? (Chapter 3). How can they be controlled to support, not distort, the structural design? How can they be controlled to avoid autokinetic illusions?

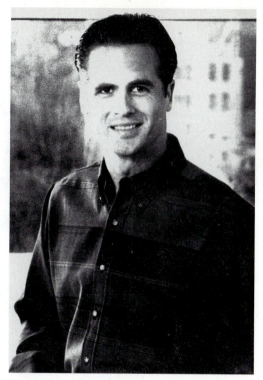

FIGURE 12-5 The structural pocket edges parallel each other, the topstitching parallels the edges of the collar and front placket, and the stripes always exemplify decorative parallelism. (Courtesy of Pendleton Woolen Mills Menswear.)

13 Sequence

DEFINITION

Sequence is the following of differing things one after another in a particular order, a regular succession. If each unit in a sequence has a meaning that determines its position, then the series does not have to be repeated for sequence to exist. For example, each of the numbers, 1, 2, 3, 4, is larger by one than the previous number. To rearrange them would destroy that order, and they do not need to be repeated for order to be important. Or if there is a clear reason why each unit is where it is (as in gradation), then again no repetition is needed. However, a series of things with no meaning or importance of succession is not sequence until it is repeated, with each unit in the same order in each repeat. For example, in a single row of different colors, it does not matter where each comes, and there is no real sequence. But if that entire grouping is repeated in the same order, then the location of each color becomes important because of its identical position in each repeat, and sequence is created. A row of identical buttons is not sequential because they are all the same and their order does not matter. In sequence, order of succession is the key.

EFFECTS

Because things following each other create a line, sequence is also a directional principle that emphasizes its direction on the figure. Psychologically it builds consistently to a climax, relaxes, and may begin again or reverse, as a completion of the sequence invites its repetition. Sequence may be gentle or abrupt, brief or prolonged, depending on what elements are used and how. Because sequence involves an order of distinct units, it is unlikely to be flowing, but it is a versatile principle of moderate power.

SEQUENCE AND THE ELEMENTS

Part of the versatility of sequence stems from its applicability to every aspect of every element. All nine aspects of line can be used, but in practice all but one or two are usually held constant to emphasize the differences of those aspects sequenced (Figures 13-1a and 13-2). Spacing can be sequenced among motifs or structural parts (Figure 13-1b). Varied shapes invite sequencing, whether their order is important by itself or because of its aesthetic position in a repeat (Figures 13-1c and 13-3). Color hue, value, and/or intensity invite beautiful sequencing in different parts of an ensemble, or in pattern (Figures 8-27 and 13-2). Texture sequence is usually found decoratively in surface contour or opaque-transparent sequences, or in textures sewn together in sequence (Figure 13-1d). Most patterns involve sequence as a particular arrangement of motifs whose order is then repeated (Figure 13-3). Sequences may develop in more than one direction, helping to unify the garment. Several patterns in one garment might be sequenced (Figures 13-1e and 13-4).

SEQUENCE AND OTHER PRINCIPLES

Sequence uses contrast to distinguish among its units, and may or may not use repetition. It is intrinsic to other principles involving order: alternation, gradation, radiation, and concentricity. Sequence can also be a strong contributor to rhythm, emphasis, balance, proportion, scale, harmony, and unity. It may not itself be a principle of major power, but it can make an important contribution to those that are.

INTRODUCING SEQUENCE

Sequence is more often used decoratively than structurally. Few structural techniques are easy to sequence.

Decorative sequences can emphasize direction in linear trims, and sequences of colors in ribbon or stripes (see Figure 8-27), but their greatest effect is in pattern (Figures 13-2, 13-3, and 13-4). Color, shape (Figure 13-3), spacing, and line sequences (Figure 13-2) are intrinsic to most patterns. The pattern repeats discussed in Chapter 10 refer to points where a motif sequence begins again. A sequence of pattern motifs should not only go in the most flattering direction, but also make appropriate use of the grain (Figures 13-2 and 13-4). For example, a one-way pattern giving a desired directional effect on grain would suffer if the structural design needed the bias for proper fit and hang.

SUMMARY

Sequence is the following of different things one after another in a specific order. It is a directional principle. If each unit in the sequence has its own meaning, no repetition is needed; but if it does not, then repetition must show each unit in the same position in each repeat. Sequence can apply to every aspect of every element and is capable of an almost infinite variety of uses. It is a simple principle and a contributor to several of the more complex ones. Sequence lends itself more easily to decorative than structural use. It helps establish priorities that create a sense of order.

CLASS ACTIVITIES

1. Invite students to wear an example of sequence of an element of their choice. Then with the class in groups, assign each group an element, and allow two minutes for the groups to find someone wearing an example of sequence of "their" element. For each group, ask the "model" of their element to stand while the group analyzes (a) what makes this use an example of sequence of that element, (b) its physical effects, and (c) whether it is introduced structurally or decoratively.

	Pure	Applied to dress

13-1(a) Line: Consistent order of aspects in each repeat.

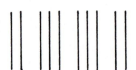

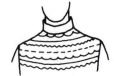

13-1(b) Space: Regular order of spacing variations in each repeat.

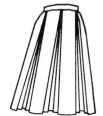

13-1(c) Shape: Each unit in its proper place without repeats, or in the same position in each repeat.

ABC 123

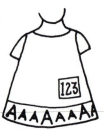

See Figure 8-27 for color sequence effects.

13-1(d) Textures: Consistent order of thickness and light reactions.

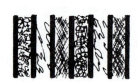

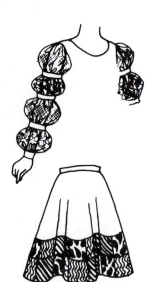

13-1(e) Pattern: Succession of patterns in the same order.

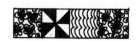

FIGURE 13-1 Sequence and the elements.

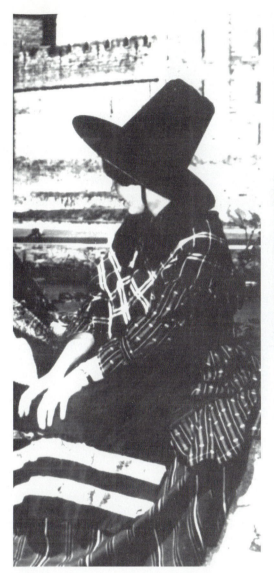

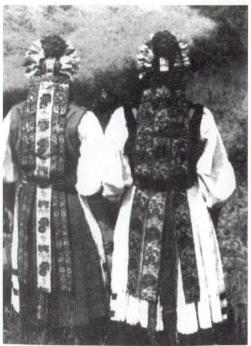

FIGURE 13-3 The motif shapes appear in the same order in each repeat of the motif group, progressing along the ribbons of these traditional Czech costume headdresses. (Courtesy of Czechoslovak Airlines.)

FIGURE 13-2 The stripes in the sleeve and upper skirt show a thick-thin sequence of line in the fabric pattern. In the lower skirt, light and dark, thick and thin lines are in the same order in each pattern repeat of this traditional Welsh costume in Caernarvon, Wales. (Courtesy of the British Tourist Authority.)

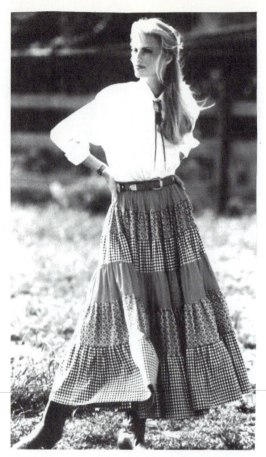

FIGURE 13-4 Not only do motifs follow in order within each pattern, but the dotted, floral, and checked patterns follow in the same order in each repeat of the group of three patterns. A graduated structural sequence appears in each tier of the skirt being slightly longer than the one above it. (Courtesy of **McCall Pattern** Company.)

2. In magazines or catalogs, find an example of sequence and identify (a) all uses of it in that outfit and all elements it is using, (b) why each is an example of sequence, and (c) its effects, reinforcing and/or countering.

3. In garments, magazines, or catalogs, find examples of structural sequence and others of decorative sequence. Which appears easiest and least costly to use? Why?

4. Find an example of a style that contains both structural and decorative sequence of:
   (a) different uses of the same element. How do they relate? Reinforce? Counter?
   (b) different elements. How do they relate to each other? Which type dominates? Do they reinforce each other? Counter? Redirect attention?

14 *Alternation*

DEFINITION

Alternation is a repeated sequence of only two things changing back and forth in the same order. A specific combination of repetition and sequence, it is a directional principle.

EFFECTS

Although it can apply to every facet of every element, alternation is not a powerful principle. It develops along a direction which it emphasizes on the body.

Any psychological effect of alternation is stronger if both items convey the same mood, but weaker if two opposing moods alternate. Regularity in alternation can be reassuring, but may become boring, a risk reduced by interesting individual units.

ALTERNATION AND THE ELEMENTS

The applicability of alternation to all facets of all elements leads to some happy surprises. Often only one facet of an element is alternated, and the others are held constant to accent the one that changes. For example, line paths alternating between straight and jagged might hold thickness, edge, consistency, continuity, and direction the same in order to accent path differences (Figure 14-1a). Alternation of several aspects in each of the two lines gives more variety (Figure 14-1b). Line directions may be alternated, as in the diagonals of zigzag (Figures 14-1c and 14-2).

The sizes or contours of shapes may alternate (Figures 14-1d, 14-3, and 14-4). Alternation of shape and space is easier to see if the space is enclosed for comparison with the shape (Figure 14-1e). Two hues, two values, or two intensities of color may alter-

	Pure	Applied to dress

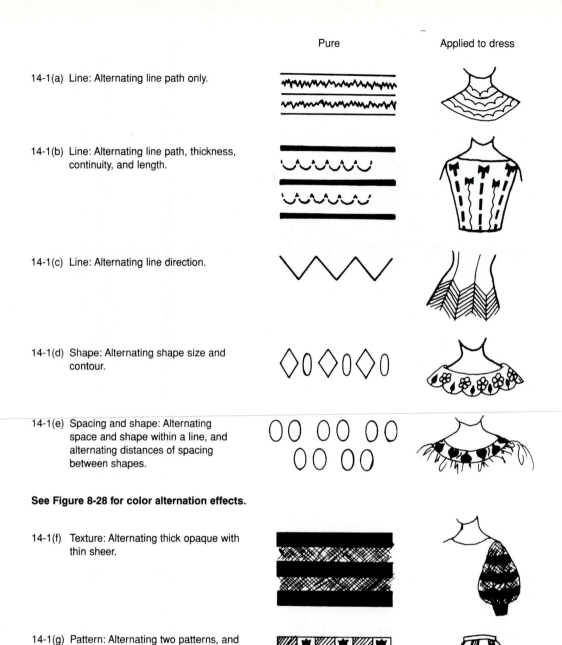

14-1(a) Line: Alternating line path only.

14-1(b) Line: Alternating line path, thickness, continuity, and length.

14-1(c) Line: Alternating line direction.

14-1(d) Shape: Alternating shape size and contour.

14-1(e) Spacing and shape: Alternating space and shape within a line, and alternating distances of spacing between shapes.

See Figure 8-28 for color alternation effects.

14-1(f) Texture: Alternating thick opaque with thin sheer.

14-1(g) Pattern: Alternating two patterns, and alternating pattern with plain area.

FIGURE 14-1   Alernation and the elements.

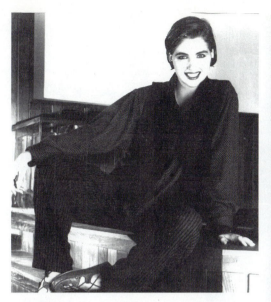

FIGURE 14-2 The diagonal zigzag lines in the shirt alternate directions; and in the pants the diagonals alternate, and the lighter and darker lines alternate. (Courtesy of Cotton Incorporated.)

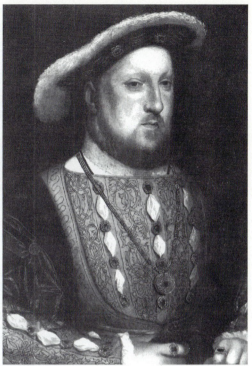

FIGURE 14-3 Vertically, the white fabric puff shapes, colors, and textures alternate with the dark, round jewels; horizontally, the thinner fabric and jewel lines alternate with the wide, patterned lines, and the two motifs in the hat brim also alternate. (*Henry VIII*, after H. Holbein; c. 1536; courtesy of the National Portrait Gallery, London.)

nate (Figures 8-28, 14-5, and 14-6). Any properties of textural surface, hand, or light reaction may alternate—shiny with dull, for example, or rough with smooth—but functional, performance, and mood harmonies are essential (Figures 14-1f and 14-3). Two whole patterns or a patterned and a plain area may alternate (Figures 14-1g, 14-3, and 14-4).

ALTERNATION AND OTHER PRINCIPLES

As a combination of repetition and sequence, alternation also involves contrast to distinguish between the two things being alternated (Figure 14-1). Often alternating lines are parallel, thus including parallelism (Figures 14-5 and 14-6). Nevertheless, alternation is a minor, weak principle, largely because it is so quickly and simply satisfied and repeated. It does not build to a climax, but it can contribute to rhythm, emphasis, balance, harmony, and unity.

INTRODUCING ALTERNATION

Alternation in clothing is more often decorative than structural. Structural alternation rarely improves a design; but it is often attractive in decorative fabric patterns, color, and applied trims.

SUMMARY

Alternation is the changing back and forth of two things, a minor directional principle which can be calming but risks monotony. It can apply to all facets of all elements, although its use is usually decorative rather than structural. It uses repetition, sequence, and contrast, and contributes to rhythm and the synthesizing principles.

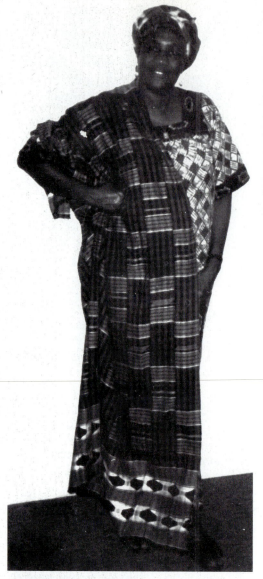

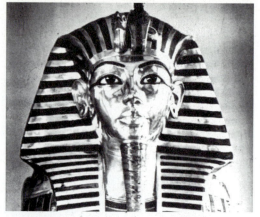

FIGURE 14-5 Ancient Egyptians alternated color value dramatically in these stripes. (Funerary mask, Egypt. Photo courtesy of Budek.)

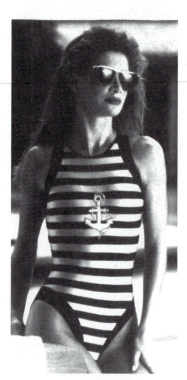

FIGURE 14-4 This Kente cloth from Ghana shows two examples each of vertical and horizontal alternation. The light and dark rectangles alternate both vertically and horizontally to form a checkerboard effect, and the lower border has horizontal alternation in the black diamonds and white "bows," and the plain and patterned bands alternate vertically. (Courtesy of Florence Dovlo, Ghana.)

FIGURE 14-6 Thousands of years later, the same light-dark alternation dramatizes this bathing suit. (Courtesy of Mark, Fore & Strike.)

CLASS ACTIVITIES

1. Invite students to wear an example of alternation of an element of their choice. Assign each group an element, and allow two minutes for the groups to find an example of alternation of "their" element. Then analyze (a) what makes this use an example of alternation of that element, (b) its effects, and (c) whether it is introduced structurally or decoratively.

2. Find an example of both vertical and horizontal alternation in the same outfit. Which is longer? What elements are used? Which one dominates? Why?

3. Find a different example of decorative alternation for each of the elements: two line qualities, two shapes, two colors, two textures, and two patterns. Which element use seems the most effective in alternation? Why?

4. Compare structural and decorative uses of alternation of the same element, such as line, in clothing. Which is easiest to incorporate? Which is most effective? Why?

15 Gradation

DEFINITION

Gradation is a sequence of adjacent units which change, usually in one respect, from one unit to the next in consistent and distinct steps. It is the process of change in a consecutive series of distinguishable increases or decreases.[1] There is no change within a unit, but each next unit differs from the previous.

Gradation is encountered in so many areas of life that we may not immediately relate it to visual design. The grades in schools are units of progressive difficulty. Test grades show distinct ranks of performance. Eggs are graded according to size, meat according to steps of quality. Any quality that can change by distinct and consecutive degrees lends itself to gradation.

---

[1]Rudolf Arnheim, *Art and Visual Perception* (Berkeley: University of California Press, 1971), p. 268.

Gradation needs more than two steps, otherwise it is simply a comparison. Change must progress consistently with each next step changing in the same aspect and to a similar degree. Any departure, such as consecutively longer lines being interrupted by a short one, destroys gradation. A progression may build toward a definite climax and stop there (Figure 15-1), or begin again, or reverse at the climax and return to the original step (Figure 15-4). Gradation does not require repetition.

EFFECTS

Gradation is a linear principle, generally stronger if used in a single, long series rather than in short, repeated sets; the longer the graduated sequence, the greater the climax. It can evoke illusions of depth or sweep the gaze compellingly to its climax and corresponding figure area. In size gradation, larger shapes enlarge, and the smaller end of the range seems smaller; so it is usually used near the waist or neck and the large end nearest the shoulders or the floor (Figures 15-1g, h, j, k, and l). Greater changes between each step seem to accent differences (Figure 15-1g) whereas slight changes lessen apparent differences (Figure 8-6).

Gradation can strengthen psychological effects of an element since step-by-step changes build intensity of feeling in neatly ranked categories. These suggest decisiveness and assurance that each next step is known and expressed precisely. There is nothing unsure about gradation; it compensates in distinctness for what it may lack in smoothness, and thus seems assertive and sure.

GRADATION AND THE ELEMENTS

Any aspect of an element that can be placed along a continuum can be graduated. Almost every aspect of line can be graduated (Figures 15-1a, b, c, d and 15-2).

Space between lines may gradually widen or narrow with each next step (Figures 15-1e and 15-3), or space within shapes may increase structurally and decoratively (Figures 15-1h, 15-4). Shapes can be graduated in contour (Figure 15-1f) or size (Figures 15-1g, 15-5, and 15-6).

Each color chart is an example of gradation. The hue wheel graduates wavelengths of the spectrum (Figures 8-2 and 8-7). The value chart graduates from light to dark (Figure 8-3), and the intensity chart graduates from bright to dull to neutral and then reverses (Figures 8-4 and 8-5). In the outer jacket of Figure 15-7, colors darken more with each line.

Textural qualities lend themselves to gradation in theory, but in practice the few advantages would rarely be worth the extra expense and technology needed to produce them in one fabric. Textural gradations are most easily achieved by seaming or layering (Figure 15-1i).

Gradation in pattern usually means increase or decrease in motif size (Figures 15-1j and 15-5) or a series of fabric sections seamed together in which all motifs within each section are all the same, but all motifs in the next section are the next size larger or smaller (Figure 15-1k). Overlapping motifs graduated in size create a strong illusion of depth (Figure 15-1l).

GRADATION AND OTHER PRINCIPLES

Gradation is a particular kind of sequence in which changes occur by distinct steps. It holds interest longer than alternation, is an intrinsic part of radiation and can make a strong contribution to rhythm, emphasis, balance, and proportion. Gradation lends itself beautifully to scaling garment parts to body part sizes, enhancing harmony and unity.

INTRODUCING GRADATION

Gradation lends itself to many structural and decorative uses. Structural darts can be graduated in length, spacing, or direction, as can pleats, seams, tucks, or draping (Figure 15-1c). A dramatic use of structural gradation is a step-by-step increase in the size of skirt tiers (Figure 15-1h and 15-4) from narrowest at the waist to widest at the bottom for walking space and aesthetic balance.

Gradation revels in decorative design. All aspects of line can be graduated (Figure 15-1a-e). Spacing between parallel lines may gradually narrow or widen (Figure 15-3). Applied trims offer a wealth of possibilities. Color can graduate dramatically in hue, value, or intensity (Figure 15-7). Pattern is ideal for gradation of motif size, spacing, or color (Figures 15-6 and 15-7).

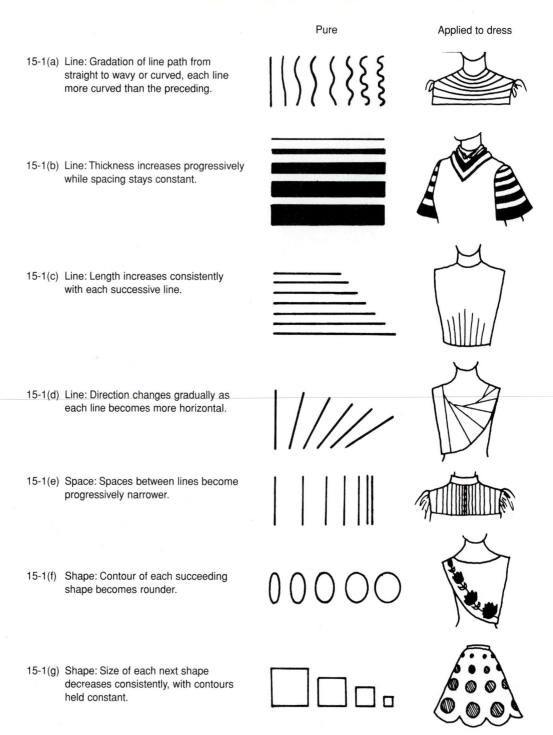

Pure   Applied to dress

15-1(a) Line: Gradation of line path from straight to wavy or curved, each line more curved than the preceding.

15-1(b) Line: Thickness increases progressively while spacing stays constant.

15-1(c) Line: Length increases consistently with each successive line.

15-1(d) Line: Direction changes gradually as each line becomes more horizontal.

15-1(e) Space: Spaces between lines become progressively narrower.

15-1(f) Shape: Contour of each succeeding shape becomes rounder.

15-1(g) Shape: Size of each next shape decreases consistently, with contours held constant.

FIGURE 15-1 Gradation and the elements.

15-1(h) Space and shape: Space in shapes may increase consecutively, changing shape proportions.

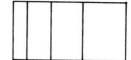
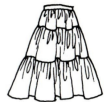

See Figures 8-2, 8-3, 8-4, 8-5, 8-6, 8-7, and 8-9 for color gradation effects.

15-1(i) Texture: Successive layers of sheer fabric gradually increase opacity.

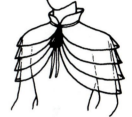

15-1(j) Pattern: Motif size increases with each repeat.

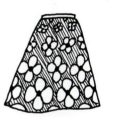

15-1(k) Pattern: Motifs identical throughout one section increase in size in the next section.

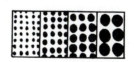
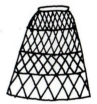

15-1(l) Pattern: Motifs which overlap as well as reduce in size consecutively create a feeling of depth.

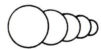
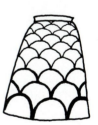

FIGURE 15-1 *(continued)*

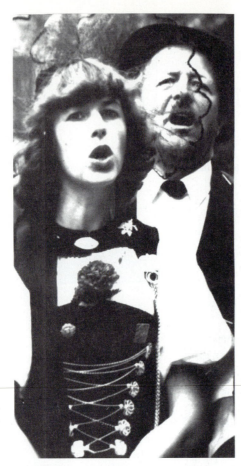

FIGURE 15-2 Progressing downward, each successive line of chain in this Swiss costume becomes shorter in length, more diagonal in direction, and straighter in path, creating a graceful lengthening and narrowing effect despite the dominantly horizontal line direction. (Courtesy of the Swiss National Tourist Office.)

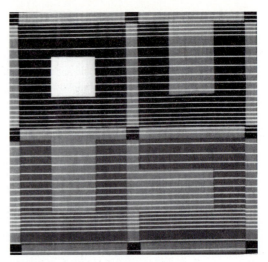

FIGURE 15-3 Each space between the white horizontal lines consecutively narrows toward the bottom of each sequence, then halts abruptly and repeats the wide to narrow gradation again. (Courtesy of and design copyright by Boussac of France, Inc.)

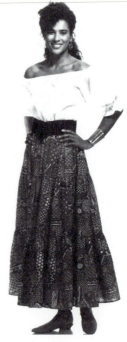

FIGURE 15-4 The space in each next descending tier is wider, putting the smaller, lighter area at the waist and the larger, heavier area at the bottom of this skirt showing structural gradation. (Courtesy of **McCall Pattern** Company.)

SUMMARY

Gradation is a sequence of neighboring units consecutively changing by degree. It is a fairly powerful directional principle, which strengthens the direction of its development and can be applied to nearly all aspects of every element. It builds to a climax more easily with one long gradation than with several short repeats. It progresses in distinct steps which invite comparisons that heighten differences, and seem assertive and decisive. Gradation uses se-

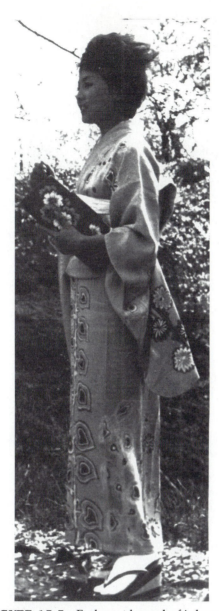

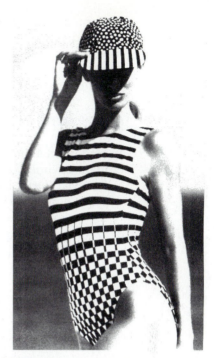

FIGURE 15-6 From the beginning of the breaks in the horizontal lines in this fabric pattern, the break is consecutively wider in each next line down until the stripes become square shaped checks and on into triangles, and the eye follows the vertical development of the gradation despite the horizontal lines. (Courtesy of Mark, Fore & Strike.)

FIGURE 15-5 Each next lower leaf is larger in this pattern down the front of the kimono, showing a gradation in size of shape, logically placed with the lower seeming larger and heavier. (Courtesy of Japan National Tourist Organization.)

FIGURE 15-7 (right) The color values in the outer jacket are graduated as each next line is darker going toward the dark cluster and lighter toward the light cluster. (Courtesy of **McCall Pattern** Company.)

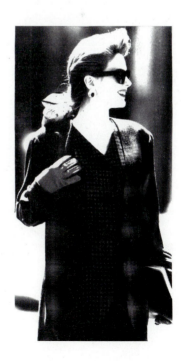

quence and proportion, is intrinsic to radiation, and can enhance emphasis, balance, scale, harmony, and unity. Almost any construction or decorative technique can use gradation to direct attention.

CLASS ACTIVITIES

1. Find nonclothing examples of gradation in the environment. Identify the element involved in each and why it is gradation. Then design a clothing adaptation of that use and evaluate its effects.

2. Invite class members to wear examples of gradation. With the class in groups, identify and analyze as many examples and elements as possible. Compare their effects when the gradation is repeated and when it is not.

3. In garments, catalogues, or other pictures, find examples of structural and decorative gradation. Which is usually larger? Which is more dramatic? Compare their effects on the figure.

4. Find or design fabric patterns each using gradation of a different element. Which element use contributes the more distinct, decisive effect? Keep your examples for future use.

16 *Transition*

DEFINITION

Transition is a smooth change in quality of a variation of an element. It changes condition as it changes location, so continuous that there is no break point, step, nor distinct pinpoint of change. It is not just a move from one place to another. Rather, something about the element changes to smoothly gradually and subtly that one is scarcely aware that change is happening. Where gradation uses distinct steps, transition glides smoothly through its changes from one variation to another within an element.

EFFECTS

Transition is a linear principle, emphasizing its direction of development on the body, a direction often the same as that of a line, thus strengthening its effect. Transition is so subtle that the gaze follows almost without realizing it is being led. It is a paradox: Too

gentle to seem powerful, much of its power comes from its subtlety. The eye seeks a break point as a point of reference, and finding none roams the entire area, gaining full appreciation of the change. Psychologically it is smooth, sinuous, flowing, soft, and graceful. Where gradation is distinct, transition is soft as it gently slides, fades, and melts.

TRANSITION AND THE ELEMENTS

Transition gracefully applies to many aspects of many elements, but not to all. Transition uses several aspects of line to make smooth changes: path can change smoothly from straight to curved (Figure 16-1a), thickness smoothly widens from a thin line into a wider shape, as in a shawl collar (Figure 16-1b). A fuzzy edge gradually fades into nothing (Figure 16-1c). Line direction curves from vertical to horizontal and back

251

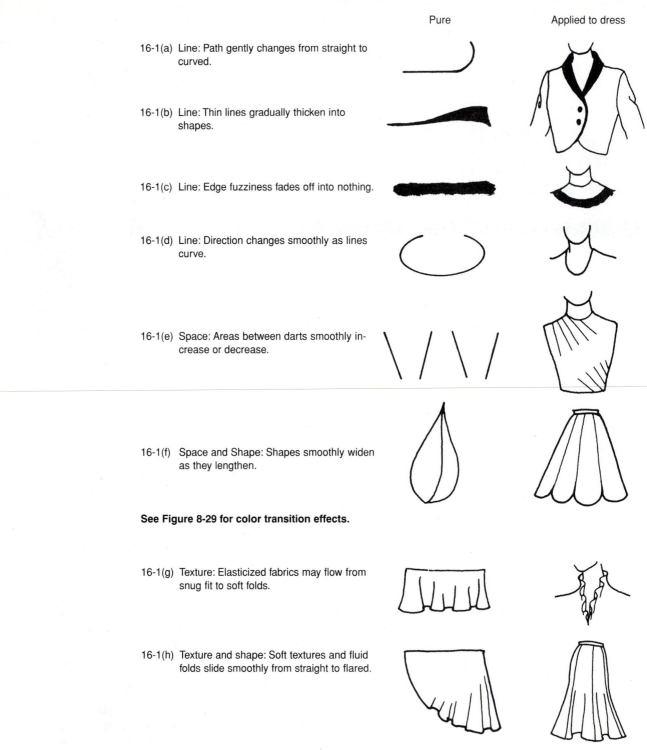

Pure   Applied to dress

16-1(a) Line: Path gently changes from straight to curved.

16-1(b) Line: Thin lines gradually thicken into shapes.

16-1(c) Line: Edge fuzziness fades off into nothing.

16-1(d) Line: Direction changes smoothly as lines curve.

16-1(e) Space: Areas between darts smoothly increase or decrease.

16-1(f) Space and Shape: Shapes smoothly widen as they lengthen.

See Figure 8-29 for color transition effects.

16-1(g) Texture: Elasticized fabrics may flow from snug fit to soft folds.

16-1(h) Texture and shape: Soft textures and fluid folds slide smoothly from straight to flared.

FIGURE 16-1 Transition and the elements.

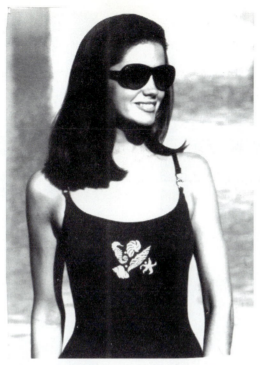

FIGURE 16-2 The neckline of the bathing suit shows smooth change or transition of path from rounder to flatter curve, and of direction, curving from vertical to horizontal and back to vertical. (Courtesy of SESSA by Apparel Ventures, Inc.)

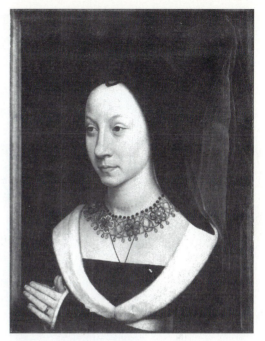

FIGURE 16-3 The graceful lines of the collar and necklace change path and direction as they curve. The collar smoothly widens toward the shoulders, and the neckline area between the lapels smoothly widens from the lower center bodice point. (*Maria Portinari,* by Hans Memling; c. 1465; The Metropolitan Museum of Art; bequest of Benjamin Altman, 1913.)

(Figures 16-1d, 16-2, 16-3). The space between lines or shapes can smoothly narrow or widen, as between darts or seams (Figure 16-1e), or in a V neckline smoothly widening from a point to wider neck opening (Figure 16-4), or within a shape, as in a skirt gore (Figure 16-1f), or a collar (Figure 16-3), helping the narrow end seem smaller, and the wider end larger.

Transition brings curved body contours from narrow to wide areas, a smooth change that flatters the human figure. A lumpy, bumpy figure of abrupt changes is a much less graceful silhouette (Figure 16-5).

Beautiful transition of color in dress reemerges in popularity from time to time, often called *ombré* in French, meaning "shaded." A transition of hues glides through the spectrum: blue melts into blue-green, which slips into green. In value a

rich, deep red slides into pink, which fades into white. In intensity, a brilliant blue melts into a duller French blue, which slips into neutral grey. No dividing lines, no break points, but a change so smooth, even, and continuous that one cannot say where it happens (Figure 8-29).

Few aspects of texture lend themselves technically to transition. However, stretchy fabric or fit of styles can cling to the figure in some places, then smoothly loosen and fall away into fluid folds (Figures 16-1g and 16-6).

Most transition in pattern emerges from curved line directions, smoothly widening or narrowing motif shapes, spacing within or between motifs, or smoothly fading colors. Pattern usually uses distinct units as motifs, so there is less opportunity for transition independent of motifs.

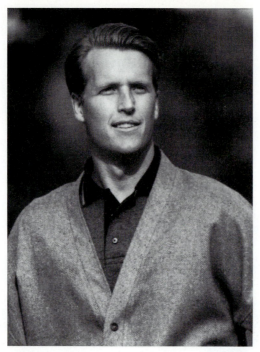

FIGURE 16-4 The space between the V neck lines in the jacket smoothly widens from the lower point to the shoulders, giving a widening and streamlined effect. (Courtesy of Pendleton Woolen Mills Menswear.)

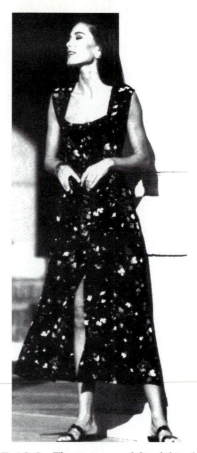

FIGURE 16-6 The texture and fit of this skirt hug snugly at the waist and hips, then gradually and smoothly fall away from the figure in soft flares. (Courtesy of Mark, Fore & Strike.)

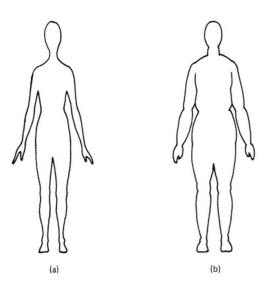

(a)   (b)

FIGURE 16-5 A figure whose silhouette lines change directions in smooth curves (a) is more graceful than one which changes direction with bumpy angles (b).

TRANSITION AND OTHER PRINCIPLES

Transition does not depend on simpler principles for components, but its smooth changes in qualities gently can contribute to a softly undulating rhythm and to a graceful sense of balance by its subtle manipulation of apparent weight (Figures 16-3 and 16-4). The smoothly widening spaces between lines bursting from a central point contribute to radiation. Transition promotes harmony as a gentle link between otherwise opposing lines, shapes, or colors; the very continuity of transitional change suggests a harmony that contributes to unity.

INTRODUCING TRANSITION

Structural seams, darts, edges, flares, or draping provide the lines that frame smoothly widening spaces (Figures 16-1e, f, 16-3, and 16-4), and they offer potential for transitional directions of line (Figures 16-1a, 16-2, and 16-3). Gathers and flares invite gradual widening, as do the shapes of many garment styles. (See Chapter 6, Figures 6-22 to 6-52, for transitional lines, shapes, and spaces in collars, sleeves, skirts, and so on.) Control of snug to loosely flowing fit provides for ease of movement as well as aesthetically graceful line (Figures 16-1g, h, and 16-6).

Decoratively, curved or gradually thickening lines bring smooth transition to applied trim lines. Colors that melt or fade into each other guide attention in the direction of color change and patterns that include curved lines and smoothly widening areas provide miniature examples of transition. Like gradation, transition is more powerful as one sustained development than as short repeats.

SUMMARY

Transition is a smooth, even, continuous change of the quality of an element as it changes location. It flows without break points, not only shifting location, but changing some quality of direction, fit, color, or other element aspect. It is a directional principle, which conveys a gentle, sinuous, graceful flow in the direction of the change. It applies to many, but not all, aspects of all elements and lends itself to structural as well as decorative use. No other principles are intrinsic to it, but it can contribute gracefully to others, including rhythm, radiation, balance, harmony, and unity.

CLASS ACTIVITIES

1. To see the difference in effects between the distinct steps of gradation and the smoothly flowing change of transition, design transition equivalents of the gradation designs you did for the previous chapter. For example, if you had gradation of color value in three distinct steps of hunter, kelly, and mint green, make a transition example that fades smoothly from dark through medium to pale green. How do their psychological effects compare? Their physical effects? Experiment with gradation/transition comparisons for other elements and aspects.

2. Invite students to bring or wear examples of transition. With the class in groups, assign each an element and allow time for groups to find a transition example of "their" element, then identify it and how transition uses that element, its effects, and how it is introduced.

3. Design a garment using transition from narrow to wide shapes or spaces between lines, such as darts, skirt gores, flares, or shawl collars. Analyze their physical effects on the part of the figure where they appear. Then reverse the wide and narrow positions and compare effects with the first use. Since the narrow/wide transition is smooth in both cases, how does it affect the apparent size differences?

4. Using reinforcing techniques, design a garment or outfit using transition in variations of several of its elements: line, space, shape, and color. How does the transition of each element variation complement and interact with that of the other element(s)? Which is most apparent in the garment?

5. Design or find a fabric pattern that applies transition to all the elements: curved lines, gradually thickening or thinning lines, smoothly widening or narrowing spaces, shapes, fading colors, and the like. Compare its physical and psychological effects with a fabric pattern that uses little or no transition.

17 Radiation

DEFINITION

Radiation is a feeling of movement bursting outward in all directions from one visible or suggested central point, the emission of rays from one source. It appears in spokes in a wheel or umbrella, petals in a flower, a sunburst, or cathedral rose window. A directional principle, any single directional effect would be along the radius of a circle (Figures 17-1a to d). Simple crossing of lines, such as an X, does not develop radiation.

Radiation may thrust out with no visible central point (Figure 17-1f). If lines were extended through the axis they would converge at one point which must be clearly suggested even though invisible (Figure 17-2a, b).

EFFECTS

Radiation commands attention, so it is most effective used sparingly. Using varying amounts of a circle creates a wide variety of effects. If only a few lines radiate in similar directions from one side of a point, then that direction dominates (Figure 17-1a); close lines thrusting outward from opposite sides of the central point further strengthen the dominant direction (Figure 17-1b). Lines that fan out in several directions reduce the area near the center, often flattering for neck and waist, and enlarge the area near the edge, an attractive use for shoulders and hem (Figures 17-1c, e, h, 17-3, and 17-4). If lines burst out in a circle all around the central point, attention is led outward in all directions (Figure 17-1d).

A suggested rather than visible point heightens interest because it stimulates imagining where the lines would converge. It hints rather than states, whether the lines are grouped (Figure 17-1e) or on both sides of an axis (Figure 17-1f).

This multiplicity of directions sometimes creates apparently conflicting effects. Some viewers may see almost as much

17-1(a) Line and space: Few lines radiating similar directions from one side of a central point give strong directional effect.

 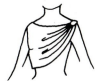

17-1(b) Line and space: Few lines radiating from opposite sides of a point give a strong directional effect.

17-1(c) Line and space: Lines radiating in a semicircle from a central point enlarge the outer edge and reduce area near the center.

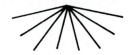

17-1(d) Line and space: Lines bursting out from a central point all around lead the eye in all directions outward.

17-1(e) Line and space: Lines fanning out from one side of another line suggest a convergence point on the other side.

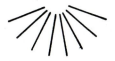 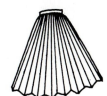

17-1(f) Line and space: Lines radiating from both sides of an axis suggest a convergence point at center.

17-1(g) Shape and Space: Closed outer ends of radiating lines create stable, self contained shapes.

17-1(h) Pattern: Radiating lines in pattern motifs enlarge outer edges, yet seem coherent.

 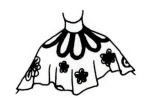

FIGURE 17-1 Radiation and the elements.

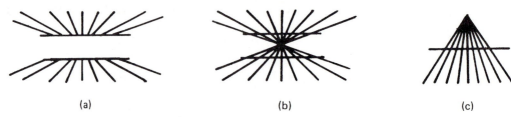

FIGURE 17-2 Radiation from an axis with no visible central point (a) clearly suggests one, and converges if extended (b). Lines radiating from one line would also converge on its other side (c).

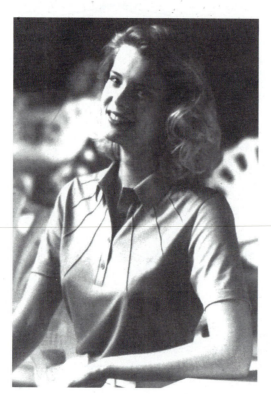

FIGURE 17-3 The narrow, structural darts radiating from the neck help provide structural fit through the shoulders and bust as well as decoratively widening the shoulders and bust, and accenting the face. (Courtesy of Mark, Fore & Strike.)

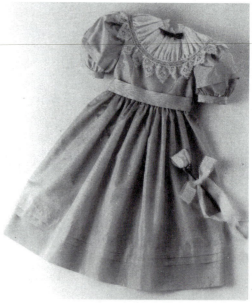

FIGURE 17-4 The gathers in the decorative shoulder yoke of this child's dress radiate out from the neck, making it seem smaller and the shoulders and bodice larger. The radiating edge lace "petals" further widen the shoulders. When the skirt is spread and flat as here, some dominant folds may suggest radiation, but lines are not at consistent angles, and hanging on the figure they fall randomly and parallel, not radiating. (Courtesy of **McCall Pattern** Company.)

movement toward the center as away from it (Figure 17-5), but the effects of radiation are primarily those of an outward thrust.

Repetition of radiating lines also leads the eye from one line to the next around the center, reducing the strength of their outward thrust and sometimes suggesting a circular, concentric effect. However, radiation is perpendicular to concentricity (Chapter 19); where radiation thrusts out from a center, concentricity circles around it. The two should not be confused. Radiation calls attention to figure areas at either end of a line, so the radiating lines should end where attention is desired.

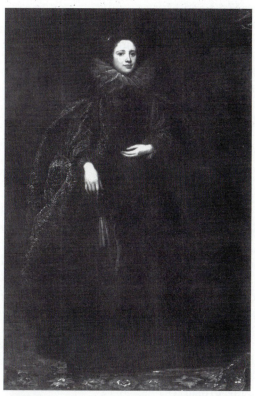

FIGURE 17-5 The invisible source point of radiation is clearly suggested in this ruff collar. It adds bulk to the neck, but is too high to widen the shoulders. With little emphasis at the outer edge, the focus is on the face as it increases size and a sense of "presence." (*Marchesa Balbi*; Sir Anthony van DYCK: 1622/1627; National Gallery of Art, Washington; Andrew W. Mellon Collection.)

RADIATION AND THE ELEMENTS

Radiation carries potent effects even though it applies only to line, space, shape, and their combinations as pattern. It uses them forcefully, though rigidly, as radiating lines are nearly always straight or only slightly curved. They are close to or meet at the center and flare outward at the other end; so spacing between the lines is critical.

Shapes containing radiating lines with closed outer ends seem more self-contained and stable (Figure 17-1g). Radiation in pattern motifs is popular, often beautiful, and may be delicate or bold: motifs such as flower petals and snowflakes seem dainty (Figure 17-1h); wheels and other mechanical radiation seem assertive.

RADIATION AND OTHER PRINCIPLES

Radiation uses four simpler principles—repetition, sequence, gradation, transition—and also contributes to more complex ones. It is a special type of sequence of repeated line and space as each ray thrusts outward at progressively graduated different angles.[1] Each line is consistently more vertical than the one below it and less vertical than the one above it. Radiation also makes a smooth transition from narrow space near the center to wide space at the periphery. Contrast emphasizes differences in line direction and apparent center-edge sizes.

For the more complex principles, radiation helps create a forceful rhythm and provides powerful emphasis between a point of convergence and outer edges. By controlling directional attention, radiation can also contribute to all the synthesizing principles.

INTRODUCING RADIATION

Structurally, darts and seams lend themselves effectively to radiating arrange-

---

[1]Maitland Graves, *The Art of Color and Design* (New York: McGraw-Hill Book Company, Inc., 1951), p. 42.

ments (Figures 17-1g and 17-3). Accordion pleats in skirts radiate gracefully from the waist, but they must be narrow at the waist and flared wider at the hem (Figure 17-1e). If extended upward they would all converge above the waist (Figure 17-2c). Gathers such as historic ruffs and yokes can also seem to radiate from a central point (Figures 17-4, 17-5), but very few pleats or gathers actually do. Some pleats are parallel, and gathers or ruffles fall at random, not in radiation. Draped folds can give a beautifully fluid radiation (Figure 17-1a), and the soft folds of a flared skirt or cape sleeve hint at it.

Radiation has unlimited possibilities in decorative design. Any radiating applied trim can be striking (Figures 17-1d and 17-4), and fabric pattern offers a fertile field with equally striking effects (Figure 10-25). The larger the radiating motif, the quicker it relates to a part of the body, such as the shoulders (Figure 17-1h); so the designer must insure that (1) the center does not fall at an awkward spot, and (2) desired size illusions are retained.

SUMMARY

Radiation is the feeling of steady outward motion from a central visible or suggested point. A graduated sequence of line directions, it is a linear principle of limited but dramatic effect. It may reinforce a directional effect or shrink apparent size near the center and expand it farther way. Radiation uses only line, space, shape, and pattern. It uses other principles of repetition, sequence, gradation, transition, and sometimes contrast; and it contributes to rhythm, emphasis, and the synthesizing principles.

It lends itself to structural radiating seams, darts, gathers, accordian pleats, and draped folds; and, decoratively, to an infinite variety of pattern motifs and applied trim.

CLASS ACTIVITIES

1. Invite students in advance to wear examples of radiation. Then with the class in groups, ask each group to find one of the following: radiation from one side of a point, from opposite sides of a point, from all around a point, from a suggested point; closed end radiation, or openended radiation. Allow time for groups to find and identify their type of radiation on anyone in the class. Then with "their" example standing, have each group identify the radiation and whether it is structurally or decoratively introduced, and analyze its effects. Discuss how the effects of each type of radiation differ.

2. Find an example of decorative radiation and cut it out. On a figure picture of appropriate relative size, place the radiation at different parts of the figure and compare their physical and psychological effects at each figure location.

3. Find an example of radiation so commanding that it demands to stand alone and another that, although self-contained, could be harmoniously repeated. What distinguishes the two?

4. Choose one example of radiation from Figure 17-1c to h, and design a decorative clothing application for it. Where on the figure would you use it? Why? Keep your results for future use.

18 *Rhythm*

DEFINITION

Rhythm is the feeling of organized movement. It may be flowing (Figure 18-1) or staccato (Figure 18-2), clearly stated or subtly suggested, and repeated or not. Its initial pattern, accent, and beat tantalize further when repeated because they anticipate continued beat that satisfies and fulfills. Since rhythm involves an arrangement of internally organized motion, it does not require repetition, but is easier and gains strength with it. Continuity gives rhythm both its fascination and its security.

EFFECTS

Rhythm suggests movement which must be in a direction; so it is a directional principle. Physically it emphasizes the direction of the movement on the body and influences apparent body size by its own size, direction, and dynamics. The more lively the rhythmic unit, the more attention it commands, and the more it enlarges. Rhythm may move in several directions, helping pull an ensemble together (Figure 18-1).

One psychological satisfaction of rhythm is its predictability. It can excite with a scintillating beat, or soothe with an undulating wave. It may swing merrily along with little anxiety (Figure 18-1), or sweep to a climax that releases suddenly (Figure 18-3). It is more subtle and sophisticated when barely suggested than when flatly stated. Shorter or smoother rhythms are usually more calming; longer developments to a climax are more exciting. But understatement is more potent; too much rhythm may seem unbalancing.

Rhythmic clothing design often seems to inspire actual movement in pictures of models, but body motion is not rhythm in clothing. The feeling of rhythm in the garment itself should exist when the wearer is standing still.

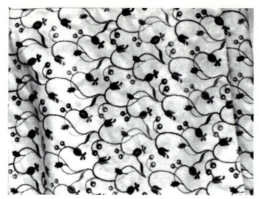

FIGURE 18-1 The curves of this lilting embroidered pattern undulate in waves and swirls, leading the eye rhythmically in several directions and reinforcing the graceful motion. (Courtesy Schiffli Embroidery Manufacturers Promotion Fund.)

RHYTHM AND THE ELEMENTS

Rhythm is a subtly powerful principle even though it applies only to the elements of line, space, shape, and pattern (Figure 18-4).

The examples of path, thickness, and other aspects of line in Figure 4-1 carry an entire repertory of potential rhythms. Wavy lines undulate (Figure 18-5a), and jagged or zigzag lines give jerky vibrations (Figures 18-2 and 18-5b). Scalloped lines are lilting. Regular broken lines give a staccato effect (Figure 18-2), and irregular ones seem syncopated. Thick lines announce an assertive, martial rhythm, and thin ones hint at a light, dainty rhythm. Curved, sea-like waves carry both undulation and sharp points in their lively effects (Figure 18-1). So, the various aspects of line lend themselves to a tremendous variety of rhythms.

Effective space relationships are vital and can inject vitality or tranquillity into a rhythm. Enough space is needed between lines and shapes to "breathe," but small enough to direct the gaze from one unit to the next (Figure 18-4). Too long a spatial pause would lose the rhythmic beat.

Shapes offer powerful rhythmic effects, jerky and abrupt (Figure 18-5e), undulating

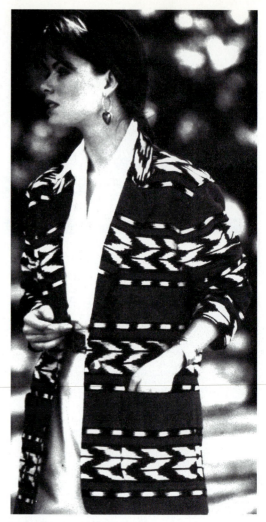

FIGURE 18-2 The fabric pattern creates several rhythms: the regular, broken lines are staccato, and the zigzag lines make a zigzag rhythm, as both types "group" into visual phrases. The straight lines and sharp-angled rhythms of the decorative fabric pattern agree well with the straight edges and angled corners of the structural jacket design. (Courtesy of Mark, Fore & Strike.)

(Figure 18-5f), or others. Unequally sided shapes create dynamic rhythms; paisleys, teardrops, and other free forms invite a range of restless rhythms (Figure 18-6). Review the geometric and free-form shapes in Chapter 6, Figures 6-2, 6-3, 6-6, and 6-7, and Chapter 10 pattern shapes. Experiment to see which ones lend themselves most read-

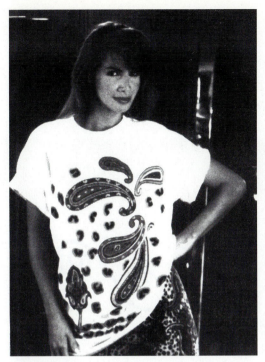

FIGURE 18-3 The dominant paisleys sweep dramatically to a line made by their points at the right, thus bringing several directions to pull the shirt composition together using similarity, but not exact repetition. (Courtesy of Mark, Fore & Strike.)

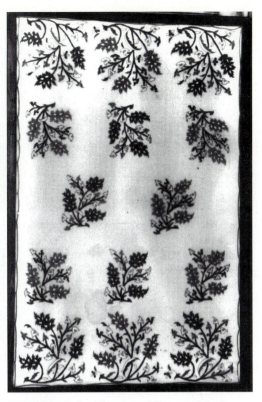

FIGURE 18-4 The curved lines and leaf shapes with ample spaces create a sense of branches swaying rhythmically to and fro in the breeze. Yet that sense is accomplished with the fabric perfectly still in this 7th century Turkish table cloth pattern. (Courtesy of Turkish Government Tourist Office.)

ily to rhythmic arrangements. Patterns that derive from these rhythmical relationships offer an infinite variety of invigorating motion (according to Chapter 10 criteria for a well-designed pattern) to entice the eye where the designer wishes it to go (Figures 18-5, 10-1 to 10-14 and other patterns).

RHYTHM AND OTHER PRINCIPLES

Although no other linear principles are intrinsic to rhythm, all of them can contribute profoundly to it. Linear rhythms can build to dramatic climaxes without repetition, as in Figure 18-5c, where the powerful swirl unwinds, pointing emphatically to the face. Or, a single, graceful line can give an elegant sweep difficult to achieve otherwise. But repetition of any element strengthens a rhythmic beat.

The limitations of parallelism and alternation create regimented rhythms (Figure 18-5e), whereas sequence is versatile and needed to retain a consistent beat and a sense of the beginning and end of a unit, or "visual phrase" (Figures 18-2 and 18-4). Gradation leads to a rhythmic climax (Figure 18-5b center), while transition glides in an undulating rhythm (Figure 18-5f).

Radiation rhythm marches line by line around its central point, and contrast accents rhythms by focusing attention where changes occur.

Rhythm can also enliven many of the more complex principles. It can playfully or forcefully emphasize a particular point. It can maneuver attention through any visual arrangement to suggest steadiness and bal-

Pure   Applied to dress

18-5(a) Line: Wavy lines convey
an undulating rhythm, moving
similarly along a path.

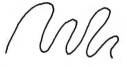

18-5(b) Line: Zigzag lines spark a regular
staccato beat.

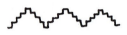 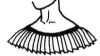

18-5(c) Line: A single swirled line gives a
powerful whirling rhythm.

 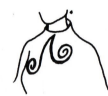

18-5(d) Line: Jagged line erupts into a
rhythmic vibration.

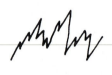 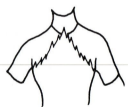

18-5(e) Shape: Sawtooth diamonds create
an abrupt rhythm with repetition.

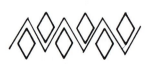 

18-5(f) Shape: Undulating shapes weave
into sinuous motion.

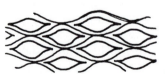 

18-5(g) Pattern: Windblown shapes in
pattern create dynamic yet graceful
rhythm.

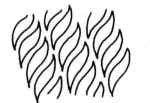 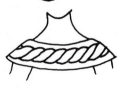

FIGURE 18-5 Rhythm and the elements.

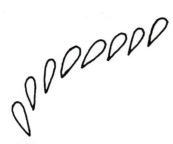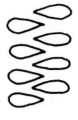

FIGURE 18-6 A single motif shape can create many rhythms. The teardrop can cascade in a sweeping flow (a), march back and forth (b), or swing playfully around a center (c).

ance. Rhythm determines eye movements that influence apparent proportions or create illusions of length, width, or size. Rhythm must harmonize its elements long enough to swing into a regular beat. Finally, rhythm contributes powerfully to unity by creating movement as it relates separate units into a rhythmic whole.

INTRODUCING RHYTHM

Structurally, flowing seams, smoothly sweeping edges, gathers, or curved, draped folds create graceful rhythms (Figure 18-5f). Straight-lined pleats that move (Figure 4-7), or tucks and series of darts that don't, create more staccato rhythms. Graduated tiers and flounces suggest both apparent and actual movement (Figure 15-4); smocking and shirring create miniature rhythms.

Decorative trims encourage rhythm, edges of gathered or flared ruffles undulate, and pleated edges march stiffly (Figure 18-5a, b). Patterns offer endless opportunity for any rhythms as contours and arrangements of any motif can create rhythm. For example, teardrops might cascade, (Figure 18-6a) or march (Figure 18-6b) or swing (Figure 18-6c).

Review the physical and psychological effects of line, space, and pattern to imagine the wealth of potential rhythms such as:

bouncing
bounding
fanning
flowing
jerky
lilting
looping
lurching
marching
regimental
sedate
skipping
staccato
stately
swaying
sweeping
swinging
swirling
syncopated
undulating
vibrating
wavy
whirling
zigzag

The rhythm sought will depend on the mood desired. Decorative design can reinforce structural rhythm (Figure 18-5g), but conflicting structural and decorative rhythms may destroy both. Interrupting or breaking the beat also destroys rhythm and accents the need for agreement of functional, structural, and decorative design.

SUMMARY

Rhythm is the feeling of organized motion which may range from a smooth flow to a stiff march. A directional principle, rhythm emphasizes the direction of its movement on the body. Psychologically, it can conjure versatile moods. It applies to line, space, shape, and pattern, and can use all the other linear principles as well as contrast. It contributes to emphasis, balance, proportion, harmony, and unity in both structural and decorative applications.

CLASS ACTIVITIES

1. Ask each group or student to choose (quietly) one rhythm from the list of rhythms under "Introducing Rhythm." Recalling the "cross-sensory interpretation" of Chapter 1, ask each to draw a line visualizing how that rhythm would look. Then (a) invite other groups or students to identify the rhythm the line visualizes, (b) analyze the physical effect and psychological mood it creates, and (c) design a garment, outfit, or fabric using it.

2. Do activity 1 using shape or pattern rather than line only.

3. In two or three different fabric patterns, analyze and compare how differing uses of space affect the impact of rhythm in each pattern.

4. Compare rhythms in several fabric patterns: (a) Which are more graceful and which are more forceful or rigid? (b) What uses of line, shape, space, and pattern give the rhythms their effects? (Review Chapter 4 on space use, Chapter 5 on line aspect variations, Chapter 6 on shape characteristics, and/or Chapter 10 on pattern criteria.)

5. For what structural garment style would the preceding rhythm be appropriate? Design a garment that harmonizes the decorative pattern rhythm with a structural style rhythm.

6. Invite students ahead of time to wear examples of rhythm. Then, with the class in groups, assign different groups line, shape, pattern, structural, or decorative rhythm. Allow time for groups to locate "their" examples, and with each "example" standing, invite the analyzing group to show how and why it is an example of rhythm of their element or technique and what effect it has.

19 *Concentricity*

DEFINITION

Concentricity is the progressive increase in size of layers of the same shape, all having the same center. Edges may be straight or curved or free form, but they retain their relationship to each other and to the center through every step. A bull's eye target is one familiar example of concentricity in which all circles share a common center and each circle is the same distance at the same points from the previous one. When a pebble hits water the ripples spread outward in concentric circles. Concentricity skirts around a central point, never pointing at it or coming in to touch it.

EFFECTS

Physically, concentricity strongly focuses attention on its central point and the part of the body it adorns and expands the outer edges, such as the shoulders (Figures 19-1, 19-2). It is a highlighting principle, but also has directional aspects: the repetition of one line leads inward to the next and climaxes at the center (Figure 19-3a-e). Limited but powerful, concentricity needs judicious use in dress.

Psychologically, concentricity is bold and commanding; there is nothing subtle about it, so its uses are generally casual. The progressive size changes that completely surround a central climax make it self-contained and offer little opportunity to link to other areas. Concentric lines carry the psychological effects of their aspects of line (Figure 5-1) and of the spacing between them; so curved, dotted lines (Figure 19-4) carry much softer effects than do thick, straight, sharp lines (Figure 19-5).

267

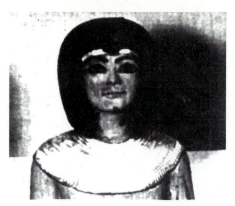

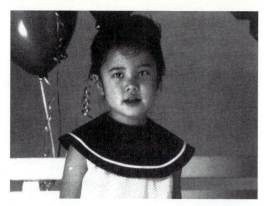

FIGURE 19-1 The concentric circles ringing the historic gold Egyptian collar accent the face and widen the shoulders. Royal *Shawabtys* or "Caller," detail, courtesy of Budek.)

FIGURE 19-2 The concentric lines of the collar in this contemporary child's dress echo historic examples with the same shoulder widening and focus on the face. (Courtesy of **McCall Pattern** Company.)

CONCENTRICITY AND THE ELEMENTS

Concentricity applies only to line, space, shape, and their combinations in pattern. Concentric squares and rectangles lend themselves to straight-edged garment styles (Figures 19-3a and 19-5), but concentric circles must be carefully placed (Figure 19-5) and usually small (Figure 19-4) to avoid resembling a walking target range (Figure 19-3b). Spacing between any two lines may be the same at all points or it may differ. If it differs, it does so in the same way, in amount and in place each repeat (Figure 19-3c). Spacing may also differ among sets of lines (Figures 19-3d and 19-5). Freeform shapes are challenging, but striking when successful (Figure 19-3e). Concentricity in pattern is usually simply a repeated series of concentric shapes (Figure 19-4), but it can produce powerful effects (Figure 19-5). The line of vision from large edge to small center crosses the concentric lines at almost right angles; so the path is rarely smooth or easy. Concentricity isolates each focal point distinctly and urges attention to remain there as much as the repetition urges it to move on (Figures 19-3e, 19-4, 19-5).

CONCENTRICITY AND OTHER PRINCIPLES

In some concentricity, there is exact repetition of lines and spaces (Figure 19-3a, b); in others the paths are merely echoed (Figure 19-6). Spacing between curved or straight lines is often parallel (Figures 19-3a, b and 19-5), and the changing sizes of the shapes involve sequence and gradation. Concentricity is perpendicular to radiation; radiation moves directly from center to edge whereas concentricity goes around a central point. However, in rare applications they can even work together, unusual for two such self-contained principles (Figure 19-7). Concentricity can be rhythmic and creates dramatic emphasis. With care it can contribute to synthesizing principles, but focus on the central point reduces that probability.

INTRODUCING CONCENTRICITY

Although some outer edges of a concentric shape might be structural (Figures 9-2, 19-3e), or a pocket might be cleverly concealed in concentric squares (19-3a), most uses of concentricity are decorative. Applied linear trims (Figures 19-2, 19-3c), pattern motifs

19-3(a) Line, space, and shape: Concentric
squares and rectangles lend themselves
to straight edged pockets and garments.

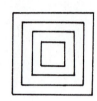 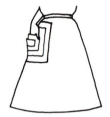

19-3(b) Line and space: Concentric circles need
care in placement.

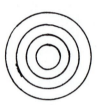 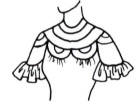

19-3(c) Line, space, and shape: Most distances
between concentric shapes are parallel,
but interesting concentricity can emerge
with non-parallel edges.

 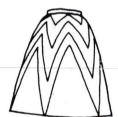

19-3(d) Line, space, and shape: Space between
concentric edges need not always be
equal among all sets of edges.

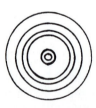 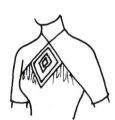

19-3(e) Line, space, and shape: Freeform as well
as geometric concentric shapes can give
interesting effects.

 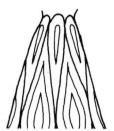

FIGURE 19-3 Concentricity and the elements.

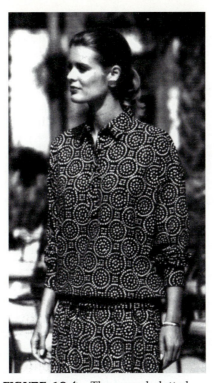

FIGURE 19-4 The curved, dotted lines and small circles help make the close repetition of concentricity in this pattern succeed. Because the circles are small and evenly spaced, and lines broken, they do not attract attention to a particular figure area as larger circles would. (Courtesy of Mark, Fore & Strike.)

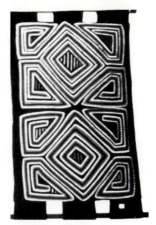

FIGURE 19-6 The concentric diamonds dramatically accent the centers in this traditional *mola* from the San Blas Islands of Panama. (Photo courtesy of Carolyn Joyner.)

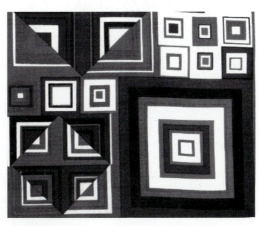

FIGURE 19-5 Spacing may differ even among parallel sets of straight lines within the concentric squares. Focus is on each center despite the repetition. (Courtesy of and design copyright by Boussac of France, Inc.)

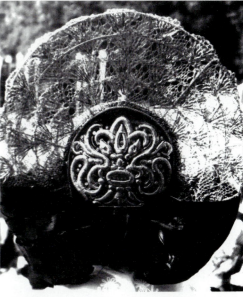

FIGURE 19-7 Each concentric ring in this decorative lace brim contains its own series of tiny radiations in an unusual combination of the two principles. The concentricity draws attention to the center cap motif of this traditional silver and gold headdress from St. Gallen. (Courtesy of the Swiss National Tourist Office.)

(Figures 19-4, 19-5), or layered appliqués, such as Panamanian *molas,* (Figure 19-6), or the lace headdress brim (Figure 19-7), embroidery, open cut-work, or beading can be arranged in concentric patterns to focus attention where it is desired (Figures 19-2 and 19-3b).

SUMMARY

Concentricity is a sequence of consecutively larger shapes all having the same center and sometimes parallel edges. It is a highlighting principle which focuses attention on the body part at the central point. It applies to line, space, shape, and pattern, always in the same singular but powerful relationship. It can include all the linear principles except radiation with which it occasionally cooperates. It contributes to emphasis, and with careful use, to some of the synthesizing principles. Although it can be introduced structurally, it is most often used decoratively.

CLASS ACTIVITIES

1. Look for examples of concentricity in a range of effects from dramatic to quiet. What body location(s) and/or uses of elements make one more dramatic? What body locations and/or uses of elements make another more quiet?

2. Invite students ahead of time to wear examples of concentricity. With the class in groups, assign groups to find concentricity in (a) lines, (b) complete shapes, and (c) fabric pattern. Allow time for groups to find examples of "their" element. Then, for each group, invite their example to stand as the group identifies (a) what makes it concentricity, (b) its physical and psychological effects on its figure area, and (c) whether it is structurally or decoratively introduced.

3. In catalogues or magazines, find as many examples of concentricity as possible, each occurring with a different principle. Identify what makes it concentricity and what makes it work with the other principle. Then analyze with which principle(s) does concentricity seem to work most easily? Why? With which is it most difficult to relate? Why?

4. Design a garment in which you use concentricity more than once to accent specific body areas, yet agree with each other. How did you do it? What elements, techniques (reinforcing, countering, etc.), and/or other principles did you use?

20 Contrast

DEFINITION

Contrast is the feeling of distinct difference, the opposition of things for the purpose of showing unlikeness. The eye most often tends to seek two types of visual relationships: similarities and differences. Repetition accents similarities and contrast accents differences. It is a highlighting principle because it focuses attention on the place where the differences occur. Contrast provides all of our visual variety and is one of the most powerful of all visual design principles.

EFFECTS

Physical

Because it so commands attention, contrast physically seems to accent and enlarge the area of the body where it occurs; the greater the contrast the more it enlarges. A juxtaposition of opposites heightens their differences and creates illusions of even greater contrast. Contrast creates a break that divides space, so a person wishing to look shorter, for example, would use contrasting color, space, line, or pattern to create a break near the waist; a person wishing to look taller would not. A gentle vertical center front contrast may narrow a bodice by breaking up horizontal space. Review the Chapter 3 illusions of geometric, size and space, and simultaneous *contrast* to see the vital role contrast plays in creating illusions.

Psychological

Psychologically, contrast is a dynamic principle that ranges from subtle to sharply aggressive. The stronger the contrast the more dramatic and assertive the effect. Bold contrast overwhelms a delicate mood, but a garment devoid of contrast is bland and insipid. Slight contrasts may seem subtle, but need care lest they seem like failed attempts to match an element. Arnheim suggests that our desire for contrast is a psychologi-

cal urge for "completeness." The eye and brain try to supply whatever seems missing in our visual environment to make a whole. An example is the after-image illusion of a hue complement to "see" the whole spectrum,[1] or the urge for a contrasting diagonal line to create a feeling of balance.

Contrast needs organization; variety invigorates as organizing relates. Too much or too scattered use of any element is spotty and disorganized; so although contrast uses opposition, it needs to be harmonious.

CONTRAST AND THE ELEMENTS

Much of the power of contrast comes from its remarkable versatility. Contrast usually occurs as differences in variations within one aspect of an element, such as curved contrasting straight line *path*, rough and smooth texture *surfaces*, or bright and dull color *intensities*. It can apply to every aspect of every element, with combinations of them, and often in several ways. The resulting opposing relationship defines and stabilizes the way an element is used at that time. The same garment might show bold contrast within one element—say light and dark color—and subtle with another—say sheer and semisheer textures. The designer can manipulate the exact kind, amount, and combinations of contrast for just the right effect.

Contrast is possible wherever qualities can change by degrees along a continuum or line. The extreme ends of any continuum provide maximum possible contrast, and points along the way control degrees of it. We can see how this works with each element. Table 20-1 shows maximum practical contrast for aspects of each element. The terms at each end of a continuum or line show extreme contrast, but many degrees are possible in between.

---

[1]Rudolf Arnheim, *Art and Visual Perception* (Berkeley: University of California Press, 1971), pp. 353, 354.

Each of the nine aspects of line lends itself to contrast. Path alone offers an almost infinite number of contrasts: straight, zigzag, curved, wavy, looped, scalloped, and more (Figures 5-1, 20-2). Every garment has directional line contrast since silhouette lines and openings are dominantly vertical, and shoulders, waistlines, yokes, and hems dominantly horizontal (Figures 20-1a and 20-3). Perpendicular plaid lines, at right angles, give maximum possible directional contrast.

Space involves several kinds of contrast: empty with filled space, and large with small space and others (Table 20-1, Figure 4-1).

The filled space of a pleated skirt contrasts the open space of a top, and its large space contrasts the small space of a pocket (Figure 20-1b, c). Their contrasts are heightened by their juxtaposition, accenting the point at which they meet.

Shapes and forms can contrast in size, contour, proportions, dimensions, mass, or—in clothing—fit (Table 20-1). Contrast in size is really a question of space (Figure 20-1c), and differences in contour—such as in the geometric shapes in Figures 6-2 to 6-5—offer an infinite variety of contrasts: curved, straight, undulating, angular, simple, complex, or others (Figures 20-1d, e, and 20-4). Garments need controlled contrast in structural form and decorative shape: too much similarity is monotonous (Figure 6-17a, d) and too much contrast is confusing (Figure 6-17b, e). Contrast in garment fit may give functionality and/or appearance variety: snug, loose, or bouffant (Figures 20-2, 20-4, and 20-5).

Color contrast is almost a science in itself. In simultaneous contrast (Chapters 3 and 8), differences in each aspect of color push each other apart as in Figures 8-14a, 8-16, and 8-21a. Combined hue, value, and intensity contrast can produce fascinating illusions (Table 20-1). An advancing red against a receding blue is blatant contrast, but contrasts are more subtle when two similar colors touch, such as a brighter and a duller blue. Then the same blue that receded next

Table 20-1   Contrast in Variations of Element Aspects

Element	Aspect	Variation	contrasted from	Variation
Line	Path	straight	⟷	crimped
	Evenness	even	⟷	uneven
	Continuity	continuous	⟷	broken
	Thickness	thick	⟷	thin
	Edge	fuzzy	⟷	sharp
	Edge contour	smooth	⟷	shaped
	Consistency	solid	⟷	porous
	Length	short	⟷	long
	Direction	vertical	⟷	horizontal
Space	Position	unenclosed (negative)	⟷	enclosed (positive)
	Division	empty	⟷	filled
	Dimension	flat, 2-D	⟷	depth, 3-D
	Pressure	concave	⟷	convex
	Distance	receding	⟷	advancing
Space/ Shape	Spacing	spotty	⟷	crowded
	Size	small	⟷	large
Shape/ Form	Contour	curvelinear	⟷	straight edged, angular
	Proportions	equally-sided	⟷	unequally-sided
	Dimension	flat, 2-D	⟷	3-D
	Mass	hollow	⟷	solid
	Fit	tight	⟷	bouffant
Light - with color and texture reactions				
Color	Hue	hue	⟷	complement
	Value	white	⟷	black
	Intensity	full	⟷	neutral
	Simultaneous contrast	hue	⟷	complement
		value	⟷	opposite
	After-image	hue	⟷	complement
		value	⟷	opposite
Texture	Surface contour	rough	⟷	smooth
	Surface friction	harsh	⟷	slippery
	Thermal character	warm	⟷	cool
	Resilience	springy	⟷	limp
	Flexibility	stiff	⟷	supple
	Compressibility	squeezable	⟷	rigid
	Extensibility	stretchy	⟷	stable
	Density	thick	⟷	thin
		porous	⟷	compact
		coarse	⟷	fine
	Light admission	transparent	⟷	opaque
	Light reflection	shiny	⟷	dull
Pattern	Source	Differing natural, man-made, imaginary, symbolic motifs		
	Interpretation	Differing realistic, stylized, abstract geometric presentations		
	Arrangement	Differing all-over, 1-way, 2-way, 4-way, border, spaced distributions		
	Composition	regularity	⟷	variety
	Mood	delicate	⟷	bold
	Motifs	similar uses of elements	⟷	different uses of elements

		Pure	Applied to dress

20-1(a) Line thickness, direction, and continuity: Thin contrasts from thick, solid from broken, and perpendicular forms maximum directional opposition.

20-1(b) Space: Filled space emphasizes differences from empty space.

20-1(c) Space and shape: Large areas are set in opposition to small areas.

20-1(d) Shape and form: Straight edged structural rings and triangles show differences from curved edge spheres.

20-1(e) Shape: Decorative shape edges of varying contours accent differences among each.

See Figures 8-11 to 8-21, 8-30 for simultaneous contrast and color contrast effects.

20-1(f) Texture: Shiny surfaces contrast from dull, and opaque form transparent in light reaction; rough from smooth in surface, and thick from thin in hand.

20-1(g) Pattern: Motifs within a pattern contrast each other and contrast between patterned and plain area accents structural edges.

20-1(h) Pattern: Juxtaposing contrasting patterns highlights differences among each.

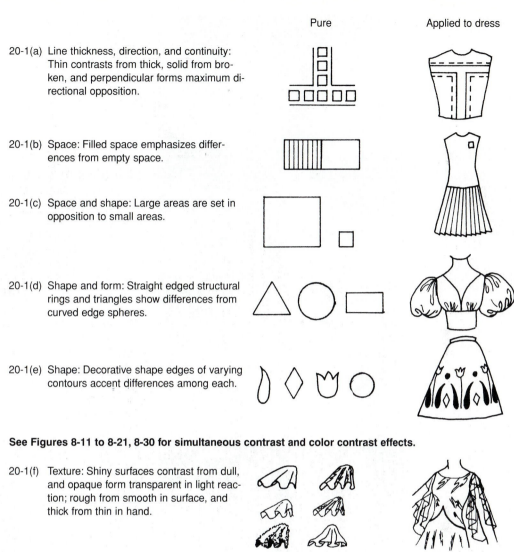
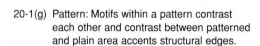
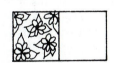
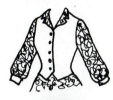
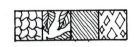
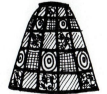

FIGURE 20-1 Contrast and the elements.

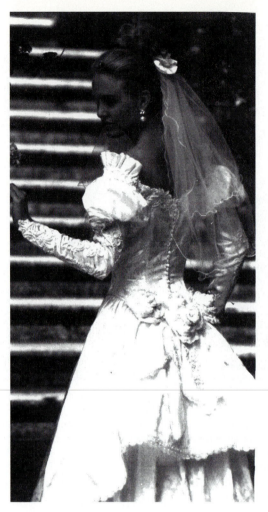

FIGURE 20-2 The same color throughout this bridal gown provides a common denominator to compare the lavish contrasts within nearly every other element: Line contrasts straight from curved from curly; short from long; horizontal from diagonal from vertical. Forms vary from spherical to tubular sleeves, hourglass bodice to conical skirt; fit contrasts the snugness of bodice and long sleeves against bouffant sleeve puffs and skirt. The applied trims of the beaded sleeves, back waistline floral trims, and embroidered neckline provide contrast for several elements: Their filled space, rough surface contour, and thicker density contrast the structurally emptier space, smoother surface, and thinner density of the gown fabric. The transparent, wispy veil texture contrasts the shiny, opaque, rich satin gown in light reaction. The degrees and kinds of contrast applied to each element create a pleasing contrast of sumptuous with delicate mood compatible with the occasion. (Courtesy of **McCall Pattern** Company.)

to red advances next to a duller blue. Opposite afterimages remind us that complements give maximum hue contrasts. Contrasting color schemes (triad, tetrad, complementary and its variations) use powerful hue contrast. But advancing and receding combinations that create autokinetic vibrations are distracting (Figure 8-24).

Contrast also enhances psychological effects of color. Green seems cooler against warm yellow; blue more serene with a lively pink, pale tints more delicate coupled with rich shades, but too stark a contrast fades tints.

Contrast in value is perhaps the most powerful element/principle use. Extreme light-dark contrasts command attention, whereas closer values are softer. For exam-

ple, the outfits in Figure 20-3 use similar straight lines, tubular forms, textures, rectangular shapes, open and closed space, and geometric patterns. But the close, light value contrast in (a) is gentle, whereas the stark opposites of the maximum black-white contrast in (b) aggressively demands attention. This single change makes a powerful mood difference in the two figures. Pure black-white contrasts with no intervening values carry the most impact (Figures 20-3b, 20-4); those with intervening, medium values soften the change (Figure 20-3a). Value contrast is usually the first noticed, as it identifies shapes and styles, just as every black and white illustration and printed word in this book depends on light-dark contrasts to identify the contents. Ex-

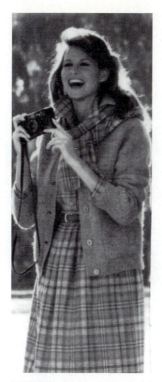 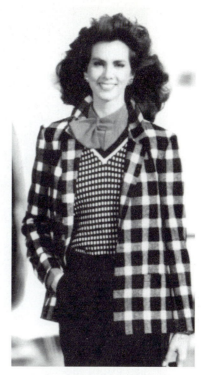

FIGURE 20-3 In both (a) and (b) the perpendicular lines of the plaids give maximum directional contrast. The filled pattern space contrasts the empty space of the pants and sweater and accents their structural edges. The rougher, bulkier textures of the tops contrast the thinner, smoother textures of pants and skirt. To this point both outfits use contrast similarly. The major difference in their over-all impact is caused by value contrast: (a) offers gentle contrast among pastels, while (b) leaps to attention with maximum contrast of black against stark white. (Ad photos courtesy of Pendleton Woolen Mills.)

treme value contrasts may overpower perception of hues (Figure 8-19), but absence of value contrast is dull; control is the key.

Natural contrasts between skin and hair (see Chapter 8) provides "built-in" appearance contrast. Contrasts in personal textures—the sheen of hair, smoothness of skin, sparkle of eyes, firmness of nails—and surface qualities of fabric all offer variety (see Chapter 9).

Every textural dimension of surface quality, hand, and light reaction invites tactile and visual contrast in any garment fabric or in notions (Figures 20-1f, 20-2, 20-4, and 9-2). Here, too, the ends of a continuum show maximum contrast (Table 20-1). The sameness in color throughout a garment or

outfit accents textural differences: rough vs. smooth, shiny vs. dull, opaque vs. sheer, crisp vs. supple, or thick vs. thin (Figure 20-2). Body movement also accents highlight-shadow and shiny-dull light reaction contrasts. Each extreme and the intervening degrees of any textural quality all require functional, structural, and decorative decisions.

Contrasts in pattern do not necessarily range along a continuum, but simply emphasize differences among motifs in sources, interpretations, or arrangements, or in use of component elements of line, sizes of shapes and spaces, between figure and ground, subjects, and color in one pattern (Figures 20-1h, 20-3), or among pat-

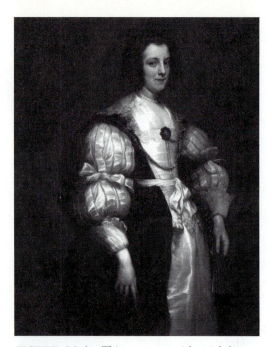

FIGURE 20-4 This gown provides rich linear contrasts in curved and straight paths; smooth and shaped edges; and varying lengths, directions, and thicknesses. Bouffant spherical sleeves and dome skirt contrast the snugly fitted, tubular bodice. Plain space in the skirt contrasts the decoratively filled space of the sleeves. The maximum black and white value contrast is dramatic. Textural contrasts emerge in the sheer, lacy collar against the crisp, smooth, shiny satin which again contrasts the deep velvet. Yet these extreme contrasts are controlled and coordinated for a dramatic effect. (*Dona Polyxena Spinola Guzman de Leganes*, by Sir Anthony van DYCK; early 1630's; National Gallery of Art, Washington; Samuel H. Kress Collection.)

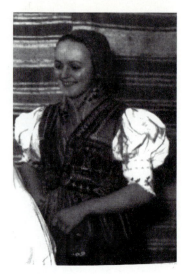

FIGURE 20-5 The spherical bouffant sleeve contrasts its snug, tubular cuff, and the snug, tubular bodice contrasts the bouffant, dome skirt. The busy, patterned, filled space of the skirt and bodice contrasts the plainer space of the sleeves and accents where they meet in this traditional Czech costume. (Courtesy of Czechoslovak Airlines.)

terns if more than one is used (Figure 20-1h). Contrast between patterned and plain areas emphasizes structural design that would be lost if all areas were patterned or all plain (Figures 20-1g, 20-3, and 20-5).

Natural and man-made sources of motifs contrast each other; combining various interpretations highlights their differences (Figure 20-1h). Directional contrast may result from combining two or more arrangements (Figure 20-3b). Using several patterns in one ensemble is tricky and needs mastery of harmony and sureness of the

mood desired; otherwise contrast may topple into conflict.

CONTRAST AND OTHER PRINCIPLES

Any principle that deals with difference or chance for comparison involves contrast. In directional principles, the break between one use and the repeat of an element is contrast in repetition. The differences among consecutive steps is contrast in sequence, alternation, gradation and radiation. The smooth change in transition does change to something different, a contrast. The pause between beats gives contrast to rhythm.

Contrast is essential to the synthesizing principles because it provides a basis for evaluating differences. For example, contrasts of length to width, or of the size of one area to that of another, are part of proportion. Contrasts of size help scale relate motif, figure, or garment part sizes. Contrast helps balance to distribute the apparent weight of forms, shapes, lines, colors, and textures; without contrast all would melt into the "balance" of an inert blob. Harmony and unity need contrast since sameness has no beginning, organization, or completion.

INTRODUCING CONTRAST

Structurally, there are infinite ways to introduce contrast. Seams, darts, hems, part edges, folds, pleats, and gathers are all lines that can contrast one another in many aspects (Table 20-1). Smooth textures contrast shirred, smocked, or quilted areas; and contrasts in fabric textural properties influence contrasts in structural design. The fullness of a gathered skirt may contrast the smooth fit of a bodice; or the spherical form of a peasant sleeve, the tube of a cuff or long sleeve (Figures 20-2, 20-5). Open space contrasts filled space; complex structural areas contrast simple ones (Figures 20-2, 20-3).

However, it is decorative contrasts that are first noticed and have the most striking impact. They usually use pattern, color, applied trims of various lines or shapes, textural light reactions, or accessories (Figure 20-2). The contrast of perpendicular lines in plaids, variety of shapes and colors in patterns, solid stripes with zigzag or broken lines, figure from ground in patterns, shape from space, patterned shirts from plain pants (Figure 20-3)—all demand instant attention. The textural glitter of beading contrasts a deep velvet (Figure 20-4). A wispy sheer veil contrasts an opaque gown (Figure 20-2). Yet color remains the most powerful kind of contrast, particularly in value (Figure 20-3). The list is endless, and the designer's joy is to select elements and apply just the right kind and degree of contrast to be as playful, subtle, casual, or shocking as desired.

SUMMARY

Contrast is the opposition of things to show differences, a highlighting principle that accents and enlarges the spot where it occurs. The more extreme it is, the more stark its effect; the milder it is, the more subtle its effect. Contrast also contributes to a sense of wholeness when differences complement one another. Every garment needs some contrast to look lively and avoid monotony; the key is to use enough contrast for interest, but not so much as to be overwhelming. Contrast can apply to every aspect of every element with versatility, but its most powerful use is in color value. Contrast is involved in almost every linear, other highlighting, and synthesizing principles by providing the means to compare differences. Possibilities for introducing contrast both structurally and decoratively are almost limitless.

CLASS ACTIVITIES

1. Choose an element aspect from the list in Table 20-1. If possible, with three copies of the same garment picture (so that all other element uses are held constant), draw a slight contrast of your element aspect on one, a medium contrast in the same garment place on the second, and an extreme contrast on the third. Or find three pictures of garments with your element aspect: one showing mild, one medium, and one strong contrast of your element. Compare their effects: What are the physical effects of the slight, medium, and extreme contrasts? How do they differ? What are the psychological effects of the mild, medium, and strong contrasts? How do they differ?

2. Repeat activity 1 with other aspects and elements. Which elements or aspects seem more powerful and which seem less powerful? Why does that seem to be?

3. Ahead of time, invite students to wear an example of contrast to class. Then,

with the class in groups, assign each group a different element or aspect, allow time to find an example of "its" element or aspect, and then, for the class, analyze how that use is an example of contrast applied to that element, its method of introduction, and physical and psychological effects.

4. Choose one element aspect and, in magazines or catalogues, find examples of structural and decorative contrast applied to that element. In general, which seems capable of more dramatic impact? Of more subtle nuance? What roles do advancing or receding uses of element aspects play in the differences of these effects?

5. List the linear and other highlighting principles, and in garments, magazines, or catalogs, find examples of contrast within those principles. In each case, how does contrast allow that principle to be fulfilled?

6. It could be said that a garment cannot exist without contrast. In magazines or catalogues or garments, find examples of garments with minimal contrast. Which element(s) always have some kind of contrast in a garment? How interesting is the garment with very little contrast? Why? Find an example of a garment with too much contrast. What makes it too much? What are the differences in element uses between the garment with too little and the garment with too much contrast?

21 *Emphasis*

DEFINITION

Emphasis is the creation of a focal point, the most important center of interest with all others subordinate. Some artists describe emphasis as the principle of dominance and subordination: one feature dominates and all others lend support. Focusing attention on one primary feature suggests mastery and control, qualities that every well-designed garment needs.

Its focal nature makes emphasis a highlighting principle, inviting the eye to scan arrangement, compare and rank its various parts to provide a satisfying hierarchy or organization. Lack of emphasis suggests disorganization; the gaze darts aimlessly, and multiple focal points are confusing. Emphasis suggests a complementary relationship of dominance and support.

EFFECTS

Physical

Emphasis focuses attention where it occurs on the figure, so one must know where and how to avoid emphasis as well as where and how to place it. Since one visual purpose of clothing is to flatter the wearer, the wearer is the real focal point; be sure that the person wears the clothes, rather than the clothes wearing the person.

Clothing can use emphasis to direct attention where it will enhance the wearer's attractiveness.

The face and neck areas are usually "safe" focal points because they are usually the first things viewed to establish identity. Most people regard their faces as one of their most attractive features, give them more grooming or makeup, and use clothing to direct attention to the face. These reasons make interesting collars and necklines important. If a culture admires a tiny waist, the person blessed with one may emphasize it; where muscles are admired, a man with bulging biceps may favor short-sleeved shirts. Cultures admiring large sizes may use voluminous robes, fullness, or stiff, bulky textures. Emphasis plays a dual role: By directing attention *to* one body area, it inevitably diverts it *away* from others.

Psychological

Any theme or mood of sophistication, sportiness, or gracefulness could be emphasized. Using all elements in a garment in the same mood reinforces each other and emphasizes that mood. So a thin, curved line suggests a soft mood that a filmy, supple texture and a soft pastel color reinforces, but stiff textures and strong colors would dilute it. So reinforcing techniques emphasize and countering techniques neutralize.

Accenting a certain area of the body physically also emphasizes it psychologically. So physical and psychological emphasis must harmonize.

EMPHASIS AND THE ELEMENTS

Emphasis can apply to any aspect of any element, although obviously not all at once. It is easier to achieve with advancing variations of elements such as sharp, straight, thick lines; assertive and unusual shapes, bold use of space, shiny fabric or glittering jewels; warm hues, bright intensities, light values, and extreme value contrasts; unusual textures; and striking patterns strategically placed (Table 21-1 and Figure 21-1). Emphasis is less with receding variations, such as thin, fuzzy lines; nondescript shapes; regular spacing; even light absorption; cool hues, dull intensities, medium values; dull, opaque textures; and small, allover, or no pattern. Larger areas of receding qualities are good backgrounds for small, advancing uses that create emphasis

TABLE 21-1

Element	Advancing Variations
Space	filled, enclosed
Line	straight, thick, sharp, continuous, solid, vertical
Shape/Form	large, solid, convex, three-dimensional
Color	warm hues
	light values
	bright intensities
	extreme value contrast
Texture	rough, thick, shiny
Pattern	above element uses

(Figure 8-22). Well-planned designs usually use advancing qualities of one element to dominate and smaller uses of the same and other elements to support (Figure 21-1).

A line may dominate the space it divides by its thickness, path, direction, or any other aspect (Figure 21-2a). Shape emphasizes the area it adorns by differences in contour or size, or by distinction from the space surrounding it (Figure 21-2b). Extremely tight or bouffant fit in structural forms emphasize the part of the body they cover (Figure 21-2c) whereas medium or loose fit is less emphatic (Figure 21-1). Closely filled space used as background emphasizes an empty space and the contour of the intervening line (Figure 21-2d).

Shiny highlights emphasize and enlarge the part of the body where they occur (Figures 21-2e, 21-3, and 21-4). Dull surfaces that absorb light help to de-emphasize an area.

Color is powerful in creating emphasis. Small areas of advancing hues, bright intensities, or extreme value contrasts provide striking accents (Figure 21-1, 21-3). Similarly, unusual textures highlight an area (Figure 21-2f).

One pattern motif usually dominates and the others are supportive (Figures 10-7 and 10-25). Border and spaced arrangements emphasize particular body or garment parts (Figure 10-29). Neighboring plain and patterned areas emphasize each other (Figures 21-2g and 10-29). Combining more than one pattern in an outfit de-emphasizes both.

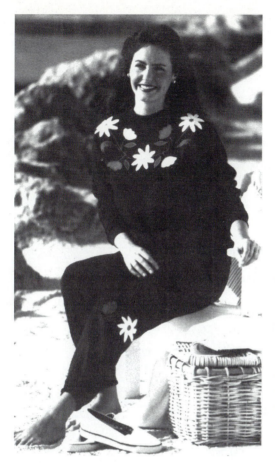

FIGURE 21-1 Advancing uses of elements are more emphatic: light against dark values, filled against empty space, sharp edges, and unconnected, convex shapes. The small, light areas provide accent against the larger, dark areas. Repetition of the flowers at the shoulder increases their emphasis, and the echoing flowers on the pants provide support. Thus contrast creates initial emphasis, and repetition reinforces it. (Courtesy of Mark, Fore & Strike.)

EMPHASIS AND OTHER PRINCIPLES

The eye initially seeks either of two kinds of relationships in any arrangement: similarity or differences. Similarity gives repetition, and differences give contrast. Extreme repetition or contrast are emphatic; so these two principles are essential to emphasis. Repetition usually evokes gentle emphasis, and contrast a stronger one.

Repetition suggests that something important is worth repeating; so repeated shapes, colors, or motifs reinforce their importance, hence emphasis (Figure 21-1), if not overdone. Most contrasts described in Chapter 20 lend themselves well to more powerful emphasis.

Initial impact of emphasis usually uses contrast, as with a motif shape contrasting background space or a light value against a dark value. Then repetition of the emphatic motif in smaller ways and other places provides support and the ranking of dominance and subordination.

Repetition and contrast in clothing may also emphasize extremes in wearer characteristics. For example, a bulky, stiff texture emphasizes heavy weight by repetition, and a supple, wispy chiffon emphasizes by contrast. Moderate textures reduce weight emphasis.

Several other linear principles can also contribute to emphasis. A climax in sequence or gradation is emphatic, and the order in sequence helps rank importance. Radiation emphasizes its center or its periphery and rhythm can lead to an emphatic climax and connect dominant and subordinate areas.

The highlighting principle of concentricity emphasizes its attention at a central point. Emphasis helps synthesizing principles control attention and relate garment areas to each other and the wearer. Clever placement of emphasis influences apparent weight distribution for balance. Well-scaled shape or motif sizes emphasize figure or garment areas. Emphasis is economical; it strips away superfluous distractions that dilute impact, and allows one feature to dominate. Emphasis organizes dominant and subordinate areas, and unity emerges more easily (Figure 21-4).

INTRODUCING EMPHASIS

Structural garment edges emphasize neighboring body parts: Skirt hems emphasize knees or legs; sleeve hems emphasize shoul-

21-2(a) Line thickness, path, continuity, and direction: Any aspect of line can dominate the area it divides.

21-2(b) Shape: Contrasting shape contours and sizes accent the area that isolates them.

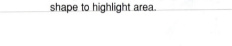

21-2(c) Form: Structural forms extended far away from or fitted very closely to the figure emphasize those body areas.

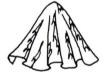 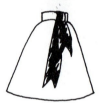

21-2(d) Space: Closely filled space used as a background allows empty space in shape to highlight area.

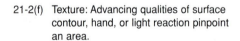

21-2(e) Lights: Shiny highlights accent an area compared to a dull background.

See Figure 8-31 for color emphasis effects.

21-2(f) Texture: Advancing qualities of surface contour, hand, or light reaction pinpoint an area.

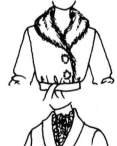

21-2(g) Pattern: One motif usually dominates a pattern, and a patterned accent will highlight a plain area.

 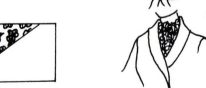

FIGURE 21-2 Emphasis and the elements.

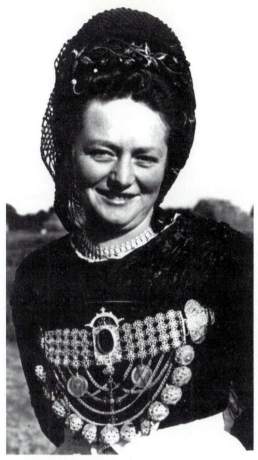

FIGURE 21-3 Most uses of elements that create emphasis also enlarge, as the filled pattern space of the metallic decoration enlarges as well as accents, and the shine of the metal and light-dark contrast reinforce the emphasis. The structural neckline edge accents the face, while the U curve of the metal chains is echoed by the reverse curve of the headdress silhouette, suggesting an oval frame to emphasize the face and bodice in this Feisen costume from Foehr in Schleswig-Holstein, Germany. (Courtesy of the German Information Center.)

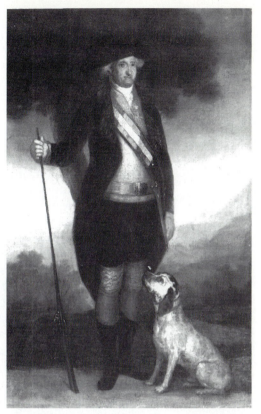

FIGURE 21-4 The shine of the sash texture helps it emphasize the chest area, and the light values accent it against the darker surrounding garments. The shine of the belt buckle and the light leg hose provide supporting emphasis. (*Carlos IV of Spain as a Huntsman;* Francisco Jose de GOYA; c. 1799; National Gallery of Art, Washington; Andrew W. Mellon Collection.)

der, arms, wrists, or hands; necklines emphasize neck or face (Figure 21-3). Exposing body areas that are usually covered by clothing emphasizes them. But in cultures or tropical climates where the body is normally exposed, body covering provides emphasis.

Any line leading to a point creates emphasis, as do unusual seams, styles, closings, or drapery folds. Structural emphasis is certainly possible, but decorative emphasis is easier and is often used to visually reinforce structural lines (Figure 10-29).

Since one purpose of decoration is to attract attention, it contributes to emphasis if it is controlled to avoid spottiness or overuse. Many applied trims command attention by contrasting their backgrounds. Jewelry is emphatic on plain backgrounds, but gets lost on patterned ones. Contrasting colors or pattern with plain is frequently a vehicle for emphasis (Figure 21-1), as are carefully chosen and placed accessories of contrasting shape, color, or texture. Emphasis is powerful, so it must be used simply and with restraint; overdone, it destroys itself.

SUMMARY

Emphasis is the creation of a focal point which draws attention to the point where it occurs and away from other areas thereby guiding the gaze around the figure. Emphasis creates dominant and subordinate relationships which can strengthen psychological moods as well as visual effects. It can apply to any aspect of any element, and is easiest to achieve with advancing qualities. Repetition and contrast are essential to emphasis, which also uses sequence, gradation, radiation, rhythm, concentricity, and scale. Emphasis can contribute to balance, harmony, and unity. It may be incorporated in dress structurally, but it is easier to achieve decoratively. It may be one of the more culturally dependent principles; what would command attention in one culture might be less emphatic in another.

CLASS ACTIVITIES

1. Using advancing qualities of selected elements, create a focal point at one figure area, and smaller, subsidiary uses at two or three other figure locations. Then switch the main focal point element uses to one of the subsidiary areas. What happens? How do its size, weight, and advancing seem to change? How does that seem to change the size, weight, and attention of that figure area? How does the change in position of emphasis affect apparent balance of the entire figure? Experiment, shifting the main focal point to other figure areas and comparing results.

2. Using the element chapters, Table 21-1, and a page of ten copies of the same, simple structural style (such as Figure 6-25b, 6-34e, or 6-44f) create a "focal point" using advancing qualities of line. In the next figure, create the same arrangement, but use receding qualities of line; then compare their effects. In each of the next pairs of figures, repeat with shape/space, color, texture, and pattern successively. For physical and psychological effects, how would you compare effects of (a) advancing and receding qualities, and (b) different elements?

3. Ahead of time, invite students to wear examples of emphasis to class. Then, with the class in groups, assign each group an element and ask them to find and analyze an example garment achieving emphasis using "their" element, what makes it an example, its effects, and how it is introduced.

4. Using the same element in the same garment locations, design one using contrast and one using repetition. Compare their effects and the reasons for them. Which is more dramatic? Which is more focused? Which is more distributed? How do their psychological effects differ?

5. Repeat activity 4, using other principles: sequence, parallelism, alternation, rhythm, radiation, gradation, transition, and concentricity, each in a different example. Which most easily creates emphasis? Which are more difficult?

22 *Proportion*

DEFINITION AND CONCEPT

Proportion is the comparative relationship of distances, sizes, amounts, degrees, or parts. It can apply to one-dimensional lines, two-dimensional shapes, or three-dimensional forms. Spatial characteristics have little meaning except as they compare to something else; so the key idea of proportion is "in relation to." A single part of the body may seem "well proportioned," but if its size or shape is inconsistent with the rest of the figure, the whole figure seems "out of proportion" (Figure 22-1). As Morton points out, designs are not judged as isolated sections; perceiving their parts in various combinations makes one aware of their relationships and able to evaluate them on that basis.[1]

---

[1]Grace Margaret Morton, *The Arts of Costume and Personal Appearance*, 3rd ed. (New York: John Wiley & Sons, Inc., 1966), p. 99.

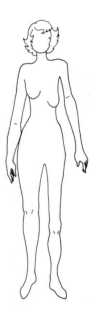

FIGURE 22-1 The key to proportion is relationships. Each isolated unit may look "normal," but seems "out of proportion" if it is inconsistent in area or dimension with neighboring areas.

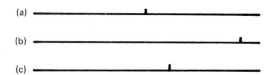

FIGURE 22-2 Unidimensional, or linear, divisions are usually least interesting when they are equal (a), less interesting when extremely unequal (b), and most interesting when they contain a variety that invites comparison (c).

Proportion is a synthesizing principle. It invites relating of parts and wholes, and in so doing, pulls them together, synthesizing and integrating our perceptions.

One mark of artistic appreciation is sensitivity to fine proportion, a feeling for dimensions, areas, or quantities that work well together. Such sensitivity is not difficult to achieve, but it does need practice.

The comparative relationships of proportion can work on any or all of four levels:

1 Within one part: as in comparing length to width in a rectangle or skirt.

2. Among parts: as in comparing the area of one rectangle to that of another, or bodice area to sleeve areas, or amount of one color to another.

3. Part to whole: as in comparing the area of a whole picture occupied by the sky, or the amount of a whole dress occupied by the skirt.

4. Whole to environment: as in comparing the size and shape of a whole house to its hillside, or relating the size and shape of an outfit to the shape and size of the wearer.

In Composition

Traditionally, proportion deals mainly with relationships of line, shapes, or areas. However, in clothing these areas contain textures, colors, or patterns in varying—or proportionate—amounts; so every element may be involved. It is not a question of whether proportion exists; it does since every shape has several dimensions which can be compared. Rather, it is a question of what makes proportions pleasing or ugly. These, like other ideas of beauty and ugliness, are subject to cultural preferences, but some guidelines have proven acceptable throughout many centuries and in many cultures.

Although some of these guidelines appear as mathematical formulas, the most beautiful applications of proportion seem to have a slight deviation that defies precise analysis. Exact multiples and divisions, equal halves, and strict mathematical equations seem sterile.

The essence of pleasing proportion is similar to our familiar guideline: enough variety for interest but not enough to overwhelm. Most people find divisions in exact halves the least interesting. On a unidimensional, or linear, level, one instantly compares the equality of the division, and there is little else to hold one's interest (Figure 22-2a). On a two-dimensional, or shape, level, the same is true of a square with all sides equal (Figure 22-3a) or equal divisions of space (Figure 22-4a). Extreme relationships have one distance or area so dominant and the other so negligible that there is little invitation for comparison (Figures 22-2b, 22-3b, and 22-4b). More interest is generated when the larger part dominates but does not overwhelm, and the smaller part is large enough to invite comparison (Figures 22-2c, 22-3c, and 22-4c).

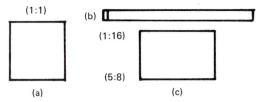

FIGURE 22-3 Two-dimensional analysis at within-part level compares shape length to width equally (a), extremely unequally (b), and with enough length to width to retain interest (c).

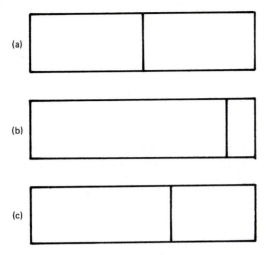

FIGURE 22-4 On two-dimensional among-part level analysis, one part equaling another gives a 1:1 ratio (a); one part overwhelming another seems unbalanced (b); and when the smaller part is large enough to hold interest, it invites comparison with the larger part (c).

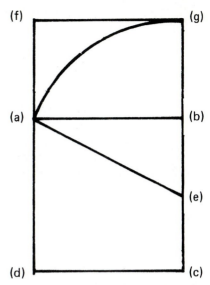

FIGURE 22-5 A rectangle of "golden mean" proportions is created from a square (abcd) with a half-way point (e) marked along one side. That point is connected to an opposite corner (a) and the line (ae) becomes a radius arcing up to (g), forming the upper corner of the new rectangle in a relationship where the smaller part (afgb) is to the larger part (abcd) as the larger part is to the whole (fgcd).

Relationships usually give more interest when one unit is about two-thirds or three-fifths the measure of the other. A line divided about three-fifths along its length (Figure 22-2c), or a rectangle about two-thirds as wide as it is high (Figure 22-3c), or two rectangles one of which is about three-fifths as large as the other (Figure 22-4c) show this relationship at "within part" and "among parts" levels. Artists and architects have traditionally labeled this proportion the "golden mean" or "golden section."

Establishing a golden mean relationship at the "part to whole" level begins with a square, with corners A, B, C, D, then marking a point E halfway along one side B - C (Figure 22-5). A line drawn from that point to the opposite corner A becomes a radius, which arcs upward to point G. This new addition is both the height of a new rectangle and the addition to the height of the original square that creates a combined rectangle of golden mean proportions in which the smaller part (AFGB) is to the larger part (ABCD) as the larger part is to the whole (FGCD). In other words, the smaller area occupies proportionately the same amount of the larger area as the larger area occupies of the whole. The length to width proportions of the small rectangle are also the same as those of the large rectangle. Neither length nor width is overpowering nor too equal, nor is one unit too large or small for the other. They invite study and reflection; they hold attention.

Such relationships are often expressed in numerical ratios. If a rectangle made of small squares were three squares wide and five squares long, it would have a ratio of 3:5 (Figure 22-6). The golden mean develops along a sequence of ratios in which the addition of any two adjacent numbers equals the next number: 1, 2, 3, 5, 8, 13, 21, 34, 55, 89, and so on. Any fraction created from two adjacent numbers, with the larger one over the smaller one, gives a fraction that translates into the same decimal figure. For example,

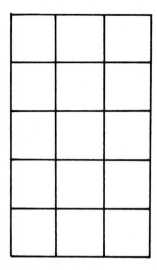

FIGURE 22-6 A rectangle composed of equally sided units, or squares, containing three along one direction and five along the other has a 3:5 ratio of width to length.

$$\frac{34}{21} = 1\frac{13}{21}, \text{ or } 1 : 1.618.$$

$$\frac{55}{34} = 1.618.$$

$$\frac{89}{55} = 1.618.$$

So the mathematic golden mean is considered to be 1:1.618, or close to 3:5 or 5:8.

Another verification uses three consecutive numbers in the above golden mean series. Multiplying the outer two, or "extremes," nearly equals the square of the center number, or the "means."[2] So the series 3, 5, 8 multiplies the extreme, or end, numbers: $3 \times 8 = 24$, and squares the center number: $5 \times 5 = 25$. With 2, 3, 5, $2 \times 5 = 10$ and $3 \times 3 = 9$. The relationship holds consistently.

Many great works of art in many cultures have consciously or unconsciously organized their linear or spatial divisions in

---

[2]Helen L. Brockman, *The Theory of Fashion Design* (New York: John Wiley & Sons, Inc., 1965), p. 84.

accordance with this relationship. Much great architecture is based on it, as are many beautiful clothes, but it is not the only way to recognize or achieve beauty and functionality in proportion.

Appropriate proportion is especially important in the applied arts of architecture, furnishings, and clothing. Functional demands on many shapes and forms in these fields often make golden mean proportions unfeasible. A thickness to length ratio of 3:5 for a table leg, or spoon, would be squat, chunky and impractical for their respective purposes and functions. An arm, leg, or total figure does not have golden mean proportions; they are narrow in relation to their length. So long evening wear, long sleeves, or pant legs will also not have golden mean proportions since they must agree with the forms they envelop to be practical and comfortable (Figure 22-7). The attention balance provided by golden mean proportion does not mean that it is the only acceptable proportion and others are "bad;" nor does the use of other proportions invalidate the golden mean. We have seen earlier that the eye usually notices first two kinds of relationships: similarities and differences. In proportion, equal proportions give similarity, and extremely unequal proportions provide differences or contrast. Proportions do not have to be golden mean to meet the criterion of a pleasing relationship between equality and such extreme inequality that one area overwhelms and another is lost. However, golden mean proportions offer a mid-range point of reference that provides balance, stability, and synthesis. Equal and extremely unequal proportions will often be part of that mix as proportions must be appropriate to the functions of their objects.

Further, shapes are not judged only as isolated units; they interact. Each subdivision of an area creates new shapes and new proportions, which relate to each other (Figure 4-12). As Arnheim notes, any shape must show the effect of interaction to avoid

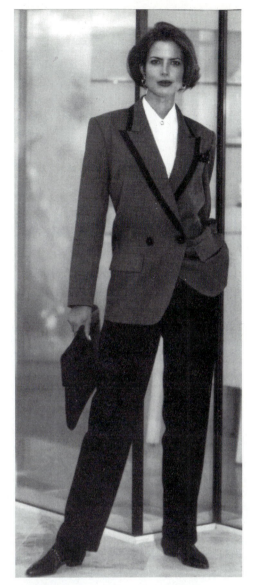

FIGURE 22-7 Proportions of long sleeves and pant legs must agree with the long, narrow, body parts they surround for comfort and function; so they are not expected to have within-part golden mean proportions. Yet as pant legs are side by side, and long sleeves widen the upper body, among-part proportions become less extreme. Compare the differences in length effects where the jacket hangs full length and the pant leg shows proportionately less, to where the pant leg is relatively longer and the jacket appears shorter. (Courtesy of Pendleton Woolen Mills.)

appearing lifeless and dead.[3] Proportions can interact to emphasize or minimize extremes. For example, two rectangles of 1:5 ratio laid end to end would be long and narrow (Figure 22-8a), but arranged side by side, as two pant legs would be, they interact in a relationship of more balanced proportions (Figure 22-8b). Proportion interaction among garment parts is one of the designer's most powerful tools in creating illusions to camouflage undesirable figure proportions.

In the Body

Proportions of clothing must relate to those of the human figure that supports them; so the clothing designer must master figure proportions. The human body has long been considered one of the most beautiful of objects because of the exquisite and complex proportions of its parts and their relationships. Rarely does it have equal multiples or divisions, and its parts offer enough artistic comparison and variety to hold admiring attention the world over. Girl- and boy-watchers are unaware that they are conducting an intricate cultural analysis of proportion. Arnheim observes that "mathematical formulae also have cultural and biological connotations." A Miss Universe whose bust is "36 inches…and 24 at the waist…" not only satisfies the Pythagorean proportion of 2:3, but fulfills the Western cultural concept of the ideal figure.[4]

Yet other writers note that some faces considered beautiful do not fit any formulas of ideal beauty proportions.[5] Such deviations suggest that beauty also springs from an informed sense that linear and spatial relationships are right for each other, not just a mathematical equation. Relationships slightly off exact ratios are often more interesting. Art by formula is rarely art.

[3]Rudolf Arnheim, *Toward a Psychology of Art* (Berkeley: University of California Press, 1972), p. 117.
[4]*Ibid.*, p. 118.
[5]Diane Ackerman, *A Natural History of the Senses* (New York: Random House, 1990), p. 275.

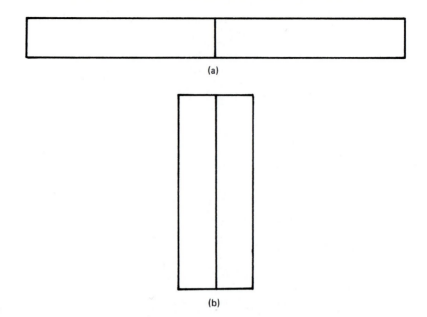

(a)

(b)

FIGURE 22-8 Proportions of neighboring shapes interact to create new proportions according to their relative positions. Two rectangles of 1:5 ratio laid end to end (a) give extreme length-width proportions, but laid side by side (b) they create a more balanced interaction.

Vertical body proportions are described as "head heights," or the number of times the height of the head could fit into the total height of the body. A person 5'4", or 64 inches tall, whose head height is 8fi" is about 7fi heads high. A man 6'3" or 75 inches tall, whose head is 10 inches high is also 7fi heads high. In both cases the proportions, or head size *in relation to* body size, are the same even though the actual measurements differ (Figure 22-9).

A figure 7fi heads high, described in head height measures shows the neck as ⅓ of a head high, chin to shoulders about fi of a head, chin to bust or chest center generally one, bust to waist about ⅔, waist to hip about one, hip to knee is about 1fl, knee to ankle about 1fi, and ankle to floor fi. The hips are about half-way from head crown to floor. The indentation at the base of the neck is usually used as the upper reference point for torso or bodice length. The widest

part of the calf is about ⅓ of the way from knee to ankle. Elbows touch just below the waist, wrists just below the hips, and fingertips about ⅓ of the way from hip to knee (Figure 22-9a, b). What ratios of length to width do you see within each part of the body? How do these change as several parts are seen together as a unit?

"Break points" occur where a silhouette line changes direction. For example, the outward direction of the line from waist to hip changes, or "breaks," at the hip and curves inward toward the knee; the inward curve from the chest changes direction, or breaks, and curves outward at the waist (Figure 22-9a). Natural body divisions or break points at the neck, bust, waist, hip, knee, ankle, elbow, or wrist usually form units of pleasing proportions, and are functionally appropriate for garment divisions because those points are where the body bends.

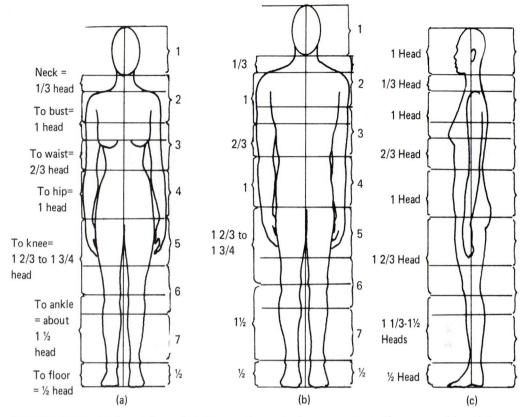

FIGURE 22-9 Different figure heights may have similar proportions. The woman (a) and the man (b) both have 7½ head heights even though their total heights differ. Profile center verticals differ among various body groups; the Western ideal (c) is not universal.

The vertical center front and back lines are common to most people. However, the traditional vertical side view balance line from ear through front shoulder, elbow, hip center, forward knee, and front ankle (Figure 22-9c) may be an ideal but also may not be common; thorough data on body measurements are not available from many parts of the world. Many cultures prize erect posture, but many people in Western cultures are round-shouldered. For reasons not thoroughly known, many Africans are swaybacked; thus the center of the waist from the side view is well forward of the knee. Differing body configurations will affect criteria of design and fit.

The Western standard of average figures 7½ heads high and ideal fashion figure of at least 8 heads high is by no means universal; other cultures may use other preferences. The lower the number of head heights, the larger the head is in relation to the rest of the body (Figure 22-10b); and the more head heights, the proportionately smaller the head (Figure 22-10c).

Other body parts may also deviate from an "average" or ideal. A woman may be low-busted in relation to her shoulder-waist length (Figure 22-10b); or short-waisted (figure 22-10a) or long-legged (Figure 22-10c) in relation to other proportions. In fact, *most figure characteristics labeled as "problems" are basically deviations from ideal proportions* for that body part for that culture. Study Figure 22-10a, b, c to see how three figures the same height have differing body proportions and head heights.

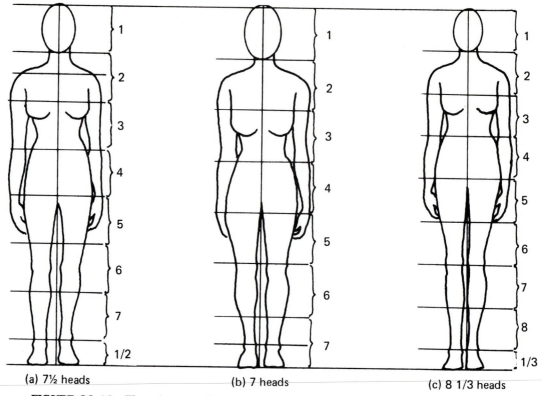

(a) 7½ heads

(b) 7 heads

(c) 8 1/3 heads

FIGURE 22-10 Three figures, all of the same height, may have differing body proportions. The larger the head in relation to other body parts, the fewer head heights the body will be (b), while a smaller head means more head heights (c). Given the same heights, one figure might be relatively short-waisted (a), another low-busted (b), and another long-legged (c) in relation to other body proportions.

Average body width, depth, and circumference proportions also vary, sometimes according to racial configurations. Many Asians tend to be somewhat smooth and flat in front and back torso, and women often have slight waist indentation. Africans tend to be narrower in hip width and thicker from front to back. Caucasian women are often wider across in the hip, with more indentation at the waist. Among most races a woman's hip and shoulder width are roughly the same. A woman's center of gravity, or greatest weight concentration is at the hips, and a man's is in his shoulders, which are usually about two head-lengths wide. Horizontal variations in proportions are as common as vertical ones. Two people could have exactly the same hip circumference, say 36 inches, but one might be 13 inches wide because of front to back thinness, and the other might be only 10 inches wide because of greater depth (Figure 6-13).

Most head and face proportions are similar, with the eyes about halfway from crown to chin and about one eye-width apart (Figure 22-11a, b). The nose tip is about halfway from eye to chin; and eye to brow or nose to mouth about the height of the eye. The hairline is about one-third of the way from crown to eyebrow, and the mouth about one-third from nose to chin. Ears usually extend from eye to nose tip in length, and are halfway from front to back of the head. These relationships help show why the 2:3 width to length ratio of oval is a well-proportioned background for facial features (Figure 6-21).

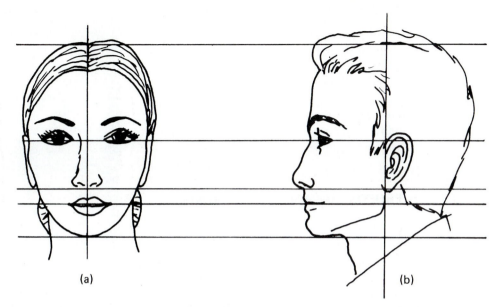

(a)   (b)

FIGURE 22-11   Front (a) and profile (b) face and head proportions are similar for both men and women, with men's features usually slightly more angular.

EFFECTS

Proportion has profound effects on apparent dimensions of the figure. When a designer changes a relationship between space and shape, establishing a silhouette and subdividing its internal space, he or she creates a new proportion and new visual arrangement (Figure 4-12).

The impact of garment proportions on apparent figure proportions reveals much of the power and challenge of proportion: it can create illusions of perfection and beauty where reality is less than ideal. For example, the long, narrow center panel in Figure 3-16 lengthens and narrows the entire figure. Equally sided shapes tend to add weight (Figures 6-2, 6-16a, b, 22-12a) and long, thin shapes accent their dominant direction (Figures 6-16c, j, k, 22-7). Proportion affects any physical property of a garment or wearer because it deals with their areas and spatial relationships (Figure 22-7).

Physical effects of shape in clothing are usually more satisfying if they follow the natural divisions of the body. For example, the skirt in Figure 22-12a has equal proportions of little interest and little relationship

to the figure. It starts in the middle of one section of the body and ends in the middle of another, ignoring body divisions and proportions. The dress in Figure 22-12b takes advantage of natural body divisions to create pleasing proportions and functional comfort.

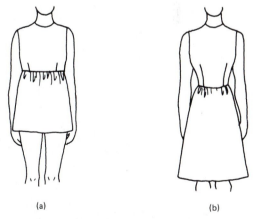

(a)   (b)

FIGURE 22-12   The nearly square skirt (a) has almost equal proportions and disregards natural body proportions and break points, while the rectangular skirt (b) has unequal and interesting proportions, and acknowledges natural body proportions.

Psychologically, proportion influences whether a shape seems stable and solid or wobbly. Usually more equal proportions seem more stable and static, and more extreme proportions seem more lithe and fragile. Larger areas of an element use suggest proportionately greater importance, and smaller areas less (unless they use advancing qualities).

PROPORTION AND THE ELEMENTS

Proportion can apply to nearly every aspect of every element. It can use every aspect of line: the width and tightness of a loop or zigzag path in relation to the dominant direction of the whole line; thickness in relation to length; broken distance in relation to solid; amount of fuzzy edges in relation to sold core, and so on (Figure 5-1). Spatial arrangements always involve proportion, whether comparing areas within differently sized shapes, or amount of empty space to filled space (Figure 4-12).

Shape inevitably has proportion. Nearly every illustration in the chapter thus far involves comparisons of dimensions, spatial divisions, or relationships of shape. Some occur only at the first level, within a unit such as the length to the width of a skirt (Figure 22-12). Others occur within and among parts and in part-to-whole relationships (Figure 22-13). The bulbous garment in Figures 6-17a, d, and g is unpleasant because of the monotonous repetition of shape, *and* because the equal proportions of the circles themselves are of little interest! The garment with a multitude of shapes in Figures 6-17b, e, and h is not only confusing, but the shape proportions have little relationship to each other or to the whole.

Interaction between body and clothing proportions at all four levels is an intricate process that we often do without realizing how, or knowing why the results strike us as pleasing or not. Isolated study of each part helps understanding of the whole. Figure 22-14a shows individual garment parts with a ratio to each other of

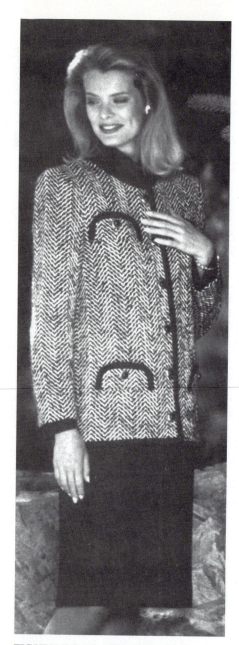

FIGURE 22-13 The individual sleeves and individual right and left jacket fronts each have long, narrow within-part proportions, and aligned side by side nearly 2:3 ratios. The visible part of the skirt has a 5:6 within-part ratio, but a 3:5 among-part ratio compared with the jacket. At part-to-whole, the jacket occupies about ⅝ of the whole outfit. The plain to patterned area also has a 3:5 ratio. (Courtesy of Mark, Fore & Strike.)

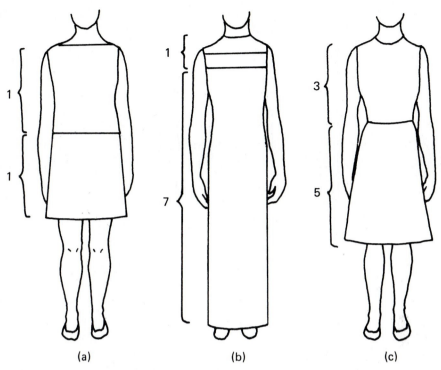

FIGURE 22-14 Equal proportions of within-part length to width and equal among-part ratios create little interest (a). Very unequal part-to-part proportions (b) invite less comparison than do gently unequal proportions (c). Compare the garments with the proportions in Figure 22-4.

1:1 and 1:2 of part to whole, still equal relationships. Figure 22-14b shows the other extreme of a narrow shoulder yoke shift. The narrow shoulder yoke has about a 1:6 within-part ratio, perched atop a long, thin shift of about 1:5 ratio. The ratio of the yoke to shift is an extreme 1:7, so the yoke almost seems negligible compared to the shift. Figure 22-14c has proportions closer to the golden mean within parts, among parts, and between part to whole. Within parts, the bodice has a width to length ratio of about 2:3, and the skirt about 3:5. Among parts, the bodice has about a 3:5 ratio to the skirt. On a part-to-whole level, the skirt provides a 5:8 ratio to the whole. Thus there is enough similarity to invite comparisons and enough variety for interest. The proportioned garment divisions follow the natural divisions of the body. Figure 22-15a, b, and c show similar relationships.

A slight change of a single line can change the entire proportions of a shape. Review the geometric and size and space illusions of Chapter 3 to see what a great change in effect every small change in distance, space, or size can make (Figures 3-6, 3-13 to 3-16). The styles in Figures 6-22 to 6-52 use relative dimensions, sizes, areas, and spatial divisions at each of the four levels to create *illusory effects on the figure.* Remember that figure proportions also interact with garment proportions (Figure 3-1).

Proportion applies to color, texture, and pattern according to the amounts used. How much light compared to dark area does a garment contain (Figure 22-13)? Or bright intensity compared to dull? Or one hue compared to others (Figure 8-32)? How much of one texture is there in relation to another, or patterned compared to plain area (Figure 22-13)? A more advancing use

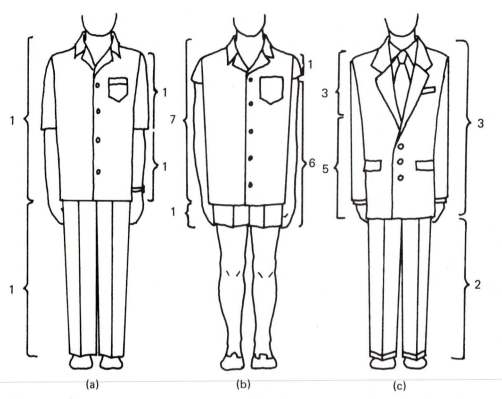

FIGURE 22-15 Trousers and shirts of equal length (a) or an extremely long shirt in relation to shorter pants (b) offer less interest than do differences that invite comparison (c).

of an element needs proportionately less space than a receding one (Figure 22-16).

Proportion applies to pattern as it does to all the other elements. It defines relationships among the lines, spaces, and shapes that define the motifs on the first three levels of proportion. Proportion in pattern compares areas occupied by figure to areas of background, in spacing between motifs compared to motif size, and in proportions of dark to light (Figure 22-16). Review illustrations in Chapter 10 and analyze how proportion is applied in pattern.

PROPORTION AND OTHER PRINCIPLES

Although no linear or highlighting principles are intrinsic to proportion, all of them can contribute to it. Distances between repeats create proportions, as do spaces among groups of parallel lines. The propor-

tion of attention directed to each step of sequence, alternation, concentrism, and gradation determines its relative importance to other steps in the series and to the whole. Even transition involves proportion in where and how its smooth changes begin, change, and end. Radiation relates its center to its periphery, and rhythm creates changing size and shape proportions as it moves. Contrast provides the variety essential for any proportion other than equal ones.

Since one dimension or area of an unequal proportion dominates, proportion and emphasis complement each other. For example, a proportionately long and narrow, central front panel emphasizes the wearer's apparent height and slimness.

Of the other synthesizing principles, proportion affects balance as sizes, shapes, and relative amounts influence apparent dimensions and weight distribution. Proportion is a close relative of scale, and it is intrinsic to harmony and unity.

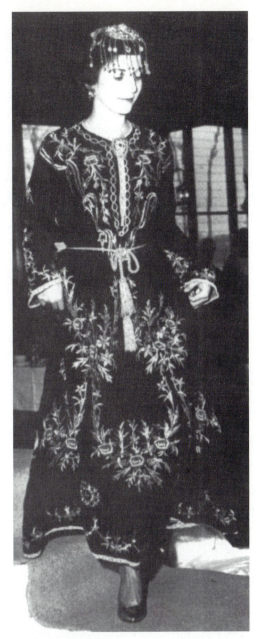

FIGURE 22-16 At within-part level, the sleeves, bodice, and skirt each offer pleasing width to length relationships which recognize natural body break points. At among-part and part-to-whole levels, each area holds interest for comparison without overwhelming. The smaller, lighter, more advancing patterned areas command attention comparable to the larger, dark, plain areas in this traditional embroidered Turkish gown. (Courtesy of the Turkish Government Tourist Office.)

INTRODUCING PROPORTION

Structurally, the location of every seam, dart, or edge influences the proportions of the shape it surrounds (Figure 22-7). If a woman perceives herself as too long-waisted, the horizontal proportions of a midriff yoke or a cummerbund can shorten the waist. A man who sees himself as thick-waisted could choose slightly longer jackets with single-breasted openings.

Review Figures 6-22 to 6-52 to see how simply changing length or width or combining different styles changes apparent body and garment proportions. These are only a few of the comparisons possible at all four levels of clothing and figure proportions, but they show how thoroughly proportion permeates every facet of one's appearance. Functionally, proportions of a garment must agree with body proportions for movement and comfort (Figure 22-16).

Decoratively, proportions emerge in every use of color, texture, pattern, or applied trim. Every line, space, or shape, every pattern motif, every cuff or button or ribbon—every item introduced into a garment interacts with every other item on one or more levels to influence apparent proportions.

Whereas structural and decorative methods of introducing proportion may remain distinct, their end effects tend to merge with each other and with the body. The eye compares structural and decorative features without distinction. Proportions allow comparison of relationships, which in clothing and personal appearance may include:

Hairstyle to head and face size, shape, and facial features

Length and width of neck to head

Size and shape of hat to head

Face, hair, and neck to collar neckline

Shoulder width to waist length

Sleeve style to shoulder and bust size

Bodice area to sleeve area

Bodice area to skirt or pant area

Sleeve length to arm length

Skirt or pant length to width

Skirt or pant length and fullness to hip and leg length

Bodice trims to skirt or pant trims

Collar width to shoulder width

Collar width to sleeve size

Lapel width to tie width

Flaps to pockets

Belt width to bodice style, size, and torso

Jacket or coat length to waist-knee length

Volume of gathers, draping, or flare to body size

Size, shape, and grouping of pattern motifs to area occupied and body size

Spacing and grouping of stripes or trims to each other, garment areas, and body size

Button size, shape, and grouping to garment edge and area

Area of one color or texture to another

Patterned area to plain area

Textural volume to body size

Light areas to dark and bright to dull

Heel height and thickness to foot, ankle, and calf shape and size

Shoe style to foot, ankle, and leg shape

Glove length to arm length and thickness

Earring size and shape to facial shape, hairstyle, and neck length

Eyeglass size and shape to facial size and shape and hairstyle

Sensitive perception of such proportions helps control apparent figure proportions and pull figure and garment together into a total composition.

SUMMARY

Proportion is the comparative relationship of distances, sizes, shapes, amounts, degrees, or parts. It operates on four levels: (1) within part, (2) among parts, (3) part to whole, and (4) whole to environment.

Mathematical formulas can guide proportion, but the most pleasing ones seem slightly off mathematical precision. Equal divisions are usually least interesting; extremely unequal divisions invite little comparison. The most pleasing proportions seem near a 3:5 ratio, which is close to the "golden mean," in which the smaller part is to the larger part as the larger is to the whole. This proportion also provides a balanced "reference relationship" to compare with more equal or extreme proportions and their effects on the figure.

Clothing proportions must also suit functional fit and movement purposes and work best when they follow the natural divisions of the body. Understanding body proportions helps master clothing proportions. Compensating clothing proportions can create desired illusions for less than ideal body proportions.

Proportion can apply to all the elements and most of their aspects. Shape and form always have it; so concern is for its qualities. More advancing uses of color, texture, and pattern need proportionately less area, and receding uses need more. Proportion can involve every linear and highlighting principle and can contribute to other synthesizing ones either structurally or decoratively.

CLASS ACTIVITIES

1. Analyze the proportions of each of the shapes and forms in Figures 6-15 and 6-16. Which are nearly equal? Near golden mean? Extremely unequal? For what body areas are they functionally appropriate? For what styles are they appropriate? Which ones would relate well together as style silhouettes to create pleasing proportions?

2. Discuss how proportion links the size and space illusions discussed in Chapter 3 with the effects of styles in Figures 6-22 to 6-50 and combinations of them.

3. With a demonstration tunic over a skirt or pants, or a series of transparencies, gradually shorten the tunic

into an overblouse and on into a shell. Analyze the changes in apparent leg length, waist-knee length, shoulder-hip, shoulder-waist, and other figure proportions that result from each step of simply lengthening or shortening the tunic length. Which proportion seems more lengthening? More shortening? Why?

4. Repeat the above activity using a range of pant leg, skirt, and/or sleeve lengths.

5. Revisit the styles shown in Figures 6-22 to 6-50. For any given style, compare likely changes in apparent figure proportions with changes in style length and/or width.

6. How would you analyze the ratios of proportions on each of the four levels in Figure 22-16?

7. With the class in groups, assign each group a level: within-part, among-part, part-to-whole, or whole outfit-to-total figure; and invite them to find and analyze an example of "their" level in the class. Then with their example standing, share their analysis of "their" level with the class. Then invite the class to relate that level to other levels.

8. In Chapters 9, 10, and principles chapters, discuss the impact of relative areas of advancing qualities related to receding qualities.

9. Choose one pair from the list of paired garment areas or garment-body areas under "Introducing Proportion," and in magazines or catalogues find several examples showing differing proportions and compare their effects. For example, find pictures of similar collar styles showing lapels in different widths, and compare their effects on apparent shoulder width, neck length, or other features.

10. Choose a particular figure "problem," and using styles in Figures 6-22 to 6-50 and/or other chapters, develop a "prescription" outfit of styles in proportions that will create the desired illusions.

23 *Scale*

DEFINITION AND CONCEPT

Scale is a consistent relationship of sizes to each other and to the whole, regardless of shapes. It is a first cousin to proportion but it compares only sizes, not other qualities. In dress it usually relates the size of smaller area accents — such as bows, pockets, collars or other style features, pattern motifs, decorative trims, jewelry, and accessories—to the size of the main parts of the garment and to the wearer. Because it is a relative size relationship, we "scale up" an object by enlarging it to agree with a larger surrounding area, or "scale down" to a smaller area (Figure 10-29). When size relationships agree, they are often described as being "in scale"; when they are clumsy or too extreme, they are "out of scale" or "in poor scale."

EFFECTS

Although scale is simple it can have powerful visual effects. Since it involves com-

parative relationships, it is a synthesizing principle.

Physically, scale invokes geometric and size and space illusions of Chapter 3, especially those illustrated in Figures 3-6, 3-16, and 3-17. Watch the Titchener and Lipps illusion of Figure 3-17 at work in Figure 23-10 as a tiny purse seems to enlarge a heavy person by contrast (Figure 23-10a), and a large handbag overwhelms a tiny person (Figure 23-10c). But an oversize handbag for a very heavy person emphasizes size by repetition, and a small purse emphasizes a person's petiteness.

Pattern, as filled space, enlarges more than plain areas (Figure 3-4a). A tiny motif makes a large person seem larger by contrast but complements a small figure (Figures 23-1a, 1b). Large motifs overpower a petite person by contrast and enlarge a heavy person by repetition (Figures 23-1c, d). It usually takes an erect, firm, smooth figure to wear a large-scale pattern well. The larger a motif the more it enlarges the figure

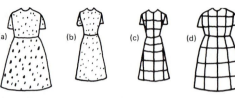

FIGURE 23-1 Pattern. Tiny motifs accent large size by contrast (a), and petiteness by repetition (b), while large motifs overwhelm the tiny figure by contrast (c), and increase already ample size by repetition (d).

(Figure 23-2). The same structural design using fabric patterns of different scale on people of differing sizes shows graphically the effects that scale has on apparent size and weight (Figure 23-1). A basic guideline is for people of either extreme large or small size to avoid extremes of scale in dress, pattern, or accessories which would emphasize figure size either by repetition or contrast (Figures 23-1, 23-10a and c, 23-11c).

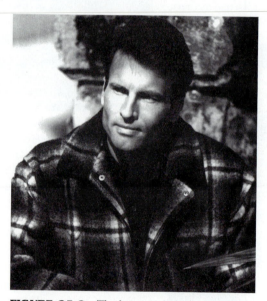

FIGURE 23-2 The large scaled plaid pattern motif in this jacket enlarges the upper figure area, seems psychologically bold, and requires a large unbroken structural area that avoids chopping up the pattern. This advancing large scale pattern may work for an average size adult, but would overpower a small person or a child. (Courtesy of Pendleton Woolen Mills Menswear.)

Psychologically, in western cultures, large scale shapes seem bold and aggressive, assertive and straightforward (Figures 23-2 and 23-3), and small sizes seem delicate and dainty (Figures 23-1b, 23-4, 23-5, and 23-10). In Western cultures small, fragile details are rarely seen in men's wear, but are common in women's wear. Similarly, large scale in women's wear is usually found in tailored wear and casual sportswear where daintiness is less emphasized (Figure 23-6). Consistent use of scale contributes to psychological satisfaction; details out of scale to each other, to the garment, or to the wearer destroy unity.

SCALE AND THE ELEMENTS

Scale can apply to all the elements, but most obviously involves sizes of shapes, their lines and spaces, and combinations in pattern motifs. Shapes may be the outlines of pockets, collars, or belts (Figures 23-6), or pattern motifs or trim (Figures 23-5, 23-6) as they relate to each other, to the garment, and the wearer. Less obviously, scale also applies to color and texture. Their advancing qualities, which enlarge, suggest more grandiose scale (Figure 23-2), and their minimizing, receding qualities suggest a smaller scale (Figure 23-7).

SCALE AND OTHER PRINCIPLES

Scale may involve the linear principles of repetition, sequence, and alternation when these involve different sizes. Gradations of size are sometimes described as progressive scales in which unit sizes increase or de-

FIGURE 23-3 Shape and space: Style features relate in size to the area they adorn, appearing dinky (a), compatible (b), or top-heavy (c).

(a)   (b)   (c)

FIGURE 23-4 Shape and space: notions. Tiny buttons well-sized for a blouse (a), seem puny on a skirt (b), and lost on a coat (c).

crease consecutively (Figure 15-1g). Scale can create gentle or dynamic rhythms, depending on the number of repeats and whether delicate or bold scale is used (Figure 18-3). Radiation suggests scale when its center seems smaller and the periphery seems larger (Figure 17-1h). We have seen that scale can emphasize either heaviness or petiteness by contrast or repetition. Because scale deals with comparative relationships, it can also contribute to balance, harmony, and unity as long as it remains consistent in size and mood with the area its use adorns.

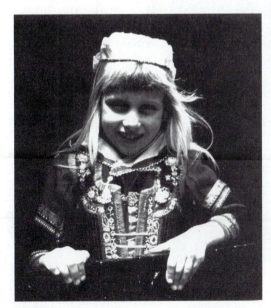

FIGURE 23-5 The small scale of the trims agrees with the small size of the wearer. The small scale of the shape and pattern elements used also suggests a delicacy appropriate to the child's age in this traditional Dutch child's costume. (Courtesy of the Netherlands Board of Tourism.)

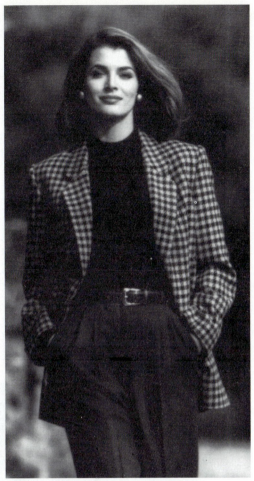

FIGURE 23-6 The assertiveness created by the larger scale collar lapels is modified by the smaller scale pattern and medium-scaled belt, giving a moderate, casual, and versatile effect to the outfit. (Courtesy of Pendleton Woolen Mills.)

INTRODUCING SCALE

Structural and decorative distinctions tend to blur with scale. Thus one might debate whether the main purpose of accessories is functional or decorative. The main ways of introducing scale to clothing include style features, notions, trims, pattern, jewelry, and accessories.

Well-scaled style features such as pockets, collars, ruffles, bows, cuffs, belts and other small parts (Figures 6-37, 23-6) seem

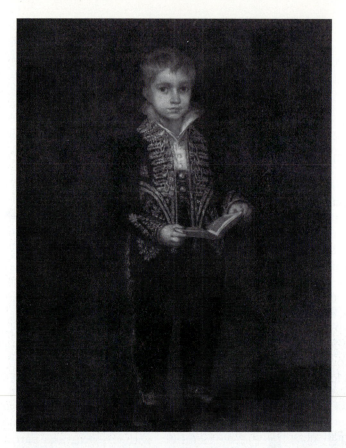

to belong to the main parts of the garment. They seem large enough to avoid resembling hesitant afterthoughts, but not top-heavy and clumsy (Figure 23-3).

In notions, a button size appropriate to a blouse would look puny on a skirt and lost on a coat (Figure 23-4). Similarly, a size pleasing for a coat might work for a skirt but be too heavy for a blouse (Figure 23-8). Hairstyles most in scale frame the face with a thickness narrower than half the face (Fig-

ure 23-9a), so the face does not seem dwarfed and the head top-heavy (Figure 23-9b).

Accessories carry strong effects of scale for both garment and wearer. Effects of purse sizes (Figure 23-10) can also apply to belt, hat, glove, and shoe sizes. Thin belts emphasize a thick waist, a large hat may seem to weigh down a small person, and chunky shoes may throw the foot out of scale to the leg.

FIGURE 23-8 Shape and space: notions. Buttons large enough to be functional and visually well-scaled for a large, heavy coat (a), seem clumsy on a skirt (b), and completely overpower a thin blouse (c).

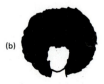

FIGURE 23-9 Shape and space: Hair styles well-scaled to head size provide a frame for the face (a); with top-heavy volume, they overpower the face and head (b).

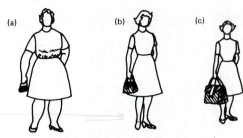

FIGURE 23-10 Shape and space: Accessories accent wearer size by repetition or contrast. A tiny purse emphasizes the wearer's weight by contrast (a), while a medium-size purse has more moderating effects for any size person (b). A large purse overwhelms a tiny person (c), but emphasizes the size of a large person by repetition.

Most purely decorative effects of scale arise from jewelry, trims, and pattern. Tiny delicate jewelry emphasizes a large person by contrast (Figure 23-11a), and long, dangle earrings emphasize a short neck. Moderately scaled jewelry suits most figures and garments (Figure 23-11b). Large, heavy jewelry visually weighs down and overpowers a small person and reinforces the size of a large person (Figure 23-11c). The same comparisons hold true for the sizes of applied trims (Figures 23-5 and 23-7).

Pattern is part of the fabric; the designer can partly control its placement on the garment and the body, but cannot rearrange it as with applied trims. A motif should be small enough to be seen completely from one angle. A small-scaled motif can be used on a structural design with seams, darts, gathers, or pleats with-

out looking chopped up; but a large-scale motif demands large, smooth, unbroken structural areas (Figure 23-2). The motif in Figure 23-2 would be much too large for the child's dress in Figure 23-5.

The age of the wearer is also important in choosing scale. Most patterns intended for small children are small-scaled (Figures 23-5, 23-7), as are those for the elderly. Small-scale patterns help camouflage stooping and the hollows and bulges that appear with age, and the resulting fabric folds do not destroy the pattern. Review pattern illustrations in Chapter 10 to see how their scale relates to the ages and sizes of the wearers.

SUMMARY

Scale is a consistent relationship of sizes to each other and to a whole. In dress it relates the size of small parts such as style features, accessories, jewelry, trims, and pattern to the size of the garment and of the wearer. Sizes may be scaled up or down to agree with the structural part of the garment or body. Extremes of scale emphasize extremes in the size of the wearer. Large-scale objects enlarge more than small ones. Psychologically, large scale seems bold, and small scale seems dainty. Scale applies especially to shape, line, space, and pattern, but advancing colors and textures also suggest bold scale. It is involved in any of the linear or highlighting principles that can offer comparisons in size, and in synthesizing principles it can contribute to balance, harmony, and unity structurally or decoratively.

CLASS ACTIVITIES

1. In magazines or catalogues, analyze how different ways of introducing scale relate to each other physically and psychologically: does the effect of the size of the pattern motif agree with the effect of the button, pocket, or collar lapel size? Does the scale of accessories agree with

FIGURE 23-11 Shape and space: Jewelry size interacts with apparent body size. Tiny, delicate jewelry seems lost on a heavy person (a); most figure types can wear moderately scaled jewelry (b); large pieces seem to weigh down the figure or accent size (c).

that of the trim? Does the scale of shoes agree with that of a belt or purse or hat in an outfit? Do these uses of scale agree with the body areas where they are used? How might you change a scale to enlarge or reduce a physical effect or change a mood?

2. Using Figure 6-21 and pictures of various hair styles, discuss and experiment with how you might use hair styles to enlarge or reduce apparent face or head size. How does this technique use Chapter 3 size and space illusions?

3. Invite students ahead to time to wear an example of scale introduced by a) collar lapels, b) patch pockets, c) buttons, d) pattern motif, e) jewelry, f) trims, or g) accessories such as purses, belts, hats, shoes, or gloves. Then with the class in groups, assign each group a different example of introduction to find and identify. With "their" example standing, each group should identify the element used and how it is introduced, and analyze its physical and psychological effects.

4. With a selection of fabric patterns, some showing large scale motifs, some with medium, and some small, compare their physical and psychological effects, and where and how you would place them on the figure to agree with body part size.

5. Using the fabric patterns from the above activity, and several structural styles from magazines or catalogues, compare how each scale of fabric would work into each structural design. Is the garment area large and unbroken enough to accommodate large scale motifs? Do seams, pleats, or gathers "break up" a motif and destroy its scale effects? Does the pattern have a variety of motif sizes that could be used in different garment part sizes, such as smaller motifs in a short sleeve or collar, and larger motifs in a skirt?

24 *Balance*

DEFINITION AND CONCEPT

Balance is the feeling of evenly distributed weight resulting in equilibrium, steadiness, and stability. Ideas about balance spring from our own experience with weight, size, density, and location. They are easy to sense if not analyze. We deal daily with our own body balance in which weights, forces, and tensions of our anatomy must interact to equalize each other around a fulcrum, or balance point, compensating for any differences and countering any extremes. Visual balance works the same way: Each part of a garment must interact with all the others to achieve stability.

There are three kinds of balance: horizontal, in which sides balance each other; vertical, in which the upper and lower parts balance; and radial, in which the center and the outer edges balance, integrating the whole around a center of gravity. As Arnheim notes, parts of a balanced arrangement seem mutually determined, creating a feeling of necessity in their relationship.[1]

In horizontal balance, the human body normally is alike on each side of an imaginary, center vertical, so the eye seeks such similarities. Artists have emphasized two types of horizontal balance: formal or symmetrical, and informal or asymmetrical. In formal balance each side of the central vertical mirrors the other; they are nearly identical. This balance is easier to achieve because everything on one side automatically determines that on the other (Figure 24-1c). In informal balance, each side of the central vertical is different, but its over-all feeling is one of equal weight distribution (Figure 24-1e). It requires a more complex interaction of parts, and consequently greater mastery of elements and supporting principles.

_____

[1]Rudolf Arnheim, *Art and Visual Perception* (Berkeley: University of California Press, 1971), p. 12.

24-1(a) Line path, direction, thickness, continuity: Curved lines help balance straight path, broken lines counter continuous ones, thick ones balance thin, and horizontals balance verticals and diagonals.

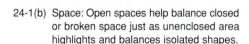

24-1(b) Space: Open spaces help balance closed or broken space just as unenclosed area highlights and balances isolated shapes.

24-1(c) Shape and space: Identical shape and space arrangements on each side of an imaginary center vertical create formal or symmetrical horizontal shape balance.

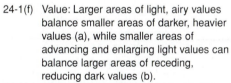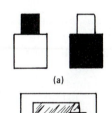

24-1(d) Shape and space: Identically sized and contoured shapes different distances from a center vertical will destroy a sense of balance.

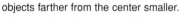

24-1(e) Shape and space: Unequal shapes and arrangements on each side of an imaginary center vertical create dynamic informal or asymmetrical balance, with objects farther from the center smaller.

See Figure 8-33 for color balance effects.

24-1(f) Value: Larger areas of light, airy values balance smaller areas of darker, heavier values (a), while smaller areas of advancing and enlarging light values can balance larger areas of receding, reducing dark values (b).

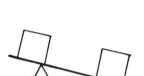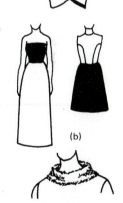

(a)   (b)

24-1(g) Texture: Advancing and heavier qualities of texture need less area to balance larger areas of lighter or smoother texture.

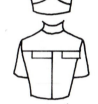

24-1(h) Pattern: Individual motifs need well-balanced proportions, well distributed weight in arrangement, and well balanced distribution throughout the garment or ensemble.

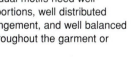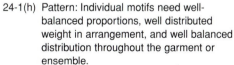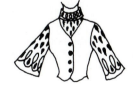

FIGURE 24-1 Balance and the elements.

Vertical balance prevents a feeling of being top or bottom heavy; radial balance keeps concentration of weight near the center. Vertical and radial balance are as important as horizontal.

The countering techniques discussed earlier are essentially ways to achieve balance and avoid extremes, illustrating the idea of "counter-balance." For example, a V yoke counters sloping shoulder curves for balance.

EFFECTS

Balance is a major synthesizing principle, as it relates apparent weights for a feeling of steadiness of the whole.

Physical

Visual effects of balance come from equal distribution of weight, density, and tension. Without horizontal balance the figure threatens to topple over or seems lopsided. The regularity of formal horizontal balance accents any figure irregularities, whereas informal balance can help camouflage them. With vertical balance the figure seems solidly based; without it, the figure seems top-heavy, bottom-heavy, or simply weighted down. With radial balance, the figure seems centrally stabilized; the center seems heaviest, and the periphery lighter. Without it, extremities seem to drag the figure down, and things seem "at loose ends."

Generally, the more attention something commands, the heavier it seems. Thus, advancing uses of elements seem heavier, and receding uses or smaller amounts seem lighter; so a smaller area of an advancing, heavy quality balances a larger area of a receding, lighter quality. Any weight seems heavier farther from the figure center, and lighter closer to the center (Figure 24-1e). The space surrounding an isolated object accents its importance, thereby adding weight. A small, shiny area attracts attention and seems heavier than a larger, dull area. Complex, broken spaces seem heavier than simple, open spaces.

Thus, it is generally the attention-commanding ability that determines apparent visual weight.

Psychological

Balance is critical to a psychological sense of security and stability. Imbalance brings a disturbed feeling, difficult to pinpoint, but easy to sense. With balance comes the calm confidence that relationships are stable, a feeling especially important in dress because the wearer moves. A well-designed garment retains a feeling of balance through a variety of figure positions. Garments that best evoke this feeling are those that avoid extremes, as balance embodies the guideline to use enough variety to avoid monotony, but not to overwhelm.

Most psychological effects relate to vertical, horizontal, or pressure balance (see Chapter 4). Feelings about vertical balance stem from lifelong experience with gravity, with heavier things lower and lighter things higher. Applied to clothing, the higher on the figure, the lighter weight the element use needs to be, and the heavier the element use, the lower it needs to be.

Formal horizontal balance is stately and regal, but it is also obvious, passive, and static. Informal balance is casual, dynamic, complex, and more subtle, but also capable of sweeping elegance. It is less rigid, more lively and rhythmic, and more challenging to create. Both formal and informal balance can be used in the same garment, but emphasizing one kind avoids competition and encourages harmony.

Radial balance suggests control and stability at the center, whereas its absence suggests undisciplined instability. Pressure balance suggests equal internal and external pressure; the figure will neither explode (Figures 4-1d and 6-17g) nor collapse. It is stable.

BALANCE AND THE ELEMENTS

Balance can apply to every aspect of every element, even though some think of it only in shape. Much of its power comes from its ability to interplay different aspects of the same or different elements. Thus, using the ability to command attention as the basis for comparison, a thin, broken line is balanced by a thicker, solid line (same element) or by a bright color (different element). Every use of every element assumes an apparent weight which relates to others. See Table 24-1 for relative weights of element variations.

Balance can apply to all nine aspects of line. So the firmness of a straight line helps counter and stabilize the fluidity of curved lines (Figure 5-4). Any line direction creates a thrust that in turn needs countering thrusts to reduce tensions and create balance. A garment of dominantly vertical lines needs some horizontal ones, just as a diagonal needs an opposing diagonal for stability (Figures 24-1a and 24-2).

Two-dimensional spatial balance results from steadiness of areas within and among shapes (Figure 24-2). The eye seeks a balance among sizes of space in bodice and skirt (Figure 24-1b), between the openness of the structurally empty space of a vest and the filled space of a patterned sleeve (Figure 24-1h), between pattern

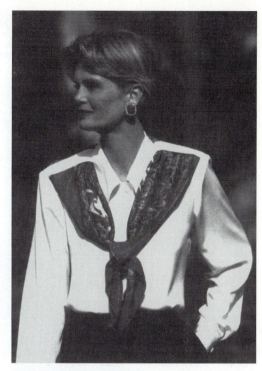

FIGURE 24-2 The strong shoulder epaulet horizontals help balance the vertical sleeve and silhouette lines, the countering diagonals of the scarf balance each other, inward and outward pressures seem to balance, the smaller filled space of the scarf balances the larger plain space of the blouse, the mirrored shapes provide horizontally symmetrical balance, and the light and dark areas balance each other in this blouse. (Courtesy of Mark, Fore & Strike.)

TABLE 24-1	Visual Weights of Element Variations		
Element	Aspect	Lighter	Heavier
Space	2-D	empty	filled
Line	Thickness	thin	thick
	Continuity	broken	solid
	Edge	fuzzy	sharp
	Consistency	porous	solid
Shape	Size	small	large
Color	Hue	cool	warm
	Value	light	dark
	Intensity	dull	bright
Texture	Surface	supple	stiff
	Density-yarn	fine	coarse
	Structure	open	compact
	Thickness	thin	thick
	Opacity	sheer	opaque
	Luster	dull	shiny
Pattern	Arrangement	widely spaced	closely spaced

motif or trim and background space (Figure 24-3). Three-dimensional spatial pressure balance equalizes internal pressures outward and external pressures inward, and convexities and concavities complement each other so that forms neither expand nor collapse; the line or surface between form and space is stable (Figure 24-2).

Although many first associate shape with balance, it is only one of the elements to which balance applies. Horizontally, if two objects are the same shape, size, color, and distance from a fulcrum, they suggest equal weight and formal balance (Figure 24-1c). But moving one of two identical ob-

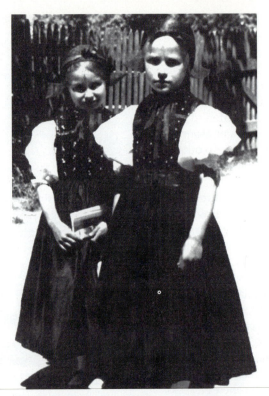

FIGURE 24-3 The patterned vests help balance the larger, plain sleeves and skirts; the light sleeves help balance the black vests and skirts, and the fitted vests help balance the full sleeves and skirts. The vest colors are scattered among each other and on the figure for balance in these traditional children's costumes from the Black Forest area of Germany. (Courtesy of the German Information Center.)

Color balance is a fascinating art in itself. Color schemes are guidelines to achieve color balance. A well-balanced color scheme has enough contrast of hues, values, intensities, and amounts for interest.

Well-balanced color schemes are possible with the narrow hue range of adjacent and monochromatic schemes, but easier with complementary schemes and their variations because they include some form of all the primaries. A balance of color value needs both light and dark values to avoid looking faded if all light or somber if all dark.

It may seem contradictory that light values enlarge, and dark values reduce, and then that light values seem light and airy in weight and dark values seem heavier. However, large or small size refers to *volume*, whereas light and heavy weight refer to *density*, or weight per volume. We relate size to weight, but objects the same size may have different weights where one is denser than the other. So a small, dark bodice could balance a large, light skirt because the smaller, heavier area balances the larger, lighter one (Figures 24-1f and 24-3). However, a small light bodice may also balance a large, dark skirt because (1) the smaller, light value advances and enlarges, and the larger, dark value recedes and reduces; or (2) the light, airy value is higher and the dense, heavy, dark value is lower where it seems consistent with gravity (Figure 24-1f). Which effect emerges depends on how the designer manipulates the sizes, shapes, differences, and locations of the values to achieve balance.

Intensity balance needs both bright and dull to avoid looking too aggressive with all bright and too blank with all dull colors. Brighter intensities seem heavier, and duller intensities seem lighter in weight.

Hence a well-balanced color scheme seeks balanced variety in all three dimensions of color (Figure 8-33).

Once balanced colors are chosen, amounts and distribution are critical to retain balance of apparent weight and density, or advancing or receding qualities.

jects farther from the center increases its weight and destroys balance (Figure 24-1d), showing that the farther from the center an object is, the smaller it needs to be (Figure 24-1e). Vertical balance of shape is easier to achieve with smaller shapes high on the figure and larger or visually heavier ones lower. Radial balance puts larger shapes toward the center and smaller ones toward the periphery. Accessories such as hats, purses, gloves, and shoes far away from the torso center need to be small and visually lightweight, with receding qualities of color and texture for radial balance with the body center of gravity.

Smaller areas of advancing qualities balance larger areas of receding qualities (Figure 8-22). Heavier qualities placed lower balance lighter qualities placed higher.

Color amount and distribution are as critical to balance as is color selection. Very different effects result when two colors are intermingled, as in pointillism, as opposed to simply being placed side by side. Colors may be distributed (1) among each other, and (2) among parts of the garment (Figure 24-3). Balanced intermingling of hues, values, and intensities emerges from a well-designed fabric pattern or applied trims. Changing color distribution in a pattern changes its balance as seen with the differences in color in each repeat of the same motif in Figure 24-4. Color distribution among garment parts depends on the effects desired, the size and shape of the wearer, the number and weights of colors used, and whether they are solid or mixed in a pattern (Figure 8-33). Larger areas of heavier color qualities are often placed toward the visual center of gravity, and lighter qualities farther away (Figure 24-3). So color balance involves a pleasing variety of hues, values, intensities, amounts, intermingling, and location in the garment and the body.

Texture is the only element with actual weight and density, so balance is essential both functionally and aesthetically. Heavier textures may seem logical lower and lighter ones near the top. But functionally and structurally it is more feasible to suspend lighter, lower textures from heavy, higher ones for strength. So textural balance depends on structural design location as well as textural selection. Table 24-1 shows weight effects of textural qualities. Both location and intermingling of textures must be functional as well as beautifully distributed for textural balance, so a small, heavy collar could accent a lighter textured bodice because the collar is small in area and structurally supported by the shoulders (Figure 24-1g). Textural weight must also balance with the size and weight of the wearer; a tiny person might seem weighted down by a thick or stiff garment.

Light reaction in texture is vital to balance. A sparkling pin or small shiny satin bow (small, advancing) on a dull velvet (large, receding) balances well, but a crepe bow (small, receding) on a sequined gown (large, advancing) might be lost. Sheer fabrics are airy, but need the stability of a solid fabric for a transparent/opaque balance.

Pattern can contribute to balance on two levels: (1) pattern arrangement and (2) distribution on the garment and figure. Review the pattern criteria in Chapter 10, recalling that patterned areas seem heavier than plain areas. Well-balanced individual motifs work more easily into well-balanced repeats which work most easily into a total fabric pattern (Figure 24-1h). Good all-over arrangements seem balanced from any angle. Other arrangements are more challenging to balance in composition, but offer greater variety in use. Distribution in the garment depends on how the pattern arrangement relates to the structural design (Figures 24-1h and 10-14d).

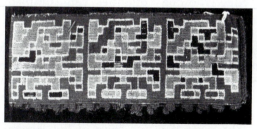

FIGURE 24-4 The three different color distributions in the same motif change the focal point and balance in each. (From the John and Mary Carter Collection of Pre-Columbian Peruvian Textiles, Department of Textile and Consumer Sciences, College of Human Sciences, Florida State University.)

BALANCE AND OTHER PRINCIPLES

Because a linear principle leads the eye in the direction it develops, that direction may either reinforce or counter another directional effect; so all the linear principles can contribute to balance. Those that develop to a climax, like sequence, gradation, and rhythm, can be especially useful in manipulating apparent weight.

Contrast enlivens balance whenever a countering technique helps avoid extremes. Concentricity and emphasis command attention with advancing, usually heavier element uses; so care is needed to maintain balance. Proportion and scale are critical to balance as they deal with relationships of dimensions, amounts, and sizes, all of which imply weight.

Balance is essential to both harmony and unity. An off-balance garment is unstable itself and does not harmonize with the figure. An off-balance garment is also missing whatever is needed for steadiness, and so lacks the completeness needed for unity.

INTRODUCING BALANCE

Because all of the elements and most of the principles can suggest weight, size, or density, there are infinite ways to introduce balance.

Structurally, the directions of seams and edges can counter or reinforce each other for balance (Figure 24-2). Diagonal draping folds might radiate from one shoulder and from the opposite hip for dynamic, informal balance, or from both shoulders, creating a graceful, formal balance. A center front buttoned opening is usually considered formally balanced even though the actual opening edge is to one side. However, if that off-center edge is emphasized, then any balance becomes informal. Since gathers, smocking, shirring, and ruffles add apparent weight, they need care for balance. Large structural forms—such as full sleeves and skirts, capes, or other styles extending out from the body—need counterbalancing visual weights near the center (Figure 24-3).

Because the human figure is different front and back, profile balance is informal but just as important for all-around balance.

Decorative balance depends in part on the size and contour of the structural forms it adorns. How the advancing or receding, heavier or lighter qualities of the elements are chosen, distributed with visually heavier weights toward the center, and related to structural forms will determine their balance.

SUMMARY

Balance is the feeling of evenly distributed weight, of equilibrium, steadiness, and stability. Like physical balance, visual balance equalizes forces, tensions, weights, sizes, amounts, pressures, and densities. Horizontal balance equalizes both sides of a vertical center either formally or informally, vertical balance equalizes upper and lower areas, and radial balance provides steadiness around a visual center of gravity. Countering techniques achieve balance by avoiding extremes.

As a synthesizing principle, balance relates all parts of a garment for physical and psychological steadiness. Physically, balance keeps the figure from appearing lopsided, top-heavy, bottom-heavy or edge-heavy. Psychologically, vertical balance suggests steadiness; formal, horizontal balance is stately, whereas informal balance is dynamic and pressure balance suggests spatial stability.

Balance applies to all aspects of all the elements, with advancing qualities seeming heavier than receding ones. Opposing qualities can complement and balance each other.

Balance can use any of the linear principles, and of the highlighting principles, especially contrast and emphasis. Proportion and scale are essential for balance, which is, in turn, essential to harmony and unity.

Most of the structural and decorative ways of introducing other principles also apply to balance. Structural forms and lines, and decorative colors, textures, and patterns all suggest varying weights. All lend themselves to techniques that can create balance.

CLASS ACTIVITIES

1. In magazines or catalogues find an example of (a) horizontal informal balance, (b) horizontal formal balance, (c) vertical balance, and (d) radial balance. Comparing them side by side, discuss (1) how each is achieved, (2) how their effects differ. Could the effects of one be achieved using the techniques (element and other principle uses) of another?

2. Invite students ahead of time to wear examples of balance to class. Then assign each class group an element and allow a given time for them to find an example of balance using "their" element in the class. Then with "their" model standing, identify the element, analyze its physical and psychological contributions to balance, and discuss how it is introduced.

3. From magazines or catalogues select a range of styles that you feel have good balance. Then using Table 24-1 identify and locate the heavier uses of the elements. Where are they? Identify the lighter uses. Where are they? How do they relate to each other to contribute to balance? How do they relate to the center and the periphery of the figure?

4. Do the above activity 3 for garment examples that have poor balance. Do the size and location of heavy and light element uses contribute to the imbalance? If so, how? Analyze them in terms of horizontal, vertical, and radial balance.

5. In pictures or garments that you feel have good balance, identify any linear and highlighting principles that contribute to the balance. How are they contributing? How are they interacting with each other for balance?

6. In actual garments or pictures in magazines or catalogues, discuss how structural contributions to balance relate to decorative contributions. How do they complement each other?

7. Ahead of time, invite volunteers to wear examples of poor balance, and ask them to analyze why they feel its balance is poor and what they would change to improve it, and invite the class to make suggestions.

25 *Harmony*

DEFINITION AND CONCEPT

Harmony is an agreement in feeling, a consistency in mood, a pleasing combination of differing things used in compatible ways. Element and principle choices avoid the extremes of boredom or conflict and seem to belong together, cooperating around a common theme. Especially in harmony, the theme must include agreement among functional, structural, and decorative design levels, as structural and decorative design are subordinate to *and agree with* functional design.

Harmony is one of the more culturally subjective principles. Different periods even within a culture differ in ideas of harmony. For example, rhinestones on sporty denim were unthinkable when their moods were considered unrelated, but were seen together when they gained a culturally common mood. But moods change, old novelties drift apart, and new combinations emerge.

What makes some combinations fleeting and others become classic depends upon (1) how widely accepted the idea or mood is; (2) how well the elements and principles combine to interpret it; and (3) how well the three levels of functional, structural, and decorative design agree. Harmony insists on clear agreement among all three, or it is lost.

EFFECTS

Functional aspects of harmony mean that a garment is comfortable, durable, moves easily, breathes with the body, performs any specialized duties well, fits, is warm or cool enough, is safe and healthy, is not sticky or baggy or otherwise hindering, and its parts function compatibly with each other and with the body. Its textures are compatible in weight, stretchability, thickness, suppleness, and performance, and they can be cleaned by the same method or are detachable. In short, the garment works; it fulfills its purpose, and meets its functional criteria (Figure 25-1). Review the functional and structural needs in Chapter 2 to recall what characteristics must work together.

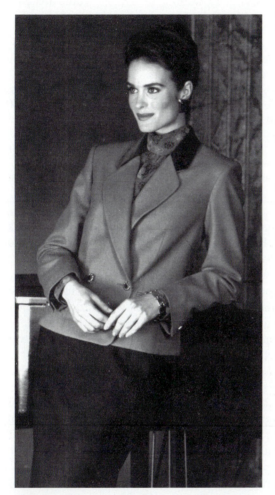

FIGURE 25-1 The firm, yet soft textures modify the tailored business styling, soft blouse texture; rounded lapel and jacket corners soften the straight structural silhouette; and the moderate value contrasts reinforce a businesslike yet gentle mood. The structural garment forms agree with body forms; and advancing and receding qualities complement each other for versatility and harmony at functional, structural, and decorative levels. (Courtesy of Pendleton Woolen Mills.)

In physical effects of harmony, garment parts are in scale, their combined proportions seem to belong with each other and the figure. Extremes of physical dimensions and the monotony of equal ones are avoided. Advancing qualities harmonize with receding qualities, countering and reinforcing techniques harmonize, and every part blends consistently with every other part (Figure 25-1).

In psychological effects harmony visually blossoms. It manipulates the elements and other principles to set the tone or mood or theme for one's appearance. The idea of "belonging together" is important in clothing, and it is harmony that most contributes to that feeling. Harmony pleasingly relates and integrates parts of a garment, and is one of the most graceful and powerful of the synthesizing principles (Figure 25-1).

HARMONY AND THE ELEMENTS

Every aspect of every element lends itself to harmony. Different aspects of the same or different elements can reinforce each other when they are all used in the same way to convey the same mood (Table 25-1 and Figures 25-2 and 25-3). Or aspects may be used in countering but compatible ways to create a more versatile and generic mood (Figure 25-1).

Harmony Within Elements

The lines of the body and the garment must agree, whether they are reinforcing or countering each other. For example, the repetition of curves in a garment reinforces the gracefulness of curved body lines, and the countering straightness of a hem and waistline add stability and harmonious variety. Using all the aspects of line in one mood reinforces and harmonizes much more than would only a few uses (Figure 25-2).

Spatial harmony emerges from agreement in size, from pleasing scale. It is easier to achieve when figure and background are easily distinguished (Figure 25-3).

TABLE 25-1 Effects of Advancing and Receding Uses of Elements and Principles

	Advancing or More Assertive Uses	Receding or More Delicate Uses
Line	straight, continuous, thick, sharp, solid, long, vertical, diagonal	curved, broken, thin, fuzzy, porous, short, horizontal
Space	large, open, unbroken	small, closed, broken
Shape	large, straight edges, solid, convex	small, porous, concave
Light	shiny, lustrous, brilliant, warm	dull, transparent, dark, cool, low
Color	warm hues	cool hues
	light values	dark values
	bright intensities	dull intensities
Texture	rough, stiff, bulky, thick, closed	smooth, supple, thin, fine, wispy, porous
Pattern	bold motifs, sharp edges, flat, bright colors, geometric, border, spaced, figure and ground sharply distinct	dainty motifs, soft edges, soft shading, soft colors, small all-over or directional
Change	gradation, concentricity, emphasis	transition
Rhythm	staccato, dynamic	smooth, flowing, gentle
Contrast	bold, extreme	subtle, close
Balance	informal, complex	formal, simple
Scale	large, bold	small, dainty

Harmony between shape and form is essential for good design. Repeated shapes or forms create emphasis and continuity; they harmonize well if their shapes are initially pleasing and the repetition not overdone. The structural forms of the garment must complement those of the body for functional and structural harmony (Figures 6-17 and 25-1). Light reactions of shiny or dull fabrics are more harmonious when they flatter the wearer's skin surface and highlights of hair (Figure 25-2).

Harmony in color bestows a psychological satisfaction combining stimulation and contentment. Monochromatic and analogous schemes harmonize in hue similarities; complementary schemes and variations harmonize by completing the spectrum (Figure 8-34). Value contrasts offer variety, and intensity contrasts offer spice (Figure 25-3). A well-balanced color scheme is essential for color harmony but does not guarantee it.

In clothing, color harmony depends on how well hues, values, and intensities (1) harmonize among themselves; (2) harmonize with the wearer's coloration; and (3) convey the psychological mood of the garment. A complementary scheme of bold contrasts in light and dark and bright colors uses hues, value, and intensity consistently to convey assertiveness (Figure 8-34 and Table 25-1); a scheme of warm-hued, muted pastels consistently conveys ethereal softness with little hue or value contrast. Harmony requires a subtlety that makes color interactions delicate but not drab, vivacious but not garish, bold but not clumsy. The designer must harmonize the colors with the garment and wearer, not only by selection, but also by placement, size, and intermingling on the figure (Figure 25-3).

Textural harmony must match textural performance characteristics with garment function. Sturdy textures agree functionally with sports and heavy work needs (Figure 25-3), just as soft, firm, smooth textures meet the physical and structural needs of business wear (Figure 25-1). Visually, surface qualities, hand, and light reactions that convey similar psychological moods harmonize well. For example, fluffy, cool, slippery, soft, thin, supple, fine, sheer and shiny qualities harmonize consistently to project a soft, flowing grace (Figure 25-2). There are textural qualities to match almost any mood, given proper choice and blend.

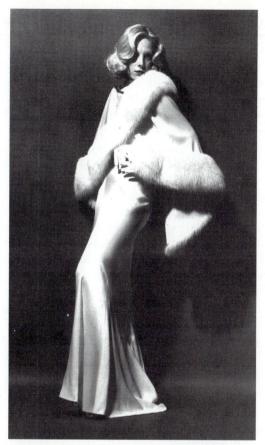

FIGURE 25-2 Use of every element employed: line, color, space, shape, light reaction, and texture are all used in similar, feminine moods to convey a harmoniously consistent feeling of soft, graceful elegance. (Photo courtesy of Du Pont, dress fabric in "Qiana" nylon.)

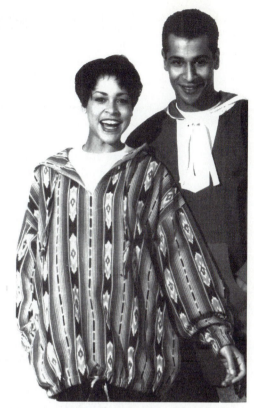

FIGURE 25-3 The straight lines, sharp angles, high value contrast, and filled space reinforce each other in pleasing scale for a brisk and sporty pattern mood consistent with the simple and casual structural design of her top, which in turn offers lively contrast with the plain, dark pants. (Courtesy of **McCall Pattern** Company.)

Harmony in pattern emerges when (1) the motif is appropriate to the occasion and the wearer's age and sex; (2) the interpretation is appropriate to the source and the occasion; (3) the arrangement is appropriate to both, is well balanced, blends with the structural design, and controls attention as desired on the wearer; (4) the pattern is in pleasing scale, proportion, and balance to the garment and wearer; and (5) all of these facets agree with each other (Figure 25-3). The same general criteria can apply to trims.

Harmony Among Elements

Harmony *within* element aspects sets the stage for harmony *among* elements. For example, soft, pastel *colors* agree with long, thin, curved *lines* and rounded *shapes*; medium-sized *spaces*; gathers and ruffles; soft, smooth, or fluffy, semi-shiny *light*-reacting *textures*; and small or delicate *pattern* or none (Figure 25-2). Each usage of each element reinforces every other use and conveys a consistent mood of soft, graceful femininity. Similarly, a crisp, tailored mood emerges from thinner, continuous, straight *lines;* medium *spaces;* vertical, straight *shapes;* neutral or dull *colors;* crisp, smooth firm *textures;* and small geometric or no *pattern* (Figure 25-1).

The consistent reinforcement in the above examples makes their effects comfortably predictable, but beautiful harmonies can also emerge from compatibly countering combinations. For example, a stately, yet sporty mood emerges with straight plaid lines, gently countered by soft, fringed textures, and draped sash (Figure 25-4).

Advancing qualities generally harmonize with advancing qualities and receding qualities with receding qualities, but carefully used, advancing and receding qualities can harmonize to create the desired mood (Table 25-1).

HARMONY AND OTHER PRINCIPLES

Any of the previously discussed principles can contribute to harmony, although certainly not all in one garment. Harmony is fragile and easily shattered if even one principle is violated.

Because all linear principles lead the eye from one place to another, they can contribute to harmony by interrelating the parts (Figure 25-1). Well-chosen and well-placed contrast is essential for variety, and emphasis is needed to establish a hierarchy of dominant and subordinate focal points. Concentricity rivets attention to one spot, and balance distributes it. Proportion and scale provide harmonious relationships of sizes, shapes, and dimensions. Harmony itself is essential to unity; without interrelatedness there cannot be wholeness.

INTRODUCING HARMONY

Harmony is a coordinating "umbrella" principle that can incorporate every other principle. So any ways of incorporating elements and other principles can also introduce harmony.

Introducing harmony also requires agreement among functional, structural, and decorative levels of design. We saw earlier that decorative design is subordinate to and must agree with structural design which must agree with functional design which is prime. So, for example, straight *decorative* plaid or stripe pattern lines and firm textures agree well with straight *structural* pleat lines which allow the *function* of space for walking (Figure 25-4). Or, muted *decorative* colors, softly edged patterns, and thin, supple textures agree with *structural* gathers and draped folds, which allow for *functional* movement and flexibility.

Thus functional harmony is achieved through the proper choices of textures and styling. Structural harmony emerges when garment parts agree with each other and the figure and allow the garment to work. Decorative harmony agrees with the structural form of the garment and the characteristics of the wearer, and conveys a pleasingly consistent mood. These interlocking relationships show the importance of fol-

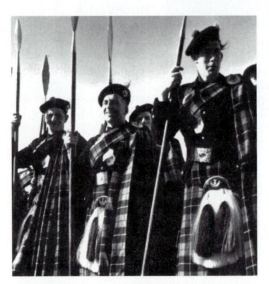

FIGURE 25-4 The straight plaid pattern lines reinforce the rigidity of the straight structural lines of the edges, pleats, and sashes, yet are agreeably softened by the fabric and pouch textures and rounded caps in these traditional kilt costumes from Aberdeenshire, Grampian, Scotland. (Courtesy of the British Tourist Authority.)

lowing design process and meeting functional, structural, and decorative criteria if a garment is to be harmonious.

SUMMARY

Harmony is agreement in feeling and consistency in mood, the culturally conditioned feeling that things belong to each other, relating all parts of a garment to each other and to the wearer. A beautiful and powerful synthesizing principle, it depends on common awareness and acceptance of a mood and its interpretation. Harmony can use all aspects of all elements which can reinforce a mood, or agreeably counter and modify a mood, depending on manipulation of advancing and receding qualities. All the other principles can contribute to harmony, and it is essential to unity. Functional, structural, and decorative agreement is essential to it, and it can be introduced by any structural or decorative technique.

CLASS ACTIVITIES

1. Ahead of time invite students to wear examples of harmony. Then with the class in groups, assign each group an element, ask them to find an example of harmony in "their" element, and with their model standing, analyze how the principle uses the "within-element" aspects and variations, its physical and psychological effects, and how it is introduced.

2. Using the above technique, or in catalogue or magazine pictures, identify and analyze examples of harmony (a) among elements, (b) among principles, (c) between elements and principles, and/or (d) among functional, structural, and decorative levels of design.

3. In garments, catalogues, or magazines, find an example of harmony among elements in which (a) variations selected reinforce each others' effects for very (1) assertive, (2) sporty, or (3) delicate moods, and (b) variations selected harmoniously counter each other for (1) versatile, (2) casual, or (3) business-like moods. Which ones use advancing qualities? Which use receding qualities (Table 25-1)? On the examples using countering, which elements use advancing qualities? Which use receding qualities? What about them makes them work well together?

4. In a garment you consider harmonious, identify the linear, highlighting, and other synthesizing principles used. To what elements does each apply? How do the principles make them interact effectively?

5. In garments of varying degrees of dressiness, sportiness, and business effects, analyze how harmony is achieved among functional, structural, and decorative levels in each, and how they compare.

6. Find examples of garments you consider in poor harmony. Does the disharmony result from within-element choices, among-element, among principles, or at functional, structural, and decorative levels? What interactions are conflicting? Why? What would you change about element and principle uses to make the garment harmonize?

26 *Unity*

DEFINITION AND CONCEPT

Unity is the sense of completed wholeness, coherence, integrated totality, of being finished. It is a relationship in which all parts belong for one consistent, complete effect, the culminating and most complex principle, and the goal to which all design aspires. In clothing it can exist in one garment but is usually easier to achieve in an entire outfit.

Unity seeks simplicity and logical organization, from "upward" perception of wholes as the grouping of parts, or "downward," subdividing complex areas into simpler units complete in themselves.[1] Unity avoids conflicts and competition by organizing a hierarchy of attention around a central theme. As in music, subordinate variations use a holistic approach to support the theme and contribute to completeness.

The distinction between harmony and unity is a fine one. Everything in harmony relates well, but is not necessarily complete. Unity gives the sense of completion, of finish. Harmony without unity is possible, but not unity without harmony. Unity is inseparable, its parts are all interdependent in agreement and in needing each other. Each part belongs reciprocally to every other part, creating wholeness.

Unity is subtle, almost defying analysis. It arises from an interdependent relationship, seeming intrinsic to the garment, not something that is done to it. Unity does not attract attention to itself, but creates a calm completed effect that makes a garment seem to be an attribute of the wearer—a major goal of visual design in dress. Arnheim notes " … that a well-mannered person is one whose manners we do not notice; that a good perfume is perceived as an aspect of the lady's own mood and character, not as an odor; that a good tailor or hair-

---

[1]Rudolf Arnheim, *Art and Visual Perception* (Berkeley: University of California Press, 1971), p. 92.

dresser fashions the person..."[2] Similarly, unity and the mechanics of its achievement do not seem separate; they are an aspect of the wearer.

EFFECTS

Unity is the ultimate synthesizing principle. It integrates every aspect of a design: garment parts, one garment with another, garments with accessories, and ensemble with person, resulting in completeness. It integrates functional, structural, and decorative design so that all three levels work together as a whole. The physical effects of unity create a feeling that all elements and principles are collaborating to flatter the wearer.

However, the most powerful effects of unity are psychological. It gives the satisfaction of design process well completed, with everything needed being present and in place. Nothing is missing or stuck on as an afterthought, for a misused element or principle destroys unity as well as harmony.

Unity requires planning to project a self-image that whispers, "Planning my appearance is part of my self-respect," but does not shout, "Hey, everybody, look at me!" It flows easily with a sense of having been studied but not labored (Figure 26-1).

UNITY AND THE ELEMENTS

Unity can involve every aspect of every element. Major lines unify more if they agree with figure contours or create pleasing illusions (Figure 26-2). Lines unify more if they converge rather than disperse, if extending ones curve back toward the body, and if they convey similar rather than conflicting messages (Figure 26-1).

Spaces are more unifying if they are comparable but distinct. Contours of shape and form unify when they harmonize with each other and the body for a silhouette

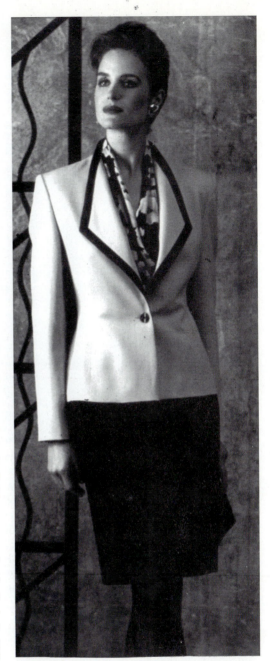

FIGURE 26-1 The repeated straight lines, sharp edges, firm textures, and extreme value contrasts reinforce each other for a consistent, bold effect that shows planned unity. Forms agree with each other and the figure functionally, structurally, and decoratively. Color, shape, and pattern all contribute to the balance, proportion, and harmony essential to unity. (Courtesy of Pendleton Woolen Mills.)

---

[2]Rudolf Arnheim, *Toward A Psychology of Art* (Berkeley: University of California Press, 1972), p. 9.

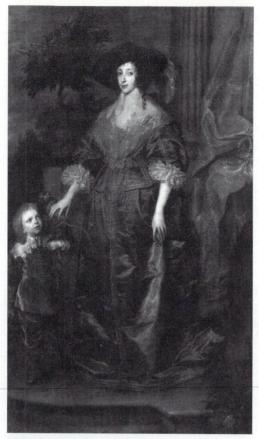

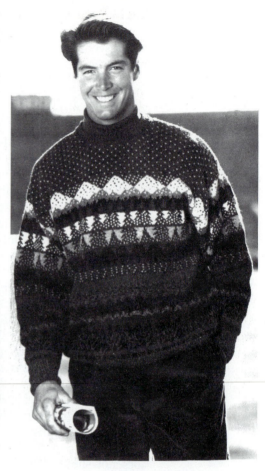

FIGURE 26-2 The lines meeting at the waist help keep attention toward the center of the figure. The soft, shiny, and sheer textures complement each other while the contrasting collar provides emphasis echoed in the cuffs. The repetition of lines, textures, values, and shapes all work together to contribute to unity. (*Queen Henrietta Maria with Her Dwarf;* Sir Anthony van DYCK; c. 1633; National Gallery of Art, Washington; Samuel H. Kress Collection.)

FIGURE 26-3 A variety of colors intermingled in a well-scaled pattern contributes to balance. Repeating color in pattern and plain areas both emphasizes and unifies. (Courtesy of Pendleton Woolen Mills Menswear.)

that seems self-contained (Figure 26-1). Colors are unified when they include a becoming variety of hue, value, and intensity that are well distributed among each other and on the figure (Figures 26-1, 26-3). Textures that harmonize qualities of surface, hand, and light reactions with each other and with structural and functional design help to unify (Figures 26-1, 26-2).

Pattern helps unify when it relates other elements. Its motifs may echo styles, spacing, or lines of parts of the garment. Repeating pattern colors in plain areas is a time-honored way of unifying an ensemble (Figure 26-3).

Illusions can play a vital role in unity when their effects make clear distinctions of figure and ground, size and space, or flattering simultaneous contrast. Distracting illusions of figure-ground reversal, auto-kinetic motion, or color vibrations create uncertainty and destroy unity.

UNITY AND OTHER PRINCIPLES

Because unity is the culminating principle and a major goal of visual design, it can use any of the linear, highlighting, or other synthesizing principles. Repeating any of the elements, especially color, is a simple but powerful unifying technique that works by arranging repeats to pull things together without looking spotty (Figure 26-1).

To the extent that sequence, alternation, radiation, rhythm, and gradation invite the eye along a path, suggesting when to pause, when to move, where to go, and building to a climax, they can contribute to unity. Transition subtly guides attention, yet can strengthen unity.

Of the highlighting principles, concentricity needs care as it focuses attention to one point. Contrast delivers the variety essential to unity. Emphasis gives unity a core; it provides a focal center around which subordinate interests gravitate (Figure 26-1).

Of other synthesizing principles, unity needs pleasing proportions of relative areas and dimensions. Scale gives good size relationships, and balance the essential equal distribution of weight (Figure 26-1). All principles involved in harmony can also contribute to unity, but not all in one garment; usually only a few well-chosen ones are used at once. It is almost impossible to use all the other fifteen principles in one garment and still create unity.

INTRODUCING UNITY

Functional, structural, and decorative design must be well integrated for unity. The garment must function, and its structural parts must be practical, comfortable, and well-related to each other and to the body (Figure 26-1). Decoratively, color, pattern, textures, surface treatment, or trim at strategic places that reinforce structural design are powerful uniting factors (Figure 26-2). Accessories can enliven and unite a well-designed garment, but accessories alone cannot achieve unity nor compensate for poor structural design.

Achieving unity depends largely on how other principles have been introduced and coordinated. One structural or decorative part may incorporate several principles. Sleeves alone will involve repetition, contrast, proportion, scale, and perhaps others (Figure 26-2). Patterns usually also involve repetition, rhythm, contrast, emphasis, proportion, scale, balance, and harmony (Figure 26-3). Unity as a cohesive principle is opposite a divisive isolation of distinct techniques of introduction.

SUMMARY

Unity is the sense of wholeness, of completion. It is the most complex principle and final, synthesizing goal of visual design. Holistic planning insures that everything needed is there; nothing is missing or extra. Subordinate parts support a focal point for interdependent wholeness.

Unity can use every aspect of every element and any of the other principles. Unity also shows that the design process has been followed well; evaluation shows that relevant influences were identified and considered; good functional, structural, and decorative criteria were set, planned, and met. Garment unity reflects functional, structural, and decorative success, and also the unity of design process and product.

CLASS ACTIVITIES

1. Ahead of class, invite students to wear an example of unity to which an element of their choice is a major contributor. Then in class invite other students to identify that element, what makes it a contributor to unity, and how it is introduced.

2. Using the example from the above activity, assign each of the following questions to different class groups: (a) How

do the elements interact with each other and with the "chosen" element: are the physical and psychological effects of their aspect variations consistent or countering? (b) What principle(s) are using the chosen element, and what other principles are contributing to unity? How? (c) How are functional, structural, and decorative levels of design relating to each other? How are they contributing to unity? (d) How does it appear that design process steps were followed to create functional, structural, and decorative unity?

3. Design or find picture examples of a garment with all of the other principles, and that still achieves unity. How are the principles interacting? If an example showing all of the principles is un-available, find one with as many principles as possible. How many are there? Which ones? Which ones work most easily together? Which are hardest to integrate?

4. Design or find picture examples of a garment with the fewest possible principles that can achieve unity. How few can there be? Which ones are always present? How do they relate?

5. Using catalogues or magazine pictures, compare the roles of linear, highlighting, and other synthesizing principles in achieving unity.

6. Select a garment or picture which shows good unity, and demonstrate how the removal of one element use or the extra addition of one can destroy unity.

IV Application

Unit I set the stage for visual design in dress by analyzing design as the fundamental process for all things intentionally created, and as a sensory and/or behavioral product. This perspective gave a context for design process applied to clothing as a sensory design product often used for behavioral design purposes. Chapter 2 narrowed design in general to clothing in particular and showed functional, structural, and decorative aspects of clothing. Functional design examined how clothing works and performs; structural design explored the assemblage that allows a garment to fit and function; and decorative design noted fabric color and pattern, construction details, and applied trim that affect appearance only. Chapter 3 described cultural importance of personal acceptability and the use of geometric, size and space, simultaneous contrast, after-image, irradiation, and other static optical illusions in clothing to enhance that visual acceptability.

Unit II examined the elements of visual design—space, line, shape and form, light, color, texture, and pattern—available to control optical illusions and visual effects influencing personal appearance. We have studied each element's characteristics, aspects, variations, physical and psychological effects, advancing and receding qualities, potentials and limitations, and ways of introducing them.

Unit III analyzed linear principles: repetition, parallelism, sequence, alternation, gradation, transition, radiation, and rhythm; the highlighting principles: concentricity, contrast, and emphasis; and the synthesizing principles: proportion, scale, balance, harmony, and unity. It examined their relative power, the elements each can use, how each relates to other principles, and ways of introducing and coordinating them.

Unit IV brings all this background together in application. Chapter 27 views sociocultural roles of effects created by clothing uses of illusions, elements, and principles, and suggests ways of coordinating them into a versatile and practical wardrobe. Chapter 28 shows "applied illusions": how use of line, space, shape, and form can combine into clothing styles of varying proportions that create geometric and size and space figure illusions of height, weight, size, and body proportions, combining information from all three Units. It also shows uses of elements, principles, and illusions to create psychological effects. Chapter 29 tours 18 countries around the world as examples showing how these same timeless and universal elements and principles have been orchestrated by cultures worldwide with tremendous diversity in ways that have become treasured traditions that identify a cultural group with pride. They show similarities of neighboring geographic areas, the influence of climate and altitude, visual application of cultural traditions and translation from architecture and other media. These applications demonstrate the potentials of the background provided in the previous units and prepare and invite the reader to use the material for further independent use.

27 *Fashionable Individualism*

APPLICATION

Application is ultimately a highly individualized matter. Even the same dress on five different women, or the same suit on five different men, will assume five different characters. Just as each garment allows a personal statement, each person brings to any style a stamp of individuality that makes it uniquely his or her own. Thus each of us is a designer, and rigid formulas are unrealistic.

1. No single set of directions or formulas applies to every culture, climate, sex, season, age, or occasion. This is why step two of the design process is to assess these relevant outside influences in light of the goal set for each design.

2. The principles provide basic guidelines that are more fundamental, comprehensive, and broadly applicable to the elements than any case by case tailored for-

mulas can be. Principles are universal and have similar effects in most cultures; so the individual must decide what effects are desired and choose and use elements and principles accordingly.

3. Specific directions usurp the designer's creativity and freedom of choice. Directions often imply "should" and "shouldn't," value judgments that make results culture-bound, sterile copies. The beginner needs to experience challenge and excitement, to learn from mistakes, and to feel a well-earned sense of accomplishment with success.

The challenge is greater than ever, not only because of a wider range of technology available, but because larger segments of more populations than ever have access to clothes categorized as "fashionable." Most studies of historic costume deal with only a tiny elite of a population who could afford "fashion" while the masses worked in survival agriculture; the functional styles the latter required changed little for centuries. Yet for festive occasions their cultural character often blossomed into delightful garments whose beauty has far outlasted the "fashionable" extremes espoused by small, often fleeting artistocracies. Peasant and aristocratic styles from around the world and through the centuries provide today's designer with a rich heritage of ideas.

SOCIETY, FASHION, AND THE INDIVIDUAL

Social Terms and Expectations

Each society, every culture has its own acceptable forms of behavior, its own methods of encouraging or requiring their observance, or of punishing their violation. *Norm* is the general term for standard patterns or behavior in any given culture. Different kinds of norms are assigned different levels of importance; *mores* are behaviors believed critical to the maintenance of social order. The violation of mores is severely punished, by arrest, imprisonment, excommunication, exile, or even death. For example, nudity in public would bring arrest in many societies. *Folkways* are less critical norms. As socially accepted and encouraged forms of behavior, their violation is chastized more gently, by teasing, ostracism, shaming, or social avoidance. For example, wearing out-dated clothes to work, or formal wear to a picnic, might cause the wearer to be made the butt of a joke or avoided with condescending disdain.

Fashion is generally considered to be a short-lived folkway. It forms a constantly changing visual expression and mute social communication of a certain period and culture. The more highly a culture values change, the more often fashions change and the more important that change is considered.

Lipovetsky suggests that the idea of fashion arose in the West as the cultural value of change used fashion to show visual distinction of social classes and give importance to timing. "Fashion goes hand in hand with a relative devaluing of the past." It attributes "prestige and superiority to new models and … downgrading of the old order."[1] There is less concept of fashion in cultures that value the past and cherish traditions. *Fads* are usually short-lived fashions. They generally involve extremes in details of minor importance, and when the novelty has worn off they die.

Style

Style is a versatile term meaning the identifying characteristics of an object, person, or period. We speak of a particular style, a sense of style, of being "in style," or of a personal style.

A particular style of garment usually refers to the cut of its structural lines in a way that has become recognized, accepted, and named. A princess style is characterized by shaping through vertical seams. It goes by that name whether or not it is in fashion at any given time. All the variations of parts—sleeves, collars, and others— shown in Chapter 6 are styles.

A sense of style is possessed by those with a flair for creating beautiful combinations, for sensing what is appropriate for an occasion and for oneself, for coordinating garments and accessories in a satisfying way, and for anticipating what will be in fashion.

Being in style means using those styles that prevail in fashions of the moment. We speak of certain fashions as the "styles of the times" or "period styles"; that is, garments are cut in the same way as those popular in the Renaissance or in another era. Traditional national or cultural dress echoed in adaptations are usually called national styles— Spanish or Mandarin, for example.

---

[1]Gilles Lipovetsky, *The Empire of Fashion: Dressing Modern Democracy*, trans. Catherine Porter (Princeton, N.J.: Princeton University Press, 1994), pp. 15, 18, 23, 41.

Adolescents groping for self-identity in many cultures are partly seeking a sense of personal style. Usually by early adulthood individuals have chosen a basic group of styles in which they feel physically and psychologically comfortable.

Just as artists are often oblivious to the fact that they paint or sculpt in their own unique manner, people don't always realize that their personal preferences in dress create a distinguishing, individual style. Our customary style seems so natural and normal to us that we often think of it as "the" normal way to dress. All other ways and those who practice them may seem a bit strange,[2] but the urge for acceptance keeps our personal styles close to generally accepted fashions. The twin urges of individuality and conformity help balance personal styles between extremes and stagnation.

Taste

Taste is a way of exercising style. It is the sense of what creates excellence, of what is appropriate, the ability to perceive beauty and harmony. Culture is a major determinant of taste, and every culture has its ideas of good and poor taste. We feel at home with what we know; the familiar is comfortable whether or not it observes the principles of art. Some people seem to appreciate beauty naturally, others only through education. In many cultures, good taste involves restraint, an understatement that implies a mastery of awareness and control. In some cultures taste prizes the elegance of simplicity, whereas others favor the flamboyant abandon of bright colors and opulence. Styles that endure as classics usually reflect what a culture considers good taste.

Individual Expression

Beyond cultural and social factors, self-image influences our unique personal taste.

---

[2]Rudolf Arnheim, *Toward a Psychology of Art* (Berkeley: University of California Press, 1972), p. 11.

One widely used comparison of self-images is the traditional Chinese yin and yang (Figure 27-1). Yin represents qualities traditionally considered feminine: delicacy, submissiveness, passivity, darkness, weakness, gentleness, warmth, softness, fragility, and subtlety. Yang represents qualities traditionally stereotyped as masculine: assertiveness, dominance, activity, light, strength, toughness, hardness, sturdiness, stability. Contemporaries may disagree with some connotations, but these traditional groupings signify the two extremes of strength and delicacy.

Yet rarely is a person all yin or yang, but rather, a combination of both, with one dominating. Individuals also differ according to their role of the moment. A coed may feel yang in the classroom, but yin on a date. A football player might feel yang on the fifty-yard line, but yin cuddling his newborn son. Physical strength does not necessarily mean strength of character, nor does a physical yin mean a yin personality. Thus yin-yang represents extremes, which in use are often blurred.

In dress, yin uses of elements and principles physically recede and are psychologically dainty, and yang uses physically advance and are psychologically bold (Table 25-1).

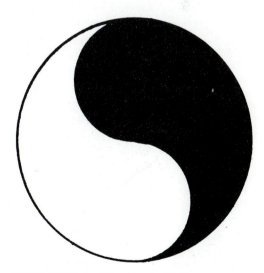

FIGURE 27-1 Yin-yang symbol.

But desired physical effects bring undesired psychological effects. Thus one may want the heightening effect of vertical lines, but not their stately mood. Here the decision becomes personal; the wearer must decide whether to use the vertical lines for height and seek a relaxed mood through other elements.

COORDINATION AND WARDROBE

There are no fool-proof formulas for wardrobe selection because people differ and their needs change as ages and social roles change. The key is to apply design process to wardrobe development according to current needs. Fashion experts have declared for years that one needn't be wealthy to dress well, attractively, and in good taste, whatever the culture. Just as unity is a goal of a garment or outfit, it is also the goal of a wardrobe; design process is the means to achieve both.

Wardrobe Development

Even within one culture, personal preferences differ widely. Some prefer one-piece and others two-piece outfits for either psychological or physical reasons; some like layered looks and others avoid them whatever the prevailing fashion. You select specific styles and garments based on your activities, finances, climate, personality, social roles, and physical and psychological effects desired. Analyzing your figure and coloration helps you decide the physical effects you want to convey, and analyzing your personality and activities helps you know what psychological effects convey the real you and accent your positive aspects. Consistency in appearance and behavior contribute to harmony and unity. Any clothing makes statements about its wearer; the challenge is to make it say what one wants it to say pleasantly. How would you organize the above points according to design process?

Selection and Combination

Few have the luxury of starting a wardrobe from scratch. Most wardrobes evolve as we grow, move homes, or change roles. Time-honored ways to coordinate outfits and increase wardrobe usefulness are suggested in the following statements.

1. Basic or classic styles last several seasons, whereas extremes or fads become dated quickly. Often a few basic items of clothing can help save money and space, vary with seasons and styles, and express personal creativity. Classic and simple styles may be focused for "now" by fashionable accessories or hemline adjustment (Figure 27-2).

2. Decoration and accessories harmonize and unify more easily if the basic garment is low-key. Simple, classic lines, versatile textures in quiet colors make good backgrounds to balance smaller fashion accents (Figures 27-3, 27-4).

3. Expensive purchases, such as coats and suits can be worn longer if they are low-key. Versatility in styling, texture, and color to span seasons provides even greater usefulness and economy. More extreme styles are usually for special occasions and ceremonies.

4. In most cultures an outfit consists of more than one garment. Indian saris are worn with the *choli* (blouse), Japanese kimono with *obi* (sash), African wrapper (skirt) with *buba* (blouse) and often headtie, and outfits in Western cultures use a vast array of separates. All invite mixing and matching, maximizing the number of possible combinations and appearances while minimizing the number of garments, the cost, and storage space (Figure 27-2).

5. Harmony is the key to coordination. Too much repetition is monotonous, and garments blend more easily if there is harmonious variation.

6. Clothing selections give most service if they reflect functional as well as struc-

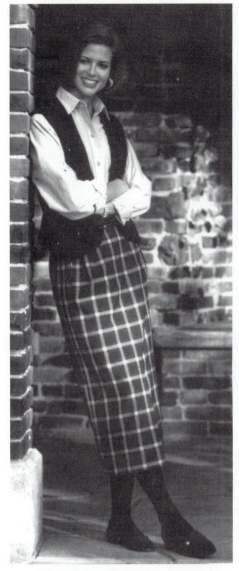

FIGURE 27-2 Mixing and matching several garments of basic styles helps maximize versatility and appropriateness to occasion, time, and season. (Courtesy of Pendleton Woolen Mills.)

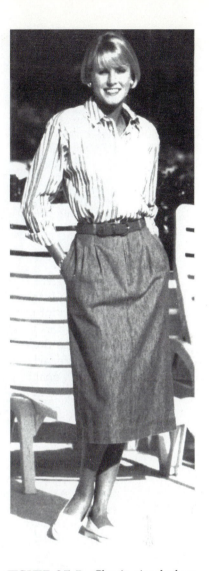

FIGURE 27-3 Classic, simple, low-key structural styles make versatile backgrounds to a variety of decorative fabric patterns or accessory accents for a range of seasons, events, physical effects, or moods. (Courtesy of Mark, Fore & Strike.)

tural and decorative needs. Graduation often means a change from a student wardrobe to a business one at a time of tight finances. A long-distance move may mean clothes for a new climate. Maternity brings changed physical and social needs. Versatile practicality means service.

7. Fewer items of good quality usually mix and last better than more items of poorer quality. Quality and versatility compensate for fewer garments. Good design and workmanship show.

8. Part of a sense of style is a sense of appropriateness of occasion which differs with cultures, climates, and times.

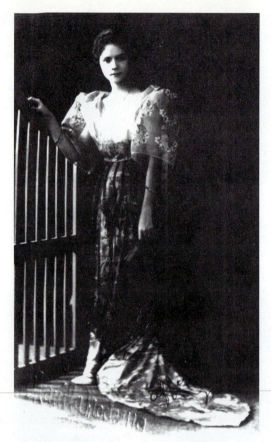

FIGURE 27-4 Structural styles that have become traditional are often those that lend themselves to great variety in decorative design such as the skirt fabric pattern and sleeve embroidery, and to a sense of cultural occasion, as in this traditional Philippine *terno*. (Courtesy of the Cultural Center of the Philippines, Manila.)

Awareness of the potential of elements and principles of visual design in dress in a specific culture helps sensitivity to cultural appropriateness (Figures 27-2, 27-4).

Clothing inventories can help wardrobe planning if garments reflect real needs and activities: Knowing what you do and what you have tells you what you need. The more a garment is worn, the less each wearing costs, but the impulsive purchase is often extreme and goes with nothing else, and so hangs unused and wastes space.

Clothing versatility results from harmonious practicality and blending advancing and receding effects.

SUMMARY

Each society has its norms of mores and folkways; fashion is a temporary folkway and fads are novel, short-lived fashions. Style identifies structural characteristics, the ability to combine garments well, and one's individual manner of dress. Taste expresses individual and social style. Yin and yang suggest extremes of delicacy and assertiveness.

Creating desired effects and illusions also means coordinating parts practically, economically and harmoniously; and realistically recognizing one's needs, finances, climate, culture, and social roles. Simple styles in good fabrics and construction are the most versatile and longlasting, made current and personal by accessories and fashion touches. Use of design process, variety, functional and structural harmony, versatility, and careful selection are the keys to success.

CLASS ACTIVITIES

1. Using clothing and textile examples, discuss the differences among mores, folkways, fashions, and fads. How might one garment be an example of all of them?

2. Compare the various uses of the term "style." How can clothing and textiles exemplify each concept?

3. Provide each student with a line drawing copy of the same basic garment structural styles. (Enlargements of examples from Chapter 6 could be used.) Then allow time for students to individualize that style for him or herself using decorative techniques of color, pattern, construction details, applied trims, and/or accessories. Then compare the varieties created by the individualiza-

tion: what physical and psychological effects are created for the wearer using the chosen decorative techniques?

4. Ask students to take a general summary inventory of their wardrobes. Assess which garments are most used and why, least used and why. How would you use present garments in wardrobe transition from school to professional wardrobe? Why would you choose some and not others?

5. For your inventory, outline design process steps for the goal of building a practical, economical, attractive, comfortable, and compact professional wardrobe. What outside factors must you consider? What criteria do they suggest? What styles and qualities will you select? Why?

6. With the class in groups, assign or select one of the above "Selection and Coordination" statements for each group, and in magazines, catalogues, or actual garments, find and analyze an example of the selected statement and share findings with the class.

28 *Applied Illusions*

We have now studied the types of illusions, the elements to which they apply, and the principles that use and result from them. For example, we have seen how geometric and size and space illusions use elements of space, line, and shape as applied in garment styles and fabric patterns employing the principles of proportion and scale to make different figure areas seem longer, shorter, larger, or smaller. We have seen how simultaneous contrast, after-image, and irradiation illusions use the element of color to create principles of contrast, balance, harmony, and others to make us seem darker, lighter, healthier, larger, or smaller. This chapter brings the illusions, elements, and principles together in their garment applications, organized according to effects for different figure areas. Each effect lists styles and techniques that incorporate the illusion, element, and principle uses to create that effect for that figure area.

PHYSICAL EFFECTS

The following suggestions are generalizations, neither iron-clad nor exhaustive. They include styles of garment parts and uses of elements, principles, and accessories where appropriate. Both Westernized styles and some non-Western styles are included. Since many "new" fashions are simply different combinations or variations of familiar styles, the following suggestions can be applied to many different "looks." Some styles may be used by either men or women; others will suggest the appropriate sex. Styles, textures, colors, and patterns recommended for different locations of the body must be considered *very* carefully so that a solution for one area does not create a problem for another, or destroy unity. Any suggestions must be considered in the context of the whole garment or outfit: its purpose, its function, its character, and its harmony and unity (Figure 28-1).

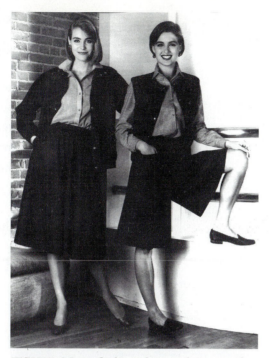

FIGURE 28-1 Styles, colors, and textures that create desired illusions for one body area interact with others and must be considered in the context of the whole. Changing any one part, such as sweater sleeves or skirt style, changes the whole. (Courtesy of Cotton Incorporated and Catalina.)

Make selections for the effect desired from that list, and avoid those listed under the undesired effect. For example, to look taller choose uses from the "taller" list, and avoid those from the "shorter" list.

Overall Height

To Look Taller

Short, close hairstyles or chignon

Small hat same color as garment

Dominantly vertical collar styles

Narrow ties and lapels

Single-breasted front openings

Narrow, center front panels or trim

Gently fitted, smooth styles

One-piece dresses

Sheath, shift, princess styles

Diagonally draped saris

Longer jackets and full-length coats, narrow capes

Long bishop or shirt sleeves

Narrow self-belts or no belts

Pointed or no waistlines

Long skirts

Straight or slightly flared skirts

Pressed pleats

Neck trim repeated at hem

Long parts

Straight, solid vertical lines

Irregular vertical lines

Same color upper and lower garment

Supple texture draped in vertical folds

Small-scale, all-over or vertical pattern

Vertically unbroken structural design

Soft textures

To Look Shorter

Bouffant hair styles

Large hats

Wide, horizontal collars

Wide ties and lapels

Short, wide jackets

Weskits, boleros

Ponchos

Trench coats

Bloused bodices

Full sleeves

Shoulder, midriff, or hip yokes

Wide or contrasting belts

Accents at waistline

Bouffant skirts

Short skirts

Bulky pants or tops

Horizontal ruffles, flounces, or shirring

Contrasting upper and lower garment

Strong horizontal lines

Irregular horizontal lines

Stiff, bulky textures

Over-All Weight

To Look Thinner

Thin, vertical collars

Accent near face

Narrow, long set-in or raglan sleeves

Gently fitted styles

Princess, sheath, coachman styles

Surplice openings

Long, slender robes

Narrow panels

Details within silhouette

Inset pockets

Pointed waist

A-Line or gently flared, long, or gored skirts

Long pants, gently fitted

Shoes following foot lines closely

Thin or vertical lines

Straight lines, sharp angles

Vertical diagonals

Cooler hues

Medium dark values

Duller intensities

Dull textures

Translucent textures

Soft but firm textures

Small-scale, vertical pattern

To Look Heavier

Bulky, horizontal collars

Large or large-brimmed hats

Bulky sleeves, elbow length or longer

Tightly fitted garments

Bloused bodices or *bubas*

Voluminous robes or capes

Double wrappers (skirts)

Wide panels

Patch pockets

Full, tiered skirts

Shoulder, midriff, or hip yokes

Extremely tiny or large jewelry, trims, or accessories

Bouffant, gathered skirts or unpressed pleats

Pants ending near knee

Chunky or delicate shoes

Details beyond silhouette

Accent on heaviest part of body

Thick or horizontal lines

Unbroken full curves, roundness

Warmer hues

Medium or darker values

Bright intensities

Extremely thin or bulky textures

Stiff, crisp textures

Shiny textures

Large-scale, bold pattern

Face

To Look Larger

Short, close hairstyle

Small or no hat

Contrasting makeup

Large eyeglass frames

Large earrings

To Look Smaller

Bouffant hairstyle

Large or large-brimmed hat

Inconspicuous makeup

Small eyeglass frames

Small or no earrings

Neck

To Look Shorter and Thicker

Hairstyle ending just below ears

Beard

Dominantly horizontal, high necklines and collars such as turtleneck, jewel, mandrin, stovepipe, rolled, high bateau

Wide collars

Scarves, bows at neck

Heavy choker necklaces

Large, dangle earrings

To Look Longer and Narrower

Hairstyle upswept or with neck showing

Clean-shaven or small, pointed goatee

Dominantly vertical necklines and collars, such as V, deep U, deep square, jabot, long tie, shawl, and the like

Narrow collars

Long pendants

Small button or no earrings

Set-in sleeves

In many Westernized cultures, extremely bony, gaunt, crepey necks or double chins are undesired.

For Smoother Chin, Neck

Built-up necklines

High, smooth-roll collars

Turtleneck, mandarin collars

High shawl collar with smooth, tie collar

No smocking and shirring or gathers in neck area

Accent at shoulder or back

For Less Crepey, Bony Neck

No scoop necklines

Closed shirt or convertible collars

Jewel neckline or high necks

Scarves, jabots, ascot ties

Medium values and intensities

Medium-heavy, medium-coarse textures

Shoulder Width

To Look Wider

Bateau neckline or collar

Wide scoop, sabrina, or cowl necklines

Bertha collar

V with point at waist, tips at shoulders

Horizontal shoulder ruffles

Accents at each shoulder

Peasant blouses, pinafores

Wide jacket lapels and ties

Horizontal bodice lines, stripes, or trim

Shoulder yokes

Same color across shoulder area

Kimono, puff, Juliet, epaulet, peasant, ruffle, leg-o-mutton, or cap sleeves

To Look Narrower

Dominantly vertical necklines; V, U, square

Deep scoop or cowl draping

Contrasting collars, scarves, or ties

Long scarves or jabots

Center front neck accent

Prominent, vertical front closings

Narrow jacket lapels and ties

Vertical or vertical-diagonal bodice lines

Princess seams shoulder to waist

Sleeveless or halter bodices, cut-in armholes

Raglan or dolman sleeves

Long cape, flared, or flounced sleeves

Round Shoulders

Choose to Look Straighter

Jewel, bateau, or sabrina necklines or collars

Short sailor or other straight-edged collars

Flat, horizontal collars

Shoulder yoke or stripes with point down at center, uplift at shoulders (V)

Shoulder seams set slightly back

Straight, horizontal lines in back shoulder area

Bloused bodices

Set-in, puff, ruffle, Juliet sleeves

Cowl, draped, or bulky necklines

Off-the-shoulder necklines

Roll or bulky collars or scarves

Diagonals meeting with upward point (∧) in shoulder area

Low-backed dresses

Peasant blouses

Curved lines in back shoulder

Raglan or long kimono sleeves

Capelets

"Dowager's Hump"

The "dowager's hump," or accumulation of fatty tissue at the back of the neck at the shoulders is an often undesired characteristic, more frequent in older women.

To Look Smoother Choose

Short, simple hairstyles

Small earrings

Choker or no necklaces

Front neck interest

High necks with front closings

Interestingly shaped shoulder yokes or back bodice draping

Bloused bodice back

Dark values in shoulder area

Medium heavy, thick textures

Small-scale, all-over or vertical pattern

To Look Smoother Avoid

Bouffant hairstyles or back chignons

Long necklaces, pendants, or scarves that make front look weighted down

Back neck accent

Low back necks or closings

Sailor or other collars flat in back

Straight lines or tucks at back shoulder

Tightly fitted bodices

Plain fabrics

Light values, bright colors in back shoulder area

Thin or shiny textures

Round lines in back shoulder area

Bust

To Look Larger

Jabot or long tie collar

Horizontal shoulder ruffles or pleats

Shoulder yoke with gathered bodice below

Bodice smocking, shirring, pleating, draping, or gathering at bust

Bodices gently bloused at bust

Cuffs or sleeve fullness at bust level

Dolman, moderately full puff, Juliet, peasant, cape, short bell sleeves

Narrow skirts

Thick or fuzzy bodice textures

Light values, brighter intensities

To Look Smaller

Straight-edge shoulder lines or collars

High cowl necklines

Single-breasted openings

Vertical bodice stripes or tucks

Full skirts

Dark values, dull intensities

Medium textures

Bodices bloused at waist

Chanel or loosely fitted jackets

Dominantly vertical collar styles

Extremely large- or small-busted women or post-mastectomy patients generally prefer to avoid drawing attention to the bust area. Full sleeves (such as short peasant, puff, Juliet, cape, bell, or lantern sleeves), trim, or large pattern at the upper arm or bust area, thin textures, or tightly fitted bodices generally call attention to the bust; bulky, large, bold shapes emphasize a large bust by repetition and a small bust by contrast. For women who consider themselves low-busted, shoulder yokes with horizontal seams break up the shoulder-to-bust length and make the bust seem higher, as will a dropped waistline, which lengthens unbroken distance from bust to apparent waist.

Waist Length

To Look Longer

Princess, sheath, shift, or A-line dresses

Princess, coachman, A-line coats

Narrow capes

Long jackets, vests, tunics

Effects that minimize bust size

Narrow self-belt or no belt at normal waist

Dropped or pointed waist

To Look Shorter

Bloused bodice

Bolero, shell

Battle jacket

Trench coat

Midriff, shoulder, or hip yoke

Waistline accents

Cummerbund

Wide, contrasting belt

Peplum

Waistline and Abdomen

Most Westernized cultures admire small waistlines and abdomens, some admire large ones, and some wish to emphasize pregnancy. (These suggestions are not intended as substitutes for maternity wear.)

To Look Smaller

Accent at neck

Single-breasted closings

Shoulder width, bertha collars

Narrow, vertical panels or skirt gores

Long jackets, vests, or tunics over pants

Two-piece outfits

Chanel or box jackets

Overblouses

Narrow self-belts

Inconspicuous or pointed waistline

Semi-full or flared skirts

Semi-fitted princess or A-line dresses or coachman coats

One-piece bathing suits

Dark values, dull colors

Small or no pattern

To Look Larger

Trumpet, shirred, or flounce sleeves with fullness at elbows

Smocks, very bloused, or very fitted bodices

Double-breasted closings

Weskits, shells or boleros ending at waist

Curved midriff yokes or hip yokes

Accent at waistline

Cummerbund, *obi*

Bouffant or pegged skirts

Hiphuggers or tight pant tops

Tent and shift or fitted sheath

Double wrappers

Bikini bathing suits

Light values, bright colors

Large-scale, bold pattern

Many cultures consider swayback and protruding ribs undesirable.

Protruding Ribs

(Effects will also depend on bust size)

Choose to Minimize

Shoulder and neck interest

Bloused bodices

Bodice draping

Boleros, shells, overblouses

Tunics, semi-fitted vests

Cape, box, A-line, coachman coats

Shirtwaist, pinafore dresses

Dark values in bodice

Small-scale pattern

Avoid to Minimize

Tightly fitted bodices or waistlines

Midriff yokes

Waist accents

Wide, tight belts

Cummerbunds

Fitted empire waistlines

Sheath, tightly fitted princess

Light values, bright intensities in bodice

Thin textures

Swayback

(Effects will also depend on abdomen size)

Choose to Minimize

Accents at neck

Low-back draped cowl with fullness at waist

Straight lines at back

Bloused back bodice

Overblouses, smocks, car coats

Box or Chanel jackets, capes

Semi-fitted tunics, vests, and ponchos

Shift, A-line dresses with waistlines

Gathered and tiered skirts

Dark values in bodice, light values in waistlines or belts

Thick textures

All-over or vertically directional patterns

Avoid to Minimize

Fitted bodice

Fitted empire waists

Curved, fitted lines at back waist

Midriff or skirt yokes

Tightly fitted, wide belts

Peplums

Contrasting bodices and waists

Thin textures in smooth styles at waist

Accents at front waist

Arm Length and Thickness

To Look Longer and Thinner

Sleeveless (if arms thin)

Sleeveless sheath or princess

Long fitted, set-in, raglan, dolman, or narrow shirt sleeves

Cap, cap kimono, or ruffle sleeve

Accent at wrist, small bracelets

To Look Shorter and Thicker

Puff, Juliet, or peasant sleeves

Full sleeves ending at or near elbow; short cape, bell, flounce, lantern (unless forearm extremely thin, then longer versions of these styles will help thicken)

Wrist and Hand Size

To Look Larger

Wrist cuffs or ruffles

Light or bright gloves

Heavy bracelets or rings

Large clutch bags

To Look Smaller

Short to narrow sleeves

Dark or dull gloves

Small, few, or no bracelets or rings

Small bags with narrow handles

Waist-Hip Length

To Look Longer

Princess, shift, sheath styles

Long jackets, vests, tunics

Empire waist

Slightly raised waistline

Skirts pleated from waist

Gored or gently flared skirts

Long skirts

Irregular vertical lines in hip area

To Look Shorter

Wide belts

Dropped waist

Hiphuggers

Peplum

Hip yoke

Flowers, bows, pockets, or trim at hips

Irregular horizontal lines or stripes between waist and hips

Hip and Buttock Size

To Look Larger

Overblouses or vests ending at hip

Sleeves with fullness between elbow and wrist: flounce, long bell, trumpet, angel, cape, lantern

Tightly fitted or halter waist

Drop waist

Peplum

Shirring, smocking, or bulk at hip area

Hip yokes

Bouffant skirts

Short or tight shirts or pants

Pegged or trumpet skirts

Double wrappers

Contrasting gloves

Extremely large or small purses

Bright intensities, light value skirt or pants

Heavy, stiff, shiny, fuzzy, or very thin textures

Large scale pattern at hip area

To Look Smaller

Shoulder width, neck interest

Vertically diagonal draping to shoulder, as in saris

Slightly bloused bodice

Unfitted empire waist

Semi-fitted A-line, princess dresses

Straight or semi-fitted coats

Longer suit jackets, tunics

Semi-fitted waist

Skirts pleated from waist

Gently flared or gored skirts

Culottes

No trim, accent, or horizontal repetition at hip

Vertical lines in hip area

Same color and texture from hem to waist; little contrast at hip

Medium size purses

Cooler hues

Dark values, dull intensities

Dull textures

Medium, firm textures

Small-scale or no pattern at hip area

Leg Length and Thickness

To Look Longer and Thinner

No hip accent

Pleats from waist

Slight skirt gathers

Gently flared or gored skirts

Palazzo or flared pants

Long skirts, pants

Longer street-length skirts

Short shorts if legs thin

Single wrappers

Ankle interest

Delicately styled shoes

Vertical pant or skirt stripes

Dark values, dull intensities

Medium-firm textures

To Look Shorter and Thicker

Full jackets or coats ending midthigh

Double wrappers

Knee or above skirts and pants, knickers

Full or tiered skirts

Accents or ruffles at knee hem

Godets at knee hem

Pedal-pushers, gaucho pants

Knee patches

Pant cuffs

Chunky shoes

Horizontal pant or skirt stripes or plaids

Light values, bright intensities

Extremely bulky, stiff, or thin textures

Foot Size

To Look Larger

Ankle or knee socks

Chunky shoes

Boots

Thick heels

Thick soles

Bright, warm colors

Complex, contrasting lines

Light values

Shiny surfaces

Bows, buckles, or bulky trim

To Look Smaller

Long stockings or no stockings

Delicate, smooth shoes

Low- or medium-cut shoes

Small heels

Medium-thin heels and soles

Simple lines

Dull, cool colors

Dark values

Dull surfaces

Small, smooth, or no trim

PSYCHOLOGICAL EFFECTS

Certain uses of elements and principles evoke similar psychological responses in many Westernized cultures. These suggestions are neither foolproof nor comprehensive.

Occasion

To Look Sophisticated, Dressy

Small or no hats

Very simple necklines

Scoop, low necklines or halters, strapless bodices

Cowl necklines, draped bodices or skirts

Tuxedo or shawl collars

Capes, long coats, tuxedos

Stoles, capelets

One-piece dresses

Long sheath or princess dresses

Long, simple or no sleeves

Soft gathers in bodice, sleeves, or skirts

Fitted or empire waists, cummerbunds

Long skirts or palazzo pants, trumpet skirts

Dressy shoes

Small accessories

Minimal, if any, trimmings

Vertical straight lines

Sweeping, continuous curves

Unbroken space

Cool, rich colors

Rich, deep or sheer, supple textures, lace, embroidery

Shiny surfaces—sequins, lamé, satin, beading

Sparkling or lustrous jewelry

Small stylized, abstract or no pattern, floral motifs

Formal balance

Striking or subtle but elegant contrasts

Fine proportions, delicate scale

Undulating rhythms

To Look Casual, Informal

Medium-sized hats

Bateau or medium-high necklines

Shirt, convertible, Italian or other versatile collar

Car coats, full-length coats

Pinafores, jumpers, shirtwaist dresses

Sweaters

Leisure suits, pant suits

Two- (or more) piece ensembles

Around knee-length skirts, pleats

Most sleeve styles except angel, trumpet, Juliet, flounce, or long cape

Shoulder, midriff, or hip yokes

Tucks, shirring, smocking

Simple, versatile trimmings: rick rack, fringe, braid, appliqué, insertion, ribbon, bows, ruffles, pom-poms

Simple costume jewelry

Medium-sized accessories

Flat walking shoes

Diagonal or vertical straight lines, plaids

Broken, thick, or shaped lines

Broken space

Warm, bright colors, light values

Flat, strong textures

Durable, firm, flexible textures

Dull but soft surfaces, semi-smooth

Rhythmic stylized, geometric, or abstract patterns

Natural or man-made objects as motifs

Bold contrast

Informal balance

Businesslike

Tailored bows, shawl or Italian collars, ties

Tailored shirts or blouses

Vests, weskits

Matching upper and lower garments

Smoothly fitted garments

Inset pockets, subtle style features

Long pants, longish skirts

Straight or gently flared skirts

Small, inconspicuous jewelry

Walking shoes

Straight, continuous lines

Restrained curves

Muted, cooled colors, medium values

Firm, crisp, smooth textures

Small-scale, geometric pattern

Reserved, restrained styling

Formal, or elegant informal, balance

Close, subtle contrasts

Sporty

Shirt, convertible, turtleneck, Italian, crew neck collars

Blazers, vests, boleros, sport shirts

Jumpsuits, gaucho pants

Pants, culottes, shorts, blue jeans

Patch pockets, yokes, conspicuous style features

Action fitting and styling, slits, tucks

Flat-felled seams

Pressed pleats

Costume (if any) jewelry

Sport shoes, sneakers, sandals

Straight lines, exuberant curves

Bright, warm colors, light values

Rough, coarse, fluffy, or sturdy textures

Bold pattern, geometric, stylized, abstract

Man-made objects as motifs

Functional formal or informal balance

Bold contrasts

Staccato rhythms

Levity

Happy

Medium-low necklines, rolled collars

Fitted or semi-fitted bodices

Short, full sleeves

Two- (or more) piece outfits

Medium-length skirts, shorts, or jackets

Full-gathered or pleated skirts

Casual, largish accessories and jewelry

Colorful trims, braids, appliqué

Straight, solid lines or exuberant curves

Broken space

Warm hues, light values, bright intensities

Medium, sturdy textures

Bold patterns, stylized, geometric

Bold contrasts

Somber

High necklines, flat collars

Semi-fitted bodices, jackets

Long, narrow sleeves, skirts, pants, jackets, and coats

One-piece dresses, A-line

Gently flared or straight skirts

Minimal, reserved trim

Restrained, small accessories or jewelry

Thin, straight lines or restrained curves

Open space

Cool hues, dark values, dull intensities

Firm, smooth, but soft, semi-fine textures

Dull surfaces

Small-scale geometric or no pattern

Subtle contrasts

Age

Youthful

Full, short sleeves, sleeveless

Stoles, capelets, vests, weskits, blazers

Pinafores, jumpers, dirndl skirts

Pants, shorts, culottes

Pleats, gathers, prominent style features, ruffles, bows

Patch pockets

Straight lines or full curves

Broken, shaped, fuzzy, thick lines

Broken space

Warm hues, light values, bright intensities, pure hues

Soft textures

Small-scale but bold patterns

Natural and man-made stylized or geometric motifs; all-over, directional, or border arrangements

Mature

Smooth, semi-fitted styles

Inconspicuous style features

One-piece dresses, A-line

Longer, semi-fitted sleeves

Full-length coats, capes

Inconspicuous waistlines

Gently flared skirts

Long skirts, pants, and jackets

Straight lines, restrained curves

Solid, thin, sharp, smooth lines

Open, smooth space

Cool hues, dark values, dull intensities

Firm textures

Small-scale, subtle, geometric or abstract motifs, any arrangement, or no pattern

Personality

Dramatic, Yang

Advancing uses of elements:

Thick, straight, solid, vertical lines

Open spaces

Straight edged style shapes

Bright, warm colors

Medium values

Firm textures, opaque, rough, or shiny

Bold patterns and geometrics or plain

Bold contrasts

Large scale

Tailored styles

Pants, vests, jackets, smooth semi-fitting

Halters, fitted bodices and waists

Wide belts, prominent accessories, style features, and jewelry

Straight, flared, pleated skirts, sharp creases

Long skirts, pants, palazzo pants

Full, flowing, or smooth sleeves

Capes, ponchos, car coats, box or Chanel jackets

One-shoulder necklines

Delicate, Yin

Receding uses of elements:

Thin, solid, curved lines

Broken spaces

Curved shapes

Muted, cool, pale colors

Soft, thin, delicate, sheer textures

Small-scale, natural, stylized, all-over patterns

Subtle contrasts

Small, delicate scale

Delicate harmonies

Small, dainty accessories, jewelry, and trims

Gathers, ruffles, flares, flounced or full skirts

Full, short sleeves

Princess, sheath, pinafore dresses

Cummerbund, sashes, bows, scarves

Palazzo, flared pants

Long, soft shirts

Capelets, fichus, weskits

Draped bodices or skirts

All of the above garment suggestions use the elements according to various prin-ciples, countering and reinforcing techniques, and selected illusions. Herein lies much of the design process step four: "planning" visual arrangements to meet criteria.

SUMMARY

Against the backdrop of cultural uses of illusions, physical and psychological effects of visual design elements and principles of design applied in dress, wearers can use the illusions to change or reinforce their apparent figure proportions or coloration, and to create effects of mood, age, personality, or occasion.

CLASS ACTIVITIES

1. Review the illusions recommended for clothing use, the ways they use the elements and principles, and how they are expressed in different garment styles.

2. Note that each figure category (over-all height, face, etc.) has two sub-categories of opposing effects (taller - shorter, larger - smaller, choose - avoid, etc.). With the class in groups, assign each group a different figure category and assign each half of a group one of the sub-categories of effects. Then give each group two identical line drawings of "their" figure area, one for each sub-group to select styles or uses from "its" sub-category list, and diagram these on the figure area drawing. For example, of the "over-all height" group, half would select uses "to look taller" and half "to look shorter." Sketch these on the line drawings and compare the effects of different uses on the same figure.

3. Invite students to list their own perceived figure problems and select choices from corresponding figure category lists. Combine the selections into one garment and analyze how it solves the figure problems yet maintains unity.

29 Visual Design in Dress Around the World

UNIVERSALITY OF APPLICATION

Dress around the world demonstrates a magnificent variety of effects, all creatively achieved with the same versatile, timeless and universal elements and principles of visual design studied here. Many traditional styles have affectionately endured for centuries in the face of fleeting, often extreme, fashions. Their distinct styles and beauty have been appreciated long enough to earn a proud rank of regional or national costume. They still visualize cultural identities, proclaiming "I am a Swede" or "I am a Filipino" or "I am a Kenyan."

Despite the spread of Western dress for daily wear, traditional dress is often such a beautiful and practical blend of functional, structural, and decorative design that its use continues for daily as well as ceremonial wear, often revealing an unsuspected versatility. So whether special or everyday, it says the world over, "I am a member of a group, yet an individual, an expressive being." This chapter does not attempt an anthropological analysis of costumes, but the following alphabetical tour through eighteen countries briefly highlights how each regional style uses the same elements and principles in its own ways to achieve its own unique and distinguishing effects that may also echo other cultural or climatic factors. You may wish to review earlier chapters showing advancing and receding, enlarging and reducing, delicate and bold effects produced by different variations of element aspect and uses of principles and illusions. As you study each country, note what reinforcing and countering techniques are used; what geometric structural forms are used, and how they relate to each other and to body forms; and how functional, structural, and decorative design relate.

AUSTRIA

Traditional Austrian costumes are characterized by gaiety, color, and styles that follow body forms.[1] The *leibkittel* from Vorarlberg province shows a traditional attached bodice and skirt (Figure 29-1). The dominant lines are vertical, structural, and well-placed so that little purely decorative design is needed.

The small-scale neck border provides value and pattern contrast. The sleeve and skirt proportions are each a pleasing length in relation to their width. Their triangular shapes show repetition, but invigorating contrasts between unbroken space, smooth texture, and light value in the full peasant sleeves, and broken space, creased texture, gathers, and dark value in the skirt help distinguish its structural parts. The bodice is fitted, yet the sleeves and skirt allow freedom of movement as well as warmth welcome in the high altitudes of the Alps.

BRAZIL

The robust full blouse, ruffled sleeves, and turban and scarf forms find happy counterpoint in the small scale beads and delicate eyelet embroidery-patterned texture which is reinforced by the shine of the bangles. The blouse and beads reflect the Portuguese Latin cultural influence, while the turban adds a local touch to this festival costume from Bahia (Figure 29-2).

CZECH REPUBLIC AND SLOVAKIA

These traditional festival costumes from Lopenikem between Slovakia and Moravia are characterized by the cap streamers and a unique combination of structural and decorative design (Figure 29-3). The proportions of the bouffant dome skirt and spherical sleeve structural forms and boots suggest a cultural value of heartiness and sturdiness. Yet this exuberance is balanced by the delicate embroidery on the sleeves and cap streamers, and the soft, sheer texture and open work embroidery of the aprons. The forceful structural forms are softly countered by the prolific variety of patterns which harmonize because they are similar in floral motifs, scale, degree of detail, interpretation, distribution, and mood, and they follow structural edges.

GERMANY

Several neighboring European countries share similar heritages and basic costume styles. Though proportions may vary, the

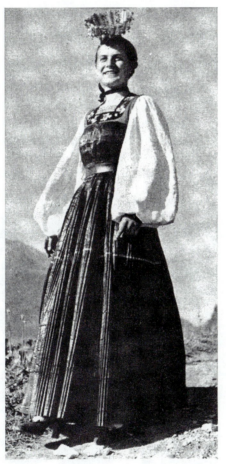

FIGURE 29-1 Austria, *leibkittel*. (Courtesy Austrian Information Service.)

[1]Wilhelm Schlag, "Austrian Costumes" (New York: Austrian Information Service).

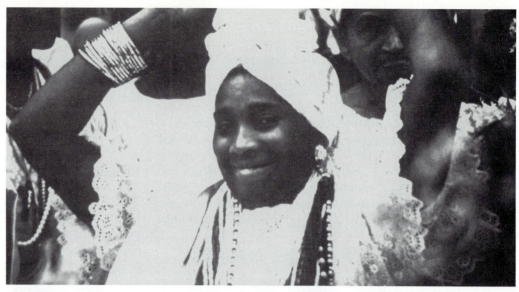

FIGURE 29-2 Brazil, Bahia costume. (Courtesy of Jonas Berger Associates/Varig Airelines.)

basic parts of the women's costumes are usually long sleeves, fitted bodices, weskits, dirndl skirts, and often aprons, and menswear often uses short pants, shirts, brimmed hats, vests or shoulder straps, and fitted jackets. These versatile, tubular functional forms provide visual variety and ex- cellent background for the decorative details that distinguish different regions. In Munich, each year the traditional *Oktoberfest* celebrates the fall harvest and brings out costumes for parades (Figure 29-4).

In women's costumes, the assertive straight lines, angular shapes, and strong

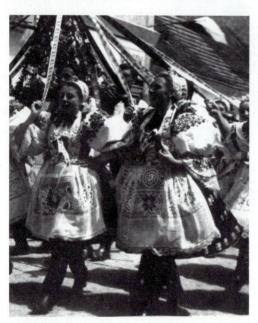

FIGURE 29-3 Czech Republic and Slovakia, festival costume. (Courtesy Pace Public Relations.)

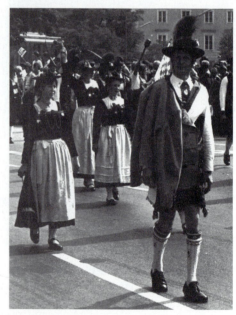

FIGURE 29-4 Germany, *lederhosen* (men), Munich Oktoberfest. (Courtesy Lufthansa German Airlines.)

value contrasts are balanced by gathers, soft textures, and small scale apron pattern. The flat brimmed hat repeats the straight lines and helps identify the region. The man's traditional *lederhosen*, short leather pants with shoulder straps, are cool but sturdy. The knee socks complement the short pants and, with the hat, plume, and pant tassels, help identify the region. Most emphasis comes from structural design lines; there is an economy of purely decorative design.

GHANA

Traditional, everyday Ghanaian dress is similar to that in much of West Africa (Figure 29-5). The skirt is usually two rectangular fabric pieces each about two yards long and used as a double wrapper giving predominantly straight structural lines. The lower, or "down," wrapper is tied about the

hips, and the "up" wrapper is tied about the waist and sometimes used to carry a baby or market purchases. The traditionally admired effects of weight and size are often achieved in two ways: the bulk and horizontal folds at the waist which help shorten and widen the figure, and the large scale fabric patterns which agree with the large, structurally unbroken areas of the wrapper. Both techniques are shown in the ensemble. The border parallels and reinforces the wrapper edges. The fitted top balances the full skirt, and the headtie adds height, even without the parcel. Mixing of fabric patterns often increases apparent size and busyness.

INDIA

The Indian sari is world-renowned for its flowing grace (Figure 29-6). Also a rectangle, it is six yards long, and its tubular form

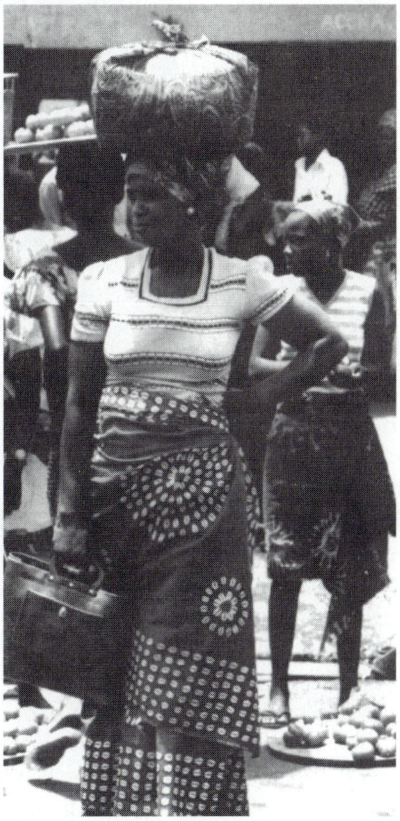

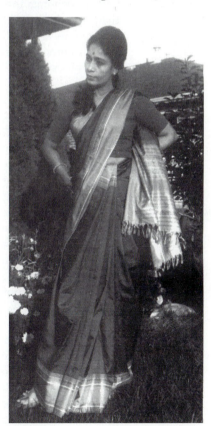

FIGURE 29-5 Ghana, wrapper and blouse. (Courtesy Ghana Tourist Office, New York.)

FIGURE 29-6 India, *sari* and *choli*. (Courtesy Manjusri.)

is achieved by wrapping, pleating, and draping. A versatile basic style, its dressiness or casualness is determined by the fabric texture and pattern. Part of the sari's distinguishing grace arises from its judicious use of receding qualities that suggest femininity and softness: the gently curved lines of the draping, spaces decoratively broken into small, delicate patterns, subtle color combinations, and soft textures. In this example, the small stripes in the border pattern, the fringe at the end, the silky texture, and gentle value contrasts add softness. The full-length, draped sweep from right ankle to left shoulder arranges the decorative borders in flattering ways, carries attention to the neck and face, gives an elegant line and informal balance and leaves the hands free; an important factor, as each hand traditionally had its own roles. Gathered drapes fall from the left shoulder in fluid folds over the bodice, echoing the soft skirt front pleats that provide walking space. The Indian use of elements and principles in the sari beautifully demonstrates the versatility and potential of a simple rectangle.

JAPAN

The graceful kimono and *obi* also enjoy worldwide recognition for their subtle beauty (Figure 29-7). The *obi* is the distinctive, wide belt-sash wrapped vertically at the back. The example here is a *furisode*, or long-sleeved kimono worn by unmarried women. The kimono is also based on the long rectangle, here derived from strips of fabric woven in standard widths so two strips form the back, two the front, and the sleeve/arm length is one strip width (Figure 6-18a). The fabric is woven or printed so pattern motifs match exactly when the narrow strips are stitched together, and sometimes patterns are visible only as the wearer moves into different positions. A distinguishing feature of many kimono fabrics is that several techniques of introducing fabric pattern, such as ikat *(kasuri)*, tie-dye *(shibori)*, printing, painting, and embroidery, may all be used in the

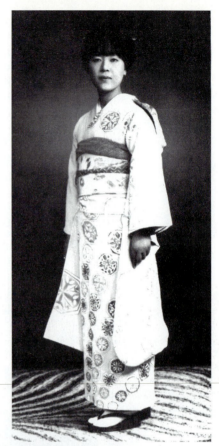

FIGURE 29-7 Japan, *furisode*. (Courtesy of Izukura-Kigyo Co., Ltd., Miss Kyoko Izumi, and Miss Reiko Izumi.)

same fabric, and so carefully planned and blended that they complement each other, match, and seem to belong together, a challenging achievement. Here, the dominantly straight structural lines accommodate the decorative patterns of curved motifs well-scaled to the area they occupy. Mild value contrasts complement strong line direction contrasts. The rectangles provide a common denominator to compare proportions among the garment divisions, and all maintain pleasing ratios. The flat neckbands in front become a narrow, stand-up collar in back as it dips and extends out, exposing the back of the neck which is considered a sensuous area. The kimono exemplifies harmony of strength, restraint, control, and delicacy in one garment.

KOREA

The traditional Korean woman's dress also exemplifies a versatile, all-purpose yet graceful garment (Figure 29-8). Like the sari, kimono, and wrapper, because the structural style is standard, its degree of dressiness is often determined by the fabric texture—lustrous silks and brocades for formal wear and cottons for everyday. The distinctive Korean style consists of a *chima*, or long, gathered dress attached to a shoulder yoke, and a tiny over-jacket or *chogori*, which ends around the bust and is held closed by long, decorative ties. The long, wide, flat sleeves curve to fit snugly at the wrist. There is ample freedom of movement, and the fullness of the dress adds some apparent bulk and weight. Except for the sleeve curve at the wrist, the structural lines are dominantly straight; so countering curved lines usually come from decorative fabric pattern. Curved or straight, decorative lines usually follow structural lines well, as in this example where the pattern filled space of the *chogori* emphasizes the upper body. The long *chogori* ties, tied into a bow, are often patterned, emphasizing their vertical direction and reinforcing upper body attention. The narrow band edging the neckline is usually white, accenting the face and neck. The proportions of the skirt and the sleeves provide pleasing comparisons of shape ratios, of dark to light, and pattern to plain in a uniquely Korean combination.

MEXICO

The Spanish Latin influence in this Mexican fiesta dress from Veracruz (Figure 29-9) echoes the Portuguese Latin influence seen earlier in the Brazilian costume. The characteristic white peasant blouse with neck flounce and ruffled, embroidered sleeves repeats the gathered skirt, allowing ample

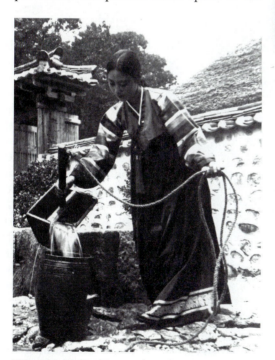

FIGURE 29-8 Korea, *chogori* (jacket) and *chima* (skirt). (Courtesy Korea National Tourism Corporation.)

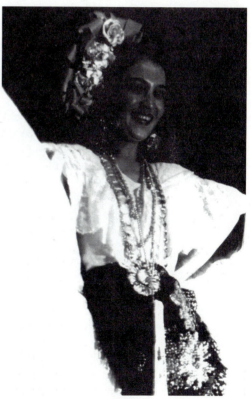

FIGURE 29-9 Mexico, Veracruz traditional costume. (Courtesy of Mexican Ministry of Tourism.)

freedom of movement and a swirling full-ness that suggests gaiety and abandon and adds weight. This drama is reinforced by the strong black-white value contrasts, and the metallic sparkle of the earrings, beads, and skirt beading. These, with the large, festive ribbon and floral headdress distribute filled-space accents vertically, lengthening the figure and balancing the structural fullness. The folded fan (hanging from a neck chain) is a classic Spanish accessory used to dramatize hand movements as much as to cool. The assertive use of many elements is softened by the supple texture which contributes a femininity to this lively Spanish Mexican costume.

NEW ZEALAND

This traditional New Zealand Maori dress uses nearly all of its elements and principles assertively to create characteristic drama through bold contrasts (Figure 29-10). The simple structural design of the bodice accommodates well the traditional geometric pattern which uses all of its elements boldly: sharp, straight, thick, solid, diagonal lines; straight-edged, sharp-angled zigzag, diamond, and triangular motif shapes; busy filled space; and extreme value contrast reinforce each other suggesting strength. The firm, ribbed texture of the bodice echoes the ribbed effect of the skirt strung of flax strips and called *"piupiu."* This traditional "strung" skirt creates unique textural contrast and reinforces straight line effects with the bodice. Alternation and parallelism find a wide range of expression: The diagonal parallel lines of the bodice pattern alternate directions, the bodice vertical line segments alternate, dark and light values alternate and contrast strongly in several skirt and bodice areas creating a crisp, sharp rhythm. Even though space is decoratively very broken, the over-all effect retains an assertiveness from the straight lines and stark contrasts.

NIGERIA

Like Ghana, Nigeria is in West Africa and traditionally uses visual elements and principles similarly in "up" and "down" wrapper skirts. In Nigeria, most blouses are overblouses, the *buba* in the west (Figure 6-25i), and in the east often peplum blouses as shown here (Figure 29-11). In this example, the desired widening effects of the structural waistline, peplum edge, wrapper hem, and their decorative borders are countered by the dominantly vertical tubular garment forms and flowered blouse pattern stripes. The peplum, especially, widens the waist/hip area. The functional and structural garment part forms and textures are practical, cool for a hot climate, and allow freedom of upper body movement. The wrapper, as a rectangle wrapped into a tube, is usually wrapped with the feet standing apart to insure walking space when finished. As here, structural space is open, and decorative space is filled by fabric pattern. The within-part,

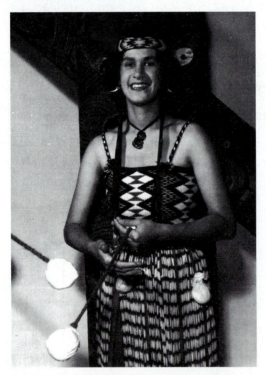

FIGURE 29-10 New Zealand, Maori *piupiu.* (Courtesy New Zealand Consulate General, New York.)

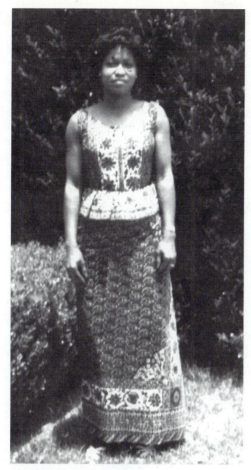

FIGURE 29-11   Nigeria, skirt wrapper, blouse with peplum. (Garments author's collection, photo courtesy of Mrs. Linda McCorvey.)

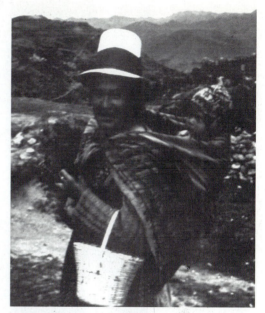

FIGURE 29-12   Peru, *chullo* (child's cap) and *q'epirina* or *inkuña* (carrying cloth), Cuzco area. (Courtesy of Carolyn Joyner.)

among-part, and part-to-whole proportions offer variety, interest, and balance. The scale of the pattern and peplum are consistent with each other, garment parts, and the wearer. The repetition of lines and pattern throughout contributes to balance, harmony, and unity in this typically Nigerian combination.

PERU

This traditional Peruvian ensemble hints at the magnificent heritage of Peruvian textiles (Figure 29-12). Forms and textures are versatile and practical, providing warmth as well as beauty for Andean mountain altitudes. The dome formed *chullo*, or child's cap, is functionally warm and decorated with pattern well-scaled to the cap and child's head size. The *q'epirina* or *inkuña* carrying cloth is a traditionally Peruvian use of shape and texture that provides warmth for both wearers and support for the child. The striped patterns echo the geometric and angular motifs and close value contrasts which characterize many historic Peruvian textiles. The banded and brimmed tube-formed hat common to many Andean regions provides both warmth and sun protection at high altitudes, and tops off a traditional village Peruvian application of functional, structural, and decorative design.

PHILIPPINES

The distinctive Philippine *terno* makes an elegant traditional ceremonial dress with its full length skirt and characteristic "butterfly sleeves" (Figure 29-13). Usually of crisp, sheer texture, the unique sleeves

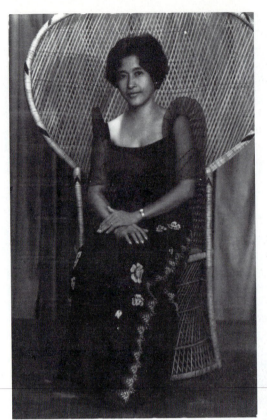

FIGURE 29-13 Philippines, *terno*. (Courtesy of Dr. Elena H. Antonio, Kabacan, Cotabato.)

SWEDEN

This child's traditional costume in Sweden echoes the adult version and shows similarities with folk costumes seen from other European countries of Austria and Germany with the fitted bodice or weskit, long sleeve blouse, gathered skirt, and apron (Figure 29-14). Functionally, this style reflects the Swedish climate, with the warmth of the cap, long sleeves, leggings, and layering of skirt, apron, bodice, and scarf. Decoratively, the straight striped trims follow the struc-

hold their shape well, and reveal at the same time they continue their vertical sweep upward beyond the shoulders and frame the face and neck. They are sometimes made detachable from the shoulder straps to increase versatility. The dress itself is usually a princess, sheath, or empire style to maximize height. The dress proportions are echoed in smaller scale in the sleeves. Line use is usually thin, long, straight or slightly curved, and smooth, all uses which suggest femininity. Historic Spanish rule left a heritage of embroidery decorative design often used in *ternos* and seen here in the skirt and up the sides, contributing delicacy. The uniquely Philippine applications of elements and principles provide both a distinctive ethnic identity and a graceful presence.

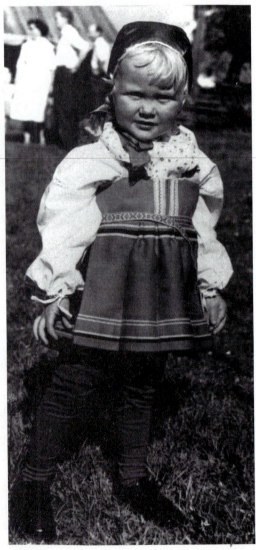

FIGURE 29-14 Sweden, child's traditional costume. (Courtesy of the Swedish Tourist Board.)

tural edges of skirt, apron, waistline, and bodice front. Their straightness, solidity, and evenness suggest strength and firmness, reinforced by the firm texture of the apron and bodice, but softened by the supple scarf texture. The small scale of the scarf and belt motifs agree with the child's size. This Swedish blend of element and principle uses suggests practicality, simplicity, stability, and attractiveness.

SWITZERLAND

The man's summer Appensell festival costume from Switzerland (Figure 29-15) shares the angularity seen in some other traditional European costumes. The straight lines of the vest, sharp angles of the lapels, and rows of square metal buttons suggest a sturdiness; yet the broken line

suggests a playfulness, reinforced by the rows of starburst motifs edging the front. The dome shaped cap provides the singular curved line. The standing back vest collar echoes that of the neighboring German jacket seen earlier, and the decorative lines reinforcing the structural edges also echo the similar use in Austria, Germany, the Czech Republic, and Sweden. While there may be similarities in approaches, like variations of a theme, each region puts its own stamp of individuality on its use of the elements. The over-all effect here is one of cheerful sturdiness that one can imagine against a backdrop of Alpine mountains and lakes.

THAILAND

These dynamically curvelinear Thai dance costumes borrow from another medium—Thai architecture to illustrate the cultural tradition of avoiding right angles in the belief that non-right, acute, or obtuse angles protect the user (Figure 29-16). So we see a rich interplay of curved line and sharp points both on traditional Thai buildings

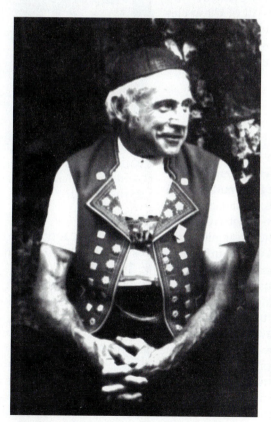

FIGURE 29-15 Switzerland, Appenzell costume. (Courtesy of the Swiss National Tourist Office.)

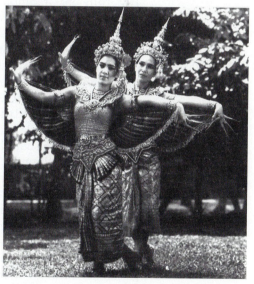

FIGURE 29-16 Thailand, traditional dance costumes, Bangkok. (Courtesy of Thai Airways International Limited.)

and costumes. However, some straight lines, and even right angles do appear in the fanned hip pleats and rich skirt fabric pattern, but on diagonals. The garment structural forms are tubular, with the skirt again derived from a rectangle, pleated in front to allow movement. The headdress and yoke collar bring sinuous grace, a gentle transition of line direction, echoed in the hand movements exaggerated by the decorative metal finger extensions with curved points. The curved lines of the headdress are countered by the sharp, straight thrust of the vertical point which contributes stateliness as well as height.

The richly textured and patterned headdress, yoke "wings," and skirt make decoratively closed, filled space which suggests intrigue and complexity as it emphasizes the figure. The close value contrasts lend gentleness which complements the busyness of the garment. All of these element and principle uses create a uniquely Thai blend of delicacy, busyness, and complexity punctuated by sharpness.

TURKEY

Two different traditional costume styles from Turkey shown here have similarities in element uses and moods despite their differences (Figure 29-17). Both make lavish use of sumptuous textures; both use a knee-length, long sleeved over-jacket style with an elongating V-neck to the waist and vertically interrupted by a belt with shiny metal, paisley motif double buckles; and beaded headdresses with short, lustrous veils reminiscent of traditional Moslem women's veils, all showing similar use of line, shape, form, and texture. The ways each differs are also indicatively Turkish. The costume at the left uses the traditional harem style, loose pants, fitted at the ankle. The unusual over-jacket is floor length in back. Its fabric pattern of stripes underlying floral bands gives a delicate and busy effect to the decoratively broken space which reinforces the elegance of the lustrous fabric, daintily scal-

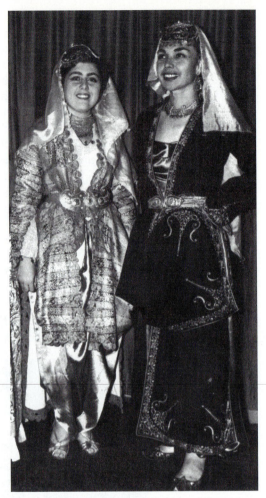

FIGURE 29-17 Turkey, traditional dress. (Courtesy of the Turkish Government Tourist Office.)

loped edges, and light, close values. The costume at the right retains a more dramatic Turkish flavor with strong value contrasts between the garments and their embroidered trim, and character contrasts between the long, sharp, straight structural edges, and the delicate, porous, curvelinear embroidered borders and three-pronged corner motifs. Like famous Turkish rugs, there is a strong sense of relating the decorative pattern to the contours of the structural shape, emphasized by the decoratively open space inside the outlines. A completing accent is the traditional shoe style with the pointed toes curving upward, a unique use of line and form. These costumes exemplify diversity in using elements and principles, yet retaining a similar cultural identity.

WALES

The traditional Welsh costume from Caernarvon (Figure 29-18) reminds some of historic Puritan dress. They are similar in the long sleeves with wide, white cuffs, the wide, white flat collar, the rectangular apron, and Puritan style hat. But important differences lighten the mood: here the hat is worn by the woman, and a gathered ruffle peeks out from under the brim, as well as narrowly edging the collar, apron, and cuffs. The jacket space is decoratively filled with bold stripes, and the apron is worn under the jacket which opens diagonally outward from the waist. The straight, long, sharp stripes and strong value contrasts are assertive, but softened by the ruffle scale,

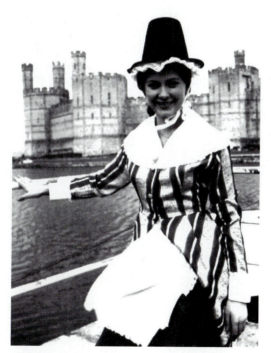

FIGURE 29-18 Wales, traditional costume from Caernarvon. (Courtesy of the British Tourist Authority.)

gathers, textures, and rounded collar edges to produce a lively individuality with a uniquely Welsh signature.

SUMMARY

This whirlwind tour of eighteen countries shows similarities and distinguishing differences in uses of the same visual design elements and principles to give a cultural identity to traditional dress. Most structural styles are related to those shown in Chapter 6; the differing combinations, proportions, and details give a unique flavor to each garment. We have seen how a number of different cultural styles are based on the rectangle. Reviewing the chapter shows other commonalities in basic forms of dress: Brazil (turban), Ghana, India, Japan, Nigeria, and Peru employ wrapped forms of dress. To the extent that full skirts are suspended, Austria, Brazil, the Czech Republic and Slovakia, Germany, and Mexico share that form; Thailand and Wales rest collars on the shoulders; and Turkey suspends veils from the head. Japan and Korea combine wrapped, suspended, and fitted, and all of the cultures shown use fitted styles in some form. Some of the styles are season spanning, some suggest warm or cool climates or high altitudes which influence functional design. Examples show a range of freedom of movement which is usually related to how "ceremonial" or "every day" a style is intended to be, or how physically active the wearer expects to be, a factor often related to occasion and/or social class. Styles that are either very full or confining allow less free movement than those that loosely follow body contours. Traditional cultural styles also use elements and principles for identification, not only of culture or region, but also sometimes of social class, specific village, or even family. Even similar structural contours, such as the tube, or the similar hat contours from Peru and Wales are given different flavors by the cultures using them. Thus the elements resemble basic musical notes, and the principles ways of harmonizing them to create innumerable melodies, each with its own use, moods, and meanings, attesting to human similarities, diversities, and creativity.

CLASS ACTIVITIES

1. With the class in groups, choose or assign an element for each group. Ask the group to review that element chapter: its aspects and their variations, its possible physical and psychological effects, and ways of introducing it. Then choose two or more of the countries and costumes shown and compare how the aspects of that element are used to create distinguishing features, physical effects, and moods that help identify that cultural dress for each country.

2. On a globe or map, locate the countries of the traditional costumes illustrated in the chapter. For each, how close to or far is it from the equator? How flat, mountainous, or insular is it? Is it primarily high or low altitude? Humid or dry? How may these factors have influenced the functional, structural, and decorative development of each costume?

3. Invite students to choose one of the countries shown and research its culture to see how it may have influenced the design and development of the costume.

4. Which costumes appear to have been "everyday wear" and which seem ceremonial? What features are common to and distinguish each type? Is there a difference in freedom of movement between the two types?

5. In several countries, such as India, Japan, Korea, and Nigeria where the basic structural style was the same for daily and ceremonial use, show how texture and decorative design might have been used to distinguish daily from ceremonial wear.

6. Invite students with heritages not shown in the chapter to share their traditional dress with the class. What are its features? How did it come to be? How does it use the elements and principles? What features could be adapted to current styles?

7. Assign each person or group one of the country costumes shown, to design a contemporary garment or outfit using it as inspiration. What would you leave the same? Why? What would you change? Why? Compare your element and principle uses with the original. What illusions is the original using? Is your design using the same ones? Compare functional design features on your design and the original.

Glossary

A-line. Garment styles with very slight widening from top to bottom, barely tapered waist. (Skirt Figure 6-31b, dress Figure 6-34e, coat Figure 6-36d)

Abstract. Fabric pattern interpretation of imaginary, non-representational shapes, lines, colors, spaces, and freeforms arranged on a surface, not depicting or portraying any object.

Achromatic. Without color.

Adaptation. Two similar hues, such as yellow-green and blue-green, appear more alike, or "adapt" each other more, when the intervening hue, such as green, is included than when it is missing (Figure 8-13).

Additive color theory. Light color theory in which mixture of all light primary hues add together to result in white.

Adjacent. Hues next each other on a color wheel or color scheme composed of such hues. Same as analogous.

Advancing technique. Use of an element or principle which makes it seem to come toward the viewer, enlarge, or seem more assertive, or use which creates depth effects of distance between foreground and background.

Affective learning. Aspect of learning dealing with feelings, values, attitudes, beliefs, emotions, and subjective value judgments.

"Afro." An extremely bouffant hair style, often with a sculptured effect in very curly hair.

After-image. Illusion in which an image is seen when the viewer looks away from a stimulus object which has tired eye receptors. In "positive" after-images the same shape as the original shape is seen; in "negative" after-images the hue or value opposite the stimulus color is seen.

All-over. Fabric pattern arrangement of motifs giving the same visual effect from any angle.

Alternation. Directional visual design principle; repeated sequences of two and only two things changing back and forth in the same order.

361

Analogous. Hues next to each other in a color wheel, or color scheme composed of such hues. Same as adjacent.

Angel sleeve. Long sleeve with normal armscye, flaring slightly from elbow, wrist length in front, extending to longer point in back. (Figure 6-27h)

Armscye. Bodice arm hole for arm passage or sleeve attachment.

Ascot. Collar style standing in back with long ends looped in half-knot (Women's Figure 6-23a); men's separate soft tie, fastened with half loop (Men's Figure 6-48a).

Asymmetrical balance. See informal balance.

Autokinetic illusion. Misperceived visual cue which appears to vibrate or move by itself.

Balance. Synthesizing visual design principle; the feeling of evenly distributed weight resulting in equilibrium, steadiness, repose, stability, rest.

Ballerina. Shoe style, soft, leather, low cut, with thin, flexible leather sole and drawstring in casing around upper edge tying in front. Originally designed for ballet dancers. (Figure 6-42a)

Balmacaan. Single breasted, loose coat style with curved collar and raglan sleeves; slash, welt pockets. Often used for rainwear. (Women's Figure 6-36a, men's Figure 6-47a)

Balmoral. Variation of oxford shoe style with seam between top and sides of upper shoe front. (Figure 6-50a)

Barrel or band cuff. Straight cuff with pointed or curved ends, overlapping to button. (Figure 6-28a)

Barrel purse. Cylindrically shaped purse with opening along one side which becomes the top, handles encircling circumference or attached to top. (Figure 6-39a)

Base hue. Pure hue from which a color is derived by varying its value and/or intensity.

Basketball shoes. Variation of sneaker style coming up high on the ankle and lacing to the top. (Figure 6-50b)

Bateau. See "boat."

Battle or Eisenhower jacket. Waist length jacket with convertible collar, shoulder yoke, front opening, banded waist, and long, cuffed sleeves. Derived from World War II military jacket popularized by then General Eisenhower. (Figure 6-35e)

Batwing sleeve. Long sleeve style, fitted at wrist, widening toward shoulder upper-arm, with deep-cut armscye seam. (Figure 6-27m)

Behavioral design. Order and content of planned events; patterns of action. Found in all behavioral sciences such as economics, politics, education, religion, and law.

Bell-bottoms. Full length pants slightly flared from knee to ankle, derived from sailor's uniform. (Women's Figure 6-33h, men's Figure 6-46b)

Bell sleeve. Normal armscye seam sleeve of any length flaring very slightly from shoulder. (Long Figure 6-27i, short Figure 6-29i)

Beret. One-piece, round cap with flat crown, often made of felt. Derived from Basque style. (Women's Figure 6-38a, men's Figure 6-49a)

Bermuda shorts. Shorts style ending at lower mid-thigh. (Figure 6-33d6)

Bertha collar. Collar style, set wide on the shoulders and forming collar and sleeve cape effect in one piece. (Figure 6-23o)

Bias. Diagonal of fabric between lengthwise and crosswise yarns.

Bib. Overlay piece of fabric attached either at neck (Figure 6-37o) or at waist as in overalls. (Figure 6-33q) May be protective or decorative.

Bishop collar. Flat collar with short tab extensions in front. (Figure 6-23b)

Blazer. Semi-fitted, hip-length sports jacket, usually with shawl or notched collar, patch hip pockets and one breast pocket, with emblem. (Women's Figure 6-35n, men's Figure 6-45f)

Bloused bodice. Bodice style with blousy gathers at the waist rather than darts. (Figure 6-24c)

Blucher. Variation of oxford shoe style with seam around front of upper and from sole to base of lacing. (Figure 6-50c)

Boat (or French "bateau"). Neckline style cut wide on the shoulders, high in front and back, slightly downward curved. (Neckline Figure 6-22h, collar Figure 6-23n)

Boater. Men's straw hat style with flat crown and brim, ribbon band. (Figure 6-49b)

Bolero. Waist length sleeveless jacket, open down front. Derived from Spanish bullfighter's uniform. (Figure 6-35a)

Bonnet. Women's hat fitted over top and back of head, brim in front, with ties under chin or in back. (Figure 6-38b)

Boot. Shoe style with firm soles and solid, closed upper, extending above the ankle, varying heel heights. (Figure 6-42b) Or waterproof covering to be worn over shoes.

Border. Fabric pattern arrangement with dominant motifs along one selvage; may have subordinate motifs throughout body of fabric and along opposite selvage.

Bowler. See "derby."

Bow tie. Narrow tie tied into crisp bow with sharp lines and corners. (Figure 6-48b)

Box jacket. Straight cut jacket, three-quarter or long sleeves, plain neckline meeting in front, open but not overlapping down front. Popularized by designer Chanel. (Figure 6-35k)

Box purse. Purse style in shape of box with top opening like hinged lid and handle looped from side to side. (Figure 6-39b)

Boy pants. Shorts ending at upper thigh. (Figure 6-33d8)

Breton. Hat style with flat crown and rolled back brim. Derived from Brittany peasant hat style. (Figure 6-38c)

Brogue. Variation of oxford shoe style with decoratively perforated toe and heel trims and seam from sole to base of lacing. (Figure 6-50d)

Broomstick skirt. Long, full, straight skirt; originally tied around a broom-stick to dry, making tiny vertical, creased gathers. (Figure 6-31t)

Buba. West African style overblouse with straight-cut sides, armscye seams, and wide, straight elbow-length sleeves. Neckline may be high or low. (Figure 6-25i)

Bustle. Back skirt fullness at skirt hip and buttocks, from padding, fabric, or frames. (Figure 6-31z)

Button-down collar. Collar style with points held down with small buttons. (Figure 6-43a)

Caftan. Long, loose, straight or slightly flared robe with slit neckline and long straight or bell sleeves. Derived from Middle Eastern style. (Figure 6-34p)

Camisole. Bodice style with upper edge straight across above bust, gathered at waist and sometimes top, with wide shoulder straps, sometimes ruffled. (Figure 6-24d)

Cap. Soft, snugly fitting headwear, often with front visor. (Women's Figure 6-38d, men's Figure 6-49d)

Cap sleeve. Very short sleeve style covering only the shoulder. May have normal armscye (Figure 6-29b) or as kimono cap be cut in one with the bodice. (Figure 6-30g)

Cape. Short, set-in sleeve style, flared from smooth shoulder cap to create soft folds. (Figure 6-29h) Sleeveless street length or longer outerwear, opening down front, gently flared from shoulders, with slits for arms. (Figure 6-36b)

Capelet. Short cape ending about hip length. (Figure 6-35h)

Capri pants. Woman's pant style ending just above ankle, closely fitted, tapering leg, very narrow, sometimes slit at bottom. (Figure 6-33d2)

Car coat. Also called "topper." Mid-thigh length coat convenient for getting in and out of automobiles. Longer than jacket, shorter than full-length coat. (Figure 6-35s)

Cardigan. Jacket or sweater style, plain neckline, long sleeves, buttoned down front, hip-length. (Figure 6-35j)

Chanel jacket. See "box jacket."

Chelsea. Flat, medium width collar with pointed ends, meeting in front in a deep V. (Figure 6-23c)

Chesterfield or box coat. Straight cut, single or double breasted coat with inset pockets and notched collar. When described as "chesterfield," upper collar is usually black velvet. (Women's Figure 6-36c, men's Figure 6-47b)

Chinese collar. Stiff, snugly fitting stand collar, nearly meeting in front. May have pointed or rounded ends. (Figure 6-23p)

Chromatic. Having or pertaining to color.

Chromatic aberration. Constant refocusing necessary when eye views bright intensities of longer and shorter wavelength hues at the same time, resulting in vibration or flicker.

Circular skirt. Very flared skirt style cut from a complete circle with center hole as waistline. (Figure 6-31d)

Cloche. Deep-crowned woman's hat style with narrow, even, turned-down brim. Derived from French "bell" shape. (Figure 6-38e)

Clutch. See "wraparound coat." (Figure 6-36k)

Clutch purse. Flat purse style without handles, open at top. (Figure 6-39c)

Coachman coat (also A-Line). Double breasted coat style, semi-fitted with princess seams and notched shawl or wide collar. (Figure 6-36d)

Cognitive learning Aspect of learning dealing with factual, intellectual, mental, objective information.

Color. Range of visible wavelengths from red through spectrum to violet.

Colorant. A substance, such as pigment, ink or dye which produces color effects by reflecting light wavelengths.

Complementary. Hues opposite each other on a color wheel.

Compressibility. Squeezability of a texture. (Table 9-1)

Concavity. Two- or three-dimensional inward hollow or indentation.

Concentricity. Highlighting visual design principle; a progressive increase in size of layers of the same shape, all having the same center and usually parallel edges.

Contour belt. Belt style shaped in a curve to fit waist-hip contours. (Figure 6-40c)

Contrast. Highlighting visual design principle; the feeling of distinct difference, opposition of things for the purpose of showing unlikeness.

Convertible collar. Straight, one piece collar with points. Worn open, blouse facing becomes lapel with seam showing. Worn closed, stand is high in back and flat in front. (Figure 6-23w)

Convexity. Two- or three-dimensional outward bulge or protrusion.

Corn-rowing. African hair style with decorative parting in long lines along scalp and braided close to the head along areas between parts.

Cossack shirt. Straight-cut, hip length shirt with standing collar, side front opening, long and narrow bishop sleeves, narrow sash tie at waist. Collar, cuffs often edged with decorated bands. Derived from traditional Russian horseman's top. (Figure 6-25f)

Countering. Use of an element, one or more of its aspects, or a principle to oppose, camouflage, distort, hide, neutralize, or otherwise reduce or avoid an existing effect or quality considered undesirable.

Cowboy hat. High-crowned hat with lengthwise crease, wide brim turned up at sides. (Figure 6-49e)

Cowboy jacket. See "Western jacket."

Cowl. Bias-cut draped neckline with folds falling in front or back from each shoulder. (Figures 6-22a and 6-22k)

Cravat. Scarf folded over and gathered in front. Worn as men's formal tie, often with wing collar. (Figure 6-48c)

Crew neck. High, plain neckline edged with knit ribbing. (Women's Figure 6-22i, men's 6-43b) Shirt style using this neckline. (Figure 6-44b)

Criteria. Functional, structural, and decorative characteristics which garment must possess to work successfully and give desired appearance.

Cross-sensory interpretation. Designs intended for one sense inspiring interpretation through another sense, such as "visualizing" music, or "tasting" sound, or "hearing" a scent.

Cuffs. Turned back garment edge (Figure 6-37m and Figure 6-46e) or attached band at lower sleeve edge. (Figures 6-28a-e)

Culottes. Knee length pants or divided skirt, looking like a skirt with a front inverted pleat when wearer stands still. (Figure 6-33j)

Cummerbund. Wide sash gathered or pleated at side seams, opening at side. Women's usually gathered (Figure 6-40d), men's usually pleated in front and plain in back. (Figure 6-48k)

Cutaway coat. Men's formal coat with peaked collar, one button, and lower edge angled diagonally from waist in front to knee in back. (Figure 6-47c)

Dashiki. Long, loose, straight or slightly flared robe with slit neckline and modified angel, pointed bell, or kimono sleeves. Derived from robe styles of Africa south of the Sahara Desert. (Figure 6-34r)

Deck pants. Long shorts ending just above knee. (Figure 6-33d5)

Decolletté. Neckline style cut wide on the shoulders and low in front, sometimes exposing bust cleavage. (Figure 6-22o)

Decorative design. Aspects of a product or plan intended only or primarily for appearance; it affects neither fit nor performance of a garment.

Demi-boot. Short boot ending just above the ankle. (Figure 6-50e)

Density. Weight per volume of a texture. (Table 9-1) May be thick to thin, fine to coarse yarn, or open to tight fabric structure.

Derby. Hat style with high, rounded crown and narrow brim rolled at sides. (Women's Figure 6-38f, men's Figure 6-49c)

Design process. Planning, organizing to meet a goal, carrying out according to a particular purpose, creating.

Design product. End result, intended arrangement or thing which is the outcome of a plan.

Dinner jacket. Men's semi-formal jacket, usually with shawl or tuxedo collar. (Figure 6-45g)

Directional illusions. Misinterpreted visual cues in which strong diagonals within a figure make the entire figure lean.

Directional or linear principle. Visual design principle which develops along a linear path, and which leads the eye in that direction to see if the principle is consistently maintained, to see what happens next.

Dirndl. Full skirt style gathered onto waistband. (Figure 6-31g)

Dolman. Long sleeve style fitted at wrist with armscye set inward on shoulder and cut deep toward waistline. (Figure 6-30d)

Draped. Set-in sleeve style draped in graceful folds in a variety of possible arrangements from armscye. (Figure 6-29k) Skirt style, usually long, draped in folds at various angles from the waist. (Figure 6-31y)

Drawn work. Decorative fabric treatment creating patterns of small holes in fabric where thread pulls yarns together. (Figures 2-9f and 10-24)

Drawstring. Blouse style with curved neckline gathered to a binding or by cord drawn through a casing and tied. (Figure 6-22p)

Dress shirt. Men's shirt style for formal occasions. Sometimes pleated down front, sometimes with wing collar. (Figure 6-44c)

Driving gloves. Glove style often with openings at back of hand and over knuckles, and leather palms and fingers. (Figure 6-41b)

Drop shoulder sleeve. Normal armscye line under arm, angling outward creating horizontal cap. Puff, lantern, or most other set-in sleeve styles may be attached to the horizontal seam created by the cap. (Figure 6-30h)

Element. Basic medium, component, ingredient, or material used to create a visual design.

Emphasis. Highlighting visual design principle, creation of a focal point, the most important or dominant center of attention to which all others are subordinate and supportive.

Empire waist. Waistline seam raised to just under the bust. (Figure 6-26d)

Envelope purse. Flat purse style without handles, with flap opening and fastening, similar to a mailing envelope. (Figure 6-39d)

Epaulet. Sleeve style following normal armscye line up to just below shoulder, then angled straight across to neckline, giving visual effect of French military shoulder tabs. (Figure 6-30c)

Ethnocentrism. Belief that one's own notions of one's own culture are "best," "true," "normal," "basic," or "most beautiful"; then making value judgments on all others on that basis.

Evening purse. Small, usually soft purse style, with or without handle; often in rich fabric or decorated with embroidery, sequins, beads, or pearls. (Figure 6-38e)

Extensibility. Stretchability of a texture. (Table 9-1)

External color. Range of visible light wavelengths coming from a light source or reflecting from a surface.

Face fabric. Fabric of exterior surface, or face, of a garment, showing from the outside.

Fagoting. Decorative, open, parallel stitching connecting two pieces of fabric, leaving small space between fabrics. (Figure 2-9d)

Fashion. Short-lived, visual folkway.

Fedora. Hat-style with lengthwise creased crown and curved brim. (Figure 6-38g)

Fez. Men's or women's hat style of tapered cylinder with tassel from top center. Derived from North African and Middle Eastern hat style. (Figure 6-38h)

Figure/ground reversal. Illusion in which foreground and background seem interchangeable. (Figure 3-25)

Flapper. Dress style, straight cut, with dropped or no waist, short skirt. (Figure 6-34n)

Flared. Garment part style wider at lower edge, sometimes falling in gentle folds. Most often seen in cape sleeves (Figure 6-29h), bell sleeves (Figure 6-27i and 6-29i), skirts (Figure 6-31c), pants (Figures 6-33c and 6-33h), trousers (Figure 6-46b), or flounces and ruffles. (Figure 2-9b)

Flattening technique. Use of an element or principle to minimize apparent depth or distance between foreground and background, and to smooth and flatten a surface.

Flexibility. Suppleness or rigidity of a texture. (Table 9-1)

Flounce. Pleated, flared, or gathered ruffle, usually extending from a sleeve (Figure 6-27g) or skirt or style feature. (Figure 6-37d)

Folkways. Social norms encouraged and accepted, but not considered essential to orderly social functioning.

Form. Three-dimensional area enclosed by a surface, hollow with volume or solid with mass.

Formal balance. Feeling of horizontally equally distributed weight resulting from each side of an imaginary center vertical line being identical or mirroring the other; also known as symmetrical balance.

Four-in-hand. Tie style of long, straight tie, tied in flat knot with under end hidden below the upper end. (Figure 6-48d)

Four-way. Fabric pattern arrangement which gives identical effects at any ninety degree angle turn, on either warp or weft.

Frequency. Number of wavelengths passing a given point in one second. Longer wavelengths are slower than shorter ones.

French cuff. Wide cuff with pointed tips at open ends, turned back till four buttonholes match allowing insertion of cuff link to hold all layers in place. (Figure 6-28c)

French dart bodice. Bodice with single bust dart placed diagonally from underarm seam near waist to bust. (Figure 6-24b)

Functional design. Primary aspect of a product or plan dealing with how something works or performs.

Funnel. Neckline cut high and standing away from, but tapering toward, the neck, cut in one piece with the bodice. (Figure 6-22j)

Gaucho pants. Slightly flared pants ending below the knee, derived from Spanish riding pants. (Figure 6-33n)

Gauntlet. Wide, stiff cuff, fitted at wrist and flared to mid-forearm. (Cuff Figure 6-28d) Glove style fitted to wrist and flared above wrist. (Glove Figure 6-41d)

Geometric illusions. Visually misinterpreted effects of line, angle, flat space, or shape relationships.

Geometric pattern. Fabric pattern interpretation using geometric shapes and lines, such as plaids, stripes, polka dots, hexagons, triangles, checks, and other nonrepresentational abstracts, but using mathematical exactness.

Ghillie. Medium-low cut shoe style, laced up front with laces sometimes wrapped around ankles, no tongue. Derived from Scottish term; also called "gillie." (Figure 6-42d)

Godet. Wedge-shape piece of fabric inserted between seams or set into lower edge of skirts, sleeves, jackets, or pants for fullness. (Figure 6-37k)

Gore. Skirt section narrower at waist and wider at hem. Skirts may have from four to twenty-four gores with fit and fullness achieved by seams rather than darts. (Figure 6-31e)

Gradation. Directional visual design principle; a sequence of adjacent units, usually alike in all respects except one which changes in consistent and distinct steps from one unit to the next; process of change happening through a consecutive series of distinguishable steps.

Grain. Directions of lengthwise and crosswise yarns in a woven fabric, or rows of loops in a knitted one. "On grain" when yarns or rows are perpendicular, "off grain" when not.

Granny. Long dress, with plain neckline, puff sleeves, high waist, gently gathered skirt sometimes with ruffle at ankles. (Figure 6-34s)

Gusset. Small diamond-shaped fabric piece (or two triangles sewn together making diamond shape) inserted in underarm bodice slash for kimono sleeves to allow freedom of movement. (Figure 6-30f)

Halter. Neckline style held by strap around back of neck with bare back and shoulders.

May be high, V, or U neck in front. (Figure 6-22c)

Hand. Tactile qualities of a substance manipulated three-dimensionally. (Table 9-1)

Handkerchief skirt. Flared skirt style cut from a square, creating uneven, pointed hemline. (Figure 6-31x)

Harmony. Synthesizing visual design principle; agreement in feeling, consistency in mood, pleasing combination of different elements, of their aspects used in similar ways, compatible compromise between boredom and conflict, cooperation around a common theme.

Headtie. Scarf tied about head in variety of arrangements, often high with tie points in back. Derived from West African headwear style. (Figure 6-38i)

Hemstitching. Decorative fabric treatment similar to drawn work with several yarns pulled out and thread wrapped decoratively around yarns perpendicular to pulled yarns. (Figure 2-9e)

Henley shirt. Short-sleeved, collarless knit shirt style edged with neck band and buttoned placket down front. (Figure 6-44d)

Highlighting principle. Visual design principle which focuses attention to the spot or area where the principle occurs.

High-rise waist. Upper edge of skirt or pants fitted at hip and waist, extending above waist, cut in one piece with garment and fitted with vertical seams or darts. (Figure 6-32c)

Hip-hugger. Skirt or pants waistline with upper edge between waist and hips. (Figure 6-32e)

Homburg. Men's felt hat style with high crown with lengthwise crease, narrow brim rolled upward at sides and back. Derived from style originated in Homburg, Germany. (Figure 6-49f)

Hood. Head cover attached to coat at neck, flexible, soft, usually fabric; crown may be rounded or pointed; sometimes lies flat as back collar. (Figure 6-38j)

Hot pants (also short shorts). Women's very short shorts ending at top thigh. (Figure 6-33d9)

Hue. Family of color on the color wheel or location of wavelength in the light spectrum.

Hue Format. Pure hues comprising the basic combination according to a particular color scheme formula. A color scheme formula might contain three hues in a particular relationship to each other on the hue wheel; that scheme would have a three-hue format. Those three hues might be lightened, darkened, and/or dulled to produce several more colors, but the final scheme would still be based on its hue formula.

Huarache. Shoe style with flat, firm sole, and soft, interlaced leather strip uppers, back of shoe separate from heel. (Figure 6-42e)

Illusions. Misinterpreted visual or other cues.

Informal balance. Feeling of horizontal steadiness and stability resulting from each side of an imaginary center vertical line differing in arrangements and/or contents, but giving effect of equal weight distribution; also known as asymmetrical balance.

Inset. Separate piece of fabric set into a garment location. Functionally includes pockets (Figures 6-37f, 6-48h, 6-48i), or decorative contrast. (Figure 6-37l)

Intensity. Brightness or dullness of a hue.

Internal color. Range of visual sensations resulting from stimulation by segments of wavelengths along the light spectrum.

Interstitial space. Unenclosed area between or among shapes.

Inverted order color scheme. A color scheme in which normal value relationship of hues is reversed, such as dark brown (from orange) and light blue.

Irradiation. Visual illusion in which perception of light area expands beyond actual shape edges and neighboring dark areas seem to shrink.

Italian collar. Notched shawl collar style with upper edge of notch pointed and lower edge curved. (Figure 6-23d)

Ivy league jacket. Men's jacket style similar to blazer but with pointed collar and inset pockets with flaps. (Figure 6-45h)

Jabot. Collar with standing band in back and cascading ruffle or frill down the front. (Figure 6-23e)

Jamaica shorts. Shorts style ending mid-thigh. (Figure 6-33d7)

Jeans. Long, sturdy, casual or work pants style usually with pockets, flat-felled seams, and sometimes reinforcing pocket studs. Often made of blue denim. (Women's Figure 6-33f, men's Figure 6-46c)

Jerkin. Sleeveless, collarless, hip-length garment worn over blouse or shirt and skirt or pants. May be pull-over or button-front. (Figure 6-35t)

Jewel neckline. Neckline following normal curve at neck base. Also called "plain." (Figure 6-22l)

Jockey cap (also "riding" cap). Men's and women's cap style with high, rounded crown, closely fitting, and front visor. Derived from cap style worn by jockeys. (Figure 6-38k)

Jodphurs. Riding pants fitted at waist, full at thighs and tapering back to fitted at knee to ankle, worn inside riding boots. (Figure 6-33m)

Juliet cap (also "skull cap"). Small, fitted women's cap following natural head crown, usually in dressy fabric, derived from Shakespeare's *Romeo and Juliet;* also called "beanie" in casual fabric. (Figure 6-38l)

Juliet sleeve. Long, two-piece sleeve with normal armscye. Lower part fitted to mid-upper arm, puffed sleeve from there to shoulder. Also from Shakespeare's play. (Figure 6-27l)

Jumper. Low-necked, sleeveless dress style to be worn with or without a blouse. May be fitted or semi-fitted, with or without waistline seam. (Figure 6-34i)

Jump-suit. One-piece step-in garment of pants and top; may or may not have waistline seam, collar, and sleeves; opens down front. Used for leisure, or as "coveralls" with sleeves and straight legs for work. (Figure 6-33r)

Juxtaposition. Colors or shapes which are touching, overlapping, or superimposed one on the other.

Keyhole. Neckline style with upper edge following normal neckline and cut-out opening below. (Figure 6-22d)

Kimono. Sleeve style cut in one with bodice. (Sleeve Figure 6-30e, with gusset Figure 6-30f, cap 6-30g) Japanese women's traditional dress composed of rectangles. (Figure 29-7)

Knickers. Knee-length pants gathered to band just below knee. Derived from "knicker-

bockers" named for fictional character. (Figure 6-33k)

Küppers color theory. Structural pattern for combining analysis of both light and pigment theories of color and their relationships on a single rhombohedron model. (Figure 8-8) Developed by Harald Küppers.

Lantern sleeve. Set-in sleeve gently flaring from smooth shoulder to seam at fullest part, then tapered back in to arm. (Long Figure 6-27j, short Figure 6-29j)

Lederhosen. Shorts style ending mid-thigh, with shoulder straps with cross-bar in front. Derived from traditional Tyrolean style, usually of leather. (Women's Figure 6-33l, men's Figure 6-46d)

Leggings. Long, fitted children's pants, usually worn as outerwear for warmth with matching coat. Sometimes fastened with strap under foot and supported with shoulder straps. (Figure 6-51e)

Leg-o-mutton. Wrist-length sleeve with normal armscye, fitted up to elbow then flared and puffed with gathers at shoulder, resembling a "leg of lamb." (Figure 6-27k)

Leotards. Snugly fitting elasticized garment of many lengths and styles, used for exercise and dance practice. (Figure 6-33s)

Light. Electromagnetic energy making things visible, radiant energy. Energy source is stimulus and visual perception is response.

Light color theory. Explanatory structure of hues as light wavelengths. Primaries are red, green, and blue, which mix to make white, described as the additive theory. (Figure 8-1)

Line. Elongated mark, connection between two points, or effect made by edge of an object.

Loafer. Slip-on shoe style with small, curved tongue and slit strap across front, seam around upper edge of front. (Women's Figure 6-42f, men's Figure 6-50g, children's Figure 6-52b)

Mackinaw jacket. Heavy, double-breasted, belted jacket with wide shawl collar and patch pockets. (Figure 6-45i)

Macrodesign. Large-scale plans, over-all or broad concepts of a plan, fundamental tenets or positions held on a topic.

Mandarin collar. See "Chinese collar."

Mary Janes. Child's flat shoe style, low cut with closed toe and heel, strap across upper instep. (Figure 6-52d)

Maternity. Dress style, usually one-piece, designed to provide for expansion of bust and abdomen during pregnancy. (Figure 6-34o)

Maxiskirt. Ankle-length skirt style. (Figure 6-31r)

Melon sleeve. Large, spherical set-in sleeve gathered at shoulder and elbow, resembling melon. (Figure 6-29g)

Microdesign. Details of a design, or small-scale plans.

Middy. Hip-length overblouse with three quarter or long sleeves, sailor collar, derived from sailor's uniform. (Figure 6-25e)

Midiskirt. Skirt style ending just below mid-calf. (Figure 6-31q)

Midriff. Fitted waistline yoke set-in between normal waistline and bust. (Figure 6-26e)

Mini-skirt. Very short skirt style ending mid-thigh. (Figure 6-31p)

Mittens. Hand covering with one section for thumb and another section for all fingers. (Figure 6-41f)

Moccasin. Soft-soled, leather shoe style with sole curved up around shoe front and fastened to top. Derived from American Indian style. (Figure 6-42g)

Mores. Social norms considered essential to social order; violations of these are severely punished.

Muff. Soft flattened cylinder with hollow center to keep hands warm. May have compartment outside one side for storage as purse. (Figure 6-39f)

Munsell color theory. Pigment color theory developed by Albert H. Munsell, containing five principal hues and organized into a solid color sphere for specific hue, value, and intensity variation locations and relationships. (Figures 8-5, 8-6, and 8-7)

Muumuu. Long, loose dress style, often with flounce from knee to hem, neck and sleeve ruffles. Derived from Westernized Hawaiian dress, often colorful. (Figure 6-34q)

Nanometer. One billionth of a meter (a meter equals 39.37 inches). Unit of measuring light wavelengths.

Natural order color scheme. A color scheme in which variations of hues are near their nor-mal or home values; yellow would be used as lighter than green.

Negative heel. Shoe style with thick sole molded to shape of foot sole, with heel lower than ball of foot and toes. (Figure 6-42c)

Negative space. Unenclosed space, area surrounding objects, background, interstitial space, ground.

Nehru cap (also called "service cap"). Brimless cap with medium crown with deep lengthwise crease, flaps like cuffs alongside crown. (Figure 6-49g)

Nehru collar. Snugly fitting standing collar not quite joined in front, from India and popularized from style of 1947-64 Indian prime minister Nehru. (Figure 6-23q)

Nehru jacket. Single breasted, semi-fitted jacket with princess seams from shoulder to hem, and standing collar. (Figure 6-45j)

Neutral. Colors of white through greys to black, true neutrals because their hue derivations cannot be traced. Also equal strengths of two complements which cancel each other out, or "neutralize" each other to produce grey.

Norm. Acceptable social behavior patterns considered standard in any given culture.

Normal or home value. Level of lightness or darkness of a pure hue on the color wheel or in the light spectrum.

Notch collar. Tailored collar style with notch at outer edge between lapel and upper collar. (Figure 6-45a)

Off-the-shoulder. Low-cut neckline extending fairly straight across below the shoulders and above the bust with straps or small sleeves. (Figure 6-22q)

One-shoulder. Neckline style extending from one shoulder diagonally under the opposite arm and up to the shoulder again in back. (Figure 6-22r)

One-way (or one-directional). Fabric pattern arrangement which gives the same effect from only one angle.

Opaque. Textural reaction to light which absorbs or reflects light rays but does not admit enough to see what is on the other side.

Ostwald color theory. "Psychological" color theory developed by Wilhelm Ostwald based on visual perception of hues that do not resemble each other. Contains four "psychologically primary" hues of red, green, blue, and yellow, plus black and white. (Figures 8-9, 8-10)

Overalls.   Sturdy working pants similar to but looser than blue jeans from waist down, with front bib over chest, and shoulder straps crossing in back. (Figure 6-33q)

Overblouse.   Loose or semi-fitted hip-length blouse worn outside pants or skirt. (Figure 6-25b)

Oxford.   Shoe style of medium-low cut, laced up front with tongue, varying heel heights. (Women's Figure 6-42h, men's Figure 6-50h, children's Figure 6-52e)

Palazzo pants.   Long, full, softly gathered pants, like long gathered skirt divided into pant legs. (Figure 6-33a)

Panama hat.   Straw hat similar in style to homburg but with wider brim and brighter headband folded under. (Figure 6-49h

Parallelism.   Directional visual design principle using lines lying on the same plane, equidistant at all points and never meeting; lines may be curved as well as straight.

Parka.   Heavy, hip-length jacket with hood attached, sometimes fur-lined. (Figure 6-35p)

Patch pocket.   Pocket attached to outside of garment. (Figures 6-37g, 6-48f, 6-48g)

Pattern.   Arrangement of lines, spaces, and/or shapes on or in a fabric, used as an element of visual design.

Pea jacket.   Hip-length double-breasted navy blue sports jacket with wide, notched collar, princess seams with inset pockets. Derived from sailors' jacket. (Figure 6-35o)

Peak collar.   Notched collar with angled seam between upper collar creating upward point or "peak." (Figure 6-45b)

Peasant blouse.   Blouse style with gathered neckline and sleeve edges, sides usually cut straight, armscye seam line from neckline to underarm. (Figure 6-25d)

Peasant sleeve (also full bishop).   Full sleeve of any length, gathered at shoulder and lower edge. (Figure 6-27f)

Pedal pushers (also clam-diggers).   Pant style ending just below knee. (Figure 6-33d4)

Pegged.   Garment part style fuller at top and tapered narrow at hem. Most often seen as

skirt (Figure 6-31m), pants (Figure 6-33o), and sometimes to describe a short leg-o-mutton sleeve.

Peplum.   Ruffle extending from bodice waistline seam to hip. May be gathered, pleated, or flared. (Figure 6-37c)

Petal or lapped sleeve.   Short set-in sleeve style with curved outer edges overlapping like petals. (Figure 6-29c)

Peter Pan collar.   Flat collar with rounded ends. Named for character in play. (Figure 6-23r)

Photon.   Unit of light measure indicating brightness, number of wavelengths determining level of illumination.

Physical or physiological visual effects.   Illusions or effects which influence apparent physical characteristics of dimensions, height, weight, shortness, slimness, width, enlargement, reduction, roundness, straightness, color, and other physical properties.

Picture hat.   Women's hat style with flat crown and wide brim to "frame" face. (Figure 6-38m)

Pigment color theory.   Explanatory structures for organizing and analyzing color according to the way a surface colorant reflects color in light.

Pillbox hat.   Women's hat style, round with flat crown, no brim, derived from traditional box for carrying pills. (Figure 6-38n)

Pinafore.   Apron-like dress usually with gathered skirt, bib-front bodice with ruffles from waist to shoulder and straps crossing in back. (Figure 6-34j)

Piping.   Covered cording stitched into seams. (Figure 2-9h)

Plaiting.   African hair style with hair parted in lines making decorative patterns on the scalp, each hair section pulled tightly together, and wrapped with special thread, creating thin, finger-like extensions which may be arranged various ways or interwoven among each other.

Platform.   Shoe style with extremely thick and stiff soles. (Figure 6-42i)

Pleated skirts.   Skirt styles with fullness achieved through various arrangements of flat, folded overlays and underlays, either sharply creased or unpressed, usually narrow at stitched top and wider at free-hanging bottom. May be seen as knife pleats with all folds going same direction (Figure 6-31h), box or inverted with underlays alternating (Figure 6-31i), accordion or sunburst with small alternating creases that widen toward hem (Figure 6-31j), cluster with series of grouped pleats then plain gore (Figure 6-31k), kilts (Figure 6-31l), or other arrangements of direction and spacing.

Pointillism.   Visual mixing of tiny dots of differing colors viewed from a distance. (Figure 8-25b, c)

Polo.   Short-sleeved, collarless, pull-over knit sports shirt or long, straight, coat style. (Women's Figure 6-36e, men's Figure 6-44e)

Poncho.   Square or triangular, hip-length, blanket-like cloak with center hole or slit for head. Derived from Latin American cowboy cloak. (Figure 6-35l)

Portrait collar.   Collar resting wide on shoulder, narrows and lowers toward center, portrait "framing" neck and shoulders. (Figure 6-23x)

Positive space.   Enclosed space, shape, foreground shape, figure.

Pouch.   Soft, deep, flexible purse gently gathered onto top frame which opens, with handle looped from one end of frame to other. (Figure 6-39g)

Prang color theory.   Pigment theory developed by Prang, patterned after Brewster's, based on three primary hues of red, yellow, and blue. (Figures 8-2, 8-3, 8-4)

Primary hues.   Prime, basic hues in a color theory from which all other hues can be mixed; no other hues combine to create primary hues.

Princess.   Garment style using vertical seams for fitting rather than darts, no waistline seam. Seams may start from shoulder or armscye and continue to hem. (Bodice Figure 6-24g, dress Figure 6-34d, coat Figure 6-36f)

Principle.   Guideline, technique, or method of manipulating a visual design element to achieve a specific effect; term used to describe that resulting visual effect.

Proportion.   Synthesizing visual design principle which is a comparative relationship of distances, sizes, amounts, degrees, or parts. Operates on four levels: within part, among parts, between part and whole, and between whole and environment.

Psychological visual effect.   Illusions or effects which influence apparent feelings or moods such as happiness, dignity, somberness, youthfulness, sophistication, daintiness, assertiveness, fatigue, exuberance, serenity, and other feelings or emotions.

Puff sleeve.   Short, set-in sleeve gathered at shoulder and lower edge, creating spherical pouf. (Figure 6-29e)

Pump.   Low-cut, slip-on shoe style with varying heel heights; usually for dressy wear. (Women's Figure 6-42j, men's Figure 6-50f)

Puritan collar.   Wide, flat collar, curved or square in back, pointed in front, meeting at neck. (Figure 6-23g)

Quilting.   Often decorative lines of stitching holding layers of fabric and padding together. (Figure 2-9c)

Radiation.   Directional visual design principle; a feeling of movement steadily bursting outward from a visible or clearly suggested central point; the emission of rays from a single source.

Raglan.   Non-set-in sleeve style of varying lengths with curved armscye seam from neckline to underarm and shoulder dart or seam. (Figure 6-30a)

Ranch boot.   Higher-heeled, stiff-soled, leather boot ending at lower mid-calf. (Figure 6-50j) Similar to cowboy boot, sometimes decorated.

Ranch pants (or "slim jims," "stove pipes"). Full length straight pants. (Figure 6-33g)

Realistic.   Fabric pattern interpretation in which the motif source object appears as it would in real life, as in a color photograph.

Receding technique.   Use of an element, one or more of its aspects, or a principle in a way that makes it seem to retreat from the viewer, moving gently away, often becoming inconspicuous or appearing to reduce in size.

Reefer.   Double-breasted, fitted coat with princess seams, flared to hem, and wide collar. (Figure 6-36g)

Regency coat.   Double-breasted coat style with wide collar rising high in back, deep notch, and wide lapels laying flat in front. Derived from Napoleonic regency styles. (Figure 6-47d)

Reinforcing technique.   Use of an element, one or more of its aspects, or a principle to strengthen or emphasize an existing effect or quality considered desirable.

Relevant outside influences. Circumstances and characteristics of the potential user's age, sex, size, weight, preferences; or climate, resources, occasion, or season that affect decisions about the design of the product garment.

Repetition. Directional visual design principle; use of the same thing more than once.

Resilience. Ability of a texture to recover its original form after squeezing, bending, stretching, or twisting. (Table 9-1)

Revers collar. Collar lapels of outward-folded facings, or reverse of outer face fabric. (Figure 6-23y)

Rhythm. Directional visual design principle of feeling of organized motion.

Ruff. High, stiff, ruffled collar ringing neck. (Figure 6-23s)

Ruffle sleeve. Short, set-in sleeve, gathered at armscye, loose at outer edge. (Figure 6-29f)

Ruffles. Strips of fabric gathered, flared, or pleated on one edge, free on the other. (Figure 6-37b)

Sabrina. Neckline style straight across shoulders with seam at shoulders from shoulder seam-neckline insets or extensions of back bodice. (Figure 6-22m)

Saddle shoe. Variation of oxford shoe style, having contrasting, curved strips across vamp and at back heel. (Women's Figure 6-42k, children's Figure 6-52f)

Safari jacket. Belted, single-breasted, hip-length sports jacket with elbow-length or long sleeves, notched collar, expandable patch pockets with flaps at hips and chest. Also called "bush jacket." (Women's Figure 6-35r, men's Figure 6-45k)

Sailor collar. Flat collar widening from V neck at front to square falling over shoulders in back. Styled after traditional sailor uniform collars. (Figure 6-23h)

Sailor hat. Women's straw hat style with flat crown and wide brim (Figure 6-38o) or men's fabric close fitting cap with turned-up stitched brim. (Figure 6-49i)

Sandal. Open, flat shoe style with uppers usually of straps of various materials. (Women's Figure 6-42l, men's Figure 6-50j, children's Figure 6-52g)

Sari. Rectangular fabric, usually six yards long, wrapped and draped into floor length skirt with unpressed pleats in front and outer end draped over left shoulder. Traditional women's dress in India. (Figure 6-31w, Figure 29-6)

Sash. Long, narrow strip of cloth tied about waist and looped over. May also be tied about head, neck, or elsewhere as an accessory. (Figure 6-40e)

Scale. Synthesizing visual design principle; a consistent relationship of sizes to each other and to the whole, regardless of shapes; in dress usually relating style features, fabric patterns, applied trims, jewelry, and accessories to garment part and wearer size.

Scalloped. Any flat neckline style given a scalloped edge. (Figure 6-22s)

Scoop. Curved neckline cut low and wide on the shoulders. (Figure 6-22t)

Scottish cap. Cap style with high front, lengthwise crown crease, low back, and no brim. (Figure 6-38p)

Secondary hues. Equal mixtures of two primary hues.

Selective absorption. Process of surface pigments absorbing all light wavelengths except one which is reflected, and that is the color the viewer perceives.

Sensory design. Design products intended to be experienced through physical senses of sight, sound, touch, taste, and smell.

Sequence. Directional visual design principle; the following of one thing after another in a particular order, a regular succession.

Shade. Hue with black added, low value.

Shape. Flat, two-dimensional area enclosed by a line.

Shawl. Square or triangular wrap, often patterned, embroidered, or fringed. (Figure 6-35d)

Shawl collar. Smoothly curved or notched collar with stand in back and flat in front tapering to nothing at lower overlap meeting. Upper lapel part may be one piece or seamed at back. (Women's Figure 6-23f and 6-23i, men's Figure 6-45c)

Sheath. Dress style with no waistline, vertical darts provide waist fitting. (Figure 6-34c)

Shell. Collarless, sleeveless top ending at or just below waist. (Figure 6-25g)

Shenandoah. Thick-soled, high-heeled leather boot ending mid-calf. (Figure 6-50k)

Shift. Dress style cut straight from underarm to hem, no waistline. (Figure 6-34b)

Shirring. Several parallel rows of gathers creating fullness; gathering cord, often elastic for fitting. (Figure 6-37e) See also virago sleeve.

Shirt. Short- or long-sleeved, high-necked top, straight sides, usually opening down the front. For wear outside pants, hem is usually straight; for tucking in, hem usually curves up at side seams to minimize bulk. (Women's Figure 6-25c, men's styles Figure 6-44)

Shirt collar. Straight, two-piece collar with seam where stand and fall join. Stand overlaps to button at front, fall may have pointed or curved ends. (Figures 6-23t, 6-43a, c, d)

Shirt sleeve. Long, straight, cuffed sleeve with normal armscye. (Figure 6-27c)

Shirtwaist. Dress style with straight, gathered, or pleated skirt; bodice resembling shirt with long or short shirt sleeves, shirt or convertible collar, buttoned opening part or all the way down front. (Figure 6-34l)

Short roll collar. Collar style extending up in back and turning down higher in back and flatter in front, ends far apart at each side of wide neckline. (Figure 6-23z)

Shoulder bag. Pouch, expandable envelope or other style purse with long strap to hang purse from shoulder. (Figure 6-39h)

Significant other. Person important to one because of the power to reward, satisfy, punish, withhold, or meet one's wants and needs.

Silhouette. Outline of an object.

Simultaneous contrast. Optical illusion in which qualities push each other apart, increasing apparent differences. Phenomenon occurs at the same time viewer is looking at stimulus.

Skort. Combination of skirt and shorts. Gathered or fuller pants ending above knee, giving short skirt appearance. (Figure 6-33d5)

Slacks. Ankle-length pants, may be cut full or fitted, usually straight-legged, cuffed, or plain. (Women's Figure 6-33d1, men's 6-46e)

Sling shoe. Variation of pump shoe style with open heel held by strap or "sling." (Figure 6-42m)

Smock. High-necked, long-sleeved, loosely fitted, hip-length top, usually opening down front. Often used to protect other clothes or for maternity wear. (Figure 6-25a)

Smocking. Stitch used to gather fabric into puckered diamond shapes, usually decorative but can provide functional fullness where edge of smocking releases into gathers. (Figure 2-9g)

Sneakers. Flat sports shoe, medium-low cut, laced up front over tongue, uppers usually of canvas and rubber soles and toe tips. (Women's Figure 6-42n, children's Figure 6-52a and 6-52c)

Space. Area or extent, a blank distance, the area within or between shapes. Flat or three-dimensional.

Spaced. Fabric pattern arrangement of a singular motif accenting a garment part, following the shape of the garment part it adorns, or forming a usually large repeat, self-contained composition, often framed with a large center motif or medallion. (Figure 10-4)

Spaghetti belt. One or more thin cords tied around the waist. (Figure 6-40f)

Spectator. Variation of pump shoe style with contrasting toe and heel trims, often perforated in decorative patterns. (Figure 6-42o)

Split-raglan sleeve. Two-piece sleeve style cut as raglan in back and set-in in front. Usually used for outerwear or rainwear. (Figure 6-30b)

Spontaneous change of position. Optical illusion in which object seen from one angle suddenly seems to be viewed from a different perspective, or when what the object is seems to change.

Stand-away collar. Slightly shaped collar standing up and somewhat away from neck all around. (Figure 6-23u)

Static illusion. Misperceived visual cue which is stationary, not moving.

Stole. Long, narrow, rectangular wrap. (Figure 6-35m)

Strapless. Self-supporting bodice style with upper edge above bust, no shoulder straps. (Figure 6-24f)

String tie. Thin cord around neck, under collar, and tied in bow falling in front. (Figure 6-48e)

Structural design. Facet of a product dealing with its plan for construction which will allow it to function. In clothing, affects fit and performance.

Style. Identifying characteristics of an object, person, or period. May refer to cut of garment, ability to create attractive clothing combinations, or using prevailing fashions of historical period or current times.

Stylized. Fabric pattern interpretation in which motif source object has been changed in some way such as outlined or flattened, but is still recognizable.

Subtractive color theory. Pigment color theories in which the mixture of all pigment primary hues results in grey or black as nearly all light wavelengths are absorbed, or subtracted out.

Surface contour. Divergence from planeness or absolute smoothness. (Table 9-1)

Surface friction. Degree of resistance of a fabric surface to slipping. (Table 9-1)

Surplice. Wrap-around garment style with one end overlapping the other and open its entire length. Bodice overlap is diagonal, skirt straighter. (Bodice Figure 6-24h, skirt Figure 6-31f)

Swagger. Women's single-breasted coat style flared from shoulders, with raglan sleeves. (Figure 6-36h)

Sweetheart. Neckline style with straight sides and down-pointed curved lower edge. (Figure 6-22e)

Symmetrical balance. See formal balance.

Synthesizing principle. Visual design principle which relates and integrates parts of a composition.

Tab. Style feature of narrow, pointed fabric strip. May be buttoned down holding something functionally or a decorative addition. (Figures 6-37a, 6-43e)

Tab collar. Standing collar with front tab placket opening. (Women's Figure 6-23j, men's Figure 6-43e) Sometimes referred to as shirt collar with points tabbed or buttoned down. (Figure 6-43a)

Tabard. Short tunic open at the sides with tab attaching front and back at waist. Worn over blouse or shirt and pants. Derived from loose tunic worn over knight's armor. (Figure 6-35q)

Tailcoat. Formal, fitted man's coat with peaked collar, open to waist, ending at waist in front with two knee-length "tails" in back. Also known as "swallow tail" coat. (Figure 6-47e)

Tam o'shanter. Soft, flat, round cap gently gathered at crown and headband. (Figure 6-38q)

Tapered or body shirt. Men's tailored shirt style fitted closely to the body. (Figure 6-44g)

Taste. A sense of what creates excellence, is fitting and appropriate; ability to perceive beauty and harmony; a way of exercising style.

Ten-gallon hat. See "cowboy hat."

Tent. One-piece dress style with no waistline, flaring from armhole to hem, like a tent. (Figure 6-34h)

Tertiary hues. Mixtures of a primary and neighboring secondary hue. Also known as intermediate hues.

Texture. Visible and tangible structure of a surface or substance. Includes surface qualities, hand or tactile manipulation qualities, and reactions to light.

Thermal character. Warmth or coolness of fabric surface compared to skin temperature. (Table 9-1)

Thongs. Flat, rubber-soled sandals with straps coming from arch to between big and second toes. (Figure 6-42q)

Tie collar. Standing collar with front extensions to tie over each other or make a bow. (Figure 6-23k)

Tiered. Skirt style of several horizontal sections, the top of each gathered to the bottom of the one above (Figure 6-31o), or successively longer layers of a skirt or cape (Figure 6-35f). Tiers may be stitched to one another, while with ruffles each lower edge hangs free.

Tint. Hue with white added, high value.

Top hat. Men's hat style of high, flat topped cylinder with narrow brim rolled upward at sides. (Figure 6-49j)

Toque. Hat style of softly draped fabric, closely fitting, without brim. (Figure 6-38r)

Toreador pants. Women's closely fitted pant style ending mid-calf, derived from Spanish bullfighter uniform. (Figure 6-33d3)

Tote bag. Large purse or bag, open at the top, with handles on each side.(Figure 6-39i)

Transition. Directional visual design principle; a smooth, flowing passage from one condition and position to another with no identifiable point of change.

Translucent. Textural reaction to light in which fabric admits enough light to perceive hazy silhouettes, but not to distinguish details within the shape.

Transparent. Textural reaction to light in which fabric admits enough light to allow clear view of sharp details on the other side.

Trapunto. Decorative quilting in which raised, stuffed pattern is edged with stitching. (Figure 2-6)

Trench. Belted, straight-cut, double-breasted coat style, with shoulder yoke and cuff tabs and wide collar to increase water repellency. (Figure 6-36i)

Trumpet. Garment part style fitted about halfway down and then flaring out. Most often seen as skirt (Figure 6-31n) and as sleeve flared from the elbow.

T-shirt. Lightweight, knit pull-over shirt with short sleeves and plain, round neck. (Figure 6-44h)

T-strap shoe. Variation of pump or sandal shoe styles with perpendicular straps in front forming a "T." (Figure 6-42p)

Tucking. Narrow, parallel stitched pleats, usually decorative. (Figure 2-7)

Tunic. Semi-fitted dress style ending around mid-thigh, usually worn over a skirt or pants. (Figure 6-34f)

Turban. Brimless hat style resembling long, soft fabric scarf wrapped or draped about head crown. (Figure 6-38s)

Turtleneck collar. Snug-fitting, flexible collar standing high on neck and turned down evenly to cover neckline seam. (Figure 6-23v)

Tuxedo. Straight, flat collar of even width, usually extending full length of garment without meeting (Figure 6-23l). Woman's coat style with tuxedo collar (Figure 6-36j), man's collar style narrowing at bottom without meeting (Figure 6-45d).

Two-piece sleeve. Long, straight sleeve style cut in two pieces with upper and under sections, fullness for elbow eased into back seam at elbow rather than with dart. Usually used for coats and tailored jackets. (Figure 6-27e)

Two-way. Fabric pattern arrangement which gives identical effects only at 180° turn.

Tyrolean cap. Cap style with peaked crown with lengthwise crease, narrow brim upturned in back, down in front. (Figure 6-38t)

Ulster. Single or double breasted coat with notched collar and flap pockets, sometimes belted. Named for Irish fabric. (Figure 6-47f)

Unity. Synthesizing visual design principle; a sense of completed oneness, wholeness, integrated totality, being coherent and finished, and the goal of visual design composition.

Value. Lightness or darkness of a hue.

Vanishing boundaries. Edges between adjacent hues of similar value and intensity tend to fade or disappear.

Vest. Sleeveless, collarless, semi-fitted garment buttoned down front and ending between waist and hips. Worn over blouse or shirt and skirt or pants.(Women's Figure 6-35g, men's Figure 6-48j)

Virago sleeve. Long sleeve style with normal armscye and periodic horizontal gathering ties or elastic creating a series of gathered puffs similar to shirring. (Figure 6-27n)

Visible spectrum. The range, within the total radiant or electromagnetic spectrum, which the human eye can see, ranging from about 400 to 700 nanometers.

Walker. Shoe style for toddlers learning to walk, having flat, firm sole, lacing up front over tongue, uppers coming high on ankle. (Figure 6-52h)

Warp. Lengthwise yarn in woven fabric.

Watteau. Women's shallow-crowned hat style worn high in back, lower in front to accommodate upswept hair style. Derived from pictures by French painter Watteau. (Figure 6-38u)

Wavelength. Distance in the radiant spectrum between the highest point of one radiation wave and the highest point of the next.

Wedgie. Shoe style with high heel in one piece with sole, forming wedge-shaped sole. (Figure 6-42r)

Weft. Crosswise yarn in woven fabric, also called "filling" or "woof."

Welt pocket. Inset with angled upper edge finish like a wide binding. (Figures 6-37h and 6-48i)

Weskit. Sleeveless, low-neck vest, buttoned down front, ending just below waist. Worn with blouse. (Figure 6-35b)

Western jacket. Jacket style with yoke and notched collar, often made of leather with decorative fringe. (Figure 6-45l)

Western shirt. Fitted, long sleeved shirt with shirt collar, opening down front, often with decorated shoulder yoke. (Women's Figure 6-25h, men's Figure 6-44a)

White light. Balanced combination of wavelengths from visible spectrum, including all hues.

Wing collar. Standing collar, open at front, with points folded and spread outward. Also know as "Gladstone collar." (Women's Figure 6-23m, men's Figure 6-43f)

Wraparound coat. Straight-cut, women's coat style without buttons. Also called "clutch coat." (Figure 6-36k)

Wraparound pant skirt. Bifurcated garment with front constructed like pants, wrapping around back and again to front as an open skirt. (Figure 6-33b)

Wrapper. Rectangular fabric usually about two yards long, wrapped around body as ankle-length skirt. Single wrapper uses one length (Figure 6-31v) and double wrapper uses two, the upper one folded and wrapped around waist and hips (Figure 6-31u). Popular in West Africa.

Yang. Traditional Chinese personality concept representing assertiveness, dominance, activity, light, and boldness. In clothing, yang usages would generally include advancing techniques.

Yin. Traditional Chinese personality concept representing delicate, fragile, dainty, feminine, passive, and submissive characteristics. In clothing, yin usages would generally be flattening or receding techniques, or reinforce usages conveying daintiness.

Yoke. Separately cut and seamed fitted section usually horizontal, sometimes with one side pointed. (Bodice shoulder Figure 6-24e, waist midriff Figure 6-26e, skirt hip Figure 6-32f)

Bibliography

The A. F. Encyclopedia of Textiles, 3rd ed. Englewood Cliffs, N.J.: Prentice-Hall, Inc., 1980.

ACKERMAN, DIANE, *A Natural History of the Senses.* New York: Random House, 1990.

ALBERS, JOSEF, *Interaction of Color,* rev. pocket ed. New Haven, CT.: Yale University Press, 1975.

ANDERSON, DONALD M., *Elements of Design.* New York: Holt, Rinehart and Winston, Inc., 1961.

ARNHEIM, RUDOLF, *Art and Visual Perception.* Berkeley: University of California Press, 1971.

———, *Toward a Psychology of Art.* Berkeley: University of California Press, 1972.

ATTNEAVE, FRED, "Multistability in Perception," *Scientific American,* Vol. 225, No. 6 (Dec. 1971), pp. 62-71.

AVERY, CAROL E., RUTH PESTLE, and PAMELA M. RADCLIFFE, "Hypothermia, Use of Textile Items, and the Elderly," *Clothing and Textiles Research Journal,* 4, no. 1 (Fall 1985), 53-59.

BARNES, RUTH, and JOANNE B. EICHER, eds., *Dress and Gender: Making and Meaning.* Providence, R.I.: Berg Publishers, Inc., 1992.

BATES, KENNETH F., *Basic Design, Principles and Practice.* Cleveland, OH.: The World Publishing Co., 1960.

BECK, JACOB, *Surface Color Perception.* Ithaca, N.Y.: Cornell University Press, 1972.

BERLIN, BRENT, and PAUL KAY, *Basic Color Terms: Their Universality and Evolution.* Berkeley: University of California Press, 1969.

BIRREN, FABER, *Color Psychology and Color Therapy.* Secaucus, N.J.: Citadel Press, 1950.

————, *Principles of Color, A Review of Past Traditions and Modern Theories of Color Harmony.* New York: Van Nostrand Reinhold Company, 1969.

————, *Color: A Survey in Words and Pictures.* New York: University Books, 1963.

BIRREN, FABER, ed., *A Grammar of Color.* New York: Van Nostrand Reinhold Company, 1969.

BROCKMAN, HELEN L., *The Theory of Fashion Design.* New York: John Wiley & Sons, Inc., 1965.

CALASIBETTA, CHARLOTTE MANKEY, *Essential Terms of Fashion.* New York: Fairchild Publications, 1986.

CLULOW, FREDERICK W., *Colour: Its Principles and Their Applications.* Dobbs Ferry, N.Y.: Morgan and Morgan, Inc., Publishers, 1972.

COLE, MICHAEL, and SYLVIA SCRIBNER, *Culture and Thought, A Psychological Introduction.* New York: John Wiley & Sons, Inc., 1974.

COLLIER, GRAHAM, *Form, Space, and Vision.* Englewood Cliffs, N.J.: Prentice-Hall, Inc., 1963.

Colour, Marshall Editions Limited. London: Grange Books, 1991.

CORBMAN, BERNARD, *Textiles: Fiber to Fabric,* 6th ed. New York: McGraw-Hill Book Company, Inc., 1982.

DELONG, MARILYN REVELL, *The Way We Look: A Framework for Visual Analysis of Dress.* Ames, Ia.: Iowa State University Press, 1987.

FIORE, ANN MARIE, "Multisensory Integration of Visual, Tactile, and Olfactory Aesthetic Cues of Appearance," *Clothing and Textiles Research Journal,* 11, no. 4 (Winter 1993), 45-52.

FOURT, LYMAN, and NORMAN HOLLIES, *Clothing: Comfort and Function.* New York: Marcel Dekker, Inc., 1970.

GARAU, AUGUSTO, *Color Harmonies,* Nicola Bruno, trans. Chicago: University of Chicago Press, 1993.

GIOELLO, DEBBIE ANN, *Profiling Fabrics: Properties, Performance & Construction Techniques,* Language of Fashion Series. New York: Fairchild Publications, 1981.

GOLD, ANNALEE, *One World of Fashion* (4th ed.). New York: Fairchild Publications, 1987.

GOLDSTEIN, HARRIET, and VETTA GOLDSTEIN, *Art in Everyday Life,* 4th ed. New York: Macmillan Publishing Co., Inc., 1969.

GRAVES, MAITLAND, *The Art of Color and Design,* 2nd ed. New York: McGraw-Hill Book Company, Inc., 1951.

————, *Color Fundamentals.* New York: McGraw-Hill Book Company, Inc., 1952.

GREGORY, R. L., *Eye and Brain: The Psychology of Seeing,* 2nd ed. New York: McGraw-Hill Book Company, Inc., 1972.

————, *The Intelligent Eye.* New York: McGraw-Hill Book Company, Inc., 1970.

————, "Visual Illusions," *Scientific American,* Vol. 219, No. 5 (Nov. 1968), pp. 66-76.

HABER, RALPH M., and MAURICE HERSHENSON, *The Psychology of Visual Perception.* New York: Holt, Rinehart and Winston, Inc., 1973.

HARLAN, CALVIN, *Vision and Invention, a Course in Art Fundamentals.* Englewood Cliffs, N.J.: Prentice-Hall, Inc., 1970.

HOLLEN, NORMA and JANE SADDLER, *Textiles,* 4th ed. New York: The Macmillan Company, 1973.

HORN, MARILYN J. and LOIS M. GUREL, *The Second Skin,* 3rd ed. Boston: Houghton Mifflin Company, 1981.

JUDD, DEANE, and KENNETH KELLY, *Color: Universal Language and Dictionary of Names,* NSB Special Publication 440. Washington, D.C.: National Bureau of Standards, 1976.

JUSTEMA, WILLIAM, and DORIS JUSTEMA, *Weaving and Needlecraft Color Course.* New York: Van Nostrand Reinhold Company, 1971.

KAUFMAN, LLOYD, *Sight and Mind: An Introduction To Visual Perception.* New York: Oxford University Press, 1974.

KAWASHIMA, MASAAKI, *Fundamentals of Men's Fashion Design, A Guide to Tailored Clothes.* New York: Fairchild Publications, Inc., 1974.

KEFGEN, MARY, and PHYLLIS TOUCHIE-SPECHT, *Individuality in Clothing Selection and Personal Appearance,* 4th ed. New York: Macmillan Publishing Co., Inc., 1986.

KUEPPERS, HARALD, *The Basic Law of Color Theory,* 1st U.S. ed., Roger Marcinik, trans., Barron's Educational Series. Woodbury, N.Y.: Barron's, 1982.

KÜPPERS, HARALD, *Color: Origin, System, Uses.* London: Van Nostrand Reinhold Ltd., 1973.

LAMBERT, PATRICIA, BARBARA STAEPELAERE, and MARY G. FRY, *Color and Fiber.* West Chester, Pa.: Schiffer Publishing Ltd., 1986.

LAND, E. H., "The Retinex Theory of Color Vision," *Scientific American,* 237, 1977, 108–128.

LEGGE, GORDON E., and FERGUS W. CAMPBELL, *Vision of Color and Pattern,* J. J. Head, ed. Burlington, N.C.: Carolina Biological Supply Company, 1987.

LIBBY, WILLIAM CHARLES, *Color and the Structural Sense.* Englewood Cliffs, N.J.: Prentice-Hall, Inc., 1974.

LIPOVETSKY, GILLES, *The Empire of Fashion: Dressing Modern Democracy,* Catherine Porter, trans. Princeton, N.J.: Princeton University Press, 1994.

LUCKIESH, M., *Visual Illusions: Their Causes, Characteristics, and Applications* (reprint of 1922 ed.). New York: Dover Publications, Inc., 1965.

MATHIS, CARLA MASON, and HELEN VILLA CONNOR, *The Triumph of Individual Style.* Timeless Editions, 1994.

MAY, ELIZABETH ECKHARDT, NEVA R. WAGGONER, and ELEANOR BOETTKE, *Independent Living for the Handicapped and the Elderly.* Boston: Houghton-Mifflin Company, 1974.

McJIMSEY, HARRIET T., *Art and Fashion in Clothing Selection,* 2nd ed. Ames, Ia.: Iowa State University Press, 1973.

MINNAERT, M., *The Nature of Light and Color in the Open Air.* New York: Dover Publications, Inc., 1954.

MOORE, CAROLYN L., "Factors That Affect Undesirable Garment Drape," *Journal of Home Economics,* 84, no. 3 (Fall 1992), 31-34.

MORTON, GRACE MARGARET, *The Arts of Costume and Personal Appearance,* 3rd ed. New York: John Wiley & Sons, Inc., 1966.

MUNSELL, ALBERT H., *A Color Notation,* 5th ed. New York: Munsell Color Company, 1919.

MURRAY, MAGGIE PEXTON, *Changing Styles in Fashion: Who, What, Why.* New York: Fairchild Publications, 1989.

PAPANEK, VICTOR, *Design for the Real World.* New York: Bantam Books, 1973.

RAINWATER, CLARENCE, *Light and Color.* New York: Golden Press, 1971.

ROACH, MARY ELLEN, and JOANNE B. EICHER, *The Visible Self: Perspectives on Dress.* Englewood Cliffs, N.J.: Prentice-Hall, Inc., 1973.

ROBINSON, J. O., *The Psychology of Visual Illusion.* London: Hutchinson & Co. (Publishers), Ltd., 1972.

ROTHENBERG, ALBERT, and ROBERT S. SOBEL, "A Creative Process in the Art of Costume Design," *Clothing and Textiles Research Journal,* 9, no. 1 (Fall 1990), 27-36.

SARGENT, WALTER, *The Enjoyment and Use of Color.* New York: Dover Publications, Inc., 1964.

SEGALL, MARSHALL H., DONALD T. CAMBELL, and MELVILLE J. HERSKOVITZ, *The Influence of Culture on Visual Perception.* Indianapolis, In.: The Bobbs-Merrill Company, Inc., 1966.

TRANQUILLO, MARY D., *Styles of Fashion; A Pictorial Handbook.* New York: Van Nostrand Reinhold Company, 1984.

WATKINS, SUSAN M., *Clothing, The Portable Environment*. Ames, Ia.: Iowa State University Press, 1984.

——, "Designing Functional Clothing," *Journal of Home Economics*, Vol. 66, No. 7 (Nov. 1974), pp. 33-38.

WORKMAN, JANE E., "Improving Uniform Design For Foodservice Workers: Criteria and Prototypes," *Journal of Home Economics*, 83, no. 3 (Fall 1991), 17-22.

ZIEGERT, BEATE, "A New System for Designing Active Wear," *Human Ecology Forum*, 16, no. 2 (Spring 1987), 15-18.

Index